Northern Arizona University Custom Edition
Invitation to World Religions

Jeffrey Brodd et al.

Religions of the World
REL 150

OXFORD
UNIVERSITY PRESS

Contents

Front Matter 1

Chapter 1: An Invitation to the Study of World Religions 5

Chapter 2: Hinduism 33

Chapter 3: Buddhism 87

Chapter 4: Chinese Religions: Confucianism and Daoism 135

Chapter 5: Judaism 187

Chapter 6: Christianity 245

Chapter 7: Islam 305

Index 363

INVITATION TO World Religions

INVITATION TO World
Religions

THIRD EDITION

JEFFREY BRODD
California State University, Sacramento

LAYNE LITTLE
University of California, Davis

BRADLEY NYSTROM
California State University, Sacramento

ROBERT PLATZNER
California State University, Sacramento

RICHARD SHEK
California State University, Sacramento

ERIN STILES
University of Nevada, Reno

Oxford   New York
Oxford University Press

3

Oxford University Press is a department of the University of Oxford.
It furthers the University's objective of excellence in research,
scholarship, and education by publishing worldwide.
Oxford is a registered trade mark of Oxford University Press
in the UK and certain other countries.

Published in the United States of America by Oxford University Press
198 Madison Avenue, New York, NY 10016, United States of America.

© 2019, 2016, 2013 by Oxford University Press

Library of Congress Cataloging-in-Publication Data
Names: Brodd, Jeffrey, author.
Title: Invitation to world religions / Jeffrey Brodd, California State
    University, Sacramento [and 5 others].
Description: Third Edition. | New York : Oxford University Press, 2018.
Identifiers: LCCN 2017060154 | ISBN 9780190690816 (pbk.)
Subjects: LCSH: Religions.
Classification: LCC BL80.3 .B754 2018 | DDC 200—dc23
LC record available at https://lccn.loc.gov/2017060154

9 8 7 6 5 4 3 2 1
Printed by LSC Communications, United States of America

1

An Invitation to the Study of World Religions

ON MOST AMERICAN COLLEGE CAMPUSES, signs of the world's religions are readily observable. Bulletin boards display fliers announcing upcoming events pertaining to Buddhist meditation or Hindu sacred art or the Islamic observance of Ramadan. Campus religious groups engage in outreach activities at tables alongside walkways or in student unions, often with posters quoting scripture or displaying religious icons. Some icons even commonly adorn the students themselves—a cross necklace, for example, or a tattoo of the yin/yang symbol.

To study the world's religions is to progress from mere observation of outward signs to understanding their meaning and relevance. Anyone who observes the yin-yang symbol can appreciate the beauty of its spiraling symmetry, but studying Chinese religion reveals a much more complex meaning. Mysterious in their origins, yin and yang are complementary primal energies that give rise to all creation. For the human being, to maintain a perfect balance of yin and yang is to live an ideal life. The nearly ubiquitous symbol of the cross similarly takes on new depths of meaning, even for many who identify themselves as Christian, when approached through the study of world religions. To Christians, God, the creator of all things, having taken on human form in the person of Jesus Christ, willingly suffered the painful death of crucifixion on the cross to save humanity from the power of sin. We can expand on our understanding of the meaning and cultural relevance of these two icons through a comparative study. Chinese religion, with its belief in the creative, complementary energies of yin and

Candlelight vigils typically draw together people of different religious perspectives in times of sorrow as well as celebration.

yang, has no need for a creator such as the Christian God. The Christian concept of sin and the corresponding need for salvation are alien to the Chinese quest for balance of yin and yang. These two icons, in other words, signify profoundly different cultural orientations.

To study the world's religions is to enhance one's understanding and appreciation of the rich variety of cultures around the globe. This chapter introduces this field of study by exploring the significance, examining the foundational concepts, and describing appropriate strategies for the academic exploration of religion. ☼

APPROACHING THE STUDY OF WORLD RELIGIONS

In order to be an educated person today, one must have an awareness of world religions. To learn about world religions is to increase one's cultural literacy—the objective that lies at the heart of this study. The religious traditions examined in this book are foundational aspects of cultures around the globe. Religion plays a crucial role in shaping, transforming, and transmitting cultures. Interacting with other cultural aspects—politics, economics, aesthetics—religion is a potent force in culture, in ways both constructive and destructive. When people believe they are acting in a manner that is condoned by a transcendent power or is in keeping with timeless tradition, they tend to act more fervently and with greater conviction. In other words, religions are powerful, sometimes even dangerous. Knowing about them is crucial for negotiating our complex world.

"World Religions" has been a course of study in American colleges and universities for nearly a century. Recently, the category has come under scrutiny by some scholars, as has the so-called world religions discourse that often accompanies it.[1] Although such scrutiny sometimes loses sight of the obvious—that "world religions" as an academic category is here to stay and that learning about its subject matter is vitally important— critics are correct to demand sound academic approaches to the study. A primary concern is that the study of world religions, and indeed the entire enterprise of the academic study of religion, arose within the nominally Christian European intellectual culture that assumed that Christianity was a model of what a religion ought to be and, commonly, that it was the only *true* religion. Until the late decades of the nineteenth century, theorists applied the term *world religion* (in the singular) only to Christianity. Eventually Buddhism, Judaism, and occasionally Islam were grouped with Christianity as "world religions" (or "the world's religions"). By the 1930s, the list had grown to include the ten to twelve religions that still today are normally categorized as world religions.

And so, to the basic need for knowing about the world religions (however they came to be categorized), we can add another vital need: that we go about studying them appropriately through awareness of what we might call the "do's and don'ts" of religious studies, which this chapter explores in some detail. We can begin by noting that an appropriate study of world religions does not privilege any religion as being somehow exemplary or the model with which others are to be compared. On a related note, we need to avoid terms and categories that are rooted in such privileging. For example, "faith" is a natural term to use when studying Christianity, but it is far less applicable to the study of Confucianism or Shinto. Other important issues involve underlying motives or assumptions that can too easily creep in. A common assumption is this: All religions ultimately say the same thing. This possibility is an intriguing one, but in fact, it is impossible to prove by way of a sound academic approach—that is, well-reasoned theorizing based on careful analysis of the evidence.

The challenge of mastering the "do's" and avoiding the "don'ts" only enriches our study. We begin by considering the rise of the modern academic field of religious studies.

Religion as a Subject of Academic Inquiry

The academic study of religion, commonly known as "religious studies" (or sometimes as "comparative religion" or "history of religions") is a relatively recent development. Prior to the European Enlightenment of the eighteenth century, it rarely occurred to anyone to think of a religion as an entity that could be separated from other aspects of culture, and therefore as something that could be defined as a distinct category and studied as such. Enlightenment thinkers, most influentially the German philosopher Immanuel Kant (1724–1804), conceived of religion as something separate from the various phenomena the human mind is capable of perceiving.[2] This impulse toward categorically separating religion, coupled with European exploration of distant lands and their unfamiliar "religions," launched efforts to understand religion that have continued to the present day. This shift means that we modern observers need to be cautious when appraising the religious aspects of other cultures, lest we make the error of assuming that all peoples have recognized religion as a distinctive category. Most cultures throughout history have had neither the conceptual category nor a term meaning "religion."

William James defined religion as "the feelings, acts and experiences of individual men in their solitude." This Orthodox Christian priest sits alone in the Amhara region of northwestern Ethiopia.

The academic study of religion is generally distinct from theology, the field of inquiry that focuses on considering the nature of the divine. Unlike religious studies, theology is an important example of *doing* and *being* religious, which naturally invites consideration of the supernatural and of the "truth" of religious claims. Religious studies, like most other academic pursuits, is to a large extent based on an approach to knowledge that depends on analysis of empirical data. The discourse and actions of human beings can be observed and studied through normal means of academic inquiry; empirical evidence can be gathered, and through rational argumentation hypotheses can be formulated and supported. Supernatural beings and events normally are held to be beyond the reach of academic inquiry. The academic study of religion, as understood by the authors of this book, is therefore not theology, however much we might admire theologians and enjoy studying their work, which is itself an important human enterprise and a major component of religion.

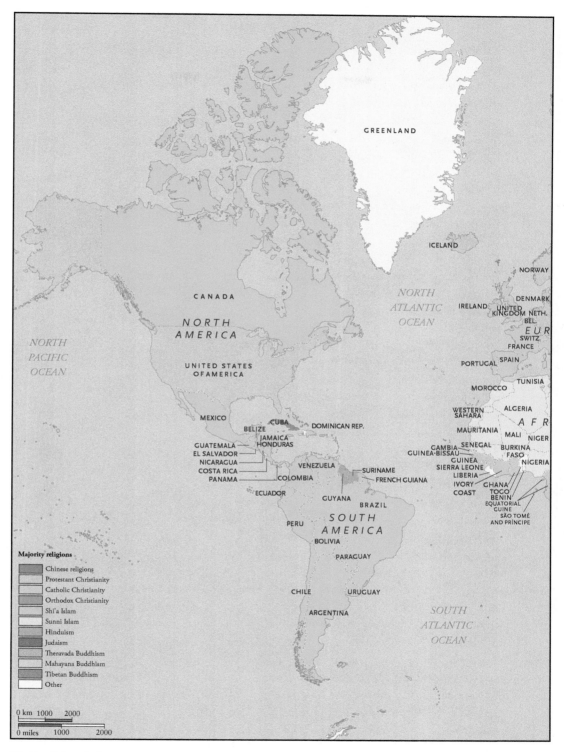

GREENLAND

ICELAND

NORWAY

NORTH
ATLANTIC
OCEAN

IRELAND
UNITED
KINGDOM

DENMARK

NETH.
BEL.
EUR
SWITZ.
FRANCE

CANADA

NORTH
AMERICA

NORTH
PACIFIC
OCEAN

UNITED STATES
OF AMERICA

PORTUGAL SPAIN

MOROCCO

TUNISIA

WESTERN
SAHARA

ALGERIA

A F R

MEXICO

CUBA

BELIZE

GUATEMALA
EL SALVADOR
NICARAGUA
COSTA RICA
PANAMA

JAMAICA
HONDURAS

DOMINICAN REP.

VENEZUELA

COLOMBIA

MAURITANIA

GAMBIA
GUINEA-BISSAU

SENEGAL

GUINEA
SIERRA LEONE

MALI

NIGER

BURKINA
FASO

NIGERIA

LIBERIA

SURINAME

FRENCH GUIANA

IVORY
COAST

GHANA
TOGO
BENIN

ECUADOR

GUYANA

BRAZIL

EQUATORIAL
GUINE
SÃO TOMÉ
AND PRÍNCIPE

PERU

SOUTH
AMERICA

BOLIVIA

PARAGUAY

CHILE

URUGUAY

SOUTH
ATLANTIC
OCEAN

ARGENTINA

Majority religions

- Chinese religions
- Protestant Christianity
- Catholic Christianity
- Orthodox Christianity
- Shi'a Islam
- Sunni Islam
- Hinduism
- Judaism
- Theravada Buddhism
- Mahayana Buddhism
- Tibetan Buddhism
- Other

0 km 1000 2000

0 miles 1000 2000

World religions today.

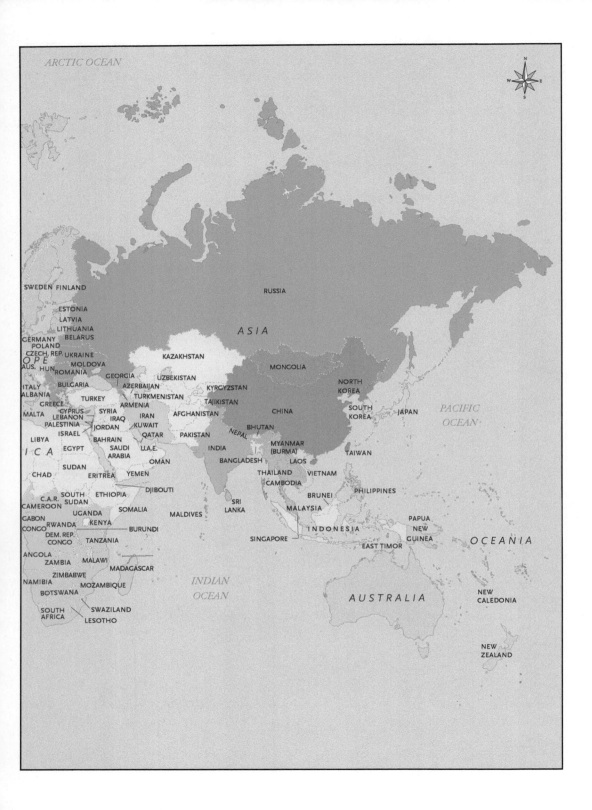

ARCTIC OCEAN

RUSSIA

ASIA

SWEDEN FINLAND

ESTONIA
LATVIA
LITHUANIA
GERMANY BELARUS
POLAND
CZECH. REP. UKRAINE
O P E
AUS. HUN. MOLDOVA
ROMANIA
GEORGIA
ITALY BULGARIA
ALBANIA AZERBAIJAN
GREECE TURKEY TURKMENISTAN
MALTA CYPRUS SYRIA ARMENIA
LEBANON IRAQ IRAN
PALESTINIA JORDAN KUWAIT
ISRAEL QATAR PAKISTAN
LIBYA BAHRAIN
EGYPT SAUDI U.A.E. INDIA
I C A ARABIA OMAN
SUDAN YEMEN
CHAD ERITREA
DJIBOUTI
C.A.R. SOUTH ETHIOPIA
CAMEROON SUDAN
GABON UGANDA SOMALIA MALDIVES
CONGO RWANDA KENYA
DEM. REP. BURUNDI
CONGO TANZANIA

KAZAKHSTAN

MONGOLIA

UZBEKISTAN
KYRGYZSTAN
TAJIKISTAN
AFGHANISTAN CHINA

NORTH
KOREA
SOUTH JAPAN
KOREA

PACIFIC
OCEAN

BHUTAN
NEPAL
MYANMAR
(BURMA)
BANGLADESH LAOS TAIWAN
THAILAND VIETNAM
CAMBODIA
BRUNEI PHILIPPINES
SRI MALAYSIA
LANKA
SINGAPORE INDONESIA PAPUA
NEW
GUINEA OCEANIA
EAST TIMOR

ANGOLA
ZAMBIA MALAWI
MADAGASCAR
ZIMBABWE
NAMIBIA MOZAMBIQUE
BOTSWANA

INDIAN
OCEAN

AUSTRALIA

NEW
CALEDONIA

SOUTH SWAZILAND
AFRICA LESOTHO

NEW
ZEALAND

10

The Definitional Challenge A natural outcome of the Enlightenment impulse toward categorically separating religion from other aspects of culture has been the attempt to produce a universal definition of the term. Scholars from various academic disciplines have struggled with this challenge without having produced a single definition that pleases everyone. Many theorists today dismiss the challenge as futile, and some even go so far as to argue that use of the term *religion* in academic study should be abandoned altogether because of its ambiguity and misleading inferences. Most scholars involved in religious studies, however, agree that they are studying basically the same subject, and for lack of a better term most are content with calling it "religion."

The relevance of defining "religion" can be understood through an analogy that compares religions to houses. Embarking on a study of religions without concern over *what*, exactly, we are studying would be akin to setting off for foreign places to explore the nature of houses without first agreeing on what counts as a house. Would we include apartments? Vacation cabins? Palaces? Defining terms helps us draw clear boundaries around the subject of study. Another challenge involves our preconceived notions of things. We might assume that everyone shares a common idea of a typical "house" (like the kind we learned to draw in grade school), but such an assumption is mainly the result of preconceptions based on our own culture's norms. People from other cultures might dwell in structures that have little in common with our standard notion of a house.

Let's consider some notable attempts to conceptualize "religion" while keeping in mind our "house" analogy. When exploring the more specific category "world religion," it will be useful to think of a similarly more specific category of house: a mansion, and more specifically, an old mansion that has undergone a long process of refurbishing. Although certainly considered a type of house, a mansion has many rooms that serve a wide variety of functions and styles. Imagine an old mansion that has kept the same foundation and basic structure over the years, but to which various inhabitants have made changes that have enabled the structure to survive into modern times. Our study of the world's religions is an invitation to explore several extraordinary "old mansions." Our tools of study—beginning with considerations of definition—are designed to help us make the most of our explorations, to take in fully the teachings, the histories, and the practices of the world's religions.

Three Classic Definitions The history of the attempt to formulate suitable definitions of "religion" is intriguing. In many instances, definitions reveal as much about the historical era and about the intentions of the individual theorist as they do about the nature of religion.

The following well-known definitions of "religion" were set forth by notable theorists in different fields:

A religion is a unified system of beliefs and practices relative to sacred things, that is to say, things set apart and forbidden—beliefs and practices which unite into one single moral community called a Church, all those who adhere to them.[3]

—*Émile Durkheim*

[Religion is] . . . the feelings, acts and experiences of individual men in their solitude, so far as they apprehend themselves to stand in relation to whatever they may consider the divine.[4]

—*William James*

[T]he religious aspect points to that which is ultimate, infinite, unconditional in man's spiritual life. Religion, in the largest and most basic sense of the word, is ultimate concern.[5]

—*Paul Tillich*

French sociologist Émile Durkheim (1858–1917), a founding figure of the sociological study of religion, emphasizes in his definition the *social* nature of religion. He insists on the unification brought about by "beliefs and practices," culminating in a "moral community called a Church." Durkheim surely hits on some central functions of religion, but most scholars contend that he overemphasizes this social orientation. In contrast, American psychologist William James (1842–1910) emphasizes the *individual* nature of religion. Although this aspect is also clearly important, his definition omits any mention of religion's social nature. The definitions put forth by Durkheim and James, though provocative, are therefore problematically limiting.

Paul Tillich (1886–1965), the eminent Protestant theologian, naturally connects religion to a focus on "man's spiritual life." His notion of religion as "ultimate concern" has been influential for several decades, probably in part because many find it true to their own experiences. But the definition is very broad, and it says nothing regarding the specific content of religious traditions. In emphasizing the existential concerns of religion, it neglects the social and institutional components of the traditions. People commonly claim to be "spiritual" while also denying that they belong to a religion. A sound definition needs to accommodate this distinction or else avoid this ambiguity altogether.

Two Prominent Definitions Let us now consider two definitions of religion that currently enjoy wide favor and that avoid these sorts of shortcomings. The *HarperCollins Dictionary of Religion*, a popular reference work, states: "One may clarify the term religion by defining it as a system of beliefs and practices that are relative to superhuman beings."[6] This definition encompasses a wide array of cultural phenomena, while at the same time restricting the category, most especially with the concept "superhuman beings."

Bruce Lincoln (b. 1948), a prominent theorist of religion, asserts in his book *Holy Terrors: Thinking about Religion after September 11* that a religion always consists of four "domains"—discourse, practice, community, and institution:

1. A discourse whose concerns transcend the human, temporal, and contingent, and that claims for itself a similarly transcendent status. . . .
2. A set of practices whose purpose is to produce a proper world and/or proper human subjects, as defined by a religious discourse to which these practices are connected. . . .
3. A community whose members construct their identity with reference to a religious discourse and its attendant practices. . . .
4. An institution that regulates religious discourse, practices, and community, reproducing them over time and modifying them as necessary, while asserting their eternal validity and transcendent value.[7]

Lincoln's definition, though lengthier than the *Dictionary*'s, is impressively precise. It also is helpfully inclusive. By basing religion on the notion of the "transcendent" rather than on "supernatural beings" or the like, Lincoln's definition encompasses Confucianism and forms of Buddhism that do not focus on belief in supernatural beings. The religions featured in this textbook conform to Lincoln's definition. This is not to say that Lincoln, or for that matter any other theorist, has determined what religion "truly" is. In the words of sociologist Peter Berger (b. 1929), commenting on the challenge of defining religion, "a definition is not more or less true, only more or less useful."[8] For purposes of our study, Lincoln's definition provides a useful means of categorizing the subject matter. It clarifies why the traditions featured in this book qualify as religions while also, especially with its insistence that a religion involves an "institution," establishing helpful limits. The general category "spirituality," for example, would not necessarily qualify as religion based on Lincoln's definition.

We now shift our focus from what religions *are* to consider what religions *do*. In the next section, we analyze various functions of religion, concentrating especially on the fundamental questions to which religious traditions provide answers.

WHAT RELIGIONS DO

Whatever one thinks a religion *is*, this much remains certain: a religion *does*. This fact is closely related to the challenge of defining religion. Some theorists have emphasized this functional side of religion in their explanations. In some cases, this results in *explaining away* or *reducing* religion to being an effect or result of other forces. Underlying Durkheim's definition, for example, is a theory that reduces religion to being an effect of societal forces, a mechanism that, having been produced in the first place by societal needs, functions in turn to promote social unity. Here is a clear case in point that definitions reveal as much about the intentions of the theorist as they do about the nature of religion. As Durkheim is a founder of sociology, it is not surprising that he emphasizes the social aspects of religion. Consider also this assertion from psychologist Sigmund Freud (1856–1939):

> Religion would thus be the universal obsessional neurosis of humanity; like the obsessional neurosis of children, it arose out of the Oedipus complex, out of the relation to the father.[9]

Freud was an atheist whose psychological theory held religion to be undesirable. Political philosopher Karl Marx (1818–1883), likewise an atheist, offers an even more antagonistic assessment:

> *Man makes religion*, religion does not make man. In other words, religion is the self-consciousness and self-feeling of man who has either not yet found himself or has already lost himself again. But *man* is no abstract being squatting outside the world. Man is the *world of man*, the state, society. . . . Religion is the sigh of the oppressed creature, the heart of a heartless world, just as it is the spirit of a spiritless situation. It is the *opium* of the people.[10]

At sites like this Confucian temple in Beijing, China, Confucius (Master K'ung) is honored for his enduring contributions to Chinese culture. Sound definitions of "religion" are flexible enough to include Confucianism as a religious tradition.

Marx, affected by what he perceived as the economic disparities of the Industrial Revolution, was a materialist who dismissed all forms of ideology as obstacles to the pursuit of true well-being. Freud similarly regarded religion as an effect of other forces, viewing it as a by-product of psychological influences. According to Freud, religion functions as an unhealthy but soothing buffer against the inner terrors of the psyche. For Marx, religion functions in a similarly unhealthy manner, as an opiate that deters the suffering individual from attending to the true cause of affliction.

Contemporary scholars largely regard these functionalist explanations as severely limited. Perhaps religions *do* function in these ways at certain times in certain situations; but surely religions do much more. In fact, neither Freud nor Marx ever actually tried to define religion; rather, they tried to explain it away. This does not diminish, however, the enduring relevance of these theorists for purposes of striving to understand the big picture of the role religion plays in the lives of individuals and in societies.

We can widen our vantage point on the functions of religion and produce a fairer and more accurate depiction by considering the variety of life's challenges that these traditions help people to face and to overcome.

Religious Questions and Challenges

It might seem disrespectful or even blasphemous to ask, Why do religions exist? Yet, this is a perfectly legitimate question. As human enterprises, religions naturally respond to human needs and readily acknowledge reasons for their doctrines and rituals. A typical reason has to do with some kind of perceived separation from the sacred or estrangement from a state of perfection or fulfillment. The human condition, as ordinarily experienced, is regarded as being disconnected from the fulfillment that lies at the end of a spiritual path. Of the questions and challenges addressed by religions, these three are especially prominent:

1. What is ultimate reality?
2. How should we live in this world?
3. What is our ultimate purpose?

The rest of this book's chapters explore the ways major religions answer these questions. For now, let's consider these questions more broadly.

What Is Ultimate Reality? It is difficult to imagine a religion that has nothing to say about ultimate reality—even if this involves asserting that "ultimate" reality consists of no more than the natural world and we human beings who inhabit it. Religions typically assert that ultimate reality is somehow divine, and explanation of the nature and role of the divine takes center stage in a religion's belief system. But the "divine" is not necessarily thought of as God or gods. When it is, we refer to that religion as a **theistic** (from Greek *theos*, or god) belief system. When it is not, the religion is said to be **nontheistic**. Some forms of Buddhism, such as Zen, are clearly nontheistic. A helpful middle ground term is **transtheistic**, acknowledging the existence of gods—but of gods that are not vital with regard to the most crucial religious issues, such as the quest for enlightenment or salvation.[11]

Theistic religions can be further categorized. **Polytheism** (from Greek *polys*, or many) is the belief in many gods ("gods" is considered a gender-neutral term and can—and often does—include goddesses). **Monotheism** (from Greek *monos*, or only one) is the belief in only one god (and hence the term is normally capitalized—God—a proper noun referring to a specific being). Here, a kind of middle ground comes in the form of **henotheism** (from Greek *hen*, the number one), which acknowledges a plurality of gods but elevates one of them to special status. Some forms of Hindu devotion to a particular god such as Vishnu or Shiva are henotheistic.

Pantheism (from Greek *pan*, or all) is the belief that the divine is identical to nature or the material world. Although not one of the world's living religions, the ancient Greek and Roman religious philosophy known as Stoicism is an example. It is important to bear in mind, too, that the world's religions often feature entities that are supernatural and yet are not necessarily gods. These quasi-divine figures, such as angels, demons, and the monsters of myths, are difficult to categorize but are important elements of religion nonetheless. To complicate matters further, scholars of non-Western religions have commonly used the term *god* to refer to supernatural beings that are more similar to angels, or even to the saints of Catholic tradition. The *theos* in the "polytheism" of such non-Western religions therefore often refers to a very different type of being than does the *theos* in "monotheism." Simplistic application of such terms is misleading.

Nontheistic belief systems include those that uphold **atheism**, which in a modern context is a perspective that denies the existence of God or gods. In ancient times, a person could be labeled an atheist for denying the significance of deities, even while believing that they exist. Among the ancient Greeks and Romans, for example, Epicureans were considered to be atheists. Even according to the modern meaning of atheism, some atheists nevertheless could be regarded as religious—depending on how one defines "religion." The *HarperCollins Dictionary of Religion* definition, with its basis in "supernatural beings," likely would not leave room for atheism, whereas Bruce Lincoln's definition could. Current trends in religiosity among young people suggest that atheism, along with its less insistent relative, agnosticism (which only refuses to assert the existence of God or gods, rather than outright denying it), are becoming more prevalent and deserving of academic inquiry. A May 2015 Pew Forum study indicates that 22.8 percent of people in the United States identify themselves as atheist, agnostic, or "nothing in particular"—a group that is labeled "Unaffiliated" or religious "nones." This marks a sharp increase. (For more on the Pew Forum study, see the Online Resources list at the end of this chapter; the issue of atheism is addressed further in Chapter 14.)

This painting, produced in 1810, depicts the Hindu deities Shiva and Parvati with their children, Ganesha and Kartikeya. Hindus believe in many gods and goddesses; these four—especially Shiva—are among the most popular.

Related to this categorical label of nontheism is **monism**, the belief that all reality is ultimately one. Some Hindus, for example, while believing in many gods and goddesses, hold that Brahman, impersonal and ultimately indescribable, is the essence of all. Those Hindus therefore embrace monism, which is also described as nondualistic, because there is no distinction between the divine reality on one hand and the rest of reality, including human individuals, on the other.

These attempts at categorizing perspectives on ultimate reality involve some complications. Some Hindus are monistic because they understand all reality ultimately to be one thing: Brahman. But some of those same monistic Hindus also pay homage to a variety of supernatural and divine beings, and thus might also be described as polytheists.

Along with asserting the existence of ultimate reality, religions describe how this reality is revealed to human beings. The foundational moments of **revelation** are frequently recorded in sacred texts, or scriptures. In the case of theistic religions, scriptures set forth narratives describing the role of God or the gods in history and also include pronouncements directly attributed to the divine. In the Jewish and Christian Bible, for example, God's will regarding ethical behavior is expressed directly in the Ten Commandments. The giving of the Ten Commandments is described in the narrative about the Exodus of the Israelites from Egypt, in which God is said to have played a central role.

Ka'ba, Mecca.

Among nontheistic religions in particular—but also among the mystical traditions that form part of every religious tradition—revelation often combines textual transmission with a direct experience of revelation. Revelation is usually experienced by a founding figure of the religion, whose experiences are later written about; subsequent believers can then experience similar types of revelation, which requires their own participation. Buddhists, for example, have scriptural records that describe the Buddha's experience of nirvana, as well as pronouncements by deities praising the ultimate value of that experience. Followers must then connect to such revelation through practices such as meditation.

Another helpful way of thinking about revelation is offered by historian of religions Mircea Eliade (1907–1986), who describes a phenomenon he calls "hierophany," or "the *act of manifestation* of the sacred," which helps a people to establish its cosmology, or religious understanding, of the order of the world.[12] Eliade emphasizes how this concept applies to indigenous or small-scale traditions. But the phenomenon of the hierophany is readily apparent within the world's major religions, often, but not always, as a theophany, a manifestation of God or of gods. The role of hierophanies in establishing places of special significance can be observed in many of the sites related to the founding figures and events of the major religions: Christianity's Church of the Nativity (and other sacred sites related to the life of Christ); Islam's sacred city of Mecca; Buddhism's Bodh Gaya, site of Gautama's foundational experience of Enlightenment; and so on. Sacred moments establish sacred spatial monuments, thus establishing a sense of centrality and spatial order.

Religions also have much to say about *this* world. Human beings have always asked searching questions about the origin and status of our planet and of the universe. Typically, these two issues—origin and status—are intertwined. If our world was intentionally fashioned by a creator god, for instance, then it bears the stamp of divine affirmation. Thus, the early chapters of the Book of Genesis in the Hebrew Bible (the Christian Old Testament) describe the creative activity of God, including the creation of humankind. In contrast, the creation stories of some religious traditions deemphasize the role of the divine will in bringing about the world, sometimes (as in the religion of the ancient Greeks) describing the advent of the principal deities *after* the universe itself has been created. The gods, like humans, come into a world that is already established; gods and humans are depicted as sharing the world, which naturally affects the relationship between human and divine. In other religions, notably Hinduism, Buddhism, and other traditions that embrace liberation as the ultimate religious objective, this world is depicted as a kind of illusion. It is thus not so surprising that liberation involves being completely freed from the confines of this world.

These are but a few examples of religious understanding of the nature of the world, a general category known as **cosmology** (from *kosmos*, the Greek term for world or universe). Along with clarifying the origin and sacred status of the world, cosmology also explains how the world is ordered. Many traditions attribute the order of the universe to the doings of divine being(s) or forces. Yet in certain respects modern scientific explanations set forth cosmologies that are intriguingly similar to some religious cosmologies taught by religious personages of the distant past, such as Gautama the Buddha or Epicurus, a Greek philosopher who espoused a theory of atomism, arguing that reality is composed entirely of a very large number of very small particles. (Recall that the Epicureans were labeled "atheists" because they denied the significance of the gods.)

Of course, a particular religion's cosmology strongly influences the degree to which its adherents are involved in caring for the world. On the one hand, religions that are indifferent or hostile toward the natural world are not apt to encourage anything akin to environmentalism. On the other hand, a religion that teaches that the world is inherently sacred naturally encourages a sense of stewardship toward the natural world. Native American traditions, for example, are notably environmentally oriented.

How Should We Live in This World?   Many religions have much to say about God or other superhuman beings and phenomena, and yet all religions are human enterprises. Their teachings are communicated in human languages, their rituals are practiced by human participants, and their histories are entwined with the development of human societies and cultures. Religions also explain what it is to be a human being.

Explanations regarding what it is to be human also figure into ethical or moral considerations. Are we by nature good, evil, or somewhere in between? Religions tend to recognize that human beings do not always do the right thing, and they commonly offer teachings and disciplines directed toward moral or ethical improvement. On the one hand, to say that we are by nature good, and at the same time to recognize moral failings, is to infer that some cause external to our nature is causing the shortcoming. If we are by nature evil, on the other hand, or at least naturally prone to doing wrong, then the moral challenge lies within and the means of improvement would need to be directed inwardly.

Religions typically prescribe what is right behavior and what is wrong, based on a set of ethical tenets, such as the Jewish and Christian Ten Commandments. In fact, the prospects of improving the human condition and of faring well in an afterlife are often understood to depend upon right ethical behavior. The ethical teachings of many religions are notably similar. The so-called Golden Rule ("Do unto others what you would have them do unto you"[13]) in the Christian New Testament is reflected in the scriptures of virtually all of the world's major traditions.

The religions differ, however, over the source of ethical truth. Some emphasize **revealed ethics**, asserting that God, or some other supernatural force such as Hindu dharma (ethical duty), has established what constitutes right behavior and has revealed

this to human beings. The divine will might be conceived of as God (or gods), or it might take the form of an impersonal principle, such as dharma. Another common approach, in some forms of Buddhism, for example, emphasizes the role of conscience in the moral deliberations of each individual. These two emphases are not necessarily mutually exclusive. Some religions, Christianity among them, teach that both revealed ethics and individual conscience work together to distinguish right from wrong.

What Is Our Ultimate Purpose?

The challenge of mortality—the fact that we are destined to die—

Sixteenth-century triptych (altar painting) depicting the creation of Eve (center), the eating of the forbidden fruit (left), and the expulsion from the Garden of Eden (right). This story of humankind's first sin sets forth basic biblical perspectives on the human condition.

is sometimes cited as the primary motivating force behind religion. And although it is true that all religions have something to say about death, the diversity of perspectives is striking. For example, whereas Christianity, with its focus on the resurrection of Christ and the hope of eternal life, can be said to make mortality a central concern, Zen Buddhism, drawing inspiration from the classic Daoist texts, simply acknowledges the natural place of death in the order of things.

Both the challenge of mortality and the issue of our moral nature relate to questions regarding the human condition. In many faiths, how we conduct ourselves in this world will determine our fates after we die. Most religions acknowledge that human beings are destined to die (although some, such as Daoism, have aspired to discover the means of inducing physical immortality). As we have noted, some religions have little to say about the prospects of life beyond death. But most religions do provide explanations regarding the fate of the individual after death, and their explanations vary widely.

Hinduism, Buddhism, Jainism, and Sikhism all maintain belief in samsara, the "wheel of life" that implies a series of lives, deaths, and rebirths for every individual. The ultimate aim of each of these religions is liberation from samsara. But most of the adherents of these religions anticipate that death will lead to rebirth into another life form (not necessarily human), one in a long series of rebirths. Furthermore, the reborn are destined for any one of multiple realms, including a variety of hells and heavens.

Other religions, for example, Christianity and Islam, teach that individuals are destined for some sort of afterlife, usually a version of heaven or of hell. Sometimes the teachings are more complicated. The traditional Catholic doctrine of purgatory, for example, anticipates an intermediary destiny somewhere between the bliss of heaven and the agony of hell, where an individual can gradually be purified from sin, ultimately achieving salvation and entry to heaven.

Given what a religion says about the human condition, what ultimate purpose is the religious life intended to achieve? Is there a state of existence to which the religious person can hope to aspire that perfectly completes or even transcends the human condition, overcoming entirely its cares and shortcomings?

One such state of existence is the **numinous experience**, as described by Rudolf Otto in his classic work *The Idea of the Holy* (1923). Otto (1869–1937), a Protestant theologian and a philosopher of religion, describes the encounter with "the Holy" as "numinous," a term he coined from the Latin *numen*, meaning spirit or divinity. A genuine numinous experience, Otto asserts, is characterized by two powerful and contending forces: ***mysterium tremendum*** and ***fascinans***. *Mysterium tremendum*, which in Latin means "awe-inspiring mystery," is the feeling of awe that overwhelms a person who experiences the majestic presence of the "wholly other."[14] *Fascinans* (Latin, "fascinating") is the contrasting feeling of overwhelming attraction. The encounter with the Holy is thus alluring (*fascinans*) even as it is frightening on account of the awe-inspiring mystery (*mysterium tremendum*). The biblical phenomenon of the "fear of God" fits this description, as the God who is being feared is at the same time recognized as the source of life and the hope for salvation.

Otto's analysis of the numinous experience remains an important contribution to religious studies, although it suffers from a significant limitation: based in his Protestant Christian outlook, it may ring true to a Protestant; from a global perspective, however, the analysis is rather narrow. For example, Otto discounts the **mystical experience**, a category that includes such phenomena as Buddhist nirvana, the complete dissolution of an individual's sense of selfhood said by Buddhists to be a state of perfect bliss and ultimate fulfillment. According to Otto, nirvana involves too much *fascinans* without enough *mysterium tremendum*.

Recall that Bruce Lincoln's definition of religion is based on the notion of the transcendent. Both the numinous experience and nirvana are examples of transcendent states of existence. For Otto, the numinous experience depends on the existence of "the Holy," or God. For many Buddhists, the experience of nirvana does not depend whatsoever on belief in God or gods. Most world religions, whether or not they embrace belief in a supernatural being, assert the possibility of such a transcendent state of existence, an ultimate objective of the religious life that brings complete fulfillment of all spiritual longings. For a Buddhist who has experienced nirvana, there is, paradoxically, no longer a need for Buddhism. The religious life has been lived to its fullest extent, and the ultimate objective has been reached. Because nirvana involves the complete extinction of individual existence, it is truly transcendent of the human condition. Other religions, in varying ways, also set forth ultimate objectives, whether or not they imply the complete transcendence of the human condition. In some cases, spiritual fulfillment can be said to consist of living in harmony with nature. Others acknowledge the supernatural—usually God (or gods)—and the need for human beings to live in perfect

Moses and the Burning Bush (1990), charcoal and pastel on paper by Hans Feibusch. In the drawing, God reveals himself to Moses in a bush that is on fire but not consumed by the flames. The event is described in Exodus, the second book of the Hebrew Bible (Old Testament).

relationship with it. Christianity, for example, offers salvation from the effects of sin, which otherwise estrange the individual from God. Sometimes spiritual fulfillment is thought to be achievable in this lifetime; other times it is projected into the distant future, after many lifetimes.

Of course, improving upon the human condition does not have to involve complete transcendence. Day to day the world over, religious people improve upon the human condition in all sorts of ways. Belief in a loving God gives hope and fortitude in the face of life's uncertainties. Meditation and prayer bring an enhanced sense of tranquility. Religious motivations often lie behind charitable acts. Belonging to a religious group offers social benefits that can be deeply fulfilling. Even for individuals who do not participate directly in a religious tradition, sacred art, architecture, and music can bring joy.

Religion and Violence

This section on religious questions and challenges has thus far emphasized what "should" be done according to religious ideals. But everyone in today's world recognizes that actions are done in the name of religion that hardly seem compatible with ideals or moral imperatives. News about the moral failings of religious leaders or the usurpation of religious institutions by groups that pervert and exploit their teachings surfaces quite frequently. Even more troubling is the constant barrage of reports regarding acts of terrorism and other forms of violence committed in the name of religion. Could there be something about religion itself that motivates such harmful acts?

Religion, as noted at the beginning of this chapter, is a potent force, in ways that are both constructive and destructive. Consider again Bruce Lincoln's four-domain definition of a religion, and note that it does not portray religion as necessarily being a force for peace in the world. The "discourse" that claims a "transcendent status," and the "practices," "community," and "institution" related to this discourse need not necessarily be based on avoiding violence. As Lincoln argues later in *Holy Terrors: Thinking about Religion after September 11*, religion has the potential to facilitate and even to escalate violence. Lincoln concludes his book with a list of fourteen "Theses on Religion and Violence," the last of which states:

> Just as the use of violence tends to elicit a violent riposte, so the religious valorization of violence prompts its victims to frame their violent responses in religious terms. In doing so, they normally invert the

signs through which their adversaries mark one side as sacred and the other profane. When both sides experience their struggle in religious terms, the stage is set for prolonged, ferocious, and enormously destructive combat.[15]

This is a frightening and, we can hope, an unlikely scenario. But as we observe frequently in today's world, even when just one side in a conflict justifies actions by belief in "transcendent" authority, there is a risk of religiously motivated violence, even to the point of taking the lives of others and of losing one's own.

Dimensions of Religions

Sound definitions strive to be universal in scope. Along with a sound definition, a means of categorizing the common, though not necessarily universal, components of a subject of study can often prove beneficial. We now explore possibilities for identifying religious phenomena, in part to bring home the important point that there is no "right" or "wrong" way to go about categorizing them. Instead, we seek the most useful means given the task at hand. This will lead naturally to clarifying how this book goes about organizing its presentation of material.

Some scholarly approaches to the world's religions feature specific categories of phenomena as the primary means of organizing information. Religious scholar Ninian Smart's (1927–2001) "dimensional" scheme, for example, divides the various aspects of religious traditions into seven dimensions:

- The mythic (or sacred narrative)
- The doctrinal (or philosophical)
- The ethical (or legal)
- The ritual (or practical)
- The experiential (or emotional)
- The social
- The material[16]

Such an approach to the content of religious traditions is very useful, especially if one focuses on a comparative analysis that emphasizes particular motifs (that is, "dimensions" or aspects thereof).

In this book, we draw on Smart's dimensions for our organizational scheme, but rather than dividing things into seven categories we divide them into three main ones: teachings, historical development, and way of life. Although each chapter of this book is organized around these three main categories, we do not devote equal attention to each category. To do so would be to ignore the varying nature of the religious traditions and to force an inappropriately rigid structure. Judaism, for example, calls for extensive attention to historical development in order to best understand the context of its teachings and practices; Jainism, for which an early historical record barely exists, does not.

We will continue to explore Smart's dimensions and their interrelationships as we proceed with an overview of these three main categories.

Teachings

Obviously, religions tend to involve beliefs. But as long as they remain private to the individual, beliefs are problematic for the student of religion. Once they are given outward expression in the form of a religion's teachings, however, beliefs can be observed and interpreted. Such public beliefs are manifested as doctrines or creeds—sets of concepts that are *believed in*. (The term *creed* derives from the Latin verb *credo*, meaning "I believe.") Among the world's major religions, Christianity most emphasizes doctrines. Most Christians, for example, regularly acknowledge belief in the statements of the Nicene Creed.

Religious teachings include another significant category, often referred to as **myth** (as noted in Smart's "mythic" dimension). In contrast to the modern connotation of myth as a falsehood, myth as understood by the academic field of religious studies is a powerful source of sacred truth. Set forth

Meditating Buddha, sixth century C.E. (Thai). Sculptures of the Buddha typically depict the serene calm of the enlightened state.

in narrative form and originally conveyed orally, myths do not depend on empirical verifiability or rational coherence for their power. Believers simply accept them as true accounts, often involving events of primordial time that describe the origin of things.

As we have noted previously, religions typically include ethical instructions, whether doctrinal or mythic, among their teachings. And as Smart readily acknowledges, the various dimensions are closely interrelated; the ethical dimension, for example, extends into the doctrinal and the mythic, and so forth.

Historical Development

The world's major religions—all of which are many centuries old—have long and intricate histories. Thus, the historical development of religious traditions incorporates a vast sweep of social, artistic, and other cultural phenomena.

The wide array of artistic, architectural, and other aspects of material culture generated within religious traditions is obvious to anyone who has studied art history. The ornate Hindu temple sculptures, the majestic statues of Jain tirthankaras, the mathematically ordered architectural features of Islamic arabesque décor—all attest to the role of religion in the nurturing of material culture. Other forms of artistic creation, most prominently music and theater, also are significant features of religions. And, as Smart helpfully clarifies when discussing the material dimension of religion, some traditions designate natural entities (mountains, rivers, wooded groves) as sacred.

Social institutions and phenomena, such as economic activities, politics, social class structures, and hierarchies, interact with the historical development of religious

Devils Tower, located in northeastern Wyoming, is regarded as a sacred place by many Native Americans.

traditions. As we have observed, Marx and Durkheim went as far as to reduce religion to being entirely the effect of economic and societal forces, respectively. Even for theorists who opt not to go nearly as far as they did, the relevance of such phenomena is obvious.

Way of Life

This main category features two types of religious phenomena: practices and modes of experience, both of which are included among Smart's seven dimensions of religion, as the ritual (or practical) and the experiential (or emotional) dimensions. Some such elements are tangible and readily observable and describable, such as a **ritual** like the exchange of marriage vows or the procession of pilgrims to a shrine. Others are highly personal and therefore hidden from the outsider's view. One of the great challenges of studying religions rests precisely in this personal, private quality. Modes of experience such as Buddhist nirvana are by definition beyond the reach of empirical observation and of description. Rudolf Otto, throughout his analysis, emphasizes the impossibility of fully describing the "numinous" experience. Even common practices such as prayer and meditation involve an inner aspect that is inaccessible to anyone who is not sharing the experience. Although the present book can adequately illustrate and explain these experiential phenomena, it cannot be expected to provide a full disclosure at certain points. Such is the nature of religion.

RELIGIONS IN THE MODERN WORLD

A sound analysis of the world's religions must take account of the rapid changes that characterize the modern world. Historical transformations, accelerated during the past several centuries by colonialism, the scientific revolution, and economic globalization, have reshaped religious traditions. This book takes into account such factors whenever appropriate. Here we introduce four phenomena that will reappear frequently: modernization, urbanization, globalization, and multiculturalism. We give special attention to two features of modernization that are especially noteworthy for our study: the increasingly visible place of women within religious traditions and the encounter of religion and science.

Modernization and Related Phenomena

Modernization is the general process through which societies transform economically, socially, and culturally to keep pace with an increasingly competitive global marketplace. Its net effects include increased literacy, improved education, enhanced technologies, self-sustaining economies, the increased roles of women in various aspects of society, and the greater involvement of the general populace in government (as in democracies). All these effects involve corresponding changes within religious traditions. Higher literacy rates and improved education, for example, facilitate increased access to religious texts that previously were controlled by and confined to the religious elite. Technological advances, strengthened economies, and increased participation in government all nurture greater equality for and empowerment of the common people. Moreover, a general feature of modernity is its tendency to deny the authority of tradition and the past. Traditional patriarchal modes, for example, have tended over time to be diminished. Around the globe, we are witnessing a general erosion of long-standing power structures within religions. Obviously, this is not the case in all circumstances; changes have tended to occur in different societies at different times, and some religious institutions are better equipped to resist change.

Bongeunsa Temple, founded in 794 C.E., is surrounded by the ultramodern cityscape of Seoul, South Korea.

Urbanization Urbanization, the shift of population centers from rural, agricultural settings to cities, is a significant demographic effect of modernization. A century ago, only about 10 percent of the global population lived in cities; today, this figure has risen to more than 50 percent. Many religious traditions developed within primarily rural settings, with calendars of holy days and rituals patterned around agricultural cycles. For most religious people, such patterns have far less relevance today.

25

Globalization   **Globalization** is the linking and intermixing of cultures. It accelerated quickly during the centuries of exploration and colonization and has been nurtured considerably by the advanced technologies brought about by modernization. The extent of this linking and intermixing is evinced in the very term *World Wide Web*, and the pronounced and rapidly evolving effects of the Internet and other technologies have been extraordinary. The almost instantaneous exchange of information that this technology allows is more or less paralleled by better means of transportation. In sum, we now live in a global community that could hardly have been imagined a few decades ago.

Multiculturalism   The most pronounced religious effects of globalization pertain to the closely related phenomenon of **multiculturalism**, the coexistence of different peoples and their cultural ways in one time and place. Many people today live in religiously pluralistic societies, no longer sheltered from the presence of religions other than their own. This plurality increases the degree of influence exerted by one religion on another, making it difficult for many individuals to regard any one religious tradition as the *only* viable one. This circumstance, in turn, fosters general questioning and critical assessment of religion. To some extent, such questioning and critical assessment erodes the authority traditionally attributed to religion. Globalization, then, like modernization, has nurtured the notably modern process of **secularization**, the general turning away from traditional religious authority and institutions.

The Changing Roles of Women in Religions

One of the more pronounced effects of modernization on world religions has been the increased visibility and prominence of women within many traditions. To some extent, this increase also has *caused* the furtherance of modernization. As women increasingly feel themselves empowered and are afforded opportunities to effect change, their momentum propels modernizing transformations. Traditional patriarchal modes have tended to give way to more egalitarian ones, and old assumptions have gradually receded. To cite just one example, in the last twenty years the percentage of clergy in Protestant Christian churches who are women has risen quite dramatically. According to a 2009 survey, whereas in 1999 only 5 percent of senior pastors were female, ten years later this figure had doubled to 10 percent.[17]

Corresponding to the increased visibility and prominence of women in many religions has been the dramatic development over the past five decades of feminist theory and its application to the study of religion. Sometimes referred to as women's studies or as gender studies, academic approaches based in feminist theory have revealed the strong historical tendency of religious traditions to subordinate women and to enforce the perpetuation of patriarchal systems. On the one hand, these studies have revealed contributions of women through the ages that have hitherto been largely ignored, while on the other hand they have prompted changes within some religions that have expanded the roles of women and have provided opportunities for their greater prominence. In other words, studies based in feminist theory have to some extent *changed* the religions themselves, along with providing new and potent means of studying them.

The Encounter of Religion and Science

Perhaps no single feature of modernization has been more challenging to traditional religious ways—and more nurturing of secularization—than the encounter of religion with science. One need only think of the impact of Charles Darwin's *Origin of Species* (1859) and its theory of evolution to note the potential for conflict between scientific and traditional religious worldviews. The question of whether the biblical account of creation should be taught alongside the theory of evolution in schools is a divisive issue in some predominantly Christian societies today. In the domain of cosmology, too, science has tended to overwhelm traditional perspectives, such as the idea that the Earth is somehow the center of the cosmos, as implied in the Bible and in the creation myths of many traditions.

Many more examples could be drawn from the history of religions and the history of science to illustrate the ongoing potential for conflict between these two domains. Of course, religions are not always hostile to science. In fact, as we have already noted, sometimes modern scientific theories seem almost to converge with ancient religious outlooks. Acquiring a more sophisticated perspective on the encounter of religion and science requires us to consider the underlying reasons for both conflict and convergence.

Fundamental to the scientific method is dependence on empirical data, the observable "facts" of any given situation. To a large extent, religions do not rely only on the observable as a source of determining truth. Religious belief is often characterized precisely by commitment to the *non*observable, such as a supernatural being.

A miniature illustration from the "Automata of al-Jazari," a Muslim scholar, inventor, engineer, mathematician, and astronomer who lived from 1136 to 1206.

This term, "supernatural," indicates another point of contention between religion and science. For whereas science takes it for granted that the universe consistently obeys certain laws of nature, religions commonly embrace belief in beings and events that are not subject to these laws.

And yet, these issues of natural laws and of the observable versus the unobservable also lead to points of convergence between science and religion. Certain basic and extremely significant scientific questions remain unanswered. For example, what is the ground of consciousness? What causes gravity? What, if anything, existed prior to the Big Bang, and what caused *its* existence? Science and religion can perhaps generally agree on one point: mystery abounds. Granted, the scientific response to a mystery is "let's solve it," whereas the religious response typically is "this is a mystery and is meant to be." But in the meantime, mystery abides, allowing for a certain kind of convergence. It is probably no accident that the percentage of scientists in the United States who regularly attend religious services is almost the same as the percentage for the general population.[18]

AN ACADEMIC APPROACH TO THE STUDY OF RELIGIONS

Scholars approach the study of religion in a variety of ways. And although there is no *single* correct approach, it is helpful to keep some basic concepts in mind.

Balance and Empathy

One concept is the maintenance of a healthy balance between the perspective of an insider (one who practices a given religion) and the perspective of an outsider (one who studies the religion without practicing it). For, although an insider arguably has the best vantage point on the lived realities of the religion, presumably the insider is primarily concerned with *being* religious and not in explaining the religion in a manner that will be most effective for those who hold other religious (or nonreligious) perspectives. It is quite natural for an insider to be biased in favor of his or her own religion. The outsider, however, has no reason to feel such bias. At the same time, the outsider would not have the benefit of experiencing the religion firsthand. It is analogous to trying to understand a goldfish in a pond. An outsider can describe the fish's color, its movements, and its eating habits, but can say very little about what it is actually like to be a goldfish.[19]

The academic approach to the study of religions attempts to balance the perspectives of insider and outsider, thereby drawing upon the benefits of each. It is not an intentionally religious enterprise. As we have noted previously, unlike theology, it is not *doing* religion or *being* religious. Instead, the academic approach strives to analyze and describe religions in a way that is accurate and fair for all concerned—insiders and outsiders alike. An instructive parallel can be drawn from the discipline of political science. Rather than advocating a particular political point of view, and rather than *being* a politician, a political scientist strives to analyze and describe political viewpoints and phenomena in a fair, neutral manner. A good political scientist could, for instance, belong to the Democratic Party but still produce a fair article about a Republican politician—without ever betraying personal Democratic convictions. A good scholar of religion, of whatever religious (or nonreligious) persuasion, attends to religious matters with a similarly neutral stance.

Another basic concept for the academic approach to religion is **empathy**, the capacity for seeing things from another's perspective. Empathy works in tandem with the usual tools of scholarship—the observation and rational assessment of empirical data—to yield an effective academic approach to the study of religions. The sometimes cold, impersonal procedures of scholarship are enlivened by the personal insights afforded by empathy.

Comparative and Multidisciplinary Approaches

Many would argue that a sound study of the world's religions requires a comparative approach. The chief benefit of this approach was emphasized by the nineteenth-century scholar Friedrich Max Müller (1823–1900), who is generally regarded as the founder of the modern field of religious studies. He frequently asserted that to know just one religion is to know none. In other words, in order to understand the phenomena of any given tradition, it is necessary to study other traditions, observing such phenomena as they occur in a wide variety of situations. This naturally requires that the study of world religions be cross-cultural in scope. As we proceed from chapter to chapter, the usefulness of comparison will become increasingly evident.

This is not to say that comparison should be undertaken haphazardly or only to discover similarities while ignoring differences. Those critics mentioned earlier who deride the "world religions discourse" tend to be suspicious of attempts at comparison, claiming that too often similarities are indeed valued over differences and that the categories used to make comparisons tend to privilege Christianity over other traditions. Sometimes the results of the comparison of religion differentiate religions into groups that are too sweepingly general: for example, "Eastern" and "Western" religions. Still, the benefits of comparative analysis outweigh the risks, and the potential pitfalls that these critics appropriately warn against can indeed be avoided through a conscientious approach.

Along with being cross-cultural, religious studies is multidisciplinary, or polymethodic, drawing on the contributions of anthropology, history, sociology, psychology, philosophy, feminist theory, and other disciplines and fields of study.

This chapter has frequently used the term *culture*, the study of which is the domain of anthropology. We have noted that religion plays a crucial role in molding, transforming, and transmitting cultures and that it interacts with other cultural aspects. An effective study of the world's religions requires consideration of the interrelationship between religion and culture; in other words, it requires a healthy dose of cultural anthropology.

The need for involvement of the other disciplines should also be apparent. Given their historical and social aspects, the appropriateness of the disciplines of history and sociology for the study of religions is to be expected. And especially when trying to make sense of the modes of religious experience, psychology offers important inroads to understanding. Along with Freud and James, Swiss psychologist Carl Jung (1875–1961) deserves mention for his vital contributions to the study of religious symbolism and of the role of the unconscious mind in the religious life. The philosophy of religion, which in certain respects is the closest to actually *doing* religion (or theology), endeavors to assess critically the truth claims and arguments set forth by religions. Questions involving the existence of God, for example, are among those taken up by philosophers. We have already noted the important contributions of feminist theory. The natural sciences also have contributed substantially, at a pace that is accelerating rapidly. Especially striking innovations have come from cognitive science, which studies both the physical capacity for thinking (i.e., the "brain"—although this category can also include computers and other systems of artificial intelligence) and mental functions (i.e., the "mind"). Cognitive science is itself a multidisciplinary field with contributors including neuroscientists, evolutionary biologists, and computer scientists, along with specialists from the social sciences.

The multidisciplinary nature of religious studies accounts for its very *existence* as an academic discipline. Without the involvement of its many subdisciplines, there could be no academic field of religious studies. In recent years, these various disciplines and subdisciplines have been pushed in new directions, with exciting results. The list of "tags" used by the Society of Biblical Literature for categorizing papers delivered at its meetings provides a glimpse of the range of disciplines and perspectives (see Online Resources at the end of this chapter). Even in this relatively confined field—although the society oversees study of much more than just the Bible—there are forty-four "Interpretive Approaches," which is only one of twelve subcategories listed under the main heading, "Methods" (the other main heading is "Texts"). These diverse Interpretive Approaches include such subdisciplines as African and African American criticism, deconstruction, disability studies, gender and sexuality criticism, Marxist criticism, postcolonial criticism, and theological interpretation. As Ninian Smart was known to say, those who study religion are "polymethod-doodling all da-day long."

CONCLUSION

In this chapter, we have explored the nature of religion and how to study it from an academic perspective. The main objective is to prepare for the study that follows, a chapter-by-chapter examination of the major religions of the world. But the theoretical and methodological content of this introductory chapter is relevant in its own right. Hopefully, readers will recognize the complexity of the ideas and the challenge of the task without feeling daunted about going forward with our study.

We have noted that the rest of this book's chapters feature a threefold organizational scheme consisting of teachings, historical development, and way of life. Although these chapters, with their focus on the religious traditions themselves, naturally are quite different from this introduction, it is worth noticing that in this chapter, too, we have featured historical development—of both the attempts to explain or define religion and the approaches to studying it—and teachings, most especially the theories of various notable contributors to religious studies. The "way of life" aspect perhaps has been less obvious, but in fact it deserves consideration as we end the chapter. On more than one occasion, we have drawn a distinction between the academic study of religion and *doing* religion or *being* religious. Where, then, does this leave the individual who wants to do (and be) both? Ultimately, this question is left for the individual reader to ponder. But it might prove helpful to know that the degree of *being* religious among scholars of religion spans the spectrum of possibilities, from not religious at all to highly devout. Either way (or someplace in between), one thing is true for all who study the world's religions: we are investigating enduring aspects of human cultures around the globe. Our understanding of things that matter is certain to be enriched.

REVIEW QUESTIONS

For Review

1. Who is Émile Durkheim, and what is notable about his definition of religion?
2. Bruce Lincoln, in his definition of religion, identifies four "domains." What are they?
3. What is "revelation," and how is it pertinent to the question, What is ultimate reality?
4. Identify and briefly describe Ninian Smart's seven "dimensions" of religion.

5. What is "empathy," and how is it relevant for the academic study of religion?

For Further Reflection

1. Sigmund Freud and Karl Marx, while tending to be dismissive of the enduring importance of religion, asserted explanations that continue to provoke and to enrich academic consideration of the role of religion. Based on their statements included in this chapter, how might their perspectives be provocative and enriching in this respect?

2. This book poses three prominent questions with regard to the challenges addressed by the world's religions: What is ultimate reality? How should we live in this world? What is our ultimate purpose? Drawing on the examples and ideas presented in this chapter, discuss to what extent and in what ways these three questions are interrelated.

3. Explore the interrelationship of these features of religions in the modern world: globalization, secularization, and multiculturalism.

GLOSSARY

atheism Perspective that denies the existence of God or gods.

cosmology Understanding of the nature of the world that typically explains its origin and how it is ordered.

empathy The capacity for seeing things from another's perspective, and an important methodological approach for studying religions.

globalization The linking and intermixing of cultures; any process that moves a society toward an internationalization of religious discourse.

henotheism The belief that acknowledges a plurality of gods but elevates one of them to special status.

modernization The general process through which societies transform economically, socially, and culturally to become more industrial, urban, and secular; any transformation of societies and cultures that leads to the abandonment of traditional religious values.

monism The belief that all reality is ultimately one.

monotheism The belief in only one god.

multiculturalism The coexistence of different peoples and their cultural ways in one time and place.

mysterium tremendum and fascinans The contrasting feelings of awe-inspiring mystery and of overwhelming attraction that are said by Rudolf Otto to characterize the numinous experience.

mystical experience A general category of religious experience characterized in various ways, for example, as the union with the divine through inward contemplation or as the dissolution of the sense of individual selfhood.

myth A story or narrative, originally conveyed orally, that sets forth basic truths of a religious tradition and that often involves events of primordial time that describe the origins of things.

nontheistic Term denoting a religion that does not maintain belief in God or gods.

numinous experience Rudolf Otto's term for describing an encounter with "the Holy"; it is characterized by two powerful and contending forces, *mysterium tremendum* and *fascinans*.

pantheism The belief that the divine reality is identical to nature or the material world.

polytheism The belief in many gods.

revealed ethics Truth regarding right behavior believed to be divinely established and intentionally made known to human beings.

revelation The expression of the divine will, commonly recorded in sacred texts.

ritual Formal worship practice.

secularization The general turning away from traditional religious authority and institutions; any tendency in modern society that devalues religious worldviews or seeks to substitute scientific theories for religious beliefs.

theistic Term denoting a religion that maintains belief in God or gods.

transtheistic Term denoting a theological perspective that acknowledges the existence of gods while denying that the gods are vital with regard to the most crucial religious issues, such as the quest for salvation.

urbanization The shift of population centers from rural, agricultural settings to cities.

SUGGESTIONS FOR FURTHER READING

Eliade, Mircea. *The Sacred and the Profane: The Nature of Religion*. Translated by Willard R. Trask. New York: Harper and Row, 1961. Eliade's most accessible work, offering a rich analysis of sacred space and time.

Hinnels, John, ed. *The Routledge Companion to the Study of Religion*. 2nd ed. Oxford: Routledge, 2010. Coverage of significant issues in religious studies by leading scholars.

Masuzawa, Tomoko. *The Invention of World Religions: Or, How European Universalism Was Preserved in the Language of Pluralism*. Chicago: University of Chicago Press, 2005. Careful historical analysis of the term and category "world religions."

Pals, Daniel. *Nine Theories of Religion*. 3rd ed. New York: Oxford University Press, 2015. The best introduction to the history of religious studies as an academic field, including chapters on Karl Marx, William James, Sigmund Freud, Émile Durkheim, and Mircea Eliade.

Segal, Robert A., and Kocku von Stuckrad, eds. *Vocabulary for the Study of Religion*. Leiden, The Netherlands: Brill, 2015. 3 volumes. Also available online, this recent, thorough work provides encyclopedic coverage of all important topics in the field of religious studies.

Smart, Ninian. *Dimensions of the Sacred: An Anatomy of the World's Beliefs*. Berkeley: University of California Press, 1996. An engaging presentation of Smart's "dimensions."

Smith, Jonathan Z. *Imagining Religion: From Babylon to Jonestown*. Chicago Studies in the History of Judaism. Chicago: University of Chicago Press, 1982. A collection of essays that exemplify Smith's impressively wide-ranging and astute approach to the study of religion.

Taylor, Mark C., ed. *Critical Terms for Religious Studies*. Chicago: University of Chicago Press, 1998. Articles on various central topics for the study of religions, written by leading scholars in the field.

ONLINE RESOURCES

American Academy of Religion
aarweb.org
The largest and most influential North American academic society for the study of religion.

Society of Biblical Literature
sbl-site.org
A companion organization to the American Academy of Religion, the Society of Biblical Literature is the premier academic organization for scholars in biblical studies and much more. The diversity and innovative nature of the Society is evidenced in its extensive list of "tags" that are used to help categorize papers presented at its various meetings: https://www.sbl-site.org/Meetings/Congresses_Tags.aspx

Pew Research Religion and Public Life Project
pewforum.org
Excellent source of information on issues involving social and political aspects of religion. The Pew Forum study of May 2015 revealed startling statistics with regard to the rapid decline of traditional forms of religion in the United States: http://www.pewforum.org/religious-landscape-study/

The Pluralism Project at Harvard University
pluralism.org
Organization that offers an impressive array of helpful resources, especially with regard to the world's religions in North America.

Hinduism

THE SKIES OVER MUMBAI are clearing and the sun is poking through the clouds, shedding rays of light on the throng of worshipers that crowd to behold the Lalbaugcha Raja sculpture of Ganesha, the elephant god. It is the last day of Ganesh Chaturthi, the ten-day festival celebrated across India in honor of Ganesha's birthday. Most of those gathered had already performed **puja,** or worship, in their homes this morning, praying before temporarily installed clay idols of the god. There and in the presence of the Lalbaugcha Raja Ganesha sculpture and many other sculptures located around the city, all having been specially prepared for the festival, Ganesha is offered his favorite foods.

At this unique temporary shrine, an exquisite idol of the god, created by a master sculptor especially for this year's festival, is colorfully painted and adorned with flowers. *Bhajan* and *kirtan*, sacred devotional songs, are performed in the god's honor. The shrine is alive with the music and the vibrant colors that seem to adorn most everything, including the worshipers. The entire city of Mumbai teems with life during Ganesh Chaturthi, one of India's most popular celebrations. Neighborhoods like Lalbaugcha sponsor their own production of Ganesha sculptures, competing with each other over the best artistic creation.

With his elephant head and human body, Ganesha is one of Hinduism's most easily recognized deities. As the patron deity of arts

A Ganesha sculpture is about to be submerged at the seashore in Mumbai on the tenth and final day of Ganesh Chaturthi, a celebration of the elephant god's birthday.

2600–1700 B.C.E.	Indus Valley Civilization.
2000–1300 B.C.E.	Migration into Northwest India of Indo-Aryans.
c. 1200 B.C.E.	Rig Veda.
c. 1200–900 B.C.E.	Later Vedas.
c. 900–200 B.C.E.	Upanishads.
400 B.C.E.–400 C.E.	*Mahabharata.*
200 B.C.E.–200 C.E.	*Ramayana.*
c. First century C.E.	*Bhagavad Gita.*
100–500 C.E.	Expansion of Hinduism into Southeast Asia.
c. 320–540	Gupta Dynasty; rise of Hindu temple culture.
300–500	Earliest Puranas; Hindu law books.
700	Flourishing of bhakti in the South.
999–1226	Mahmud of Ghazi; repeated raids of India.
Fifteenth century	Bhakti movement begins in northern India.
c. 1398–1518	Kabir, bhakti poet
1526–1757	Mughal rule in India.
1651	The East India Company opens first factory on the Hugli River in Bengal.
1786	Sir William Jones lectures on the common ancestry of Sanskrit and many European languages.
1828	Brahmo Samaj founded by Ram Mohan Roy.
1834–1886	Sri Ramakrishna.
1869–1948	Mohandas (Mahatma) Gandhi.
1875	Arya Samaj founded by Swami Dayananda Saraswati.
1893	Swami Vivekananda at the World Parliament of Religions, Chicago.
1925	RSS (Rashtriya Swayamsevak Sangh) founded.
1947	India gains independence; partition with newly established nation of Pakistan
1964	VHP (Vishwa Hindu Parishad) founded.
1992	Destruction of Babri Masjid and widespread riots.
2014	BJP (Bharatiya Janata Party) wins Indian elections by a landslide.

and sciences and the god of wisdom, new beginnings, and commerce, he is especially venerated by students, writers, travelers, and businessmen. Ganesha is worshiped at the beginning of every new undertaking, and he is the first deity invoked in almost any Hindu ritual context. He is often depicted as carrying objects in his four arms (including an axe, a noose, and an elephant goad) that he uses to destroy, subdue, or control the obstacles of life. He also often holds a bowl of sweets, symbolizing his benevolent and loving nature.

Later this afternoon, at the conclusion of Ganesh Chaturthi, the shrine's clay idol will be carried in a procession to the seashore and, to the accompaniment of music, will be submerged in the ocean where it will soon dissolve, becoming one with the natural world and thereby nourishing it. The worshipers celebrate this event, as Ganesha is believed now to return home to his parents, Shiva and Parvati, who live on Mount Kailash high in the Himalaya. ☀

Unlike many other religions discussed in this book, Hinduism has neither a single founder nor a single sacred book. There is no single historical event that marks its birth. The history of Hinduism embodies both continuity and change. Having never had a sole central authority, Hinduism's fluid character has always allowed it to adapt to a variety of social and cultural contexts. This diversity has led many scholars to argue that Hinduism is not one religion at all but a constellation of many religious sects that share some common aspects. Others see enough by way of common beliefs and practices to regard Hinduism as a single religious tradition. In this chapter, we will explore Hinduism's variety of sects, beliefs, and practices and seek to understand what unites a tradition that is the religion of over one billion of the world's people.

THE TEACHINGS OF HINDUISM

Prior to the nineteenth century, the word "Hinduism" did not exist. Most Hindus identified themselves by their sectarian orientation and their communal or caste affiliations. The word "Hindu" was initially a term used by the ancient Persians to describe the people who lived beyond the Indus River in the northwestern corner of the Indian subcontinent. By 325 B.C.E., Alexander the Great had crossed the Indus; the Greek conquerors adopted the Persian convention of calling the river the "Indos" and the land beyond it "India." In the centuries that followed, the term *Indu* or *Hindu* became a territorial, as well as a racial, social, and cultural, designation for the people of India. After the sixteenth century C.E., the word appeared occasionally in Indian literature to distinguish "Hindus" from Muslims or other "foreigners." Although the "-ism" was added to "Hindu" in the early 1800s, only toward the end of the nineteenth century did the word "Hinduism" become widely used by Hindus themselves.

Some Hindus look to the authority of a group of texts known as the **Vedas** and may rely on **brahmin** priests to officiate at various rituals. Others reject the centrality of the Vedas and brahmins. Some Hindus join organizations built around saints or sages. Others seek solitude to practice contemplation, meditation, or yoga. Some Hindus believe that God is a divine person with identifiable attributes. Others say that divine reality is so expansive as to be beyond all description.

A photograph taken of a Hindu temple in Trinidad in 1931. The presence of Hindus in the Caribbean and South America can be traced back to the nineteenth century, when Hindus came as indentured workers on sugar cane plantations.

Despite Hinduism's diversity, it is possible to identify common core concepts in which most every Hindu believes. For instance, the law of **karma** determines the nature of one's incarnations in **samsara**, the continuing cycle of death and rebirth. At the end of this cycle is **moksha**, or liberation, the final release from the trials and tribulations of samsara.

For the sake of simplicity, in this chapter we have organized our investigation of Hindu teachings around four main topics: beliefs about God or divine reality; Hinduism's key doctrines and social concepts; Hinduism's foundational texts; and Vedanta, a philosophical school, and Hinduism's three major sects.

Hindu Beliefs about Divine Reality

In keeping with Hinduism's general diversity, Hindu beliefs about divine reality are wide ranging. Indeed, one of the most fundamental differences in Hinduism is the split between monistic and dualistic (or devotional) viewpoints. Monism, as explained in this book's introductory chapter, is the doctrine that all reality is ultimately one. It is nondualistic in that there is no distinction between the divine reality and the rest

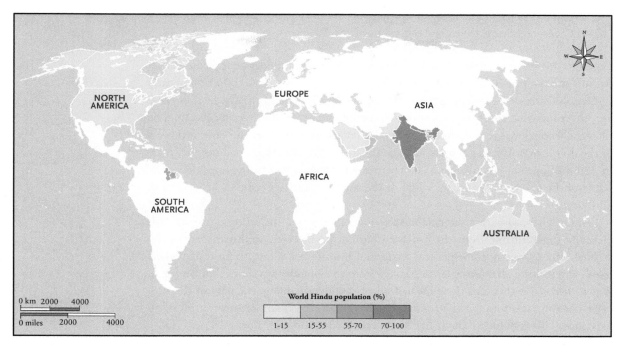

World Hindu population.

World Hindu population (%)

1-15   15-55   55-70   70-100

0 km 2000   4000
0 miles   2000   4000

of reality. The Hindu dualistic viewpoint, in contrast, understands divine reality as God, a personal being separate from the rest of reality. This means that God is separate from the individual, and therefore devotion to God is natural. Devotional practice of this sort is a primary religious activity of Hindus who hold this dualistic viewpoint. The majority of Hindus understand divine reality in this dualistic manner.

Names of the Divine Reality   Hindus refer to divine reality in a variety of ways. In this chapter, in order to maintain clarity between references to the monistic and the dualistic viewpoints, we use two distinct terms. When referencing monism, we use the term **Brahman** (lit. "expansive") to denote the divine reality, which monistic Hindus believe is the supreme, unitary reality that is the source of all being and all knowing. When referencing dualistic or devotional Hinduism, we use either "God" or the name of the specific deity under consideration.

In actual Hindu practice, conventions of naming the divine are often not so simple as our chapter's use of these two distinct terms might imply. Sometimes monistic Hindus, for example, refer to Brahman as "God." Many dualistic Hindus use "God" to denote a universal being that encompasses all the various deities worshiped in Hinduism, and sometimes they use the term Brahman. When dualistic Hindus refer to a particular deity, they often use the specific name, such as Krishna, Rama, or Shiva. Devotees of the goddess traditions refer to God as *Mahadevi* ("Great Goddess") or *Mataji* ("mother"). Sometimes Hindus use Sanskrit terms such as *Bhagavan* (lit. "Magnanimous One;" also an epithet for Vishnu) and *Svami* (or Swami, lit. "Master"; also denoting an initiate of a monastic order).

One Divine Reality, Many Gods   The monistic viewpoint does not preclude belief in gods and goddesses. In a famous passage from the **Upanishads** (a collection of early philosophical texts), a sage is asked how many gods there are. Initially, he says there are "three hundred and three, and three thousand and three," but, upon reflection, he ultimately concludes that there is only one.[1] The sage explains that the various powers of the divine manifest as countless deities. In later times, the traditional number grew to 330 million. The passage from the Upanishads concludes with the sage giving the name of the one god: Brahman, which is the supreme, unitary reality, the ground of all Being.

Although Brahman is the true nature of all that exists, including ourselves, it is virtually indescribable from the ordinary human perspective. Brahman can be described only by way of some general attributes: infinite being (*sat*), infinite awareness (*chit*), and infinite bliss (*ananda*). A passage from the Upanishads states that Brahman is *neti, neti*: "not this, not this."[2] When all of the identifiable particulars of the universe are subtracted away, what remains is Brahman, the essential substratum of all existence. This is monism, the belief that all reality is ultimately one.

These passages from the Upanishads influence how later monistic Hinduism forms its understanding of the mystery and majesty of Being. Many monistic Hindus believe that the divine reality is simultaneously one—as Brahman, the ground of all Being—and many. Given the worship of many deities, along with affirmation of the ultimate singularity of the divine, and indeed of *all* reality, this form of Hinduism can be described as both polytheistic and monistic. Unlike polytheistic religions that see the various gods as limited, Hinduism regards each god as a manifestation of Brahman.

Divine Reality as Sound   The primordial sound **OM** (or, more literally, *AUM*), is constituted of three sounds of the Sanskrit language: *A* (the first vowel), *U* (the final vowel), and *M* (the final consonant). OM therefore encompasses all words and all things they represent. OM is the sound through which the universe is manifested and thus is the very expression of Brahman. Some Upanishads also identify it with four states of consciousness: *A* is waking consciousness, *U* is dreaming consciousness, *M* is deep sleep without dreaming consciousness, and *AUM* in its entirety is the fourth and final state, oneness with Brahman. In later Hinduism, the sounds are identified with the gods Brahma, Vishnu, and Shiva and their functions of creating, preserving, and dissolving the universe.

God as Image   Paradoxically, given the difficulty of comprehending the nature of divine reality, Hinduism is an intensely imagistic religious tradition. This is especially true of dualistic Hinduism, as imagistic representations of God are naturally well suited for devotional practices.

Shiva as Lord of the Dance (Nataraja) performs his Five Activities: creation (represented by the drum in his upper right hand), preservation (signified by the positions of his lower right and left hands), destruction (symbolized by the fire in his upraised left hand), illusion (personified by the Demon of Forgetfulness crushed beneath his right leg), and liberation (offered by surrendering to his upraised left foot). Chola period, c. eleventh century. India, Tamil Nadu.

Images of supernatural beings and mythical beasts decorate Hindu temples, as well as Hindu homes. These images can be richly adorned stationary icons enshrined in temples or beautifully crafted bronze icons carried in religious processions. Today, some Hindus revere print and online images of the divine. This love for the divine form emerges from Hindu notions of the simultaneous immanence and transcendence of God. An image of a deity is a symbolic representation meant to aid devotees in contemplating the deity's divine attributes, but the image is also believed to be suffused with divine presence, as we saw in the opening narrative about the Ganesha festival and temple. Thus, Hindus believe that God becomes accessible to devotees through images. For Hindus, an image of a god *is* God.

The Divine in Nature   If Brahman is everywhere and everything, it follows that the natural world is an expression of the divine. This belief is held by most Hindus, whether inclined toward the monistic or the dualistic viewpoint. The worship of such natural entities as rivers, the earth, mountains, and the sun, as well as a reverence for certain trees and animals, can be traced back to the roots of Hinduism.

Many sacred sites arose in conjunction with the worship of rivers and mountains. Rivers in particular are worshiped as embodying the creative energy that generates the universe, as well as being powerful places of crossing between the divine and terrestrial worlds. It is for all of these reasons that many Hindus bathe in rivers—of which the Ganges in India is the most important—believing that they wash away one's sins. For centuries, the awe-inspiring peaks of the Himalayas have attracted monks, yogis, and pilgrims seeking an experience of the divine. Mount Kailash, believed to be the home of the god Shiva, draws devotees who perform a ritual circumambulation of the mountain over the course of several days, reaching elevations of greater than 18,000 feet on the trek. Hindu mythology portrays the sun, planets, and other celestial bodies as gods.

For Hindus, all living things are sacred, and some especially so. For example, the type of fig tree under which Gautama the Buddha attained enlightenment (Chapter 5) is sacred to the god Vishnu. As is well known, Hindu society gives a special place to the cow, a practice that has deep historical roots in the pastoral, cattle-tending communities found throughout India. Because a child, once weaned from its mother's breast, is frequently given cow's milk, Hindus revere the cow as a second mother. Cows are worshiped on the first day of the important Hindu festival of Diwali, as well as on the first day of a harvest festival observed in southern India. For Hindus, the worship of cows is an expression of respect for creatures that help humanity.

Although Hinduism has a long history of reverence for natural entities, this has not always translated into ecological awareness and activism. The worship of rivers does not mean that India's sacred waterways are pristine. Because rivers are divine, they are said to be able to absorb the sins of worshipers and still remain unaffected. Thus, for many Hindus, rivers remain pure even if they are polluted by waste. In recent years, Hindu environmental activists have begun to challenge these assumptions by employing Hindu beliefs about the divinity of the natural world to promote more informed ecological awareness.

God Comes Down: Avatars Two of the most popular deities in Hinduism are Krishna and Rama. Each is an **avatar**, a "descent" (Sanskrit, *avatara*) of God to earth in a physical form with the specific goal of aiding the world. Like most avatars, they are manifestations of Vishnu, whose primary function is the preservation of order in the world. Vishnu is believed to have ten such forms, of which nine have already appeared. As noted, the most popular of the avatars are Rama, Vishnu's seventh form, and Krishna, his eighth. It is said that Vishnu's final avatar, Kalki, will arrive at the end of the present age to usher in an era of peace.

We have seen that Hindus often use the names of particular gods as a way of referring to divine reality.

A Hindu devotee performs rituals dedicated to the Sun God as he takes a holy dip in Allahabad, India, at the confluence of the Ganges and Yamuna rivers, one of Hinduism's important centers.

This is the case with avatars. For example, Hinduism's best-known sacred text, the *Bhagavad Gita* ("The Song of the Lord"), presents Krishna as a manifestation of the supreme Being.

In the *Bhagavad Gita*, Krishna asserts the principle that although God's essential nature is unchangeable, God chooses to descend into the world in the form of an avatar when intervention is necessary to reinstate peace and harmony. Krishna says (4.6–8):

Though myself unborn, undying,
the lord of creatures, I fashion nature,
which is mine, and I come into being
through my own magic.

Whenever sacred duty decays
and chaos prevails,
then, I create

myself, Arjuna.
To protect men of virtue
and destroy men who do evil,
to set the standard of sacred duty,
I appear in age after age.[3]

We will learn more about the *Bhagavad Gita* later in this chapter.

The Individual and the Quest for Liberation

Having explored Hindu perspectives on divine reality, we turn now to basic concepts that form the framework of the Hindu outlook on the individual and the quest for liberation. Some of these concepts, such as samsara and karma, are also significant for other Indian religions (Buddhism, Jainism, and Sikhism).

Atman   All Hindus believe in an undying soul or self, the **atman**, whose nature is neither limited by the physical body nor defined by its relationship to the world. It is the atman that moves from body to body through successive incarnations.

The task of recognizing the true nature of the essential self is understood to be arduous and rarely achieved. Most Hindus assume that this will require many lifetimes. One's life ordinarily revolves around a sense of selfhood that is limited, constrained by desires and by ignorance of the true nature of atman. Therefore, life ordinarily is lived by the egoistic "self" that is by nature selfish and stuck with false identification of the self with the physical body. This leads to suffering, as the body undergoes painful changes brought on by disease, old age, and death.

Monistic Hinduism, true to its basic premise that all reality is ultimately one, teaches that the atman *is* Brahman. Another famous passage from the Upanishads conveys this idea through the story of a young man named Svetaketu, who receives instruction from his father on the true nature of the atman. Using a number of analogies, the father explains that despite the appearance of multiplicity, all reality is one. The father emphatically declares: *Tat tvam asi svetakato iti* (*"You* are that, Svetaketu!").[4] Atman *is* Brahman.

Karma   The course of the atman through successive incarnations is determined by karma. In its original, most basic sense, karma means "action," but for Hindus it means the consequences of action as well. Karma functions in accordance with the law of cause and effect: good actions produce good effects, bad actions produce bad effects. Karma encompasses all kinds of action, physical as well as mental. A person's situation in any given moment has been shaped by all previous actions. Similarly, the karmic forces that we set in motion in our present lives will determine the nature of our future incarnations. To ensure that the future will be good, our actions now must be good—and that means living in conformity with dharma.

Dharma For Hinduism, the term **dharma** can mean law, duty, righteousness, or even "religion," all of which have to do with living in a way that upholds cosmic and social order. Dharma is traditionally believed to have been divinely revealed to the *rishis,* the poet-sages who composed the Vedas.

Through the centuries, Hindu texts have set forth ritual and social obligations that define a good life. The *Laws of Manu,* for example, a classic juridical text from the period 200 B.C.E. to 200 C.E., contains detailed prescriptions for correct behavior in all aspects of life. The two ancient and enormously influential Indian epic poems, the *Ramayana* and the *Mahabharata,* depict the simultaneous particularity and universality of dharma. As we will consider in more detail in a later section, both poems present epic heroes who must resolve conflicts between social or family obligations and their own personal sense of what duty demands from them.

Samsara Hindus use the term samsara in two closely related ways. Samsara is the continuing cycle of birth, death, and rebirth. *It* is also the this-worldly realm in which birth, death, and rebirth recur. When the physical body dies, the eternal self or soul, the atman, moves on to another body. This process continues until the true nature of the atman is recognized. As noted previously, the nature of each rebirth is determined by karma. Virtuous acts of kindness and generosity over lifetimes ensure favorable rebirths, perhaps even in the blissful heavens of the gods. Selfish action and meanness lead to undesirable rebirths.

Hindus believe in a multitude of heavens and hells, as well as other regions in between. A rebirth in a heaven or hell could last thousands of years but is still only temporary. The most desirable rebirth of all is as a human being in a situation that offers the greatest opportunity for realizing liberation from samsara; for example, as a sage or an ascetic.

The concept of samsara presents some basic questions. What gives rise to samsara? And why are human beings so prone to remain stuck in this samsaric realm? Through the ages, Hindus have offered various answers to these questions. Some of these answers have involved the concept of **maya**, which in the Vedas refers to the magical power the gods used to create this world. Is the world an illusion, as is often the case with magic, or real? Hindus are divided on this issue. In either case, they agree that human beings are powerfully attracted to this world, with its many particulars—our egoistic selves, our relationships, our possessions, and the seemingly countless objects of our desires. Our attachment to such things in all that we think and do and the karma it generates steer us after each lifetime back into the samsaric realm of particulars.

All of this leads to another basic question: Why should anyone *want* to escape from samsara? After all, the prospect of a future filled with numerous lifetimes would seem to be appealing. Hinduism's answer is simple: beyond the samsaric realm lies something inexpressibly better.

Moksha Freedom from the bondage of samsara is achieved through moksha, "release" or "liberation." Having overcome attachments to this world, the atman realizes its true nature. For monistic Hindus, moksha is the union of the atman with Brahman, such that no sense of individuality any longer exists. For dualistic or devotional Hindus, for whom the divine reality is identified with their supreme God (be it Vishnu, Shiva, or another), moksha involves the eternal existence of the atman in the company of God. Hindus also have differing opinions on whether moksha can occur for a living person or whether it must await death of the physical body. For all Hindus, however, moksha marks the end of the samsaric cycle of rebirth and the end of the effects of karma. Like Brahman, moksha is virtually impossible to describe, beyond being characterized—also like Brahman—as infinite awareness and eternal bliss.

The quest for moksha, for liberating oneself from samsara even while constrained to the limits of this world, is extremely challenging. Hinduism offers three main paths to moksha, each of which provides the means of eradicating ignorance and egoistic attachment and thus freeing the atman.

A sannyasi, or Hindu ascetic. His sectarian affiliation is indicated by his forehead marking, which demonstrates that he is a worshipper of Vishnu.

Three Paths to Liberation

Typical of the diverse nature of Hinduism, there are a variety of approaches to the goal of liberation. Traditionally, they have been categorized as three paths, or margas (also called yogas), each one featuring its own set of practices and being suited to certain personality traits and life situations. **Karma marga**, for those engaged in the activities of family and career, emphasizes ritual and ethical works. **Bhakti marga**, for the vast majority of Hindus who regularly worship in temples and in their homes, is devotion to a deity. **Jnana marga**, for those privileged to devote time and energy on study and contemplation, focuses on spiritual insight. The paths are by no means exclusive of one another: Hindus commonly engage in more than one. Almost all Hindus, for example, practice some form of bhakti marga, and karma marga is a natural way to approach life's everyday tasks. All three margas function to diminish the ignorance, attachment, and false identification of the self with the physical body that characterizes life in the samsaric realm.

The *Bhagavad Gita*, which was composed in about the first century of the Common Era, sets forth all three margas, explaining characteristics common to all three and making clear their mutual compatibility. Of fundamental concern is the need to eradicate the ignorance and attachment born of an egoistic sense of selfhood. One passage puts it this way: "He who abandons all desires and acts free from longing, without any sense of mineness or egotism—he attains to peace."[5]

Karma Marga As noted previously, all Hindus are required to act in conformity with dharma, the duty to live in a manner that upholds the cosmic and social order. Karma marga combines focus on dharma with an attitude of detachment with regard to acting and to the results, or "fruit," of action. In the words of the *Bhagavad Gita* (5.11–12):

> Relinquishing attachment,
> men of discipline perform action
> with body, mind, understanding, and senses
> for the purification of the self.
> Relinquishing the fruit of action
> the disciplined man attains perfect peace;
> the undisciplined man is in bondage,
> attached to the fruit of desire.[6]

When the self, or atman, is devoid of attachment to the results of action, the problems of egotism and the suffering brought about by birth, disease, old age, and death are resolved.

Bhakti Marga The path of devotion, bhakti marga, is the most widely practiced of the three paths to liberation. This chapter's survey of the history of Hinduism includes a section detailing the rise of the bhakti tradition. In an important manner, the tradition is grounded in the *Bhagavad Gita*, which, along with prescribing the other two margas, gives pride of place to bhakti. In the *Bhagavad Gita*, the featured deity is Krishna. Bhakti, however, can be directed toward whatever deity one chooses. The deity is perceived as the supreme divine reality, as is clearly shown with regard to Krishna in the *Bhagavad Gita*. Hindus typically worship more than one deity, depending on personal preference and on the occasion. For instance, during the festival in honor of Saraswati, goddess of education, Hindu schoolchildren offer devotion to her. There are numerous such festivals of the gods in the Hindu year.

In the *Bhagavad Gita* (12.6–8), Krishna makes clear to his devotee Arjuna the great benefits of bhakti:

> But men intent on me
> renounce all actions to me
> and worship me, meditating
> with singular discipline.
> When they entrust reason to me,
> Arjuna, I soon arise
> to rescue them from the ocean

of death and rebirth.
Focus your mind on me,
let your understanding enter me;
then you will dwell
in me without doubt.[7]

Like karma marga and jnana marga, bhakti marga functions to eradicate egotism, ignorance, and attachment to the objects of desire. By devoting one's time and energy to a deity rather than to one's individualistic yearnings and concerns, ultimately the true nature of reality can be realized, the effects of karma neutralized, and liberation from samsara achieved.

Jnana Marga   Generally agreed to be the steepest ascent to liberation, jnana ("knowledge") marga requires disciplined study of sacred texts and intensive contemplation, typically through the practice of meditation. In the words of the *Bhagavad Gita (4.38–39),*

No purifier equals knowledge,
and in time
the man of perfect discipline
discovers this in his own spirit.
Faithful, intent, his senses
subdued, he gains knowledge;
gaining knowledge,
he soon finds perfect peace.[8]

The knowledge gained through jnana marga is wisdom or insight of a special kind. To attain this wisdom is to become aware of the true nature of atman. For monistic Hindus, this is to become aware that the atman is none other than Brahman, the ultimate, unitary reality.

We now turn our attention to the two most prominent forms of jnana marga and of Hinduism's six philosophical schools: Vedanta and Yoga. The Yoga school, which teaches specific physical and mental exercises designed to promote jnana, is so distinctive and historically significant that some Hindus classify it as a fourth marga. With its meditative practices often performed in the lotus position, Yoga is commonly envisioned by non-Hindus when pondering the spiritual life of India. The Vedanta school has been even more influential in the history of Hindu thought.

Vedanta: The Predominant School of Hindu Philosophy

The philosophical system that emerged out of the Upanishads is called **Vedanta,** which in Sanskrit means "the end of the Vedas"—"end" not only as conclusion but also as culmination. The Vedanta school asserts that the Upanishads reveal the truth about the fundamental questions of existence. The Upanishads are both profound and challenging and are open to a variety of interpretations. Following the composition of the early Upanishads, philosophy became a very important part of Hinduism. Predictably, there even arose a number of different schools within Vedanta. Each school of Vedanta sought to understand the precise nature of the relationships between Brahman, atman, and the world.

The impact of Vedanta on the development of Hinduism cannot be overestimated. As different Hindu sects emerged, their distinctive understandings of Vedanta shaped their philosophical orientations. Of the many schools of Vedanta, the three most important are *Advaita*, *Vishishta-Advaita*, and *Dvaita*.

Advaita Vedanta Known as Hinduism's uncompromisingly monistic school of philosophy, *Advaita* ("Non-dualist") Vedanta teaches that the atman is identical to Brahman and denies any distinction whatsoever between Brahman and everything else. This school of thought grew directly out of the Upanishads but was further developed in the eighth century C.E. by Shankara, its most famous proponent. Shankara posited that the world is maya, "illusion." Earlier in this chapter we noted that the Vedas present maya as the magical power the gods used to create this world. For Shankara, maya veils the mind, such that it does not discern the true nature of the self (atman). According to Shankara, it is this lack of discernment, or ignorance, manifesting as attachment and desire, that keeps one bound to the cycle of death and rebirth (samsara). When one uses wisdom and discernment, one can cut through ignorance and recognize the inherent unity of all things, including the oneness of Brahman and atman. This in turn results in moksha and the complete dissolution of one's sense of individual selfhood.

Vishishta-Advaita Many of the sects that worship Vishnu differ on the subtler aspects of the relationship between Brahman and atman. For Vaishnavas, Brahman is identified with Vishnu. The school of *Vishishta-Advaita*, founded by the twelfth-century C.E. philosopher Ramanuja, declared that all is Brahman and that the material world and individual souls also are real. The world is not illusion (maya); rather, it is the body of God. All beings are a part of God, eternally connected to Vishnu but not the same as him. We are more like cells in the divine body. Unlike Shankara, Ramanuja interpreted the ignorance that obscures true knowledge as forgetfulness—in particular, the devotee's forgetfulness of our eternal relationship with Vishnu. In this manner, Ramanuja's Vedanta marries philosophy to the devotional, sectarian traditions of Vaishnavism.

Dvaita Vedanta The school of *Dvaita* ("Dualist") Vedanta, founded by the thirteenth-century theologian Madhva, advocates a complete distinction between Brahman and atman. It posits that there are five acknowledged aspects of complete separateness or difference: between the atman and Brahman, between Brahman and matter, between the various souls, between the souls and matter, and between various forms of matter. This philosophical strain, too, is associated with the worship of Vishnu, particularly in his avatar as Krishna.

Yoga

Yoga in its most basic sense means a "yoking" or "uniting." In religious discourse, it refers to the uniting of the self with God. Most of us are familiar with hatha yoga, which makes use of physical exercises to promote the health of the body. As a form of jnana marga, Yoga—often called Raja ("Royal") Yoga—employs both physical and mental techniques in order to make liberation from samsara possible.

By the fourth century C.E., the principles and techniques of Raja Yoga had been systematized in the *Yoga Sutras* of Patanjali. The *Yoga Sutras* consist of 196 instructional sayings about the moral, physical, and mental conditions and techniques that can enable the

A Hindu ascetic sits in the lotus position, a prominent bodily posture for the practice of yoga.

individual to achieve moksha. These are evident in the eight steps through which practitioners move in their quest for liberation. The first two steps have to do with moral preparation. Prohibitions against harming other beings, lying, stealing, sexual irresponsibility, and greed must be observed. In addition, the five virtues of cleanliness, contentment, discipline, studiousness, and devotion to a god must be practiced. The next three steps involve preparation of the body. The practitioner learns postures (especially the lotus position) that promote comfort and alertness and the ability to breathe in rhythmic patterns that calm the body. Once these ends have been achieved, it becomes possible to withdraw the senses so that they no longer demand the mind's attention. The next two steps prepare the mind for liberation. By focusing its attention on a single thing, all other particulars fade away. All that remains is to remove this single object of attention from the mind's awareness. This brings the practitioner to the eighth step, which is also the ultimate goal: samadhi, a state in which one's awareness is of the self as Brahman.

The Individual and Society

The Hindu individual's quest for liberation is determined by such factors as gender, caste status, and age. Like all aspects of the religion, the rules governing these factors admit to diversity even while conforming to basic patterns that have persisted through the centuries. Collectively, these rules are known as *varnashrama dharma*: the religious law regulating caste (*varna*) and stage of life (ashrama). Traditionally, all Hindus are required to comply with *varnashrama dharma*.

The Caste System

The Sanskrit term ***varna*** (literally, "color"), commonly translated as "caste," refers to a system of hierarchical social organization. A more accurate way of expressing the meaning of *varna* in this context is through the English term "class." There are four main classes in Hindu society: brahmin, the priestly class; **kshatriya**, the warrior and administrator class; **vaishya**, the producer class (farmers and merchants); and **shudra**, the servant class. *Varna* is determined by birth and is propagated through endogamy, or marriage only within a particular group. The caste system, and *varnashrama dharma* generally, has traditionally been most important for males of the three higher classes, the so-called "twice-born" castes.

We encounter the first mention of *varna* in a poem known as the *Purusha Sukta*, an early Sanskrit poem found in the tenth book of the Rig Veda (c. 1200 B.C.E.). The poem, which describes the primordial sacrifice of the cosmic man, ascribes a mythical origin to the *varna* system. From the various parts of the cosmic man emerge the component parts of the universe—the sun, the moon, the breath, and fire among them. At the very end, people emerge. From his mouth emerge the brahmins, from his arms the kshatriyas, from his thighs the vaishyas, and from his feet the shudras.

The *varnas* are organized along a continuum of purity and pollution. A person's state of purity or pollution is determined by the degree of contact with substances that are considered polluting (corpses, for example). Although it might appear from the *varna* system and from the *Purusha Sukta* that brahmins are at the top of the hierarchy, we know that from the earliest period brahmins and kshatriyas (and to some extent vaishyas as well) existed in close, mutually dependent relationships. The brahmins, with their ritual knowledge, gave legitimacy to kings and ambitious chieftains who might come to power. In turn, kings supported the priestly class with gifts of wealth and land, while merchants and landlords paid taxes and sponsored priestly activities.

A fifth group below the shudras, called the "untouchables" or "outcastes," was added. Today, this lowest group constitutes nearly 20 percent of the population of India. During the Indian Independence movement of the early twentieth century, Mohandas (Mahatma) Gandhi (whom we will discuss later in the chapter) sought to uplift this class socially, referring to them as Harijans, "Children of God." Many people of this class now refer to themselves as **dalit**, a word that means "oppressed." In modern India, educational institutions and government jobs have been opened to the *dalits* and have helped many with social and economic mobility. Nevertheless, *dalits* continue to suffer terrible oppression, especially in rural communities in India.

The caste system is further classified through thousands of subcastes called *jatis*. **Jati** literally means "birth group." Usually, a *jati* is composed of an endogamous group. One can marry within *jati* communities that are equal in social and ritual status, but not into a *jati* above or below one's own position. Marriage across *jatis* is usually undertaken to widen communal alliances. Over time, the *jati* system has made social hierarchy more fluid.

The Hampi Bazaar in Karnataka, India, a sacred town where doorsteps and houses are decorated by *rangoli* or *kolam* ritual protective drawings.

In modern times, the strictures of caste have broken down. Many Hindus have embraced a more egalitarian outlook formulated by nineteenth-century Hindu reformers. These reformers regarded intercaste marriage as essential to bringing about social equality and the development of the Indian nation. In urban areas, caste status has often given way to a modern class-based system in which one's marriageability is based on education, current employment, and financial status, rather than solely on caste. But caste remains a challenging issue for many Hindus, particularly those living in rural settings.

The Four Stages of Life Another main aspect of the *varnashrama dharma* system involves the ashrama, or "stage of life." Traditional Hinduism describes four ashramas:

1. The student
2. The householder
3. The forest-dwelling hermit
4. The renouncer (the sannyasi)

As affirmed by the *Laws of Manu,* the repository of dharma discussed earlier, fulfilling the duties of these stages is said to repay three debts of life, which are:

1. To the ancient seers (by studying the revealed texts known as the Vedas)
2. To the gods (by making offerings as a householder)
3. To the ancestors (by having a son—again, as a householder—who will continue to perform ancestral rites)

The specific regulations pertaining to each stage of life are meticulously spelled out in Hindu texts. For example, the *Laws of Manu* prescribes the ritual of initiation for boys who are about to enter the student stage:

> In the eighth year after conception, one should perform the initiation (*upanāyana*) of a *brāhmin*, in the eleventh [year] after conception (that) of a *ks'atriya*, but in the twelfth that of a *vaiśya*.[9]

The student's main duty is to acquire a sufficient understanding of the Vedas. Upon getting married, a Hindu enters the stage of the householder, whose duties include supporting those in the other three stages of life. Hindus in the last two stages focus primarily on seeking moksha or liberation, first by detaching themselves from the worldly concerns of the householder and then, once this detachment has been achieved, by entering the fourth stage of the renouncer, or **sannyasi**.

Renunciation is understood to be the most effective life situation for working to achieve moksha. As we have seen, attachment to objects of desire binds one to samsara. Renouncing, or no longer clinging to, such objects is empowering. By not indulging one's desires for the impermanent things of this world, the true nature of the self (the atman) can be realized. Most renouncers are ascetics, celibate wanderers who engage in meditation and yoga. Some take formal vows and join a monastic order. Although estimates of the number of sannyasis vary, there may be as many as 15 million in India.

The four stages define the ideal life for men. Women participate primarily in vaguely defined supporting roles through the last three stages and thereby assist in repaying the three debts. Some Hindu texts, including the *Laws of Manu*, emphasize that women hold a place of honor because of these roles. In general, however, Hindu society has been highly patriarchal. (The place of women in Hinduism is explored in more detail in a later section of this chapter.)

The Four Aims of Life Whereas the four stages of life describe an individual's social and familial responsibilities from birth to death, the four aims of life set forth Hinduism's primary spiritual purposes and goals. The four aims are dharma, duty or righteousness; kama, sensual enjoyment; *artha*, material wealth and social prestige; and moksha, liberation. A Hindu is meant to diligently pursue all four of these goals.

As we have seen, dharma applies throughout life. Along with taking care to observe regulations governing everyday routines, some Hindus may take vows to practice nonviolence, perhaps maintaining a vegetarian diet as part of that goal. Others have strict rules for maintaining ritual purity or they observe a complex ritual regimen each day to ensure the harmony and well-being of their household and family members.

The next two aims of life—kama and *artha*—apply especially to the second stage of life, that of the householder. Kama is directed at the fulfillment of desire. It encourages Hindus to enjoy the human experience and celebrate the sensual aspects of life. *Artha*, the pursuit of wealth and social prestige, is also encouraged. It is a Hindu's duty not only to provide security for loved ones but also to savor and share life's bounty. Of course, kama and *artha* must conform to dharma.

Moksha, the ultimate aim of human existence, is the special focus of the last two stages of life (the forest-dwelling hermit and the renouncer). Having fulfilled the duties and obligations of student and householder, one is ready to turn inward, to contemplate the nature of the atman.

The four stages and the four aims of life represent traditional ideals intended primarily for upper-caste men. We do not know the extent to which the prescriptions of the stages and aims have been followed in the long history of Hinduism. These ideals, though to some extent impractical in today's contemporary society, still inform the beliefs and practices of many Hindus.

Jayashree Venkatesan is a wife, a mother, and a retired accountant who lives in Chennai, India. She is a devotee of the goddess Sharada (a form of Saraswati, Goddess of Wisdom), whose most important temple is in the town of Shringeri in southern India.

As a Hindu, what is the most important part of human existence? What should Hindus do or focus on in life?

As a Hindu, I believe that God is in all things, in every aspect of creation and in every aspect of life. Consequently, one must practice compassion and nonviolence towards all things. It is how we learn to see and experience the divine presence all around us. I also believe in the tenet that work is worship. It is an act of surrender. You don't shirk your responsibilities, whatever they may be—whether as a mother, a student, a professional—but do not cling to the fruits of work. As a Hindu I trust that when you surrender fully, God will provide you with the solution and guide you through both the happy and difficult moments of life.

What aspect of your day-to-day life as a Hindu would you characterize as being most spiritually gratifying?

Every morning and evening, I light an oil lamp in my puja room (home shrine) before the image of the Supreme Mother, Sharada Ambal. I see Sringeri Sharada Ambal as my mother, as one who takes care of everyone in this world. In these moments of quiet peace, I feel Her presence and Her guidance. I begin my day by surrendering myself into Her loving care.

What is your favorite Hindu holiday, and why?

I would not say I have a favorite Hindu festival. I like them all, as they are all so different. However, one of the most important festivals for me is Navaratri, which celebrates the Great Goddess. The festival falls sometime between September and October. We worship the goddess in Her three forms as Durga, Lakshmi, and Saraswati over nine nights and ten days. During this festival, I recite the *Lalita Sahasranama*, the one thousand names of Devi, several times a day. I do more elaborate puja (home rituals) to the goddess. Most importantly, it gives me the opportunity to invite several women of all ages to my home to feed them and give them clothes as I honor them as aspects of the Great Goddess.

Jayashree Venkatesan

Hindu Sacred Texts

The great diversity within Hinduism is reflected in its astonishing array of texts, composed in many different languages over the course of centuries. Down to present times, Hindu texts have facilitated the asserting of new ideas, the overturning of old ones, and the reasserting of the dominance of fading traditions. In this next section, we undertake a brief survey of Hinduism's main texts and their continued relevance.

The Vedas The term *Veda* ("knowledge") is used in two ways when categorizing Hindu texts. In the broader sense, the Vedas refers to all of Vedic literature. These texts are regarded by most Hindus as revealed. That is, they are believed not to have been composed by man but rather "heard" by the *rishis*, the poet–sages of ancient times who were divinely inspired. Vedic literature thus belongs to the category of Hindu texts known as **shruti** ("that which is heard"), as opposed to the other category, **smriti** ("tradition").

In the more narrow sense of the term, Vedas refers to four collections (Sanskrit, samhitas) of texts. Composed in Sanskrit between 1200 and 900 B.C.E. and drawing on centuries of oral tradition, these are the earliest Hindu texts and are generally considered to be the world's oldest scriptures. The four Vedas are the Rig Veda, a collection of hymns to the gods; the Sama Veda, melodic renditions of hymns from the Rig Veda; the Yajur Veda, ritual formulas; and the Atharva Veda, hymns, spells, and incantations.

Following upon the four samhitas, the *Brahmanas* set forth instructions for brahmin priests. The next collection of texts, the *Aranyakas* (or "forest treatises," so-named because they record esoteric teachings conveyed to students in secret), form a bridge from the samhitas to the Upanishads by exploring the hidden meanings of rituals. The Upanishads are speculations with regard to the deeper truths of the samhitas, especially the Rig Veda.

The 1,028 hymns of the Rig Veda, the oldest and by far the most important of the samhitas, praise the gods and ask for their blessings. The gods include Indra, god of lightning, thunder, and rain and king of the gods; Agni, god of fire and messenger of the gods; and Varuna, god of law and order (who later becomes god of the sea). New deities emerged in the later portions of the Rig Veda. One deity that has enduring influence is the *Purusha* (literally, "Man"), who is praised and described in the famous Vedic hymn known as the *Purusha Sukta,* which was discussed earlier in connection with the caste system. This later Vedic hymn is also significant for the ways in which it asserts the centrality of sacrifice, and it continues to be recited in Hindu rituals even today. The *Purusha Sukta* describes the sacrifice of a primordial, cosmic man out of whose body the universe is created. As a creation myth, it has parallels in numerous Indo-European traditions. As we have seen, the *Purusha Sukta* not only details the first sacrifice but also delineates the structuring of society.

The Upanishads (900–200 B.C.E.) The Upanishads, also known as Vedanta ("end of the Vedas"), are so distinctive from the earlier Vedic texts and so important as to deserve their own treatment here. The term *Upanishad* means "sitting down near [a teacher]." The term Vedanta, while identifying these texts as the concluding portion of Vedic literature, implies for some Hindus—for example, followers of the Vedanta philosophical school—that the Upanishads contain the culmination of the wisdom of the Vedas.

HINDU SACRED TEXTS

SHRUTI ("THAT WHICH IS HEARD")
Samhitas ("Collections")

Rig Veda
Yajur Veda
Sama Veda
Atharva Veda

Brahmanas
Aranyakas
Upanishads

SMRITI ("TRADITION")
Dharma Shastras (including *Laws of Manu*)
Epics and *Puranas*

Ramayana
Mahabharata
Bhagavata Purana
Markandeya Purana

Darshanas (treatises of the philosophical schools)
Tantras (scriptures of the various sects)
Writings of Hindu gurus

Departing from the Vedic focus on ritual, and especially sacrifice, the Upanishads feature philosophical speculation on the nature of the divine, the self, the world, and the relationships between them. These texts signal a significant shift away from emphasis on the external performance of sacrifice characteristic of the Vedic era. The Upanishads also mark a new stage in the development of religious texts, having been composed in part by people of nonbrahmin backgrounds. The newfound emphasis on philosophical speculation, no longer the sole domain of the brahmin class, had an enormous impact on the development of Hinduism. It propelled the development of the contemplative disciplines of yoga and meditation and influenced the philosophical concepts found later in the *Bhagavad Gita*.

What advantages and disadvantages can you think of when comparing the flexibility of Hindu beliefs with that of other religions?

The Upanishads are also significant for describing for the first time the concepts of karma, samsara, reincarnation of the soul, and the soul's immortality, which were initially closely guarded secrets. We had occasion earlier in the chapter, when discussing Brahman and the monistic concept that atman is Brahman, to draw from the *Brhadaranyaka* and *Chandogya Upanishads*. They are two among the thirteen so-called principal Upanishads (some scholars set this number at ten). Traditionally, there are 108 Upanishads, although the term has been applied to some 200 texts, some of which were written in recent times.

Ramayana   For most Hindus, belief and practice are informed by and disseminated through storytelling traditions and narrative texts. Two of the most significant of these texts are the Sanskrit epics the *Ramayana* and the *Mahabharata*, both of which are categorized as smriti rather than shruti—although this in no way diminishes their relevance as Hindu sacred texts. Both epics are among the most important sources of Hindu notions of duty, or dharma.

The *Ramayana* ("The Journey of Rama"), composed between 200 B.C.E. and 200 C.E., is a compelling tale of political intrigue, romance, and philosophical speculation. It tells the story of a ten-headed demon king named Ravana, who was rewarded for his austerities with the granting of a wish by Brahma. Ravana asks for protection from gods, celestial beings, and other members of his own demon race. Protected in this way, he and his demon hordes dominate the earth and eventually enslave the gods of heaven. But in his arrogance, Ravana neglects to ask for protection from humans and animals.

Hindu priests perform *arati,* waving a lamp of burning camphor before an image of Hanuman (the monkey god of the *Ramayana*) at a temple in Kuala Lumpur, Malaysia, during the festival of Diwali.

In the meantime, King Dasharatha of Ayodhya and his three queens, desiring an heir, perform a sacrifice in hopes that the gods will grant their wish. The king is blessed with four sons—Rama, Lakshmana, Bharata, and Shatrughna. Rama, as we have noted earlier, is an avatar of Vishnu. Rama eventually marries a princess, Sita. As Rama is beloved for his righteousness and virtue, King Dasharatha, wishing to step down from the throne, announces that Rama's coronation will soon be held. Then Kaikeyi, Dasharatha's favorite wife, suddenly calls in two wishes that the king had once granted her. She demands that Rama be banished to the forest for fourteen years and that her own son, Bharata, ascend to the throne of Ayodhya instead. Distraught, King Dasharatha grants Kaikeyi's wish but dies of a broken heart.

Rama accepts his exile without protest and is accompanied by his wife Sita and his brother Lakshmana into the forest, where they spend many years, until one day Ravana kidnaps Sita and carries her off to the island of Lanka.

A despairing Rama and Lakshmana wander in search of Sita. They eventually meet Hanuman, a messenger from a kingdom of monkeys. Hanuman helps to search for Sita. At the citadel of Ravana on Lanka, Hanuman finds Sita held prisoner in a garden. He tells her not to lose hope, promising that Rama will soon come to free her.

Upon hearing Hanuman's news, Rama and his army march to Lanka. During the battle that ensues, Rama kills Ravana and is reunited with Sita. However, after spending a year in another man's house, Sita must publicly prove her chastity through a trial by fire. With the fire-god Agni as her witness, she passes through the flames and into Rama's embrace. Their exile concluded, Rama, Sita, and Lakshmana return to Ayodhya, where Rama is reinstated as the rightful king. All are happy for a time, but later, because of rumors circulating about Sita's chastity, Rama is compelled to abandon Sita in the forest. He doesn't know she is pregnant with their two sons, who are raised by the hermit Valmiki. Valmiki, who, while meditating, has seen all that

Rama and Lakshmana, with their army of monkeys and bears, are camped outside the palace of the demon-king Ravana on the isle of Lanka, while the demons try to rouse Kumbhakarna, the giant brother of Ravana. India, Mughal period, c. 1595–1605.

has come to pass, composes the *Ramayana* and teaches it to the two boys, who eventually sing it before their father. Rama dies shortly thereafter, sadly pining for Sita.

For many Hindus, the characters in the *Ramayana* serve as exemplary social role models. Sita is the faithful wife, Rama is the ideal man and perfect king, Lakshmana is the loyal brother, and Hanuman is the selfless devotee. The text grapples with issues involving dharma, both in the public, political realm and in the private, familial realm. The characters of the *Ramayana,* however, are also understood to be divine. Thus, the *Ramayana* is as much a text that imparts religious and ethical knowledge as a text that reinforces Hindu beliefs about the accessibility and immanence of God.

Mahabharata   The other great Hindu epic, the *Mahabharata*, is composed of over 100,000 verses and is the world's longest epic poem. Like the *Ramayana*, this work is deeply concerned with issues of dharma. The epic also introduces Krishna, the beloved avatar of Vishnu.

The main storyline of the *Mahabharata* concerns a dynastic conflict between two groups of royal cousins. These are the *Pandavas* (the five sons of King Pandu), the heroes of the epic who are all descendants of the gods, and their antagonists, the *Kauravas* (the hundred sons of the blind king, Dhritarashtra). Their dispute ultimately results in a terrible war that marks the end of an epoch for humanity.

On the eve of the battle, the great Pandava warrior Arjuna experiences crippling doubt. When Arjuna asks his charioteer, Krishna (an avatar of Vishnu), to pull the chariot into the middle of the battlefield, he sees his friends and relatives on both sides clamoring for war. Not wanting to commit the sin of killing his kinsmen and overcome with sorrow, he refuses to fight. It is at this key point in the story that the profound philosophical discourse known as the *Bhagavad Gita* begins. Many Hindus regard this conversation between Krishna and Arjuna as the most significant philosophical work in Hinduism.

The *Bhagavad Gita* (The Song of the Lord)   The *Bhagavad Gita*, the conversation between Krishna and Arjuna, was probably composed around the first century C.E. The text, which seeks to reconcile the tension between renunciation and worldly life, also presents radical new ideas about the pursuit of moksha, including the three margas or paths to liberation that we explored in an earlier section.

The *Gita* begins with Arjuna refusing to act on his dharma, as is demanded of a member of the kshatriya, or warrior class, out of fear of the consequences of killing his kinsmen. Krishna responds to his dilemma by revealing that one does not need to give up action to achieve moksha. Rather, as we noted before, one gives up the *fruit* of action. That is, one cultivates "desireless action," or acting without attachment to the fruit or benefit of the action.

Arjuna must honor his dharma as a warrior and fight his own kinsmen. But he transcends the karmic repercussions of this act by relinquishing personal attachment and realizing that Krishna is the primary cause leading all the individual actors toward this inevitable outcome.

As you have seen in the earlier section on bhakti marga, the *Gita* emphasizes the path of devotion, which later comes to dominate Hindu practice and belief. The *Gita* also teaches that it is possible to achieve moksha by being active in the world, provided that, through selfless devotion, one surrenders attachment to the expectation of any particular result. This contrasts with earlier teachings that advocated complete detachment through renunciation as the primary means of escaping samsara.

Puranas   In addition to the rich storehouse of narrative material in the epics, there are equally important collections of mythic stories known as **Puranas** (Sanskrit *purana*, "ancient"). Like the epics, the Puranas existed in oral form before being committed to writing—in this case, between the fourth and sixteenth centuries. The Puranas contain useful historical data, such as the genealogies of regional kings, but they also reflect the rise of dualistic or devotional Hinduism. This is evident primarily in their narrations of the deeds of the great deities such as Shiva, Vishnu, and Devi. They also consider the genealogies of gods, rules governing the proper worship of the gods, the construction of temples, the observance of festivals, the undertaking of pilgrimages, and similar topics.

There are eighteen major Puranas, two of the most influential of which are the *Bhagavata Purana* and the *Markandeya Purana*. The *Bhagavata Purana* focuses on Vishnu and his incarnations, most especially Krishna. It is one of the most widely recited, performed, and studied texts in contemporary Hinduism. The tenth book, which serves as the primary source for Krishna's life story, is particularly important. The *Markandeya Purana* includes the *Devi Mahatmya,* which is an important text of Shaktism, one among various Hindu sects that we explore in the next section.

The Sects of Hinduism

The most prevalent devotional sects in Hinduism are Vaishnavism, Shaivism, and Shaktism. Each features veneration of one of the major deities at the center of Hindu

Krishna, in the guise of Arjuna's charioteer, counsels the warrior on the verge of battle against his kinsmen. The battle scene in the Mahabharata is the setting of the *Bhagavad Gita.*

cosmology. The devotees of these sects are called **Vaishnavas** (devotees of Vishnu and his avatars), **Shaivas** (devotees of Shiva), and **Shaktas** (devotees of the Great Goddess, Devi). Within each of these sects are numerous individual orders that differ in the sacred texts and saints they revere, their modes of worship, and their philosophical orientation.

Vaishnavism   Vaishnavas worship Vishnu and his consort (wife) Lakshmi as supreme. Vishnu mercifully intervenes in the world through his avatars (such as Rama in the *Ramayana* and Krishna in the *Mahabharata*) and is inseparable from his beloved Lakshmi, who is the goddess of auspiciousness and good fortune. For Vaishnavas, Vishnu is the source of all existence. These ideas about Vishnu's fundamental nature are expressed in myths and poems that invoke him as the lord who created the universe.

Hindus worship Vishnu in a number of different forms. He is often depicted reclining with Lakshmi on a thousand-headed serpent that floats on the cosmic ocean. From his navel rises a lotus, upon which Brahma the Creator-God is seated. Visually, this image asserts that the world is born from Vishnu and that he is its sole originator and sustainer. Brahma, Vishnu, and Shiva constitute a triad of gods whose roles are, respectively, to create, preserve, and dissolve the universe as it moves through cycles. For Vaishnavas, Vishnu is not just the preserver but the supreme god who performs all three roles.

In Hindu sacred art, Vishnu typically is shown holding objects in his four hands that symbolize his powers and characteristics. In his upper right hand, he holds a flaming discus (symbolizing the sun and omniscience); his upper left hand bears a white conch shell (the moon and creativity). In his lower right hand, he holds a mace (power), and in his lower left hand, he holds a lotus (purity). Most Vaishnavas have special devotion for Vishnu's avatars, Rama and Krishna.

Shaivism   Shiva is the destroyer and at the same time a benefactor. He embodies both the ideal of ascetic renunciation and sensual participation in the material world. Beyond being the god of spiritual insight and of yogis and ascetics, Shiva is also the god who destroys the universe at the end of time before a new cycle of creation can begin. Most Shaivas worship Shiva as a god with no beginning or end who transcends time but also presides over its endless cycles. Some Shaivas emphasize that Shiva is also a family man, to be venerated with his divine queen Parvati and their two sons, the divine princes Ganesha and Skanda.

Shiva is usually depicted sitting in deep meditation on Mount Kailasha in the Himalayas, with a tiger skin wrapped about his waist and wearing serpents for jewelry. His third eye is turned inward in meditative contemplation, and he wears the crescent moon and the holy river Ganges in his matted hair. A common symbol of Shiva is the linga, an abstract phallic symbol that represents his creative potential. His consort Parvati is also believed by Shaivas to represent the creative energy of the universe.

Shaktism   The cults of the Great Goddess venerate her as the supreme cause and end of the universe. Although she has many names and many forms, the Great Goddess is most often referred to as Devi, Mahadevi, or Shakti. Devotees of the Goddess are referred to as Shaktas.

The primacy of Devi is definitively asserted in the fifth century C.E. Sanskrit text called the *Devi Mahatmya* ("The Greatness of Devi") which, as noted previously, is part of the *Markandeya Purana*. The *Devi Mahatmya* posits that the supreme cause of the universe is feminine. The text argues for Devi's greatness through three main myths, the most important of which tells how she killed the buffalo-headed demon, Mahisha, who threatened the world and whom even the gods Vishnu and Shiva were not able to vanquish.

Accompanied by a legion of other goddesses and fierce creatures and riding a lion, Devi, in the form of the goddess Durga, protects the world by battling the buffalo demon Mahishasura. (The buffalo is associated with Yama, the God of Death.) Pallava period, seventh century, Mahishasura Mardini Cave, Mamallapuram Tamil Nadu, India.

To Shaktas the Goddess is all-powerful and pervades the entire universe. She is the one who creates, preserves, and destroys the universe in harmony with the rhythms of cosmic time. The *Devi Mahatmya* teaches that the goddess is eternal and that she manifests herself over and over again in order to protect the universe as a mother would her child.

Shaivas and Shaktas have much in common, as Shiva and Devi (also called Parvati) are believed by both sects to be married to each other. So the difference between Shaivism and Shaktism is a matter of emphasis regarding the importance of each of these two primal forces. For Shaivas, Shiva is pure consciousness that pervades all existence, and Devi is his creative (but subordinate) power. In contrast, Shaktas believe that Shiva is entirely passive and that Shakti is the creative energy that constitutes and governs the whole of existence. Thus, the Shaktas say that "Shiva without Shakti is *shava*" (Sanskrit, "a corpse"), an idea that is iconographically represented in the form of the goddess Kali dancing upon the inert body of Shiva.

Gurus, Saints, and Sages Entire sects of Hinduism are constantly forming around the veneration of gurus, saints, and ascetics. In the words of one scholar, "saints still remain . . . as they have always been, the generating centers of Hindu religion."[10] The fully enlightened are regarded as being the most immediate means of accessing the divine reality directly, either to obtain material and mundane blessings or to receive spiritual teaching to quicken one's own journey toward moksha. Some saints are venerated as embodiments of God, others for being humble and perfectly surrendered devotees.

Gurus are sometimes powerful religious authorities who preside over well-established institutions in which the divine authority of a guru has been passed down to his senior disciple in an unbroken lineage for many generations. Certain important

A modern painting of the goddess Kali, whose name means both "Black" and "Time," dancing on the body of Shiva. From the Indian state of Odisha.

gurus and saints have been responsible for the formulation of the specific philosophical orientation of various sects and monastic orders, making interpretation of sacred texts and belief more systematic and consistent. We have noted, for example, the founding roles of Shankara, Ramanuja, and Madhva in, respectively, the Vedanta schools of Advaita, Vishishta-Advaita, and Dvaita. The roles of guru as founder and authority are characteristic of Hindu movements outside of India, such as the International Society for Krishna Consciousness (commonly known as the Hare Krishna Movement), the Osho Rajneesh Movement, and Transcendental Meditation—all of which are explored in Chapter 14.

THE HISTORY OF HINDUISM

Hinduism is a vibrant tradition that has exhibited dynamic change and a willingness to embrace innovations in thought and practice. At the same time, Hinduism has preserved many of its most ancient elements to the present day, cherishing some traditions that go back more than 3,000 years.

The history of Hinduism can be traced back to the Indus Valley Civilization (c. 2600–1700 B.C.E.) and to the Indo-Aryan peoples who composed the Vedas (c. 1200–900 B.C.E.).

The Indus Valley Civilization

As its name suggests, the Indus Valley Civilization developed along the Indus River, which flows through modern Pakistan. It reached its developmental peak between 2300 and 2000 B.C.E., when its thriving cities, such as Harappa and Mohenjo-Daro, enjoyed a high standard of living. Archaeological excavations at Indus Valley sites have yielded evidence of trade with regions as far away as Mesopotamia and impressive skill in metallurgy, handicrafts, and urban planning. The archaeological finds include a vast number of stone seals that were perhaps used to stamp products for trade. These are decorated with depictions of animals and people and with a script that has not yet been deciphered.

Some scholars believe that in the Indus Valley seals we can detect very early elements of Hinduism. For example, the most famous seal has been called the Proto-Shiva seal because its central image may be an archaic form of Shiva. The male figure is seated in a yoga posture, wears a buffalo-horned headdress, is surrounded by animals, and appears to have three faces. Later images of Shiva often show

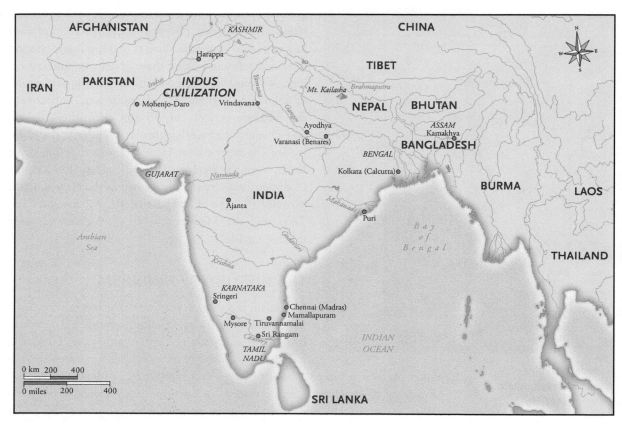

Significant sites in the history of Hinduism.

him meditating in a yoga posture, being in the company of animals, and having three faces. Of course, without a decipherment of the script it is difficult to understand fully this and other images depicted on the seals.

Archaeologists working in the Indus Valley have also discovered a number of terracotta figures depicting women. Some scholars have identified these as representations of a mother goddess. It may be that the widespread worship of goddesses in later Hinduism originated in the

The Proto-Shiva seal. The male figure, sometimes called the "Lord of the Animals," is surrounded by various totemic animals, such as an elephant, a tiger, a rhinoceros, a water buffalo, and two antelopes or deer.

The great bath can be seen amid the ruins of the ancient cityscape of Mohenjo-Daro, an important city of the Indus Valley Civilization. A towering granary can be viewed in the distance.

veneration of female deities in the ancient Indus Valley Civilization.

At some point early in the second millennium B.C.E. there was a sudden decline in the Indus Valley Civilization, which would collapse by 1300 B.C.E. Although most scholars believe that the primary cause of the fall of the Indus Valley Civilization was climatic change that disrupted agriculture, it is possible that the migration of Aryans into the Indus Valley was a contributing factor.

Who Are the Aryans?

The English linguist Sir William "Oriental" Jones (1746–1794) described how Sanskrit, Latin, Greek, and several other ancient languages shared a common linguistic ancestor. These languages are referred to as "Indo-European" and probably stem from a lost language we call "Proto Indo-European." Jones's discoveries astounded Europeans, who soon learned that Sanskrit was closest to the original language spoken by the earliest Indo-Europeans.

The ancient speakers of Sanskrit who moved into the Indian subcontinent around 1500 B.C.E. referred to themselves as the *Arya*—that is, those who are "noble," "cultivated," and "civilized." Today, we call them Indo-Aryans or, more simply, Aryans—although this use of the term is more specific (and accurate) than the general label "Aryan race" as used by the Nazi Party in the twentieth century. Skilled in handling the horse and chariot, the Aryans were a warlike and nomadic people who were well prepared to make themselves the dominant elite soon after they entered the Indian subcontinent.

Like other Indo-European peoples, the Aryans revered the horse, placed special importance on sacrifice, and organized their society into a three-part structure. For the Aryans, sacrifice was a means to maintain order in the universe. The priests (brahmins) who conducted sacrificial rituals occupied the top rung of the social order because of the religious power they wielded. The rulers and warriors (kshatriyas) were equally important. Last were the traders and farmers (vaishyas). As the Aryans did not place a great deal of emphasis on agriculture, one can see why the vaishyas would occupy a lower social position. The servant class (shudras) probably derived from the indigenous people at the time of the Aryan immigration. This social structure has remained fundamental to Indian society until today.

The Aryans, who eventually settled across northern India, have left us a body of texts composed in Sanskrit, of which the earliest example is the Vedas. It is to the era of these texts that we now turn.

The Vedic Period

Ritual was of ultimate importance in Vedic times, as rites of sacrifice were performed to sustain the cosmic order and please the gods. Much of ritual sacrifice involved the pouring of offerings into a sacrificial fire as Vedic hymns were recited. Although the construction of their fire altars became quite elaborate, Indians of the Vedic period inherited from their nomadic ancestors a very "portable" religion with no fixed buildings or icons and with sacred knowledge maintained by priests.

In Vedic times, as today, fire was considered a god. Known as Agni, he was the mouth of the gods and the gateway to the celestial realms, so offerings were magically transported through Agni to whichever god was invoked.

A *yajna* or fire sacrifice, one of the most archaic of Hindu rites, is performed by priests before an image of Durga during the Durga Puja festival in Calcutta, India.

In Vedic mythology it is Indra, god of lightning, thunder, and rain, and the virile god of fertility itself, who, as the most powerful, is king of the gods. More hymns in the Vedas are addressed to Indra than to any other god, but in later Hindu tradition and mythology he is somewhat comical: haughty, proud, and often drunk. Many of the Vedic gods continue to play a part in the later Hindu pantheon but endure only in a subordinate status.

In the later Vedic period, philosophical innovations began to supplant the older Vedic emphasis on sacrifice. It is in hymns from the later period that Vedic religion begins to take a decisive turn, shifting away from an emphasis on myth, cosmology, and sacrifice to a keener interest in philosophy and introspection. In these hymns, the perception of the nature of existence emerges as being more important than upholding the cosmic order through sacrifice. Late Vedic hymns mark a transition toward what would be the philosophical revolution of the speculative texts known as the Upanishads.

During the time of the Upanishads (c. 900–200 B.C.E.), contemplative and philosophical reflection became more widespread. Many philosophers moved from urban areas to the forest in order to lead simpler lives. Some lived as hermits, some lived in colonies of contemplatives, and others practiced strict ascetic disciplines in the solitude of the jungle. Still others became wanderers, going from town to town begging for food and engaging in lively philosophical debates.

The Age of the Guptas

Most scholars characterize the time of the Gupta Empire (c. 320 to 540 C.E.) as a period of remarkable creativity. The Guptas, who ruled much of northern India, patronized the arts, sciences, religion, and literature. Their reign was an era of relative peace and prosperity, often described as "the Golden Age of India." It was during this period that the epics took on their definitive forms and the first of the Puranas was compiled.

The Gupta rulers practiced religious tolerance and sponsored groups and institutions associated with Buddhism, Jainism, and other religions. The Guptas, who were themselves Hindus, promoted Hinduism and sought to organize society in accordance with Hindu beliefs. Thanks in part to Gupta patronage, the worship of Vishnu and Shiva became increasingly popular during this period, which also saw a shift from worship at open-air sacrificial altars to worship in temples. As temple institutions arose, so did special forms of temple art and architecture. These developments quickened the spread of bhakti and the emerging devotional sects.

A very significant religious development during the age of the Guptas was the rise of devotional Hinduism. The two great Sanskrit epics, the *Ramayana* and the *Mahabharata,* had been completed and were well established by this time. As we have seen, these epics are concerned with political problems, dynastic successions, duty, and obligations. But they also feature the exploits of the gods and have much to tell us about popular deities and avatars and forms of devotion to them. Composition of the Puranas commenced during this period, indicating the growing popularity of devotional Hinduism.

The Development of Bhakti

The devotional aspects of Hinduism became increasingly popular under the Guptas, but they took on new life in southern India between the sixth and ninth centuries C.E. through an ecstatic form called bhakti marga, the path of devotion. This movement eventually spread all over India, changing and adapting to new regional and linguistic circumstances. Devotion now came to be expressed through poetry, art, architecture, and temple building. Bhakti was instrumental in the development of the various sectarian orientations of Hinduism and in its vibrant temple cultures.

By the late fifth century C.E., Buddhism (Chapter 5) and Jainism (Chapter 6) were deeply entrenched in southern India. Bhakti arose as a challenge to these traditions. Over the next four centuries, wandering poets roamed the countryside and converted royalty and commoners alike to the devotional ethos of bhakti. Royal patronage for Jainism and Buddhism waned, and kings sought legitimacy through poets' songs that praised the kings as the representatives of the gods Shiva and Vishnu. The religious networks forged by the itinerant poets sometimes developed into political networks and strengthened alliances between religion and politics.

By the twelfth century, the bhakti movement had transformed once again, becoming an adversary of caste and gender prejudice. In this new transformation, practitioners of bhakti often rejected ritual and temple-based worship, insisting that the body is itself a temple and that God dwells in every individual. Many scholars argue that the bhakti movement had such a far-reaching impact because it was egalitarian, revolutionary, and frequently anti-brahmin. Bhakti poet-saints represented a variety of caste backgrounds. Furthermore, rather than using Sanskrit, the language of the Vedas and of priestly authority, the bhakti poets used vernacular languages such as Tamil, Kannada, Marathi, and an early form of Hindi. The bhakti poets asserted that caste and other circumstances of one's birth did not determine one's access to God. Rather, it was the quality of one's surrender to God that mattered.

Tantra

Bhakti was not the only revolutionary new development to challenge the strictures of gender and caste. **Tantra**, another new system, emerged alongside it. Making use of symbols, rituals, yogic postures, breathing techniques, mantras, and other spiritual practices—sometimes in shocking or forbidden ways—Tantra offered the possibility of sudden liberation from samsara. Likely having arisen among mystics in the northern Indian region of Kashmir and perhaps also in eastern India, by the seventh century Tantra had come to influence not only Hinduism but Buddhism and Jainism as well.

Tantra (Sanskrit, "loom") assumes the interweaving and interconnectedness of all things. These include pure consciousness, which is identified with Brahman or Shiva, and material reality in its most basic state, which is identified with Shakti. Similarly, samsara and moksha are understood not as two different things but as aspects of a single continuum of being. For practitioners of Tantra, the material world is a manifestation of the divine energy associated with pure consciousness. Their spiritual practices are said to give them the ability to manipulate or channel that energy in order to gain liberation. Unlike the ascetics who renounced the material world and its sensual pleasures, practitioners of Tantra made use of material things and the senses as the means by which to transcend them. For them, moksha could be found in the midst of everyday experience.

Tantric practitioners taught that the ritual transgression of social boundaries could create ideal conditions for transcending the egocentric self and achieving instantaneous moksha. Recognizing that people's egos are embedded in caste identity and in taboos regarding purity and pollution, practitioners of Tantra performed rituals in which they identified their bodies as deities, ritually consumed meat, fish, and wine, and engaged in ritual sex with low-caste partners.

As Tantra increased in popularity, it also became increasingly secretive. While many were attracted by the promise of achieving liberation in this life, others alleged that some practitioners exercised seductive magical powers and that others suffered mental breakdown. For these reasons, along with disapproval of rituals that violated social conventions, Tantra for the most part remained hidden during its later development.

Hindus and Muslims During the Mughal Dynasty

One of the first sustained encounters between Hindus and Muslims in India was initiated by the raids of Mahmud of Ghazni (Afghanistan) early in the eleventh century C.E. Mahmud repeatedly raided the subcontinent, annexed states headed by Hindu,

How does the criticism of special knowledge and power wielded by brahmins compare to criticism of the power of priests and religious authorities in other religions?

Buddhist, and Jain kings, and made the kings his vassals. His most famous incursion involved the looting and destruction of the great temple of Shiva in Somnath (1025). According to Muslim sources, more than 50,000 defenders of the temple were killed, and its immense wealth was taken back to Ghazni. These Muslim accounts also speak of the forced conversions of Hindus to Islam. Contemporary Hindu nationalists often point to this early encounter with Islam as the beginning of centuries of oppression and persecution under Muslim rule.

The Mughal Dynasty was established in India in 1526, by which time Islam already had a strong foothold there, particularly in the northern regions. The Mughals were Muslim rulers of Turkic-Mongol origin. The Mughal Dynasty endured until 1857, although it reached its apex of power in the eighteenth century, declining thereafter with the rise of British influence. Under the Mughals, a complex relationship existed between Hinduism and Islam. Some Mughal emperors were hostile to religions other than their own and to Hinduism and Jainism in particular. Others, such as Akbar (1542–1605), were open to them. Akbar encouraged dialogue with representatives of different religions at a weekly salon. He even invented his own religion, the "Divine Faith" (in Arabic, *Din-I-Ilahi*), which incorporated elements of various religious traditions including Hinduism, Islam, and Zoroastrianism. Akbar was a clever political strategist who understood non-Muslims as subjects rather than infidels, counted Hindu kings among his closest advisors, and married the daughters of Hindu kings to cement political alliances with them. Good relationships between Mughal emperors and high-ranking Hindus helped to produce a vibrant pluralistic culture.

Under the Mughals, the conversions of Hindus to Islam do not appear to have been forced. Instead, Hindus converted for a variety of reasons, the most common one being improved economic and social standing and sincere belief in the teachings of Islam. There were also conversions of Muslims to Hinduism, especially when Muslims married into Hindu families.

Some of the greatest Hindu thinkers, poets, and philosophers lived during the time of the Mughals. The influential poet-saint Tulsidas (1532–1623), a member of Akbar's court and a devotee of Rama, wrote the *Ramcharitmanas*, an epic retelling in Hindi of the original Sanskrit *Ramayana*. The Muslim weaver-mystic Kabir (c. 1440–1518) was inspired by a Hindu teacher and composed poetry that seamlessly combined Hindu and Islamic philosophical ideas, while at the same time critiquing the social policies of Hindu and Muslim rulers.

Colonial Critique and the Hindu Reformers

When employees of the British East India Company established an imperial presence in India in the late eighteenth century, they initially adapted themselves to local customs and practices. They learned regional languages, married into local families, and even embraced local religious beliefs. One particularly colorful example is Charles

Stuart (1758–1828), an Irish general in the Bengal Army ("Bengal" in this case refers to the area of eastern India between the Bay of Bengal and the Himalayas). Stuart was such an avid admirer of Hinduism that his colleagues nicknamed him "Hindoo Stuart." His book, *Vindication of the Hindoos* (1808), was intended to discourage the ever-growing support for British missionaries who sought to convert Hindus to Christianity. When these missionaries tried to embarrass Stuart by calling attention to aspects of Hindu mythology that seemed strange to Westerners, he eloquently wrote in response: "Whenever I look around me in the vast region of Hindoo Mythology, I discover piety in the garb of allegory: and I see Morality, at every turn, blended with every tale; and, as far as I can rely on my own judgment, it appears the most complete and ample system of Moral allegory that the world has ever produced."[11]

But not everyone involved with the British East India Company admired Hindu beliefs and customs. Many felt that the "primitive backwardness" of Hindu belief was enough to warrant colonial intervention. By the middle of the nineteenth century, and certainly after the 1857 Indian Uprising (referred to as the "Mutiny" by British chroniclers, but as the "First War of Independence" by many Indian historians), the attraction to Hinduism and Indian culture represented by figures such as "Hindoo" Stuart and the linguist William "Oriental" Jones (whom we met earlier in this section) began to fade. As the commercial and administrative presence of the British East India Company gave way to the colonial control of the British Crown, critiques of Hinduism became an increasingly important means of exerting political power over the subcontinent.

One of the major effects of the British presence on Hinduism was a shift to English as the common language of religious written discourse (although Sanskrit retained its role as the primary priestly language). Other major effects on Hinduism resulted from the prevalence of Christianity and its Bible. In the nineteenth century, Hindus began to reassert the place of the Vedic texts, especially the Upanishads, as the authoritative foundation of their religion. This trend toward a more book-based religion continued, although by the early twentieth century, it was the *Bhagavad Gita* rather than the Upanishads that emerged as the most popular text of Hinduism. To this day, Hindus tend to regard the *Bhagavad Gita* much as Jews and Christians regard the Bible.

By the mid-nineteenth century, amid the movement to reassert the authority of the Vedic texts, English-educated Hindus took up the work of reform as a response to colonial critiques of Hinduism. They, too, began deriding Hinduism's many gods, erotic symbolism, temple worship, and rituals as crass corruptions of the purity of the authentic Hinduism embodied in the Vedas and Upanishads. They sought to transform Hinduism from within.

One of these reformers was Ram Mohan Roy (1774–1833), a member of a wealthy Bengali brahmin community who in 1828 established the Brahmo Samaj (Community of Brahman Worshipers) as a neo-Hindu religious organization open

Temple volunteers unveil a statue of Swami Vivekananda at the Hindu Temple of Greater Chicago, Saturday, July 11, 1998, in Lemont, Illinois. The statue honors Vivekananda as "the first man to bring Hindu religion and the practice of yoga to America."

to all, regardless of religious orientation. Roy believed that British rule offered India considerable opportunities for progress, and he devoted his life to religious, social, and educational reform. He was particularly concerned with issues involving the protection of women, such as child marriage, polygamy, dowry, and the practice of *sati*, an upper-caste practice in which a widow immolated herself on her husband's funeral pyre. This ritual suicide was believed to bring great honor to the family and to raise the status of the dead widow to that of a goddess. Roy campaigned for the abolition of *sati,* arguing that there was no scriptural basis in the Vedas for this practice. Finally, in 1829, *sati* was made illegal in Bengal. Roy was among the first members of the Indian upper classes to visit Europe, traveling there in 1830 to ensure that the British would not overturn the *sati* law. He died in 1833 and was buried in Bristol.

Another influential reformer was Dayananda Saraswati (1824–1883). Having become a wandering monk early in life, Dayananda studied under a blind sage who urged him to campaign for a return to what he considered the pure and original Vedic religion. Following his advice, Dayananda rejected the epics and Puranas as departures from the purity of the Vedas and spoke out against all aspects of temple tradition, image worship, and pilgrimage. In 1875, he founded the Arya Samaj (the Noble Community) as a "Vedic" religious organization whose social reform platform condemned child marriage and untouchability while promoting the equality of women. Dayananda rejected social hierarchies based on *jati*; *rather,* he believed, caste status should be based on one's character, which the organization would determine in a public examination. Although Dayananda Saraswati, like Ram Mohan Roy, favored a return to Vedic religion, his Arya Samaj distinguished itself from Roy's Brahmo Samaj in its encouragement of Hindu nationalism, anticipating the more extreme Hindu nationalist groups that would appear in the early twentieth century.

Other figures, less influenced by colonial and Christian critiques of Hinduism, were not as concerned as Ram Mohan Roy and Dayananda Saraswati with reforming Hinduism in ways that would appeal to the West. One of these figures was the enormously popular Bengali mystic, Ramakrishna (1836–1886). A devotee and temple priest of the goddess Kali, Ramakrishna devoted himself to spiritual exercises drawn from different religious traditions, including Vaishnavism, Advaita Vedanta, Tantrism, and even Islamic Sufism and Roman Catholicism. These served as the basis for his teaching that all religions are directed toward the experience of a God who creates religions to suit the spiritual needs and tastes of different peoples. Seen in this way, Hinduism could claim the same legitimacy as any other religion.

Among Ramakrishna's disciples was Narendranath Datta (1863–1902), a former law student who took monastic vows during Ramakrishna's last days and was thereafter known as Swami Vivekananda. In 1886, shortly after the death of Ramakrishna, he oversaw the founding of what would become the Ramakrishna Math, an order of monks devoted to the teachings of Ramakrishna. Swami Vivekananda had an enormous impact on the representation of Hinduism in the West, particularly in the United States. In 1893, he visited the United States to speak on behalf of Hinduism at the World Parliament of Religions in Chicago. Quoting from the *Bhagavad Gita*, he represented Hinduism as a tolerant and universal religion. Like his teacher, Ramakrishna, Vivekananda asserted that all religions are true. His stirring speech proved a milestone in changing Western attitudes toward Hinduism. It also ensured his fame in America, and he went on to establish the Vedanta Society of New York. Today, Vedanta Societies throughout the world are dedicated to the study, practice, and promotion of Hinduism.

Gandhi and the Struggle for Indian Independence

Mohandas Karamchand Gandhi (1869–1948), a towering religious, political, and social reformer in India, recast many Hindu ideas in the service of the fight for Indian independence. Born into a middle-class family of merchants, Gandhi was an English-educated lawyer and a deeply religious man. As a law student in England, he had read the *Bhagavad Gita,* and it had a profound impact on him.

Gandhi's political career began in South Africa, where he worked as a lawyer. It was here, in a struggle against racial discrimination, that he began to develop his political philosophy of nonviolent resistance. He characterized nonviolent resistance as *satyagraha* (Sanskrit, "grasping the truth") and explained that its strength lay in converting wrongdoers to justice rather than striving to coerce them.

Gandhi returned to India in 1915 to join the fledgling Indian independence movement, which sought to free India from British colonial rule. Deeply influenced by the American writer Henry David Thoreau (1817–1862), especially his thoughts on civil disobedience, Gandhi established an ashram (a place of religious seclusion) to train freedom fighters. The ashram chose as its motto a statement from the Upanishads: *satyameva jayate,* "the truth alone will prevail." Like his Upanishadic forebears, Gandhi believed that truth could be sought only through selfless service and humility, which could in turn be achieved by disciplining the body through fasting and celibacy.

Gandhi did not hesitate to criticize certain Hindu beliefs and practices, particularly that of *varnashrama dharma*, the ancient system by which society was ordered into various classes or castes. He worked tirelessly to abolish untouchability, calling the untouchables Harijans ("Children of God"), thereby seeking to increase their respectability. Gandhi also strove to improve the status of women.

Gandhi's charisma and influence were so great that even in his lifetime he was revered as a saint or Mahatma (Sanskrit, "Great Soul"). A lifelong Hindu, Gandhi also advocated the universality and truth of all religions and sought throughout his life to reconcile Hinduism and Islam. Tragically, on January 30, 1948, he was assassinated by Nathuram Godse, a Hindu nationalist who thought Gandhi was too accommodating of Muslims. Godse was later executed for the crime despite the pleas of Gandhi's two sons and Jawaharlal Nehru (1889–1964), India's first prime minister, who believed that violence would dishonor everything Gandhi represented. After decades of struggle, Gandhi had lived to enjoy just five months of freedom after Great Britain had partitioned colonial India into the independent states of India and Pakistan in mid-1947.

Hindutva and Hindu Nationalism

Whereas reformers such as Ram Mohan Roy, Vivekananda, and Gandhi sought to build bridges with the West through calling attention to the commonalities between Hinduism and other religions, other figures, such as V. D. Savarkar (1883–1966), insisted on the distinctiveness of Hinduism. Savarkar called this concept **hindutva** (Sanskrit, "Hindu-ness"), a term he coined in a 1923 pamphlet. For Savarkar, *hindutva* was a force to unite Hindus in repelling all dangerous foreign influences. As president of the Hindu Mahasabha, a Hindu nationalist political party that embraced this concept, Savarkar argued that India was an exclusively "Hindu Nation."

In 1925, the Rashtriya Swayamsevak Sangh (RSS; National Volunteer Corps) was founded. Although it has presented itself as a Hindu cultural organization, its members have a long history of political actions that have intensified communal tensions, precipitated violence, and propagated religious intolerance. The founder of the RSS, K. B. Hedgewar (1889–1940), was himself inspired by V. D. Savarkar's concept of *hindutva*. The RSS was meant to be a training ground for the self-empowerment of Hindu youth who were committed to defending a Hindu nation from the perceived threat posed by the Muslim world. Gaining independence from oppressive foreign rule can often rob nationalist movements of their momentum, but this was not the case in India after 1947. Hindu nationalists continued to be a major force in that country. The political backlash following Gandhi's assassination led many Mahasabha members to leave the party and ally themselves instead with a new political organization, the Bharatiya Jana Sangh (Indian People's Alliance), which was founded in 1951. Its founder, Syama Prasad Mookerjee (1901–1953), had been a member of both the

Mahasabha and the RSS. Bharatiya Jana Sangh was a Hindu nationalist party specifically created to oppose the Indian National Congress, the more moderate party of Jawaharlal Nehru and Mahatma Gandhi. In 1981, the Bharatiya Jana Sangh became the Bharatiya Janata Party (BJP). Today, the BJP and the Indian National Congress are the two major parties in India's political system. In 2014, the BJP won a landslide victory in India's national election. Prime Minister Narendra Modi has been one of the party's most visible leaders.

Today, organizations espousing Savarakar's *hindutva* ideology are under an umbrella group called the Sangh Parivar (Family of Associations). The RSS is the cultural wing, the BJP is the political wing, and the Vishwa Hindu Parishad (VHP; World Hindu Council) is the religious wing of the Sangh Parivar. The RSS continues to attract mostly lower-middle-class male youth, who feel empowered by the strong sense of cultural identity that it advocates. The RSS has awakened a deep sense of cultural pride among Hindu youth, but in recent years some of its members have been leading participants in sectarian violence against Muslims.

Hindu Nationalism and Violence

In 1991, the BJP led a pilgrimage around India gathering bricks to build a temple to Rama in Ayodhya, India. This was to be no ordinary temple. The pilgrims claimed that a fifteenth-century C.E. Islamic mosque called the Babri Masjid had been erected over an older Hindu temple that marked the exact birthplace of Rama. Their purpose was to tear down the mosque and build a grand Rama temple in its place. Members of Sangh Parivar rallied around the cause, which culminated in more than 200,000 participants converging on Ayodhya and demolishing the mosque with their bare hands. RSS youth then targeted the local Muslim community, destroying other mosques, ransacking Muslim homes, raping Muslim women, and murdering Muslim men. The backlash of these events echoed throughout India and Bangladesh, resulting in more than a thousand incidents of riots and communal violence perpetrated by both Hindus and Muslims. By the time calm had been restored, more than 4,000 people had been injured and at least 1,100 had lost their lives.

The BJP has also employed less aggressive strategies in its campaign to create a thoroughly Hindu India. For example, in the 1980s and 1990s, it attempted to rewrite Indian history by distributing new school textbooks throughout India. These textbooks reflected the BJP's vision of India as a Hindu nation and Hinduism as a unified, monolithic tradition. Most important, and dangerously, this historical revisionism minimized Muslim contributions to the development of India and described India's Muslim rulers as foreign invaders. The RSS also has a strong presence in the Hindu diaspora communities in Europe and North America. Many Hindu emigrants send their children to RSS youth camps to give them a sense of their Hindu identity and cultural pride.

About 90 million Hindus live outside of India, making for an extensive diaspora with a great variety of Hindu communities. In the United States alone, there are well over two million Hindus. In Iowa, Hindus account for less than 1 percent of the population (the states with the highest percentage, at about 2 percent each, are California and Delaware).[1] And yet, the Hindu diaspora is well represented there, with organizations that promote very different ways of practicing Hinduism.

The Des Moines Balagokulam is one of over 140 meeting centers in the United States of the Hindu Swayamsevak Sangh (HSS), which is historically rooted in the Rashtriya Swayamsevak Sangh (RSS; National Volunteer Corps), the conservative organization inspired by *hindutva*. HSS, as it states on its website, "is a voluntary, non-profit, social and cultural organization" that "aims to organize the Hindu community in order to preserve, practice and promote Hindu ideals and values. . . . We encourage maintaining Hindu cultural identity in harmony with the larger community."[2] True to its RSS roots, HSS is highly conservative in orientation, seeking to preserve traditional beliefs and practices among those living in the diaspora.

About a two-hour drive southeast of Urbandale, Fairfield (pop. 9,750) is home to Maharishi University of Management, founded in 1971 as Maharishi International University. This is one of the original institutions of Transcendental Meditation (TM), the new religious movement—or so most scholars would call it; the organization itself denies that it is religious—established by Hindu guru Maharishi Mahesh Yogi (1918–2008), who taught many Westerners, including the Beatles and the Beach Boys, how to meditate. Like HSS, Maharishi Foundation USA (the official name of the TM organization) is nonprofit, although there is a fee for learning Maharishi's unique method of meditation. Whether or not labeled as "religious," TM is highly innovative relative to most traditional forms of Hinduism.

For more details on TM and other diasporic movements inspired by Hinduism, see the section "The Rediscovery of Eastern Religious Thought" in Chapter 14.

Maharishi Mahesh Yogi.

[1]http://www.pewforum.org/religious-landscape-study/religious-tradition/hindu/#demographic-information

[2]https://www.hssus.org/about-us

The Future of Hinduism

Encouraged by nationalist groups and political parties in India, some of today's Hindus see Hinduism as monolithic, homogeneous, and impermeable, closed off from what they perceive as the corrupting influences of the West and foreign religions. At the same time, an emerging global movement is seeking to transcend traditional boundaries to better serve the needs of an increasingly diverse Hindu community. Hinduism has always displayed a unique ability in the face of changing conditions to sustain ancient traditions within new and ever-changing contexts. How this ability will manifest itself in the future remains to be seen, but it seems certain that the efforts of both Hindu traditionalists and progressives will ensure the continuing vibrancy of the world's oldest religions.

HINDUISM AS A WAY OF LIFE

Hindus often insist that Hinduism is more a "way of life" than a system of beliefs. Indeed, Hinduism does place greater emphasis on what one *does* rather than on what one *believes*. The emphasis on doing rather than believing might explain the disconnection between textual injunction and actual practice that one often encounters in Hinduism. For example, the *Laws of Manu*, as we have seen, provide prescriptions for how to live based on the *varnashrama dharma* system, but these do not always translate into actual lived practice. In this section, we will explore Hinduism as a way of life.

Temples and Icons

Hinduism encourages a sensory religious experience in its adherents. This experiential aspect is nowhere more evident than when a Hindu goes to a temple. As religion scholar Diana Eck observes, the devotee doesn't say, "I am going for worship." Rather, the devotee asserts, "I am going for *darshan*." The Sanskrit word **darshan** means "to see," but in the Hindu context it refers specifically to the interlocking gaze shared by the deity and the devotee. That is, *darshan* is the intimate act of both seeing the deity and being looked upon by the divine, an act that establishes a loving relationship between devotee and God.[12]

In Hinduism, folding one's hands and offering salutations by saying *namaste* (nom-us-tay) is a simple way of giving a respectful greeting, as well as saying, "I bow to the divine in you."

Hindu forehead markings: bindi, *tripundra*, and *namam*. Bindi (drop) is a decorative mark on the forehead signifying auspiciousness. An additional "dot" is often applied by married women to the top of the head where the hair is parted. The mark between the eyes signifies the "third eye" (perception beyond ordinary sight). Some forehead markings denote sectarian affiliation, such as the three horizontal lines worn by worshippers of Shiva and the vertical "V" of the worshippers of Vishnu. The red "drop" in the middle represents Lakshmi, the goddess of fortune.

The mandala (Sanskrit, "circle") is a sacred device that varies in form and function: to map cosmology, to embody deities, to serve as talismans, or to facilitate meditative contemplation.

As we learned earlier in this chapter, the image of a god in a temple or a personal shrine at home is not just a representation of the deity; rather, it is imbued with the divine presence. Thus, devotees believe that to see an image of a deity is to see the deity itself. In turn, the gaze of the deity's image is believed to confer blessings on every person who comes into its presence. In many ways, the act of *darshan* is often the most meaningful experience for Hindus.

Today, most Hindus go to a local temple or on pilgrimage to a sacred site for *darshan*. For this reason, the temple is a central religious and cultural institution in Hindu religious practice.

Temples generally house two different kinds of icons. The first type is the main image (or images), which resides at the center of the temple. These images are usually made of stone and are permanently fixed in the shrine. The second type of icon is the processional image, typically cast from an amalgam of five metals. Smaller and more mobile than fixed images, processional images are brought out of temples on special platforms or chariots for temple festivals and are usually adorned in elaborate costumes and jewels. Hindus gather for a *darshan* in the presence of the divine form embodied in these mobile images. Although both types of icons are made by human hands and are constituted of material substances, while the icon is being worshiped it is understood not to be *merely* stone or metal but the very body of God.

In temple rites, deities are treated as royal guests. Temple worship usually involves sixteen different offerings. Of these, the most significant is the eighth offering, which involves pouring auspicious substances over the icon. These substances might include scented water, milk, and sandalwood paste. After the ritual, the deity is adorned in ornaments, textiles, and flowers. The temple rituals end with a waving of lamps before the image. For Hindus, this is the ideal moment for *darshan*.

Divine images can also directly convey religious teachings. For instance, Nataraja, Lord of the Dance, is one of the most iconic forms of Shiva (see the photo on p. 96). In his dance, Nataraja represents what Shaivas call the Five Activities of Shiva, which can also be understood as the five principal manifestations of divine energy: creation, preservation, destruction, illusion, and liberation.

Forms of Worship

The Sanskrit word *puja* is commonly used to describe worship in Hinduism. In its simplest form, puja involves making some offering to the deity (such as fruit, incense, or flowers). The deity is then believed to partake of the devotion inherent in the offering. The material aspect of the offerings left behind is thought to be infused with the deity's blessing.

Puja can be simple or elaborate. Along with material items, offerings can consist of washing or clothing the image of the deity, greeting it, prostrating oneself before it, and similar gestures. Puja can be offered almost anywhere—before a home shrine,

Clouds of incense billow from a censer as devotees pray before a multi-armed clay icon of Durga (upper center), Ganesha (lower left), and other deities. This is the final opportunity for *darshan*, as the icon is about to be dissolved by immersion into the Ganges River at the conclusion of the festival of Durga Puja. Kolkata, India.

The majestic gate of a Shiva temple in southern India is reflected in one of the two ritual bathing tanks found within its precincts. These towers are erected in the four directions and are often covered in sculptural imagery that refers to the sacred myths of the gods venerated within. Arunachaleswar Temple, Tiruvannamalai, India, eleventh century.

at a temple, at pilgrimage sites, by sacred trees or rivers, at roadside shrines, or within temporary structures specially made for a specific rite. Rituals may be carried out as an expression of love for the deity, in a rite of passage, in celebration of a holiday or festival, when asking for blessings, in order to create an atmosphere of peace and harmony, or in propitiation of the gods in times of trouble. Ritual occasions are ideal for maintaining and strengthening community ties.

Certain forms of Hindu worship are so popular as to deserve special attention, especially *arati*, mantras, and sacrifice.

Arati   A common form of puja, **arati** involves an offering of light. *Arati* is so common that some Hindus use the term *arati* rather than puja to refer to worship generally. A lamp fueled with *ghee* (clarified butter) or camphor is lit and waved in a clockwise direction in front of the deity. The five flames used in *arati* symbolize the five elements (earth, water, fire, air, and ether), as well as the totality of the universe. This waving of the lamp is thought to remove evil influences and to return the object or recipient of the offering to an auspicious state, regardless of any negative thoughts or desires that might have been projected onto it. At the end of the ritual, participants wave their hands over the flame and touch them to their foreheads, taking the divine light of the deity into their innermost being.

Mantras   Nearly all rituals in Hinduism are accompanied by the recitation of **mantras**. These are ritual formulas used to produce a spiritual effect. Mantras can be used for a variety of reasons: to heighten awareness of God, to enhance the efficacy of an offering, to aid the practice of meditation, or to produce some magical effect. Mantras are usually—but not always—in Sanskrit.

The mantra that we have considered previously, OM, is prominent throughout Hinduism. The intonation of OM, the sound through which the universe is manifested, is thought to attune the mind to the essence of reality. Various Hindu sects use specific mantras especially suited to them. For example, the most important mantra for Vaishnavas is *Om Namo Narayanaya,* which means "obeisance to Narayana" (another name for Vishnu). For Vaishnavas, this mantra articulates the relationship between God and the devotee while also asserting the unity of Vishnu. Reciting and contemplating the mantra is an act of devotion that brings the devotee closer to Vishnu.

Sacrifice   Fire sacrifice has been an essential component of Hinduism since the Vedic period. Sacrifice usually involves building an altar, kindling a fire, feeding it with *ghee*, and casting offerings (milk, cereals, fruits, flowers, etc.) into the fire while chanting mantras. Although fire sacrifice is usually performed by a brahmin priest, these rites can be performed by any married upper-caste man. A fire sacrifice is a crucial component of life-cycle and temple rituals.

Although sacrifice has persisted as an important feature of Hindu worship through the centuries, perspectives on the relevance and meaning of sacrifice have varied. In the Vedic period, sacrifice was seen as essential to maintaining cosmic order. This is the reason that one of the most important Vedic myths describes the universe as being born from the sacrifice of the cosmic man. The Upanishads, however, tend to diminish the relevance of sacrifice as an effective means of liberation from samsara. These texts argue that the true sacrifice takes place internally, with the breath itself fueling an inner sacrificial fire that awakens one to knowledge. The *Bhagavad Gita* follows in this line of interpretation, asserting that it is the surrender of the fruit of action that is the true meaning and purpose of sacrifice.

In the earliest period, the sacrifice of animals was an important aspect of Hindu ritual. However, over time (and particularly under the influence of Jainism and Buddhism), animal sacrifice ceased to play a role in upper-caste sacrificial rituals. In such sacrifices, coconuts and pumpkins came to act as substitutes for the animals. Animal sacrifice continues to play a significant role in folk Hinduism.

Rites of Passage

Hindu rites of passage are intended to invoke blessings and divine favor during important times of transition. In addition, they help socialize individuals, assisting them as they move into new roles and stages of life. Some rites of passage occur very early in life. These include the naming ceremony of a child, typically held on the tenth or twelfth day after birth; a child's first haircut, usually performed between the first and third years of life; and ear piercing, which is typically done for both boys and girls before age five. The following are also major rites of passage.

Initiation Rituals   Boys of the brahmin, kshatriya, and vaishya classes traditionally underwent initiation by means of the *upanayana,* or sacred thread ceremony. Today, it is performed almost exclusively for brahmin boys at about the age of eight, giving them permission to perform certain religious functions. Beginning with a fire sacrifice, the ritual culminates in the promotion of the initiate to the category of "twice-born." The initiate is given a sacred thread that symbolizes a kind of umbilical cord linking the boy to the sun, the source of all light and knowledge. The sacred thread consists of three cotton threads, each composed of three strands, which are joined together by a single knot. It lies across the chest, resting over the left shoulder and under the right arm, thus being a highly visible sign of caste status.

Girls from all castes undergo initiation at the onset of the first menstrual period, which marks the transition from childhood to adulthood. Sometimes in these ritual observances the girl will spend the first three days of her first period secluded, although friends can visit. Now considered a young woman, she takes a ritual bath on the fourth day, and a feast is held in her honor. This transition is a public affair because it announces her availability for marriage. Often the young woman is taken to the local temple to receive a special blessing from an older married woman in her community, who will perform an *arati* ceremony to honor her new potential to bear children. Her life radically changes afterward, and, for many communities, her freedom to have unsupervised interaction with boys may be greatly curtailed.

Marriage   Marriage is a very important rite of passage. It is through marriage that one enters the householder ashrama, which provides the main support for society as a whole. In the past, marriage was traditionally arranged by the parents between a bride and groom of the same *jati* after consulting an astrologer, who determined the couple's compatibility. In the last few decades, caste strictures have eased somewhat. As a result, marriages for love have become more commonplace.

The marriage ceremony is sanctified through a fire sacrifice in which the gods are asked for blessings and offerings are poured into the fire. A thread is tied around the bride's wrist, and she is asked to step three times on a grinding stone from the groom's family as a demonstration of her fidelity to the new household she is joining. At the high point of the rite, the bride and groom walk together seven times around the sacred fire. The bride's family then provides a sumptuous meal for all guests. After the last day of celebration, the bride goes to the home of her husband.

Death   Hindus most often cremate the dead. The cremation pyre is likened to a fire sacrifice so that the funerary ritual is regarded as "the last sacrifice." Cremation usually takes place on the same day as death. The body is washed, smeared with sandalwood paste, wrapped in a cloth, and then carried on a litter by male relatives, who chant a holy name or phrase as they bear the body to the cremation ground. It is usually the duty of the eldest son of the deceased to conduct the last rites and light the pyre. An ancient practice that is still often observed requires him to also crack the skull of the deceased in order to release the soul from the body.

Although cremation is the typical means of disposing of the body, there are exceptions. Earth burial is practiced for babies and among some low-caste communities. Saints, yogis, and ascetics are also buried. Their bodies are placed in special tombs, around which shrines are sometimes erected and worship is performed.

Following the funeral ceremony, the family and home of the deceased are considered to be polluted for a period of about ten days. The bereaved are expected to keep to themselves until the rites of ancestral offerings are completed. During this period, the deceased is offered balls of rice with which he or she is believed to construct a body in the spirit world or intermediate realm. This rite, which reflects the gestation of a human embryo for ten lunar months, may very well predate the formulation of a belief in reincarnation that was developed by the time of the Upanishads.

Pilgrimage

In Hinduism, sacred pilgrimage sites are believed to lie at the border between this world and that of the divine. Many of the earliest pilgrimage sites were located at sacred rivers and pools, and pilgrimage specifically involved ritual bathing as a means of purification. Some revered sites, marked by a shrine or temple, commemorate a sacred event or the life of a holy person. For pilgrims, these sites allow immediate, tangible access to the sacred.

One of the most important Hindu pilgrimage sites is the sacred city of Varanasi (Benares) on the banks of the Ganges. Many Hindus believe that to die in Varanasi is to be immediately released from samsara. For this reason, many old and sick people travel to Varanasi to die. However, because the Ganges is held to be the most sacred river in India, people who are unable to go to Varanasi to die arrange to have their ashes scattered in the river. In this way, the sacred river is believed to carry the dead from this life into the divine realm.

How do Hindu pilgrimage practices compare to those of other religions, such as Buddhism, Islam, and Christianity? How do pilgrimage sites arise, and how do they serve the practical and spiritual needs of the visiting pilgrim?

The largest pilgrimage in India is to the sacred city of Allahabad (Prayag), where the Ganges and Yamuna rivers (as well as the Sarasvati, a now-vanished river mentioned in sacred texts) come together. To bathe at the confluence of these three rivers is considered especially auspicious. Every twelve years, the Kumbha Mela festival takes place at Allahabad. During the Kumbha Mela, the largest gathering of humans on earth takes place as pilgrims converge to bathe in the holy waters in the hope that all their sins will be washed away.

There are many other important pilgrimage sites in India. Some are dedicated to the goddess Devi and are referred to as *Shakti Peethas* ("Seats of Power"). Still others, like

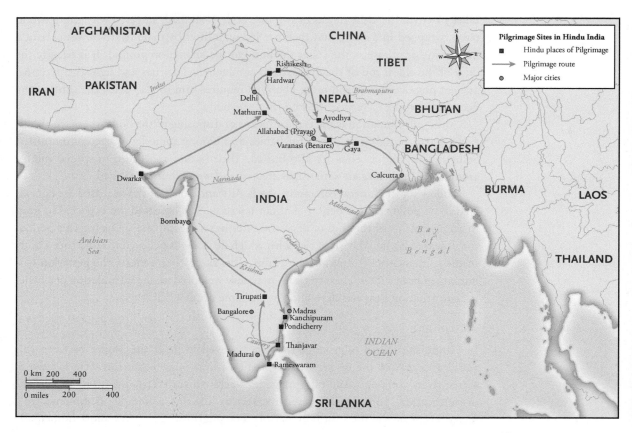

Hindu pilgrimage routes in India.

the city of Vrindavan in northern India, attract devotees of Krishna, who believe that it is not only the site of the god's birth and childhood but also where he continues to live.

Women in Hinduism

Hindu tradition has tended to be patriarchal, both subordinating and marginalizing women. Some evidence in the Vedic literature suggests that some women participated in early philosophical movements or dialogues. But for the most part, throughout the history of Hinduism the public roles of women have been secondary to those of men. In the domestic sphere, however, Hindu women have played a significant role.

The *Laws of Manu,* in the course of its extensive coverage of *varnashrama dharma,* includes some statements that confer upon women a relatively high place; for example: "Where women are honoured, there the gods are pleased; but where they are not honoured, no sacred rite yields rewards."[13] At the same time, numerous passages in the *Laws of Manu* and other classical texts subordinate and marginalize women, clearly asserting the predominance of father, husband, and even sons.

The bhakti movements enabled women to overturn social hierarchies. Women poets and saints such as Meera, who lived during the fifteenth century in Rajasthan, rejected marriage, devoted themselves to a spiritual life, and challenged the limits of gender, class, and caste. Today, Hindu women are increasingly assuming leadership roles in India and in the Indian diaspora. Women sometimes act as priests and are beginning to wield influence as spiritual teachers, monastics, and theologians. One of the most important contemporary female gurus is Mata Amritanandamayi Devi (b. 1953). Known to her followers as Ammachi ("Mother") and popularly referred to as "the hugging saint," she is believed by her devotees to be the embodiment of Devi, the divine mother.

In contemporary South Asian and Southeast Asian Hindu society, women are regarded as the custodians of traditional beliefs and ritual for the family. Generally, the social roles of men and women are expressed through clothing and other outward signs. While men wear contemporary slacks, dress shirts, and ties, women prefer traditional modes of dress. Although many men eschew sectarian forehead markings except on ritual occasions, most Hindu women, especially those who are married, adorn their foreheads with the bindi. In addition to performing puja at the home shrine, observing festivals, and encouraging regular temple visits for the family, women also perform pujas for the spiritual welfare of their husbands and children on certain holidays. They also commonly take vows—*vratas*—which we now consider.

Vrata   A *vrata* is a vow of temporary self-denial usually undertaken by a woman. This generally involves a short period of fasting, but a *vrata* can also be a vow of silence or a short-term renunciation of anything to which one is attached. A woman usually undertakes a *vrata* for a specific purpose, such as to ensure the health and well-being of her husband and family. There are many special *vratas* observed at specific times throughout the calendar year. One of the most popular, observed by married women throughout southern India, always falls on a Friday in early August. This *vrata* involves a period of purification and fasting, after which the woman invites the goddess Lakshmi into her home. The hope is that Lakshmi, goddess of wealth and good fortune, will bring these things to the home. All *vratas* are vows taken by women on special festival days.

Festivals and Holidays

Hindus make use of both solar and lunar calendars, as well as a calendar based on twenty-seven different constellations. All three calendars are consulted to determine when festivals and holidays will be observed. Many Hindu festivals link mythic events to the agricultural cycle. There are also innumerable holidays and observances that commemorate saints and sages, historical events, and sacred sites of regional interest.

Three popular Hindu festivals that are celebrated with many regional variations serve to illustrate the diversity of observances in Hinduism.

Navaratri and Dussehra Navaratri (Sanskrit, "nine nights") is a holiday cycle celebrating the end of the monsoon season in India. In some regions, Navaratri also commemorates the conclusion of a great war between Rama and the demon-king, Ravana. In other regions, such as southern India and in Bengal, the festival celebrates Devi's battle against the buffalo-demon, Mahisha. To commemorate this conquest, altars are set up with images of the Goddess. For the first three days of the festival, devotees worship Devi in her manifestation as Durga. They then turn their attention to worshiping her as Lakshmi. On the concluding three days, she is worshiped as Sarasvati, the embodiment of knowledge. In Bengal, the eighth day is especially important, as it celebrates Durga slaying Mahisha and is marked with the sacrifice either of black goats or a substitute sacrifice of pumpkins. The festival culminates with street processions of large painted clay icons of Durga that are later dissolved in the nearby river or the sea.

Dussehra, also called Vijayadashami (Sanskrit, "victorious tenth day") is celebrated on the day after Navarati throughout India as Rama's final victory over the demon Ravana. Dussehra occurs annually on the day of the full moon in the Hindu month of Ashvin (and so, this also determines the calendar dates of Navaratri).

Diwali Diwali, the five-day "Festival of Lights," is celebrated between mid-October and mid-November (like Dussehra and Navaratri, the dates of Diwali are determined on the basis of the lunar calendar). For many Hindus, it commemorates Rama's rescue of Sita and their heroic return to Ayodhya. Other myths are invoked as an explanation for the festival in different regions of India. During Diwali, oil lamps are set out on doorsteps and window ledges, and floating lamps are placed as offerings in rivers and reservoirs to signify the triumph of good over evil. Fireworks are lit on the night of the new moon, when Lakshmi is worshiped. The third day of Diwali marks the end of the harvest season, and Lakshmi Puja is performed to thank the goddess for the abundance that she has given. New clothes are worn and gifts are exchanged. Diwali is also celebrated by Sikhs and Jains.

Holi The spring festival of Holi, always celebrated at the vernal equinox, is Hinduism's most colorful holiday. Celebrated in late February or early March (commencing on the full moon day of this period), its festivities take place over two days. On the first night, bonfires are lit, and coconuts are offered as a sacrifice. The following day is a carnival celebration during which social and gender hierarchies are temporarily inverted, as crowds of young and old alike frolic in the streets, spraying colored water and staining one another with brightly colored powders.

Performance Traditions

There is a multitude of performance traditions in Hinduism, many of which cross over into the realm of ritual. Even the act of publicly reciting the *Ramayana* is believed to transform the performance site into sacred space. Hindu sacred performance traditions include many different genres: theater, puppetry, dance, music, storytelling, processions, and street festivals.

Fun and frolic characterize the spring festival of Holi, as participants mischievously smear colored powders or spray colored water on each other.

Ram Lila The *Ram Lila* ("The Play of Rama") is one of Hinduism's most popular performance traditions. During the month of September, northern Indian villages and cities host *Ram Lila* festivals to coincide with the festival of Dussehra. These festivals, lasting anywhere from ten days to a month, are costume dramas based on the *Ramayana*. The most famous and elaborate *Ram Lila* is sponsored by the Maharaja (the hereditary ruler) of Ramnagar, a city located across the Ganges from Varanasi. The Ramnagar *Ram Lila* attracts pilgrims from all over northern India who come not only to participate in this annual festival but also to have *darshan* of Rama. The roles of Rama, Lakshmana, and Sita (the three principal characters of the *Ramayana*) are played by young upper-caste boys. For the duration of the *Ram Lila*, these boys are worshiped as the embodiments of divinity. Every evening, a priest waves a lamp, illuminating the principal characters who give *darshan* to the assembled pilgrims and devotees. Just as in a temple, where God is actively present in the icon, here too the very act of performing the *Ramayana* enables the young boys to embody divinity.

A performance in Mumbai, India, of *Ram Lila*, the very popular enactment of the *Ramayana*.

Sacred Songs: *Bhajan* and *Kirtan* The term *bhajan* refers specifically to devotional songs in Hinduism and Sikhism. The *bhajan* helps the gathered community to contemplate the divine. This is usually achieved through repetition of key phrases and lines and also through a call-and-response format of singing. Often, profound mystical concepts are presented in simple language that everyone may understand.

Bhajan may be contrasted to *kirtan*, which is not formal in either form or structure, nor is it constrained by setting. *Kirtan* may be performed in lively sing-along processionals that roam the streets. Instruments are not necessary for *kirtan* performance, although they are often used. There are two different types of *kirtan* performances: in one type, the *kirtan* leader and the chorus alternate singing the divine name; and in the other, a hymn is communally recited. *Kirtan* continues to be popular today, especially for the Vaishnava sect. As explained in Chapter 7, *kirtan* is also a vital component of Sikh worship.

Storytelling   An important way in which Hindus learn about the content of their religion is through storytelling. Even today, as in centuries past, professional storytellers continue to travel particular routes throughout India to visit local festivals, where they sing the epics and other myths in all-night performances.

Modern Hindus enjoy sacred narratives through new and equally vibrant media, such as movies, television, and even comic books. Throughout the history of Hinduism, there have been numerous versions of sacred narratives, the *Ramayana* being perhaps the most obvious example. In recent decades, sacred narratives have been invigorated through print, radio, and television, as well as the Internet, with ever-new and imaginative retellings of these ancient stories.

CONCLUSION

Throughout this chapter, we have explored the rich diversity of the Hindu tradition. The extent of this diversity has prompted some observers to remark that "there are as many Hinduisms as there are Hindus." But we also have noted aspects of Hinduism that tend to unite Hindus. For example, all seek moksha, the ultimate liberation from samsara, and the realization of the true nature of the self and its relationship to the whole of reality. Hindus traverse three main paths to liberation: karma marga, jnana marga, and bhakti marga. In these various paths, we see diversity and unity together, with three different sets of teachings and practices all leading to the same goal. We see a similar blending of diversity and unity when we consider the detailed system of *varnashrama dharma*, which assigns to each individual Hindu a specific place and stage in life, while asserting the overall duty to conform to that which upholds the cosmic and social order.

For the most part, Hinduism developed in a rural setting, in small villages, and even in forests. In recent decades, however, there has been a pronounced shift in population from rural to urban settings. Furthermore, India, the world's second largest country in population and its largest democracy, has become a leader in high-tech industries, with cities like Bangalore and Mumbai now epicenters of international corporations. Hinduism, in the face of significant challenges brought on by modernization and the accompanying phenomenon of globalization, is constantly being reshaped. But as this chapter has shown, the diversity of the Hindu tradition is integral to its identity, in the present just as in the ancient past. Whatever shape Hinduism takes in the future, it is likely to thrive, drawing on its age-old ability to adapt and to reform with even greater diversity and vitality.

What Is Ultimate Reality?

Monistic Hindus believe that Brahman is the supreme, unitary reality, the ground of all Being. Understood as undifferentiated and without attributes, Brahman manifests itself as the world, in all its particular forms. Thus, all things are inherently divine. Humans are unable to apprehend this ultimate reality because of attachment, delusion, and identification with the limited ego-self. For dualistic or devotional Hindus, ultimate reality is typically understood to be fully embodied in a deity, such as Vishnu or Shiva.

How Should We Live in This World?

Powerfully attracted to the samsaric realm of particulars—our egoistic selves, our relationships, our possessions, and the seemingly countless objects of our desires—we are caught up in the continual cycle of death and rebirth. Hinduism prescribes living in a manner that moves the self toward liberation from samsara. Three paths (margas or yogas) lead to moksha: karma (action), jnana (knowledge), and bhakti (devotion). All the while, Hindus are required to live in conformity with dharma, upholding the cosmic and social order.

What Is Our Ultimate Purpose?

Moksha is liberation from samsara—the continuous cycle of death and rebirth, and the this-worldly realm in which this cycle recurs. Impossible fully to describe from the perspective of this world, the experience of moksha is said to be one of infinite awareness and eternal bliss. For monistic Hindus, moksha involves the full realization of the identity of the self with Brahman rather than with the world. For dualistic or devotional Hindus, moksha is the complete realization of the soul's perpetual and deep loving relationship with God.

REVIEW QUESTIONS

For Review

1. What were the essential features of Vedic religion? How was it different from Hinduism as it is practiced by most Hindus today?
2. In what ways do Hindus seek an experience of the divine?
3. What is the relationship between the ideas of karma, samsara, and dharma?
4. Describe the three margas, or paths, to liberation.
5. Describe the Vedas, Upanishads, epics, and Puranas. What are the most important features of each?

For Further Reflection

1. What are the various ways in which Hindus understand divine reality? How do these compare with those of other religions?
2. What is an avatar? How does the concept of avatar compare with the ways in which other religions speak of God on earth?
3. How does the traditional system of *varnashrama dharma* compare to systems of social organization with which you are familiar?
4. How were Hindus and Hinduism affected by British colonialism?
5. What are the most important turning points or milestones in the history of Hinduism?

GLOSSARY

arati (aah-ra-tee; Sanskrit) Worship with light, involving the waving of a lamp in front of the deity.

atman (aat-mun; Sanskrit) The eternal self or soul that is successively reincarnated until released from samsara through moksha.

avatar (ah-vah-taahr; from Sanskrit *avatara*) A "descent" of God (usually Vishnu) to earth in a physical form with the specific goal of aiding the world.

bhakti marga (bhah-k-tee; Sanskrit) The path of devotion.

Brahman (braah-mun; Sanskrit, "expansive") For monistic Hinduism, the supreme, unitary reality, the ground of all Being; for dualistic Hinduism, Brahman can refer to the supreme God (e.g., Vishnu).

brahmin (braah-mun; Sanskrit) A member of the priestly class of the *varna* or caste system.

dalit (daah-lit; Sanskrit, "oppressed"; Marathi, "broken") Self-designation of people who had traditionally been classified as untouchables or outcastes.

darshan (dur-shaan; Sanskrit, "to see") Worship through simultaneously seeing and being seen by a deity in the presence of its image.

dharma (dhur-mah; Sanskrit) Duty, righteousness, "religion"; basis for living in a way that upholds the cosmic and social order.

hindutva (hin-doot-vah; Sanskrit, "Hindu-ness") A modern term that encompasses the ideology of Hindu nationalism.

jati (jaah-tee; Sanskrit, "birth group") One of thousands of endogamous groups or subcastes, each equal in social and ritual status.

jnana marga (nyah-nah mar-guh) The path of knowledge.

karma (kur-mah; Sanskrit, "action") Action; also the consequences of action.

karma marga (kur-mah mar-guh) The path of ethical and ritual works, or "action."

kshatriya (kshut-ree-yuh; Sanskrit) A member of the warrior and administrator class of the *varna* or caste system.

mantra (mun-trah; Sanskrit) A ritual formula recited to produce a spiritual effect.

maya (my-yah: Sanskrit, "magic" or "illusion") In the Vedas, the magical power the gods used to create this world; in Vedanta philosophy, illusion that veils the mind.

moksha (mohk-shah; Sanskrit, "release") Liberation, the final release from samsara.

OM (oh-m; from three Sanskrit letters: *A-U-M*) The primordial sound through which the universe is manifested.

puja (poo-jah; Sanskrit, "worship") Generally, worship; usually the offering before an image of the deity of fruit, incense, or flowers.

Purana (pooh-raa-nah; Sanskrit, "ancient") A compendium of myth, usually with a sectarian emphasis.

samsara (sum-saah-rah; Sanskrit) The continuing cycle of birth, death, and rebirth; also the this-worldly realm in which the cycle recurs.

sannyasi (sun-nyaah-see; Sanskrit) Renouncer in the fourth stage (ashrama) of life.

Shaiva (shay-vah; Sanskrit) A devotee of Shiva.

Shakta (shah-k-tah; Sanskrit) A devotee of the Great Goddess, Devi.

shruti (shroo-tee; Sanskrit, "that which is heard") Term denoting the category of Vedic literature accepted by orthodox Hindus as revealed truth.

shudra (shoo-druh; Sanskrit) A member of the servant class of the *varna* or caste system.

smriti (smree-tee; Sanskrit, "tradition") Term denoting the vast category of Hindu sacred texts that is not shruti.

Tantra (tahn-truh; Sanskrit, "loom") System of ideas and practices that potentiates sudden liberation from samsara; also a form of sacred text detailing the ideas and practices.

Upanishad (ooh-pah-nee-shud; Sanskrit, "sitting down near [a teacher]") A philosophical text from the later period of Vedic literature, also called Vedanta ("end of the Vedas").

Vaishnava (vie-sh-na-vah; Sanskrit) A devotee of Vishnu and his avatars.

vaishya (vie-sh-yuh; Sanskrit) A member of the producer (farmer and merchant) class of the *varna* or caste system.

varna (vaar-nah; Sanskrit, "color") Caste or class; the four main classes form the basis of the traditional hierarchical organization of Hindu society.

Vedanta (veh-daan-tah; Sanskrit, "end of the Vedas") Synonym for Upanishads; prominent Hindu philosophical school.

Vedas (veh-duh; from Sanskrit *veda*, "knowledge") Broadly, all Vedic literature; narrowly, four ancient collections (samhitas) of hymns and other religious material.

yoga (yoh-gah; Sanskrit, "yoking" or "uniting") Generally, uniting of the self with God; sometimes used as an alternative to marga when referring to the three main paths to liberation; also (normally capitalized: Yoga) one of the six philosophical schools, focusing on moral, physical, and spiritual practices leading to liberation.

SUGGESTIONS FOR FURTHER READING

Eck, Diana. *Darsan: Seeing the Divine Image in India.* New York: Columbia University Press, 1998. An excellent discussion on the significance of *darshan* and traditions of Hindu temple worship.

Flood, Gavin. *An Introduction to Hinduism.* Cambridge, UK: Cambridge University Press, 1996. A concise and in-depth study of Hinduism.

Flood, Gavin, ed. *The Blackwell Companion to Hinduism.* Oxford, UK: Blackwell, 2003. A presentation on select special topics that are key to understanding Hindu belief and practice.

Hawley, John Stratton, and Mark Juergensmeyer. *Songs of the Saints of India.* Oxford, UK: Oxford University Press, 2006. A survey of the lives of medieval *bhakti* saints, with excellent translation of some of their poetry.

Hawley, John Stratton, and Vasudha Narayanan, eds. *The Life of Hinduism.* Berkeley: University of California Press, 2006. Special topical articles that explore personal voices and perspectives on Hindu life experience.

Klostermaier, Klaus K. *Hindu Writings: A Short Introduction to the Major Sources.* Oxford, UK: One World Publications, 2000. A keen survey of excerpts from many of the important textual sources that inform Hindu belief.

Knipe, David M. *Hinduism: Experiments in the Sacred.* New York: HarperCollins, 1991. A dependable and clear study organized based on the history of the tradition; includes a helpful timeline and glossaries.

ONLINE RESOURCES

Internet Sacred Text Archive (Hinduism)
sacred-texts.com/hin
The Internet Sacred Text Archive provides an excellent array of the many genres of Hindu sacred texts with multiple public domain translations of key works.

The University of Wyoming Hinduism Website
www.uwyo.edu/religionet/er/hinduism
The University of Wyoming Hinduism website offers concise but in-depth discussions on numerous aspects of Hindu tradition, literature, and belief.

Understanding Hinduism
hinduism.co.za
An informal collection of articles and information on key topics offering some range of viewpoints.

Internet Sacred Text Archive (Yoga)
sacred-texts.com/hin/yoga
The Internet Sacred Text Archive offers an extensive array of works on Yoga, including both original

sacred texts in translation and modern explorations of the subject.

The Sri Vaishnava Home Page

ramanuja.org

The Sri Vaishnava homepage is designed primarily for adherents to this important sect of Hinduism, yet is accessible and informative for outsiders.

The Shaivam.org Site

shaivam.org

The Shaivam.org site, self-described as the "Abode of God Shiva On the Internet," is designed primarily for devotees but is also useful for academic study.

Buddhism

TODAY IS <u>VESAK</u>. Here in Chiang Mai, northern Thailand's largest city, throngs of Thais and tourists crowd the streets and fill the city's 300 Buddhist temples. This is a day to honor the Buddha, the "Awakened One," who taught great truths about the cause and cure for human suffering. It is also a day for expressing gratitude to the order of Buddhist monks who have preserved the Buddha's teachings, known as the Dharma, for twenty-five centuries. More than 1,500 monks will receive gifts of food and drink from thousands of laypeople during this celebration in Chiang Mai.

Known as Visakha Bucha Day (the day of "honoring the Buddha in Visakha") in Thailand, Vesak commemorates three events: the birth, enlightenment, and death of the Buddha. According to tradition, all three miraculously took place on the same day of the year: the full moon day of the Indian lunar month of Visakha. On the Western calendar, this places Vesak sometime in May or, less frequently, in June.

Throughout the Buddhist world, Vesak is a time for visiting temples, meditating, listening to "Dharma talks" given by monks, and other forms of devotion, such as walking around a temple three times in recommitting oneself to the "Three Jewels" of Buddhism: the Buddha, the Dharma, and the order of monks (Sangha). Some Buddhists bring offerings of flowers or candles to temples as reminders that, just as flowers fade and candles burn out, so are all things subject to change. Most take care to observe the Five Precepts (which forbid such things as stealing and

Buddhists offer alms to monks during a celebration of Vesak in Chiang Mai, Thailand.

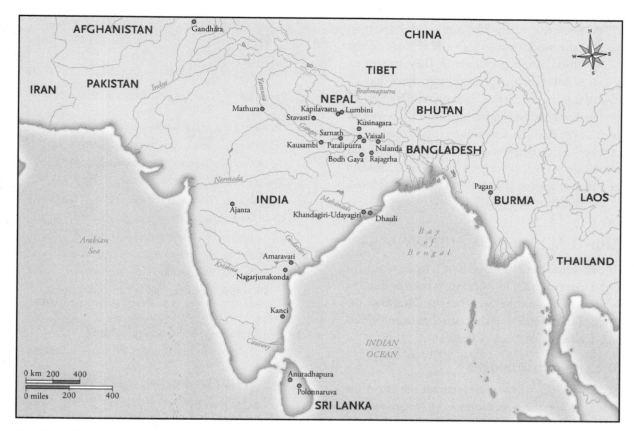

Significant sites of early
Buddhism.

drinking intoxicants) and, for good measure, three other precepts otherwise required only of monks: abstaining from food after noon, not wearing jewelry or perfume, and not using soft beds or chairs. In Chiang Mai, there is a very special way of expressing devotion. At sunset on the day before Vesak, devotees begin a nine-mile trek from the bottom of Doi Suthep Mountain to Wat Phrathart Doi Suthep, a famous temple perched near the summit of Doi Suthep that holds relics of the Buddha. Holding paper lanterns lit by candles, incense sticks, and lotus buds, adherents circle clockwise around the temple's Bhote chapel. Then, at dawn, they make offerings to the temple's monks.

According to an ancient story, as the Buddha lay dying, he told his disciples that there was no reason to weep, for his death and the disintegration of his body would be in accordance with the universal law that nothing escapes change. His followers were welcome to honor him with offerings and devotions, he said, but it would be more important for them to honor the Dharma when he was gone and to strive to follow its teachings. Like the Buddha's disciples, those who understand the meaning of Vesak today honor the "Awakened One" with both simple expressions of devotion and their commitment to follow his teachings. ☀

There are nearly 500 million Buddhists in the world today, about 7 percent of the total world population.[1] They belong to a vast number of Buddhist groups. Each has its distinctive characteristics, and their differences are sometimes remarkable, but all trace their origins back to the Buddha, our point of departure in this chapter. After examining the Buddha's life and teachings, we will survey the history of Buddhism and then take note of the more important features of the Buddhist way of life.

THE TEACHINGS OF BUDDHISM

The **Buddha**, the "Awakened One," lived in northern India more than 2,500 years ago. It was the Buddha who set in motion the "wheel of the **Dharma**," the body of teachings about the cause and end of suffering that lies at the heart of Buddhism.

The Life of the Buddha

We know little with certainty about the life of the Buddha. The many accounts we have are legendary rather than historical, although their agreement on many points suggests they are based on a genuine historical figure. While reliable historical sources might satisfy our curiosity about the course of the Buddha's life, the legends about him are more helpful to us here. This is because they are didactic in character, telling the story of the Buddha in a way that educates us about the essential features of his teaching.

The earliest accounts of the Buddha's life and teaching are recorded in Sanskrit and Pali, two closely related languages of ancient India. We will follow scholarly convention in this chapter by using the Sanskrit forms of important terms except when the Pali form is more commonly used.

The Early Life of the Buddha
Siddhartha Gautama, who was to become the Buddha, was probably born in the sixth century B.C.E. Western

TIMELINE
Buddhism

c. 563–483 B.C.E.	Traditional dates for the life of the Buddha
c. 483 B.C.E.	First Buddhist Council.
c. 383 B.C.E.	Second Buddhist Council.
c. 360 B.C.E.	Council of King Mahapadma.
c. 272–231 B.C.E.	Reign of Ashoka in India.
c. 247 B.C.E.	Third Buddhist Council.
250–200 B.C.E.	Buddhism arrives in Southeast Asia.
65 C.E.	Buddhism arrives in China.
100–200	Composition of the *Lotus Sutra*.
300–400	Buddhism arrives in Korea.
400–450	According to tradition, Bodhidharma brings Chan (Zen) Buddhism from India to China.
552	Buddhism arrives in Japan.
775	The first Buddhist monastery in Tibet is built at Samye.
c. 800	Borobudur Stupa built in Java.
c. 1200	Destruction of Buddhist universities at Nalanda and Vikramasila.
1185–1333	Pure Land, Zen, and Nichiren flourish in Japan during the Kamakura period.
c. 1500	Virtual disappearance of Buddhism in India.
1890–1921	T. W. Rhys-Davids, professor of Pali at the universities of London and Manchester, translates Buddhist texts into English.
1899	The Buddhist Churches of America is founded in San Francisco by Japanese immigrants of the Jodo Shinshu sect.
1900	Over 40,000 Buddhist and Daoist texts are rediscovered in a cave at Dunhuang, in western China.
1956	Indian social activist B. R. Ambedkar (1891–1956) converts to Buddhism along with 400,000 others to protest Hindu oppression of "untouchables."
1959	The 14th Dalai Lama flees to India from Tibet.

scholars have traditionally set the dates for his life at 563–483 B.C.E., though arguments can be made for moving them as much as a century earlier or later. According to tradition, Siddhartha's father was the ruler of a small kingdom that straddled part of what is now the border of India and Nepal.

Siddhartha's father was determined that his son would follow in his footsteps. Fearing that Siddhartha would be drawn to the spiritual life if he became aware of the existence of suffering in the world, the king tried to shield him from the harsh realities of life. And so Siddhartha grew up living a sheltered and luxurious life with no hint of pain. In time, he married a princess, Yasodhara, with whom he had a son. And yet, despite his happy life, Siddhartha grew restless.

Finally, at the age of twenty-nine, Siddhartha ventured outside the sheltered world of the palace. Accompanied by his charioteer, he saw things that were to change the course of his life. Buddhists call these the "Four Sights." The first was a frail old man. Siddhartha, who had never seen old age, asked if he, too, would become old and decrepit. He was dismayed when his charioteer assured him that he would. The second sight was a man afflicted by disease. Sickness, said the charioteer, is also a part of human life. The third sight, a corpse being carried off to a cremation, was terrifying. Death, too, said the charioteer, is something no one can escape. Siddhartha now saw through the illusion that his father had created and was filled with despair by the inescapable truths of old age, sickness, and death. It was not until he witnessed the fourth

Siddhartha cuts his hair. Mural depicting the life of Buddha, Jogyesa Temple, Seoul, South Korea.

sight that he found some reason to hope. Sitting by the side of a road, he saw a wandering ascetic, homeless and without possessions, who seemed to be content.

The "Great Going Forth" For Siddhartha, the ascetic pointed the way. To return to life within the palace would be to hide from the truth. He resolved instead to face it. He would renounce the life he had lived, take up the life of an ascetic, and search for the truth about suffering. One night, he kissed his sleeping wife and son good-bye and silently slipped away. As soon as he was alone in the forest, he took off his expensive clothing and used his sword to cut off his hair, symbolically severing the bonds that tied him to his old life.

At first, Siddhartha turned to ascetic sages who were acknowledged for their wisdom, becoming a disciple first of one, then another. They taught him meditation techniques and yogic disciplines, but although he mastered them all, they left him unsatisfied. He then committed himself to extreme asceticism. After a time of wandering, he found a grove of trees by a river. Joined there by five other ascetics who wished to follow his example, he began to practice severe austerities in the hope that they would somehow clarify his thought. For five years,

Siddhartha wore rags and did not bathe. He slept on thorns and in cemeteries strewn with half-burned corpses. Eating as little as a single grain of rice a day, he became a skeletal figure whose mind was tormented by searing pain.

One day, after a long period of intense fasting, Siddhartha set out for the river. On the way, he overheard a music teacher explaining to his student that an instrument string wound too tight will break, whereas one that is too loose makes no sound at all. These words brought Siddhartha to the realization that neither sensual indulgence nor self-denial is helpful in the quest for understanding and liberation from suffering. Because both weaken the body and the mind, the best path lies between them. This principle of the **Middle Way** was to become foundational in Buddhism. According to tradition, it was at this moment that a woman came to Siddhartha with a bowl of porridge. He ate the porridge and also bathed himself. He then returned to his ascetic companions, but they left him when they learned he had abandoned their way of life.

Enlightenment   Siddhartha's determination was now absolute. At a village in northern India now known as Bodh Gaya, he sat down beneath a fig tree and vowed to remain there in meditation until he gained the understanding he sought. Restored to health by his practice of moderation, he sat and meditated for forty-nine days. Then, one night, his enlightenment came. Siddhartha first recalled all of his past lives. He then saw how **karma**—the law of actions and their consequences—had been at work throughout time, conditioning the existence of all beings as they took form and then passed away. Finally, Siddhartha realized that desire is the cause of suffering and that for suffering to end there must be an end to desire.

According to Buddhist tradition, Siddhartha was not the first to attain enlightenment. Buddhists believe that others before and after him became, and will become, buddhas. But it is from *this* buddha that they have received the Dharma, and so for them he is *the* Buddha, the "Awakened One." His enlightenment brought an end to the desire that causes suffering. It also brought freedom from rebirth, which results from attachment to the world. Freed from the disturbances caused by attachment, his mind came to rest in its natural state, and he was filled with joy. He had attained **nirvana**, the "extinguishing" of desire and suffering. For many days the Buddha remained close to the site of his enlightenment. Then, moved by compassion for others, he set out to teach what he had learned.

Beginnings of the Buddhist Community   The Buddha went first to a deer park at Sarnath (near modern Varanasi in India), where the five ascetics who had earlier abandoned him were still practicing harsh austerities. Seeing that he had broken through to some new understanding, they gathered around the Buddha, who gave them his first teaching. This was the "Sermon in the Deer Park," in which he told them of the Middle

"Calling the Earth to Witness." According to tradition, the demon Mara afflicted the Buddha with powerful temptations to give up his quest for enlightenment. Ignoring them, the Buddha touched his right hand to the ground, thereby calling upon the earth to witness his unshakeable resolve. Immediately thereafter, he experienced nirvana.

Rock-cut reclining statue of the Buddha preparing to enter *parinirvana*, in a cave shrine at Ajanta, Maharashtra State, India. Fifth century C.E.

Way and set forth the Four Noble Truths and the Noble Eightfold Path, which describe the cause and cure of suffering (pp. 152–154). The ascetics became followers of the Buddha, the first Buddhist monks and the first members of the Buddhist **sangha** (Pali, "community").

From Sarnath, the Buddha began to retrace his steps back home, attracting more followers to the sangha along the way. Many were relatives, including his father and his son, Rahula. A cousin, Ananda, became one of the Buddha's most devoted disciples and later played such an important role in remembering and transmitting the Buddha's teachings that he has been called the "Guardian of the Dharma." The Buddha wandered across northern India for more than four decades, teaching, ordaining monks and nuns, and accepting lay followers.

The Death of the Buddha   The life of the Buddha came to an end in his eightieth year, forty-five years after his enlightenment. He and Ananda had stopped to eat at the home of a blacksmith. Something in the meal was tainted, causing the Buddha to become fatally ill. In a grove on the outskirts of the village, Ananda made a bed for him between two trees. His monks soon began to gather at the scene, frantically seeking a final bit of the Buddha's wisdom. When they asked what they would do without him to teach them, he responded that the Dharma would always be their guide. Not long afterward the Buddha closed his eyes, went deep into meditation, and died. Without attachments to the world, and unbound by karmic forces that would have brought another incarnation, he passed into ***parinirvana***, the complete and final entry into nirvana.

What Did the Buddha Teach?

The Buddha sought both the cause of human suffering and the means to end such suffering. His enlightenment had revealed to him the truths he sought, and these truths constitute the core of the Dharma. We saw in Chapter 4 that in Hindu usage the Sanskrit word *dharma* has a wide range of meanings, including "law," "duty," and "righteousness." In Buddhist contexts, *dharma* is more often used to describe the body of the Buddha's teaching. As we will see, the teachings of the Buddha are based on his observations of nature and its laws.

Interdependent Origination   We will begin our investigation of the Buddha's teaching with the doctrine of **Interdependent Origination,** also known as Dependent Origination, because so much of the Dharma is based on it.

To most of us, the world seems to be a composite system consisting of different and separate things. The chair you are sitting in certainly appears to exist on its own, apart from all other things in the room. And it is likely that you see yourself as existing independently of everyone and everything else you encounter.

Probing deeply into the nature of reality, the Buddha saw things very differently. He taught that reality is a complex of interrelated and interdependent phenomena in which nothing exists apart from anything else. Instead, all things depend on other things for their coming-into-existence—that is, for their origination. Of course, everyone recognizes at some level that this is the case. Someone built your chair, for example, and your parents had something to do with you. But the Buddha's teaching, augmented by later Buddhist thinkers, goes far beyond this in identifying a cycle of twelve causal factors (such as ignorance, desire, and rebirth) that bring about a coming-into-existence once any one of them is set in motion.

Of course, things also *remain* in existence—or at least they *seem* to. How can this be explained? And what *are* things, really? Here, again, the Buddha taught that all things are interdependent—so much so, in fact, that they have no existence whatsoever *in and of themselves*. Once again, take your chair as an example. Probing deeply, you will find that it is constituted of different elements: height, width, leather, legs, texture, firmness, color, and so on. But you will not find "chair." Instead, your chair exists only as a complex of "not chair" elements, and only for as long as these constituent parts remain together. And so it is with all things. Each thing exists as a collection of other elements, having no independent existence of its own.

The Three Marks of Existence Building on his teaching about the interrelatedness and interdependence of things, the Buddha taught that there are **Three Marks of Existence**—Impermanence, Suffering, and No-Self.

The Buddha's doctrine of **Impermanence** (Pali, **anicca**) holds that all things are always changing. Nothing remains the same, even for a moment. All things are always in a state of *becoming*. For example, imagine a blade of grass. Although it may seem static, the truth is that it is growing and therefore becoming a *different* blade of grass in every moment.

The Buddha's teaching about **Suffering** (Pali, *dukkha*) is central to the Dharma. He once said, "I have taught one thing and one thing only, suffering and the cessation of suffering." Suffering is caused by the desire to hold on to things when, in fact, nothing can be held. Uncomfortable with constant change and the impermanence of things, we want them to remain as we want them to be. Buddhists describe this wanting in a variety of ways—as desiring, craving, clinging, and thirsting. However it is described, desire is made possible by ignorance (and, in particular, ignorance of impermanence) and can take the form of an attachment to something we want in our lives or an aversion to something we don't want. These three qualities of attachment, aversion, and ignorance (sometimes labeled as greed, hatred, and delusion) are known as the "Three Poisons." The suffering that arises from them can take innumerable forms.

Wanting is suffering. Lacking is suffering. Fearing that something you have might one day be lost is suffering. Believing that you cannot be happy unless you have something is suffering. Being averse to something is suffering. Wanting things to stay the same is suffering. Wanting things to be different is suffering. Stress and worry are suffering. Envy and jealousy are suffering. Anger, hatred, grief, loneliness, and frustration are suffering. Finally, the unhealthy effects many of these mental or psychological states have on the body constitute suffering.

The third of the Three Marks of Existence is the doctrine of **No-Self (anatman)**. Of all the things we desire, it is likely that our greatest attachment is to our notion of self. As we saw in Chapter 4, Hinduism includes the belief that at the core of one's self is the unchanging and eternal soul or *atman*, which survives the death of the body through successive incarnations. The Buddha rejected this idea, teaching that just as there are no other things that remain unchanged, there is no static self that remains the same. The doctrine of No-Self does not mean that there is no "you." Clearly, you exist. You have a body, a mind, movement, interests, and other qualities. The Buddha taught that these are rooted in the *skandhas* (Sanskrit, "bundles"), the five basic components of every self: the body, perception, feelings, innate tendencies, and thought—all of which are always in flux. Thus, the Buddha taught that each of us is a shifting self that is always changing in response to changes happening elsewhere in the web of interrelated, interdependent, and impermanent phenomena that make up reality.

It can be difficult to accept this idea. After all, most of us are attached to our individual identities and to the notion that for as long as we live (and, perhaps, even after we die) there are some ways in which we will remain the same. No-Self might seem to imply a destruction or annihilation of something we like very much—ourselves. But this is not the case. Instead, the Buddha urged only that his followers recognize that the self is not concrete, permanent, or independent of other things. The great benefit he saw in this teaching is that it opens the way to living without the suffering that arises from a false notion of self and from clinging to things that cannot be held. The Buddha found the full realization of this ideal in his enlightenment and in the bliss of nirvana.

Compare the Buddha's teachings about the self or soul with the teachings of other religions.

THE FOUR NOBLE TRUTHS

1. Suffering is inherent in life.
2. The cause of suffering is desire.
3. There is a way to put an end to desire and suffering.
4. The way is the Noble Eightfold Path.

The Four Noble Truths and the Noble Eightfold Path   We saw earlier that the first teaching the Buddha offered to the sangha was the Sermon in the Deer Park, in which he told the five ascetics who had been his companions about the **Four Noble Truths** and the **Noble Eightfold Path**. He structured his most fundamental teaching about suffering as if it were a medical diagnosis and prescription for a cure. The Four Noble Truths follow the four steps ancient Indian doctors used to diagnose and treat illness: (1) identifying a symptom, (2) discovering its cause, (3) determining if there is a way to remove the cause, and (4) prescribing a therapy to effect a cure. As a process of identifying and treating the disease of suffering, the Four Noble Truths empower those who follow them to understand the root cause of suffering and to cure themselves.

Now that we have investigated some of the Buddha's other teachings, we are in a good position to understand the Four Noble Truths. In teaching that suffering is inherent in life, the Buddha was pointing to the inevitability of suffering and its everyday presence in people's lives. In identifying the cause of suffering as desire, the Buddha was not teaching that all forms of desire are unhealthy. Satisfying our desire for nourishment, employment, and a decent place to live certainly makes sense. But when we desire to grasp and hold on to things that cannot be held, we will always be disappointed. The good news is that there is a way to deal with desire and to minimize, even to end, the suffering it causes.

The Buddha's prescription for a cure for suffering is the Noble Eightfold Path. In treading the Eightfold Path, one follows in the footsteps of the Buddha in eradicating attachment, aversion, and ignorance, putting an end to desire, and ultimately achieving enlightenment and nirvana, just as the Buddha did.

THE NOBLE EIGHTFOLD PATH

1. **Right View**: seeing things as they are, in accordance with the Buddha's teachings.
2. **Right Intention**: cultivating an unshakeable commitment to tread the path to enlightenment in accordance with the Buddha's teachings.
3. **Right Speech**: cultivating the virtue of addressing others with kindness, while abstaining from lying, divisive or abusive speech, and idle chatter.
4. **Right Action**: abstaining from killing, stealing, and sexual misconduct.
5. **Right Livelihood**: making a living in a way that harms no one and benefits all.
6. **Right Effort**: striving to abandon all thought and action that is harmful to oneself or others and to cultivate virtues that benefit oneself and others.
7. **Right Mindfulness**: focused awareness of the body and mind and the phenomena arising within and affecting each.
8. **Right Concentration**: cultivating the four stages of concentration leading to equanimity beyond pleasure and pain.

The eight aspects of the Noble Eightfold Path are sometimes divided into three divisions, each with its own goal. The first is the *prajna* (Sanskrit, "wisdom") division, which includes Right View and Right Intention. Here, the aim is to ensure that one understands and accepts the Buddha's teachings about Impermanence, Suffering, and No-Self and is committed to striving for goals consistent with them. The second division has the purpose of cultivating ethical conduct through Right Speech, Right Action, and Right Livelihood. The Buddha taught that unethical conduct is an obstacle to mental clarity. For this reason, destructive speech, immoral behavior, and making a living in a way that is harmful to oneself or others are to be avoided. The third division promotes concentration. Through Right Effort, one seeks to eliminate all qualities of the mind that give rise to unwholesome thought and action and to encourage those that produce more positive effects. Right Mindfulness is the observation of thoughts, feelings, and all other phenomena that occur in the body and mind. Finally, Right Concentration involves progress through four stages of concentration until one achieves a state of nonattachment and equanimity.

Karma and Rebirth   The Buddha taught a doctrine of rebirth that differed from the Hindu view in denying that there is an eternal and unchanging soul (Sanskrit, atman) that passes through many incarnations. According to his doctrine of No-Self, one's sense of self arises from the interrelationship of the five *skandhas* and exists only for as long as they function together in such a way as to give rise to that sense of self. When they separate at death, that sense of self ceases to exist, and so there is nothing substantial that passes from one incarnation to another. And yet there is a definite connection between one life and the next; there is a type of rebirth. The Buddha's teaching on this point is obscure and much debated. What *is* clear is that one's actions and the karma they generate bring about the conditions for the coming-into-existence of a new set of *skandhas*. This, in turn, gives rise to another sense of self. Nothing concrete passes from one life to the next; there are only the karmic and character-related elements of the previous life, which shape a new life in some ways consistent with the old. Buddhists have used a variety of analogies to illustrate this idea. According to one analogy, rebirth is much like what happens when one candle is used to light another. A light appears where none had existed before, and yet nothing has passed over other than the energy (which we might compare to karmic energy) generated by the first candle.

Of course, these teachings about karma and rebirth do not apply to those who have found enlightenment. The Buddha taught that these individuals no longer set in motion the karma that leads to rebirth and are also freed entirely from the karma produced in earlier lives. There is no rebirth for them. Only those who continue to thirst for things and seek to satisfy their desire through attachment to them are reborn in **samsara** (Sanskrit, "continuous flow"). For Buddhism, as for Hinduism, samsara has two closely related meanings: the continuous cycle of birth, death, and rebirth and the this-worldly realm in which this cycle recurs.

Nirvana   The ultimate goal of Buddhist practice, nirvana is liberation from suffering in the cyclic existence of samsara. A Sanskrit word, nirvana means a "blowing out" or "extinguishing," and refers to the extinguishing of desire that leads to suffering. The Buddha taught that all people have the potential to attain nirvana, which brings perfect bliss and an end to suffering. Beyond this, any description of nirvana is uncertain. Being utterly unlike anything one might experience with ordinary awareness, no comparison is possible. For this reason, the Buddha said very little about nirvana, as it is something that must be experienced in order to be understood.

Gods in Buddhism?   It is often said that Buddhism is an atheistic religion. And, indeed, some Buddhists are atheists. Many other Buddhists, however, believe in a wide variety of divine beings.

The Buddha had little to say about the gods. His view concerning them is perhaps best described as "transtheistic" (Chapter 1) because, although he appears to have acknowledged the existence of gods, he insisted that they are not helpful in bringing an end to suffering and in making progress toward enlightenment.

As we will see, many Buddhists acknowledge the existence of supernatural beings, such as celestial buddhas and **bodhisattvas**, who are objects of devotion and are believed to bestow benefits on those who call upon them. Whether or not these supernatural beings are gods depends on how one defines "god." We will explore the roles of celestial buddhas and bodhisattvas later in this chapter.

Early Buddhism also assimilated an astonishing variety of supernatural entities from the religions and folk traditions of the regions to which it spread. These include Hindu gods, nature spirits, mythical creatures, demons, dragons, serpents, protector deities, heroes, heavenly musicians, and many others.

VOICES: An Interview with Katherine Sei

Katherine Sei is an American Buddhist who lives in California. She is a practitioner of Vajrayana Buddhism and has been a student of Lama Lodru Rinpoche for nearly three decades. She is the facilitator of a Buddhist study center in Sacramento.

As a Buddhist, what is the most important aspect of human existence? What should Buddhists do or focus on in life?

The most important aspect of human existence, to me, is that we have an opportunity to evolve as beings. This evolution encompasses uncovering our true nature. This true nature is comprised of a spontaneous, natural compassion and a clear wisdom as to "what is really going on here." I've found through all the years of meditation that we all tend to really limit our minds, and the expression of our true wise and benevolent nature. As I uncover and begin to understand my mind's true nature, and learn to let go of my limiting definitions of self, others, and events in my life, suffering diminishes. Life becomes more joyful, more peaceful, and I feel more interconnected with everyone. Life also becomes very, very interesting as I begin to become aware of all the interconnections of karmic causes and effects, and I can relax into the "play" of events.

Katherine Sei.

Does Buddhism give you a unique outlook on life? How so or why?

I'm not sure if Buddhism gives a unique outlook as much as a useful outlook on life in this culture. The teachings of Lord Buddha are not necessarily unique to Buddhism—I think many aspects of Hinduism, Christianity, Judaism, and Islam provide a framework for becoming a more loving and wise person. What may be unique in terms of Buddha's teachings is that one can examine one's mind and one's life through meditation practices. It's more like a science than a religion, analogous to a physicist learning mathematics to explore the universe. I've found through meditation that life isn't quite as rigid as we often make it out to be. Knowing that, one can learn to let go of many of the emotional habits and knee-jerk reactions. One can find many creative solutions to life's problems, big and small, from "What is death?" or "What does it all mean?" to "How do I deal with my angry boss?" "How do I deal with the stress in my life?" and so on.

What single event in your life would you characterize as your most meaningful religious experience?

It's hard to pick one single event in my life that I consider most meaningful. Three come to mind. First would be when I took refuge with Trungpa Rinpoche in the 1980s. At that time, I discovered that I could treat others and myself with more gentleness. The second event would be when I met Ven. Lama Lodru Rinpoche, my direct teacher for the past twenty-seven years. Lama Lodru has taught me the same meditation practices that Tibetan lamas go through in a formal three-year retreat, but spread out over fifteen years. In doing this, he demonstrated that anyone can learn to meditate and apply it in their day-to-day life. One doesn't have to become a monk or nun to become liberated. The third event was having the nature of my mind pointed out by Mingyur Rinpoche. Mingyur Rinpoche is a Tibetan lama who had to overcome panic attacks when he was a teenager. He showed me how applicable Buddha's teachings on meditation are to all aspects of life.

THE HISTORY OF BUDDHISM

In this section, we explore the early history of Buddhism in India, its expansion into other parts of Asia and beyond, and the development of the three great traditions in Buddhism: **Theravada**, **Mahayana**, and **Vajrayana**.

The Period of the Buddhist Councils

According to early Buddhist accounts, immediately after the death of the Buddha, a council of monks was convened at the town of Rajagriha in northeast India. This was the first in a series of councils that would define Buddhism by addressing key doctrinal and practical issues as they arose at particular times and places in its early history.

The First and Second Buddhist Councils   The First Buddhist Council was convened c. 483 B.C.E. According to an ancient tradition, this was an assembly of 500 of the Buddha's direct disciples. Recalling that the Buddha had urged them to look to the Dharma as their guide after his death, they established an oral canon of his teachings. In this way, the First Council established the Dharma as the primary authority in the sangha.

The Second Council was occasioned by developments within the order of monks. During the Buddha's lifetime, he and his monks, or **bhikkus,** had been wanderers who remained in one place only when they needed to take shelter during the annual rainy season. This practice changed during the centuries after the Buddha's death as formerly

Diffusion of Buddhism across Asia.

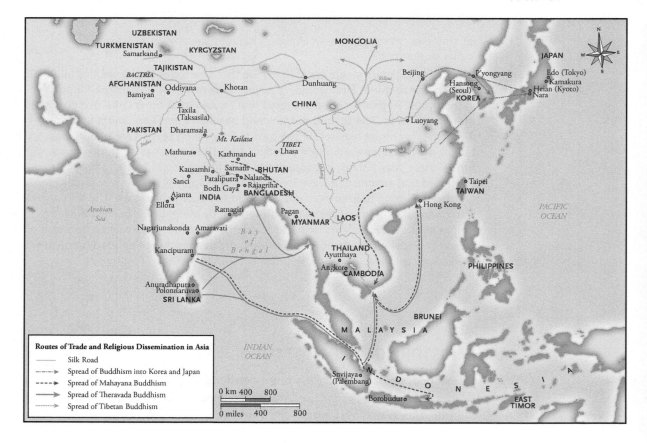

itinerant monks and nuns began to settle in permanent monastic communities. Over time, these communities became increasingly insular and geographically dispersed. Without a unifying authority, there was a proliferation of variations in teachings and practices that led to sectarian splits. The Second Buddhist Council (c. 383 B.C.E.) was called to address this issue. It took a special interest in differences of opinion on matters related to monastic discipline. For example, monks were split over the issue of whether it was permissible to accept payment for performing ritual services to laypeople. Although the historical record is not entirely clear, it appears that differences among monks were exacerbated rather than resolved at the Second Buddhist Council.

Ashoka and the Third Buddhist Council   While early Buddhist monks were working out their differences, the political situation in India was changing dramatically. In the third century B.C.E., it produced a ruler who was the first great champion of Buddhism.

This was Ashoka (r. c. 272–231 B.C.E.), the renowned emperor of India's Mauryan Dynasty. Ashoka united the subcontinent of South Asia on a scale unseen before his time, and it was not until the British colonized India in the eighteenth and nineteenth centuries that such a large portion of the subcontinent was again unified under a single ruler.

One of many marble slabs containing text and commentary from the *Tripitaka* or Pali Canon, Kuthodaw Pagoda, Mandalay, Myanmar (Burma).

Despite his success as a conqueror, Ashoka came to regret the violence and suffering he had imposed on others during his conquests. According to legend, he underwent a conversion experience after triumphing over his rivals in 260 B.C.E. He now abandoned his expansionist policies and began to channel his efforts into social reform grounded in Buddhist ethics.

Although Ashoka had been influenced by Buddhist ideals even before his victory, his conversion was clearly the pivotal moment in his reign. His sincerity was evident in his edicts, which promoted moral purification, self-awareness, nonviolence, and respect for all religions. The edicts were promulgated across his empire. Often carved on stone pillars, some of which are still preserved today, Ashoka's "rock edicts" are our earliest evidence for the widespread promotion of Buddhist ideals.

Ashoka convened the Third Buddhist Council in his capital at Pataliputra c. 247 B.C.E. According to tradition, the 1,000 monks who attended sent out missionaries—monks who had memorized much of the Dharma—to other countries. The council also attempted to settle disputes concerning interpretation of the Dharma. Ultimately, it concluded that one sect, which eventually gave rise to Theravada Buddhism, represented the authentic and orthodox viewpoint of the Buddha.

Theravada Buddhism

Theravada (Sanskrit, "Way of the Elders") views itself as representing the original and authentic teaching of the Buddha. Theravada has also been called *Hinayana* (Sanskrit, "Lesser Vehicle"), but this term, once favored by adherents of the much larger Mahayana tradition, is rarely used today. Theravada is the predominant Buddhist tradition in Sri Lanka, Thailand, Cambodia, Laos, and Burma.

Theravada emphasizes pursuit of nirvana through the individual's own efforts. The Buddha is revered as one who achieved nirvana and gave the Dharma to humanity, so that others could attain nirvana as well. But the Buddha himself is beyond the reach of the individual and is no longer available to provide direct assistance. For this reason, Theravada emphasizes the Buddha's admonition in his last words to his disciples: "Work out your salvation with diligence." The individual pursues nirvana primarily through meditation, for which the monastic lifestyle is best suited. Theravada therefore also emphasizes the central role of the monastic community, or sangha.

There are perhaps ten times as many monks as nuns in Theravada countries, and monks have always had the greatest influence over the sangha, but both devote themselves to attaining nirvana through study and meditation. Those who attain it, known as **arhats** ("those who are worthy"), represent the religious ideal for Theravada. In many countries where Theravada is dominant, the monastic body acts as an advisor to governments or rulers and provides teaching to the lay community, while its monks also serve as ritual specialists during festivals, at funerals, or in rites that confer blessings and supernatural protection. The central role of the monastic community can also be seen in the support it receives from laypeople, who seek to accumulate karmic merit by making offerings to support the monastic community.

Theravada Texts Theravada claims to follow the original teachings of the Buddha as found in an early collection of Pali texts known as the **Pali Canon**, or *Tripitaka*. According to tradition, four centuries after the Buddha's death a group of 500 monks met in Sri Lanka to commit his teachings to writing for the first time. As there were already significant differences in oral reports of what the Buddha had said, these monks were intent on ensuring that the most accurate account of the Buddha's teachings was preserved in written form. *Tripitaka* ("Three Baskets") reflects the ancient practice of storing manuscripts, often written on palm leaves, in baskets. Theravada's collection is the only complete version of the *Tripitaka* that has survived to the present day.

The first of the three baskets, the *Vinaya Pitaka* ("Discipline Basket"), contains hundreds of monastic rules reportedly prescribed by the Buddha and stories that illustrate how these rules originated. The second basket, the *Sutra Pitaka* ("Discourse Basket"), consists of teachings of the Buddha recorded in the **sutras** ("discourses" or "sermons") of the Buddha. Although one cannot assume that everything recorded in the sutras is the literal word of the Buddha, their overall content is remarkably consistent in portraying the Buddha's teaching, suggesting to a significant extent the ideas, practices, and personality of the Buddha himself. The third basket is the *Abhidharma Pitaka* ("Basket of texts about the Dharma"). These texts reorganize and systemize the teachings in the *Sutra Pitaka* while also elaborating upon them, exploring the nature of consciousness, epistemology (the nature of knowledge), cosmology, and meditation.

The opening verses of the **Dhammapada**, an early collection of sayings of the Buddha found in the Pali Canon, allows us to see how sutras are structured and how they present ideas in a poetic fashion. They also illustrate a key feature of Theravada thought: we are responsible for our own happiness.

> What we are today comes from our thoughts of yesterday, and our present thoughts build our life of tomorrow: our life is the creation of our mind.
>
> If a man speaks or acts with an impure mind, suffering follows him as the wheel of the cart follows the beast that draws the cart.
>
> What we are today comes from our thoughts of yesterday, and our present thoughts build our life of tomorrow: our life is the creation of our mind.
>
> If a man speaks or acts with a pure mind, joy follows him as his own shadow.[2]

Mahayana Buddhism

With origins in the early years of the Common Era, the period to which we can trace its earliest sutras, **Mahayana** Buddhism soon grew to become the largest of the Buddhist traditions. This is suggested by its very name—the Sanskrit word *mahayana* means "Great Vehicle"—as well as by its great variety of schools and sects, which make Mahayana a large and accommodating "vehicle" with room for Buddhists of all kinds. Mahayana Buddhism sees itself as a tradition that penetrates the teachings of the Buddha more deeply than does Theravada. Its careful analysis and elaboration of the many aspects of the Dharma help to explain its flexible doctrines, which allow for an easy coexistence among the many sects within the Mahayana tradition. Sometimes called "Buddhism for the masses," Mahayana, unlike Theravada, understands that everyone is capable of attaining nirvana, not just monks and nuns. Today, the great majority of Buddhists belong to the Mahayana tradition, which is the dominant form of Buddhism in East Asia and in parts of Southeast Asia.

As we have seen, Theravada Buddhism regards Gautama the Buddha as only a man, albeit an extraordinary man. Mahayana Buddhism understands the Buddha as something far greater: the earthly expression of ultimate reality. According to the Mahayana doctrine of Trikaya (Sanskrit, "three bodies"), reality exists at three levels called "Buddha Bodies." At the lowest level is the *Nirmanakaya*, the "earthly body," which is ultimate reality expressed rather crudely in material forms. These forms can be personal and are always limited by factors such as time and space. Gautama Buddha, the man who was known to other human beings as he traveled and taught across northern India, was ultimate reality expressed at this level. The second Buddha

Body is the *Samboghakaya*, or "bliss body." This is ultimate reality expressed at what we might think of as a "heavenly" level; at this level, particulars exist but are beyond space and time. This is the level at which many bodhisattvas and "celestial buddhas" exist. At its highest level, the *Dharmakaya,* or "truth body," ultimate reality exists as it is: undifferentiated, impersonal, absolute—and completely beyond all forms and labels. Mahayana Buddhists describe ultimate reality at this level in a variety of ways: Void, Consciousness, Nirvana, Buddha–Nature, and Buddha Mind.

Understood in this way, the universe is the great setting in which the Mahayana ideal of compassion makes enlightenment and freedom from suffering possible for everyone. Instead of having to "go it alone" in seeking nirvana, the Mahayana Buddhist can benefit from the compassion of others.

Indeed, one characteristic that distinguishes Mahayana from Theravada is its teaching that compassion for others and working to bring about *their* liberation is a higher goal than attaining one's own enlightenment. Many Mahayana Buddhists take a "bodhisattva vow" to subject themselves to rebirth until all other beings have been liberated from suffering. Whereas Theravada Buddhism makes the arhat its spiritual hero in recognition of his detachment from the world and attainment of nirvana, Mahayana recognizes as its ideal figure the compassionate and selfless bodhisattva, who remains devoted to others in the samsaric realm of suffering.

THE MAHAYANA DOCTRINE OF TRIKAYA AND VISION OF REALITY

In Mahayana Buddhism, the essence or ground of all reality—that is, the fundamental reality from which all things arise—is often called Buddha–Nature (also, Void or Emptiness). According to the doctrine of Trikaya (Sanskrit, "three bodies"), Buddha–Nature assumes three "bodies" or modes of expression. These are the *Nirmanakaya* ("earthly body"), in which Buddha–Nature is manifested in particular forms, such as that of the historical Buddha, and is present in human and all other beings; the *Samboghakaya* ("bliss body"), in which Buddha–Nature exists at a "heavenly level" populated by celestial buddhas and bodhisattvas; and *Dharmakaya* ("body of truth"), in which Buddha–Nature exists as it is, undifferentiated and beyond all forms, labels, and other limits. The doctrine of Trikaya has greatly influenced Vajrayana as well as Mahayana Buddhism.

The five "celestial buddhas," also known as Dhyani (contemplative) Buddhas, have postponed their final entry in nirvana, when they will give up their particular forms, in order to minister to the needs of human beings. Each is distinguished by color, symbol, and the direction it faces. Each presides over a "pure land." Amitabha, for example, is lord of his "Western Paradise" in which practitioners of Pure Land Buddhism seek rebirth.

Each of the celestial buddhas is associated with a bodhisattva. For example, Amitabha is linked with Avalokiteshvara. The personification of compassion, Avalokiteshvara has a special concern for human beings and helps them overcome moral vices and avert threats to their physical well-being. It is said that Avalokiteshvara has come into the world at various times and in different forms to save those in danger who have called upon him for help.

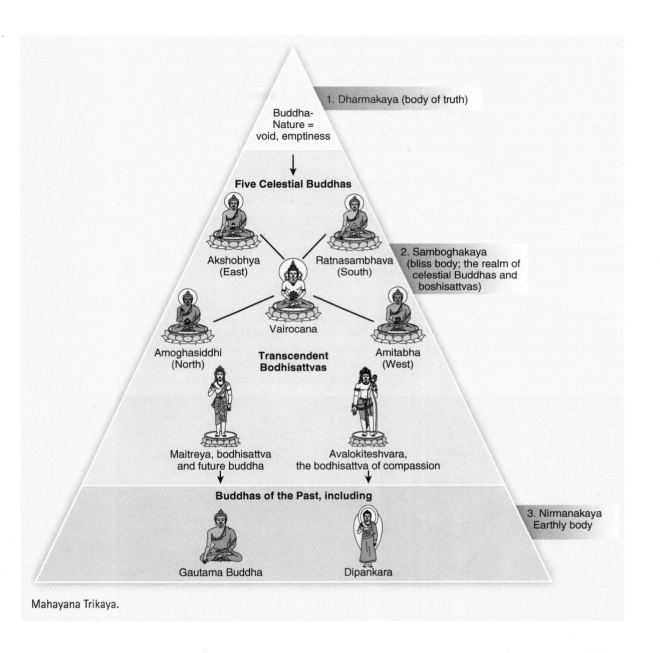

1. Dharmakaya (body of truth)

Buddha-Nature = void, emptiness

Five Celestial Buddhas

Akshobhya (East)

Ratnasambhava (South)

2. Samboghakaya (bliss body; the realm of celestial Buddhas and boshisattvas)

Vairocana

Amoghasiddhi (North)

Transcendent Bodhisattvas

Amitabha (West)

Maitreya, bodhisattva and future buddha

Avalokiteshvara, the bodhisattva of compassion

Buddhas of the Past, including

3. Nirmanakaya Earthly body

Gautama Buddha

Dipankara

Mahayana Trikaya.

Bodhisattvas   In the early years of Buddhism, **bodhisattva** (Sanskrit, "enlightenment being") was a term used to denote the Buddha in the lives he lived prior to that in which he achieved enlightenment. It was also used to refer to future buddhas (in fact, many Buddhists today look to the bodhisattva Maitreya as the next buddha to arise in the world). Later, Mahayana Buddhists began to describe a multitude of bodhisattvas. Some were simply people who had taken a bodhisattva vow to help others. This was done by practicing the "Six Perfections" (generosity, morality, patience, energy, meditation, and wisdom), thereby generating merit that could be transferred to those not as advanced on the path to enlightenment. Other bodhisattvas were figures who had already attained insight and power nearly equivalent to that of a buddha. Many legends describe them intervening in the lives of both ordinary people and aspiring saints with their pithy wisdom, psychic powers, and skillful magic. Some of these legendary bodhisattvas no longer required human bodies, dwelling instead in celestial realms and appearing to those who prayed to them.

One of the earliest and most popular bodhisattvas is Manjushri, Patron of Buddhist Scholars and Lord of Wisdom. He is often represented with his flaming sword of discriminating insight in one hand and the *Perfection of Wisdom Sutra* in the other. Without a doubt, the most widely venerated of all the bodhisattvas is the Bodhisattva of Compassion, Avalokiteshvara. A male deity in South Asia, in East Asia this bodhisattva is known as Guanyin, the Goddess of Mercy.

Gilded bronze Sitting Maitreya icon. Maitreya ("Loving-kindness") is the future Buddha. Like Rodin's Thinker, he is seated on his throne in deep contemplation with his hand touching his chin. Three Kingdoms period, seventh century. National Museum, Seoul, Korea.

"Manjushri, Bodhisattva of Wisdom" appearing with the flaming sword of discrimination and a copy of the *Prajnaparamita Sutra* in the blooming lotus of enlightenment. Kopan monastery, Kathmandu, Nepal.

Mahayana Texts Mahayana schools revere a wide array of texts that build upon the Pali Canon, or *Tripitaka*. These texts address widely varying subjects. Some investigate profound states of consciousness reached in meditation. Others elaborate on the implications of doctrines such as Interdependent Origination. Still others analyze the qualities of bodhisattvas or explain the benefits of calling upon various buddhas. All are thought to be thoroughly grounded in the teachings of the Buddha, whose implications they identify and explain.

One of the earliest Mahayana texts is the *Perfection of Wisdom Sutra*, which can be traced back to South India in the first century B.C.E. Over time, a body of related texts appeared, so that the *Perfection of Wisdom Sutra* is best understood as a collection of sutras. The most influential of these are the *Diamond Sutra* and the *Heart Sutra*. Both emphasize the cultivation of **bodhichitta** (Sanskrit, "awakened thought"), the aspiration to achieve enlightenment in order to benefit others. They also emphasize the Six Perfections, which were to become important in relation to the ideal of compassion in the bodhisattva path.

Among the most widely venerated Buddhist works in East Asia is the *Lotus Sutra*, composed in Sanskrit in the second century C.E. While exploring the path of the bodhisattva, it places particular emphasis on "skillful means," the thoughtful application of knowledge and insight in making decisions related to ethics and spiritual progress. Another interesting feature of the *Lotus Sutra* is its teaching that the death of the Buddha did not bring about his absolute dissolution. Instead, he is an eternal entity who remains in the cycle of samsara in order to benefit those who have not yet achieved liberation. Another important Mahayana text, the *Lankavatara Sutra* (fourth century C.E.), provides a detailed study of the nature of consciousness and explores how the mind has both the propensity to generate illusory, dualistic misperceptions and the potential to clearly apprehend the unity of existence. Another theological innovation appears in the *Pure Land Sutras* (second century C.E.), which describe Amitabha Buddha, "The Buddha of Boundless Light," who brings those who call upon him to rebirth in his Buddha Realm, "the Pure Land." The Pure Land is a kind of heaven where the faithful enjoy happiness and affluence. The *Pure Land Sutras* became foundational to Pure Land Buddhism (also known as Jodo Buddhism).

Two Mahayana Schools: Pure Land and Zen Pure Land Buddhism, popular throughout East Asia, is arguably the most important of all the schools within the Mahayana tradition. Based on belief in the infinite compassion

"The Laughing Buddha." This form of Maitreya is popular in China, where his fatness symbolizes prosperity and joy. It is customary for Buddhists to rub his belly for good luck. Here, people try to improve their luck by touching an image of Maitreya during the New Year fair at the Huayan Temple on the Laoshan Mountain in Qingdao, China.

of the Amitabha Buddha—known in China as Amito and in Japan as Amida—Pure Land Buddhism is best known for its practice of reciting the Buddha's name as a way of guaranteeing entry into his Pure Land at death. For those who join Amitabha in his Pure Land, there will be no more rebirth in the samsaric world. Instead, their reward for their devotion to him is happiness in his heavenly paradise. There is also the possibility of attaining full and complete enlightenment in Amitabha's Pure Land. Pure Land

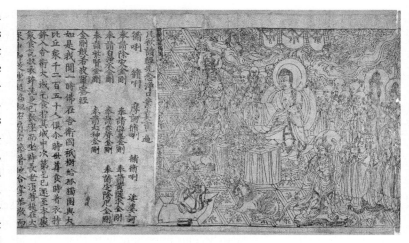

Frontispiece of the *Diamond Sutra* of Dunhuang, 868 C.E. This manuscript is the oldest known printed book in the world; it appeared 587 years before the Gutenberg Bible.

Buddhism's reliance on the grace of Amitabha Buddha stands in stark contrast to Theravada Buddhism's insistence on self-reliance and individual effort.

One of the best-known Mahayana Buddhist schools in the West is **Zen** Buddhism (known in China as **Chan**). Although Zen traces its teachings back to the Buddha himself, it traditionally holds that it became a distinct school when the South Indian sage Bodhidharma (early fifth century C.E.) brought it to China. From China, it spread throughout the rest of East Asia.

Zen emphasizes practice over doctrine, considering doctrine to be a distraction from the sudden, spontaneous experience of enlightenment called *satori*. Even devotion to the Buddha can be an obstacle to satori. This helps to explain the well-known Zen saying: "If you meet the Buddha on the road, kill him." Any form of attachment, even to the Buddha, is an obstacle. The Zen sayings called koans present the mind with paradoxes. Two well-known examples of koans are: "What is the sound of one hand clapping?" and "What was the appearance of your face before your ancestors were born?" As a means of resolving these paradoxes through logic, the impotence of rational cognition is exposed—and ultimately abandoned. What remains is direct intuition of reality, which is enlightenment.

Zen practitioners often use artistic mediums such as poetry, calligraphy, and garden design to enable the insights gained in meditation to find articulation outside the constraints of language. This creative aspect of Zen, its deeply ingrained sense of humor, and its emphasis on direct apprehension over doctrine helped to popularize this form of Buddhism in American pop culture and subculture. This is particularly evident in its influence on the 1950s "Beat" poets Gary Snyder and Allen Ginsberg.

Zen asserts the total efficacy of the mind rather than unswerving devotion to a savior figure as the only path to enlightenment and liberation. In other words, it rejects the Pure Land reliance on the Buddha's compassion for salvation in favor of gaining personal insight into the true nature of all things. Zen is the most radically self-reliant tradition among all Buddhist traditions.

Buddhist bodhisattvas can be understood as intermediary figures who serve others. What kinds of intermediary figures exist in other religions, and what are their functions?

Vajrayana Buddhism

Although **Vajrayana** Buddhism began in India in the sixth or seventh century C.E., it has little presence there now. Today, it is the dominant form of Buddhism in Tibet, Nepal, Bhutan, and Mongolia. Although it is generally understood as deriving from Mahayana Buddhism, Vajrayana Buddhists say their tradition can be traced back directly to the Buddha, who began expounding its teachings sixteen years after his enlightenment. Vajrayana is a unique form of Buddhism that combines elements of Mahayana—and, in particular, the bodhisattva ideal—with secret teachings found in the Tantras (see also Chapter 4), ancient Indian texts that teach esoteric knowledge about special methods for attaining enlightenment and liberation.

The Tantric texts reveal Tantra as a system of thought and practice based on the idea that the material world is a manifestation of divine energy. Practitioners of Tantra seek to gain control of this energy and to channel it in ways that will allow them to break through the confines of the ego, thereby finding enlightenment and liberation. Some of the most prominent features of Tantra are its emphasis on secret knowledge, ritual use of mantras and mandalas, worship of deities, visualization of deities and identification with them, and the deliberate breaking of taboos. Taken together, these and other features of Tantra are said to give practitioners powerful and even shocking means for shattering the illusion of self. One scholar has defined Tantra as "a technique for magically storming the gates of Buddhahood."[3]

As a Buddhist tradition that combines Tantra with Mahayana Buddhism and shamanism, Vajrayana was originally conceived as a spiritual method so powerful that it could catapult an ordinary person to the level of an advanced bodhisattva—a level of awareness that would normally take many eons to attain—in a single lifetime. Adherents of this tradition refer to it as the "Diamond Vehicle" because of the clarity of its wisdom and its ability to cut through all misperceptions of reality. It is also known as the "Thunderbolt Vehicle" because of its power. Among Vajrayana's most visible features are its **lamas**, the spiritual teachers (such as the Dalai Lama) of Tibetan Buddhism; its devotion to vast arrays of buddhas and bodhisattvas and to fierce gods and goddesses; its complex rituals; and its special meditation techniques designed to propel one to full enlightenment and Buddhahood.

The most fundamental practice in Vajrayana Buddhism is "deity yoga." This exercise, which involves visualizing oneself as a deity, ultimately leads to the experience of becoming one with the deity and attaining its heightened perspective of reality. In "guru yoga," the practitioner seeks to unite his mind with that of his guru, or teacher, thereby gaining and experiencing his wisdom. Other forms of Vajrayana practice take advantage of states in which the mind is more attuned to the true nature of things and well positioned to gain enlightenment. These can occur in meditation, while dreaming, during sex, and at death. "Death yoga," for example, is based on the belief that there are moments during the death process in which the mind's vision is especially clear. If the dying person makes skillful use of such a moment to meditate on the "emptiness" (*sunyata*) of all things—that is, the absence of any enduring identity or quality in them, as the Buddha taught—then enlightenment can be achieved.

Vajrayana Texts Tibetan Buddhism preserves two canonical collections of sacred texts, including traditional sutras (such as those found in the Pali Canon and Mahayana sutras), as well as Buddhist Tantras. In addition, Tibetan Buddhism has also maintained a tradition (dating back to the eleventh century C.E.) of "hidden texts." Often called "hidden treasures," these texts are attributed to Padmasambhava, the Tantric master who is credited with bringing Vajrayana Buddhism to Tibet in the eighth century. According to Tibetan tradition, Padmasambhava hid these texts away with the intention that each would be found at the proper time. The "treasure finders" who discover them do so only when Padmasambhava's "time-lock spells" unravel—always at a time when the world is ready for a new revelation.

What general tendencies do you see in the Theravada, Mahayana, and Vajrayana forms of Buddhism? Do you see similar tendencies in divisions within other religions?

COMPARISON OF THE THERAVADA, MAHAYANA, AND VAJRAYANA TRADITIONS

GEOGRAPHY
THERAVADA: Thailand, Myanmar (Burma), Sri Lanka, Cambodia, and Laos.
MAHAYANA: China, Japan, South Korea, and Taiwan.
VAJRAYANA: Tibet, Nepal, Bhutan, and Mongolia.

SCRIPTURES
THERAVADA: The Pali Canon, or *Tripitaka*
MAHAYANA: In addition to the Pali Canon, there are foundational Mahayana sutras attributed to the Buddha such as the *Prajnaparamita Sutra* ("*Perfection of Wisdom Sutra*"), which includes the *Lotus Sutra*, the *Heart Sutra*, and the *Diamond Sutra* as well as other texts. There is no formal and exclusive Mahayana canon acknowledged by all Mahayana groups.
VAJRAYANA: In addition to the Pali Canon and foundational Mahayana sutras, there is a Tibetan canon that includes two collections of texts: the *Kangyur* (texts said to contain the Buddha's own words) and the *Tangyur*

(commentaries and other treatises). Vajrayana also makes extensive use of Tantric texts. There is no formal and exclusive Vajrayana canon acknowledged by all Vajrayana groups.

REALITY
THERAVADA: Reality is a system in which all things are in constant flux. All phenomena are interdependent and interrelated; nothing exists apart from everything else.
MAHAYANA: Mahayana elaborates on the Theravada view of reality. The Mahayana doctrine of sunyata ("emptiness") states that reality is "empty" of fixed identities or qualities. Reality, or Buddha-Nature, has three levels or modes of being, often called "Buddha Bodies."
VAJRAYANA: Vajrayana beliefs are essentially the same as those of Mahayana.

THE BUDDHA
THERAVADA: Acknowledges the historical Buddha, Siddhartha Gautama, as a man whose teachings have been of great benefit to others.

(continued)

MAHAYANA: In addition to the historical Buddha, there are nonhistorical celestial buddhas who personify Buddha–Nature. The most important is Amitabha, who is the focus of Pure Land Buddhism. Mahayana Buddhists also honor Maitreya, the future Buddha.

VAJRAYANA: Vajrayana beliefs are essentially the same as those of Mahayana.

BODHISATTVAS

THERAVADA: The Buddha in his previous lives is considered a bodhisattva, as is Maitreya, the future buddha.

MAHAYANA: Bodhisattvas are enlightened beings who remain in samsara in order to help others. The most important bodhisattvas and their special qualities are Avalokiteshvara (mercy), Manjushri (wisdom), Ksitigarbha (who helps others achieve a better reincarnation), and Samantabhadra (devout practice and meditation).

VAJRAYANA: In addition to Mahayana beliefs concerning bodhisattvas, Vajrayana recognizes the existence of "Dharma guardians," who help individuals to transcend negative thoughts and emotions.

ULTIMATE GOAL

THERAVADA: The attainment of enlightenment and nirvana through one's own effort alone.

MAHAYANA: The attainment of enlightenment for all beings, as well as for oneself—hence, the emphasis on compassion and serving others as a bodhisattva.

VAJRAYANA: Vajrayana beliefs are essentially the same as those of Mahayana.

RITUALS

THERAVADA: Theravada makes less use of ritual than Mahayana and Vajrayana. Common rituals include bowing before images of the Buddha; honoring the Buddha by chanting and offering incense, flowers, and fresh fruit on altars; chanting the Three Refuges and the Five Precepts; observing annual holidays; performing rituals that mark important life events; and going on pilgrimages.

MAHAYANA: In addition to Theravada rituals: chanting the name of the Buddha; adopting devotional practices honoring bodhisattvas and celestial buddhas; taking the bodhisattva vow; reciting mantras; and chanting sutras and other texts.

VAJRAYANA: In addition to Theravada and Mahayana rituals: visualization rituals; Deity yoga; tantric practices; turning of prayer wheels; ritual hand gestures (*mudras*); and contemplation of mandalas.

GODS

THERAVADA: Local and regional gods might exist, but they cannot be helpful in bringing an end to suffering and liberation from samsara.

MAHAYANA: Local and regional gods might exist. Mahayana Buddhists also describe as "gods" those whose accumulation of good karma has won them rebirth in the highest of the six realms of rebirth. Some of these "gods" have specific roles in maintaining the cosmic order.

VAJRAYANA: Vajrayana beliefs are essentially the same as those of Mahayana but also include an elaborate pantheon of deities and tantric helpers.

Buddhism in India

During the centuries after Ashoka, Buddhism thrived in India and expanded into Central, East, and Southeast Asia. We will soon turn to the story of Buddhism's expansion, but it is important first to say something about its early history in its Indian homeland.

The Theravada, Mahayana, and Vajrayana traditions all began their historical development in India. Of these three, Theravada had the least impact in India. As we will see, its future lay instead in Sri Lanka and Southeast Asia. Mahayana and Vajrayana maintained a longer cultural presence in India.

The Mahayana tradition, which originated in the first centuries of the Common Era, was fortunate in receiving financial and political support from the Gupta Dynasty (320–550 C.E.) of northern India. As we saw in Chapter 4, the Guptas succeeded in bringing about a partial restoration of the great empire of Ashoka. Many Indian monasteries adopted Mahayana ideas and practices during the Gupta period. This is made clear by records of donations made by laypersons to monasteries, many of which praise monks for embracing Mahayana ideas. The vibrancy of Mahayana in India is also attested to by the fact that from the fifth century onward East Asian monks regularly traveled to India to study and bring home copies of Mahayana texts. The accounts of these East Asian pilgrim monks confirm that Mahayana ideas and practices were widespread among Indian Buddhists. By the seventh century, many of India's monasteries had formally allied themselves with the growing Mahayana tradition, with the greatest concentration of these being in northern India.

By that time, some influential teachers in northeast India were promoting Vajrayana Buddhism. Vajrayana was transmitted to nearby Tibet and Nepal, and subsequently to Mongolia and Bhutan, as well as to parts of East and Southeast Asia. Also, a number of Buddhist universities were founded in India during this period.

The Decline of Buddhism in India Even as Mahayana and Vajrayana Buddhism were flourishing in India, the forces that were to bring about their decline had already been set in motion. The fall of the Gupta Empire in the mid-sixth century brought political fragmentation and an end to much of the royal support and protection given to Buddhists and Buddhist institutions in earlier years. At the same time, Indian Buddhism had to contend with a resurgence of Hinduism. The Hindu brahminical establishment began to regain and enforce its supremacy in Indian society and culture. In southern India, Buddhism was challenged by the flourishing bhakti movement (Chapter 4). By the tenth century, Hinduism had won back both royal and popular support across India, and Buddhist monasteries had fallen into a decline from which they would never recover.

The final stage in the decline of Indian Buddhism was initiated by Muslim Turks, whose raids into northern India in the eleventh and twelfth centuries disrupted all of society but were particularly damaging to Buddhist monasteries and universities, which the Turks looted and destroyed. The Turkish destruction of the Buddhist universities at Nalanda and Vikramasila c. 1200 delivered the final blow. When the Tibetan Buddhist monk Dharmasvamin wrote of his travels in India in the mid-thirteenth century, he despaired that almost no one would openly profess to being a Buddhist. Nevertheless, small pockets of Buddhism did endure in India, particularly in its southern regions, until the seventeenth century.

Buddhism Beyond India

Even as Buddhism faded in India, it was thriving and spreading along three major routes that took it far from its homeland: a southern transmission into Sri Lanka and Southeast Asia, a northern transmission into Central Asia and East Asia, and a western transmission in the colonial period that brought Buddhism into contact with Europe and North America.

Lokeshvara peers out in all directions from the temple towers at the Angkor Wat temple complex in Cambodia.

The Southern Transmission Sri Lankan legend recounts that King Devanampiyatissa (250–210 B.C.E.) was converted to Buddhism by Ashoka's son, Mahinda. The newly converted king built a huge monastery complex in his capital at Anuradhapura. It is said that Ashoka's daughter, Sanghamitta, came to the island to plant a sapling from the Buddha's bodhi tree and to establish the first order of Sri Lankan nuns. From the beginning, monastic institutions were strong in Sri Lanka, nourishing a society dedicated to the Dharma and making Sri Lanka a bastion of Theravada Buddhism until the present day.

In Burma (Myanmar), the pivotal moment for Buddhism occurred in 1057 when Anwar, the Bamar king of Pagan, invaded the Mon kingdom of the south to establish the first Burmese empire (1057–1287). Along with other spoils of his conquest, Anwar carried off relics said to be those of the Buddha, Pali texts, and a retinue of monks to whom he granted control of the sangha. As a result, Theravada became the state religion of this new empire. These events spurred the spread of Theravada Buddhism throughout Southeast Asia. In Thailand, Laos, and Cambodia between the twelfth and fifteenth centuries, an earlier mingling of various Buddhist sects, Hinduism, and indigenous traditions gave way to state-sponsored Theravada.

Mahayana also had a significant place in the history of these regions. In Cambodia, kings frequently identified themselves as bodhisattvas, and the worship of Lokeshvara (another name for Avalokiteshvara) was of prime importance during the latter part of the Angkor period (twelfth–fifteenth centuries C.E.). Mahayana also reigned supreme in Indonesia and on the Malay Peninsula. By the seventh century, sites such as Srivijaya in Sumatra were important centers of Buddhist training and attracted monks from as far away as China. The renowned Indian monk Atisha (982–1054) came to study in Srivijaya under the great master Dharmakirti before journeying in 1042 to Tibet, where he founded the Kadampa sect of Vajrayana, from which the Gelugpa school of the Dalai Lamas eventually arose.

In Java, Mahayana Buddhism was promoted by the native Sailendra Dynasty, which ruled much of Indonesia, including Sumatra and Bali, in the eighth and ninth centuries. One of the great monuments built by the Sailendras is the Borobudur Temple (c. 800). This gigantic complex includes 540 statues of the Buddha, some of them hidden within perforated screens of stone. There are also another 2,672 relief sculpture panels depicting the Buddha. Buddhism thrived alongside Hinduism in Indonesia until both were eclipsed by Islam, originally introduced by Muslim traders, in the thirteenth through fifteenth centuries.

The earliest known image of the Buddha appears on the reverse of a coin minted by the second-century Kushan king, Kanishka I. Previously, the Buddha was depicted more as an absence than a presence, symbolized with images such as footprints or an empty chair.

The Northern Transmission Buddhist communities were also founded in Central Asia during the time of Ashoka's reign (r. c. 272–231 B.C.E.). Ashoka sent Buddhist missionaries to Afghanistan. Legend says that he sent his son, Kustana, to the region northwest of Tibet, where he founded the Buddhist kingdom of Khotan in 240 B.C.E. Later, the Central Asian ruler Kanishka I (r. c. 110–139 C.E.), after inheriting the portions of Bactria and northwest India conquered by his Kushan predecessors, is said to have embraced Buddhist tradition. Some of the earliest Buddhist images date from the period of his reign. Indeed, the oldest extant image of the Buddha appears on a coin of Kanishka.

Buddhism Comes to East Asia Buddhism may have first appeared in China as early as the first century C.E., brought by monks and missionaries from Central Asia who accompanied merchants along the Silk Road. When Buddhism arrived in the refined world of China's Han Dynasty (206 B.C.E.–220 C.E.), it was received as an exotic import.

China The first dated proof of Buddhism's entry into China is found in the Han chronicles, which assign this event to 65 C.E. In that year, they say, the Han emperor Ming dreamed of an encounter with a golden-robed flying figure his diviners later identified as the Buddha. The chronicles also describe imperial relatives and aristocrats making offerings to the Buddha. Translation of Buddhist texts into Chinese began as soon as they appeared in China. This was especially true of texts relating to meditation and breath-control techniques. These were of great interest to Daoists (Chapter 8), who at first regarded Buddhists as like-minded seekers of physical health and immortality. Not unexpectedly, the process of translation sometimes resulted in deviation from the original sources. Early on, for example, Daoist equivalents stood in for Buddhist philosophical terms; only later were new Chinese words coined to better convey abstract Buddhist concepts. Daoist interest in the new religion diminished only when Buddhism's teachings were better understood and after its differences with Daoism had become apparent.

After the fall of the Han Dynasty (c. 220 C.E.), the Chinese Empire split along a north–south division that lasted more than three centuries. The north was ruled by successive groups of non-Chinese tribes, while the south was colonized by fleeing Chinese elites. The Chinese Buddhist community experienced a similar split. Many Buddhist clerics and their followers remained in the north, while others fled to the south, taking the Dharma into new territory where it quickly found acceptance among locals. Confucianism, which had always supported the aims of the state, lost much of its influence as a consequence of China's political upheavals, and Buddhism was in a position to take its place. Moreover, Buddhism appealed to the Chinese in both the north and the south because it reflected the contemplative and mystic introversion of native Daoism. In northern China, Buddhist intellectualism had given way to an emphasis on practice. "Barbarian" kings who ruled in the vacuum created by the fleeing native Chinese rulers patronized Buddhist ascet-

Borobudur Temple, Java, Indonesia, c. 800 C.E. Here, one of the hidden statues of the Buddha is revealed. In order to see others, pilgrims would have to peer through holes in bell-shaped stupas, such as those visible in the background.

ics and magicians who had roots in Central Asian traditions. In the south, there was an intense expression of faith and piety in the plea for Buddha's compassion, as well as a movement toward meditation and enlightenment.

The golden age of Buddhism in China lasted from the fifth to the eighth centuries C.E. During this period, many Mahayana texts were translated into Chinese. Pilgrim monks from China also journeyed to India in search of Buddhist wisdom from its point of origin. New sutras were authored by Chinese patriarchs to proclaim equal authority with the Indian and Central Asian texts. Of the Mahayana schools of today, many took on their definitive forms in China. In particular, the Mahayana convention of devotion to a particular text can be clearly seen as informing the primary character of these schools.

The two major schools that would eventually signal the final stage in the Chinese transformation of Buddhism into a native faith were Pure Land and Chan (known as Zen in Japan and as Seon in Korea). Pure Land appeared at the beginning of the fifth century C.E. According to its own tradition, Chan was introduced to China at nearly the same time by the legendary Bodhidharma. It was in the eighth century, however, that it began to make its mark on the Chinese religious scene thanks to a succession of Chinese patriarchs (masters of particular sects of Buddhism).

Korea and Japan Buddhism arrived in Korea in the fourth century C.E. and closely emulated the text-based Chinese systems by developing the Five Doctrinal Schools.

115

The new religion from China soon blended with native Korean shamanism, with the result that it took on a distinctive flavor. Many Buddhist temples, for example, also became centers for the veneration of Korean mountain spirits and local deities. Moreover, Korean Buddhists ignored many of the sectarian differences that plagued the Indian and Chinese Buddhist establishments. Seon (Chan, Zen) has long been the dominant form of Buddhism in Korea.

In Japan, Buddhism was first introduced in 552 C.E., when the Korean king of Paekche presented Emperor Kinmei of Japan (r. 531–571) with a gift of sutras and an icon of the Buddha. The leader of a clan with the least vested interest in native Shinto (Chapter 9), Kinmei embraced Buddhism and promoted its adoption by the imperial family. Its success was evidenced by the accomplishment of Prince Shotoku (574–622), a prominent member of this clan. According to tradition, Prince Shotoku produced for the newly institutionalized Japanese state a constitution that stressed the ideals of the Buddhist Three Jewels as well as the Confucian virtue of harmony. By the Nara period (710–784), six schools of Buddhism had been imported directly to Japan from China. In the Heian period (794–1185), Tantric Buddhism and the Tendai sect were added, and by the Kamakura period (1185–1333), Pure Land, Zen, and Nichiren added to the sectarian complexity of Buddhism in Japan. Among these sects, Pure Land would later have the most enduring impact on Japanese culture and values. Today, its presence is ubiquitous in almost every Japanese home. Zen Buddhism is embraced by the Japanese cultural and military elite and has influenced many Japanese art forms.

Vietnam Mahayana Buddhism also made major inroads in Vietnam. Because of Vietnam's cultural and geographical proximity to China (it was twice annexed by China, and it sent tribute to China for much of its premodern history), Vietnamese Buddhism shares a great deal with its Chinese counterpart. Because Vietnam served as the point of convergence between the northern and southern routes of Buddhist expansion out of India (north from China and south from Sri Lanka and Indochina), Vietnamese Buddhism displays Theravada influence as well.

Tibet Although Buddhism took root in Tibet later than in China, its transmission came directly from India. Since its arrival in Tibet (around 650 C.E.), the region has remained a stronghold of Vajrayana Buddhism. Initially, the new religion met with resistance, for the shamans and court wizards of the indigenous Tibetan *Bön* religion had strong influence over the nobility. But legend has it that when King Songtsen Gampo (c. 617–649) arranged alliances with the king of Nepal and the emperor of China through marriages to their daughters, he found that his new wives were Buddhists. It was not long before the king built Tibet's first Buddhist temple and made arrangements for the translation of sutras into Tibetan. As monks and teachers poured into Tibet, Buddhism flourished. Trisong Detsen (c. 742–798), Tibet's first Buddhist king, consecrated the Samye monastery in 775 C.E. and also ordained members of the Tibetan aristocracy.

In the early ninth century, Buddhism was again under siege in Tibet and forced underground during the reign of King Lang Darma (r. 838–842 C.E.). When the king was assassinated and his dynasty collapsed, Buddhism was blamed for instilling weakness in the military. The scholarly monk Atisa, who arrived in Tibet in 1042 C.E., provided Tibet with an effective synthesis of the Theravada, Mahayana, and Tantric forms of Buddhism and united the Tibetan sangha. Atisa instituted the practice of formal initiation into lineages of Tantric teachers, which still characterizes Tibetan Vajrayana today.

During the thirteenth century, Tibetan Buddhist masters entered into a "patron–priest" relationship with the Khans (descendants of Genghis Khan), who ruled an empire that extended from China to eastern Europe. In 1578 C.E. the head of the Gelugpa monastery, Sonam Gyatsho (1543–1588), converted Altan Khan, the ruler of the Mongols. The Great Khan bestowed upon Sonam Gyatsho the title Dalai Lama ("Ocean [of Wisdom] Teacher"). Because this title was later assigned to two of his predecessors, tradition calls him the third Dalai Lama. It was the fifth Dalai Lama (1617–1682) who took full advantage of Mongol patronage. Backed by Mongol troops, he took over all of Tibet and sent other sects with conflicting political aspirations fleeing to other parts of the Himalayas. By the seventeenth century, with the Dalai Lama as the primary ruler of Tibet, great efforts were made to identify and reinstate him in this role each time he died and took rebirth.

Across all of these regions and countries, Buddhism adapted to local cultures and integrated indigenous beliefs. These patterns of transformation have also extended to Buddhism's encounter with Europe and America in the modern and postmodern contexts.

The Western Transmission

Only during the last two centuries have Buddhist traditions come to the attention of the West. Many of those who were among the first to understand Buddhist teachings and practices and share them with Western audiences were also among the first Western converts to Buddhism. These early Western Buddhists both anticipated and inspired the growing popularity of the religion in Europe and America today.

Some say that the story of the Western transmission begins in the early nineteenth century with T. W. Rhys-Davids (1843–1922), a British colonial administrator who "discovered" Buddhist teaching while stationed in Sri Lanka. His translations of Buddhist texts sparked the interest of an English-speaking audience, many of whom saw the Buddha as embodying the modern values of the era as a radically independent, rugged individual who relied entirely on his own introspection and insight. These early Western readers of Buddhist texts understood Buddhism as a philosophy whose teachings differed radically from what they saw as the irrational dogmas of Western religion.

As the young Thich Nhat Hanh, a Vietnamese monk, looks on,
Dr. Martin Luther King Jr. calls for a halt to the bombing of Vietnam
(May 31, 1966).

In 1963, the Vietnamese
Buddhist monk Thich
Quang Duc, while seated
in meditation, burned
himself to death in
Saigon's Market Square
to protest his govern-
ment's religious policies.

Although Chinese and Japanese immigrants had established Buddhist institutions on American soil many years earlier, the first notable conversion of an American to Buddhism did not occur until 1893. But it was the American subcultures of the 1950s and 1960s, and particularly those of the Beats and hippies, that helped spark a deep and abiding interest in Buddhism among Americans. The perception of Buddhist leaders as political dissidents and peace activists helped to inspire new generations of American Buddhists. Martin Luther King Jr.'s nonviolent approach to civil rights activism was informed in part by Buddhist thought and practice. King's admiration for the Vietnamese Buddhist monk and peace activist Thich Nhat Hanh (b. 1926), whose commitment to community service helped to heal the emotional wounds of many American veterans of the Vietnam War, led King to nominate Hanh for a Nobel Peace Prize in 1967. The ever-growing popularity of the fourteenth Dalai Lama, Tenzin Gyatso (b. 1935), who was awarded the Nobel Peace Prize in 1989, also exemplifies the identification of Buddhism with peaceful political dissidence in America.

Buddhism and Sectarian Violence: Myanmar and Sri Lanka

Although Buddhism has a well-deserved reputation as a religion that promotes peace, we would be mistaken in assuming that Buddhists never lose sight of this ideal. Recent events in Myanmar and Sri Lanka demonstrate that when ethnic and religious identities become more important than peaceful coexistence, the results can be disastrous.

Myanmar, also known as Burma, is a small country in Southeast Asia with a long history of ethnic and religious strife. Ruled by a military junta from 1962 until 2011, its parliament is now in the hands of the National League for Democracy, whose leader, Aung San Suu Kyi, was awarded the Nobel Peace Prize in 1991. Despite its democratic ideals, Myanmar's Buddhist-dominated government has persecuted ethnic and religious minorities. Its most visible victims are the Rohingya people, Muslims who have been denied citizenship and have suffered killings, house burnings, and the displacement of thousands.

Ethnic and religious conflict has also plagued Sri Lanka, a small island country southeast of India. Here, the majority Sinhalese, who are Buddhists, fought Hindu Tamils in a civil war (1983–2009) in which more than 80,000 were killed. More recently, there has been violence against Muslims, much of it incited by Bodu Bala Sena (BBS; Buddhist Power Force). An organization led by monks, BBS sees Islam as a threat to Sri Lanka's Buddhist culture, which reaches back to the third century B.C.E. It makes effective use of public rallies and social media to attract supporters.

Buddhists in the World Today

Today, teachings about the Dharma are delivered as podcasts. Apps that help Buddhists time their meditations or look up specific sutras are available for mobile devices. In Japan, vending machines sell pocket-sized plastic replicas of some of the most revered Buddhist icons. Chinese animated hagiographies of saints and bodhisattvas can be easily downloaded. In America, Trey Parker and Matt Stone, creators of the television show *South Park*, offer online versions of old Zen lectures by Alan Watts (a twentieth-century philosopher and proponent of Buddhism), accompanied by their own cartoon commentaries. In the world of American comic books, an increasing number of superheroes are turning Buddhist (such as "Xorn" of the X-Men; even Batman has been revealed to have received Buddhist training in Tibet). Even as far back as the 1930s and 1940s, there were mystic American heroes trained in Buddhist practice, such as the Shadow and the Green Lama, who appeared in pulp magazines, radio serials, and comic books.

Today, new technologies and media challenge Buddhists to adapt, expand, and explore new environments. But Buddhism has encountered a multitude of cultures in its spread throughout Asia (and beyond) over the past 2,500 years and has always found skillful ways of applying new technologies. Buddhists continue to develop innovative ways to integrate modern realities into an ancient Buddhist worldview, as they convey traditional teachings through contemporary media that preserve the sacred sutras, stories, and songs that comprise Buddhist traditions.

A Cambodian monk at work on his computer.

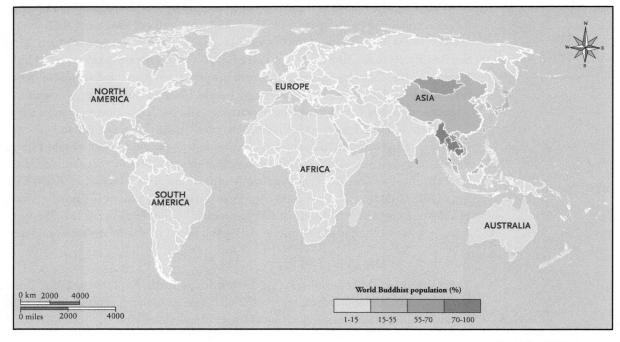

World Buddhist population (%)

| 1-15 | 15-55 | 55-70 | 70-100 |

World Buddhist population.

BUDDHISM AS A WAY OF LIFE

Buddhists practice the teachings of the Buddha in many ways. Seeking to observe the ethical principles he taught, they aspire to proper conduct in daily life. Many of those who seek to observe the workings of the mind and to see reality more clearly make use of meditative disciplines. Some become members of monastic orders. Most Buddhists participate in observances that commemorate important events in the history of Buddhism and participate in rituals that mark important transitions in life. In this part of our investigation, we will look at several Buddhist practices to gain an understanding of the meaning they have for followers of the Buddha.

Who Is a Buddhist?

You will recall that the first followers of the Buddha were the five ascetics who had once practiced severe austerities with him. Convinced by his example and by his Sermon in the Deer Park that he had found what they, too, had been looking for, they became the first members of the sangha. Their formal conversion was solemnized by their recitation of the "Three Refuges," also known as the "Three Jewels":

I take refuge in the Buddha.
I take refuge in the Dharma.
I take refuge in the Sangha.

For centuries, Buddhism was known exclusively in Asia, where one or another of its schools and sects predominated in every region. Today, Buddhism is becoming increasingly popular in the West, especially in North America and Europe, where sanghas of many kinds often coexist in the same neighborhoods.

Developments in California are typical of those occurring elsewhere in the West. In Sacramento, for example, there are sanghas representing many Buddhist traditions. Some, founded by immigrants, continue to cherish rituals, languages, and cultural practices with roots in Asia. At the same time, Buddhism's cultural roots can be less important for sanghas whose members come from non-Asian and non-Buddhist backgrounds. Because Buddhism is beginning to thrive in the West, the question arises: What form will its emerging Western tradition take?

The Reverend Bob Oshita served for many years as priest at the Sacramento Buddhist Church, a sangha in the tradition of Japanese Jodo Shinshu, a form of Pure Land Buddhism. Although his sangha has an unmistakably Japanese flavor, Reverend Bob is pleased to see that Western Buddhism is taking the form of something larger—a "Dharma buffet," as he puts it, that will offer Western Buddhists the benefits of all of Buddhism's many traditions.

Across town, members of the Sacramento Dharma Center (SDC) have created a space in which only a single image of the Buddha and a few Tibetan *thangkas*, or painted mandalas, suggest a connection with traditional forms of Buddhism. Many SDC members say their commitment to meditation as a practice that reduces suffering is more important than the religious and cultural aspects of Buddhism. As for the future of Buddhism in the West, they agree with Reverend Bob that wisdom and compassion are certain to lie at the heart of the emerging Western tradition.

Buddhists have always prized these two virtues: wisdom grounded in an understanding of the true nature of reality—which is characterized by the impermanence of all things and the absence of a continuing "self"—and a compassion for all beings that arises from awareness of the oneness and interconnectedness of all things.

Members of the Sacramento Dharma Center participate in a group mediation session.

Since then, followers of the Buddha have affirmed their Buddhist identity by reciting this formula, Buddhism's most fundamental ritual practice and the closest thing the Buddhist tradition has to a creed. To take refuge in the Buddha is to acknowledge the Buddha as the supreme example of the potential of human life. To take refuge in the

Dharma is to recognize it as the path to enlightenment and an end to suffering. To take refuge in the sangha is to recognize one's reliance on the Buddhist community—and, in particular, the order of monks—as the custodian of the Dharma, responsible for its preservation and transmission.

The Buddha's Teachings on Ethics and "Skillful Means"

Like most religions, Buddhism includes a body of teachings on ethics, the principles and practices associated with moral conduct. For Buddhism, these principles and practices have nothing to do with those produced by human societies, which change over time. Rather, they are rooted in the nature of reality, as described in the Dharma. In general, speech and actions based on compassion and the intention of promoting happiness and progress toward nirvana for oneself and others are ethical. On the other hand, unethical speech and actions arise from the Three Poisons of greed, aversion, and delusion, which are based on a false understanding of reality and lead to suffering.

Pema Chodron is an American-born Buddhist nun whose books describe skillful ways of dealing with everyday suffering.

Most Buddhists recognize the Five Precepts as the most important of ethical principles. These are: (1) not killing or causing harm to living beings, (2) not stealing, (3) not engaging in sexual misconduct; (4) not lying, and (5) not using intoxicants. These precepts, intended for laypeople, are supplemented by additional principles found in the Eight Precepts and Ten Precepts, which are followed by novice monks and nuns as well as by laypeople who wish to make an extra effort in purifying their thought and behavior, especially during sacred or ceremonial times of the year. For ordained monks and nuns, there are also the many rules for monastic conduct found in the *Vinaya* "basket" of the *Tripitaka*. Although some Buddhists consider these precepts to be rules that must always be followed to the letter, others see them as general principles that are subject to interpretation. This helps to explain why practices such as eating meat and drinking alcoholic beverages are acceptable for some Buddhists.

For the Buddha, the distinction between "ethical" and "unethical" is not something that can be reliably discerned with reference to absolute standards of "right" and "wrong." Such standards, which often hold that an action is *always* right or wrong, do not necessarily result in ethical behavior when applied in particular circumstances. Thus, one must bring compassion, insight, and creativity to every situation in order to determine how to speak and act. This practice, known as **upaya** or "skillful means," is an important feature of Mahayana and Vajrayana Buddhism and emphasizes the importance of taking into consideration the needs, interests, and awareness of those with whom one interacts. The *Lotus Sutra* offers numerous examples of how skillful means might be applied with the compassionate intention of helping others find relief from suffering. For example, it describes the bodhisattva Avalokiteshvara as appearing to those who suffer in the form to which he knows they will be most receptive. Thus, to some he appears as a monk, to others as a king, to still others as a boy or girl, and so on. This same principle is also useful in more ordinary situations. Interaction with others is most likely to promote happiness when our speech and actions are skillfully adapted to the needs, interests, and awareness of others.

Meditation and the Cultivation of Mind

The Buddha encouraged his followers to practice meditation, which enables practitioners to identify, understand, and eliminate patterns of thought that perpetuate desire and suffering. It is sometimes said that the full implications of the Buddha's teaching cannot be understood without devoting oneself to meditative practice. Of course, most of the Buddha's followers were monks and nuns who had given up ordinary life in order to devote themselves entirely to monastic practices. For them, there was no obstacle to meditation. Others, who continued to meet their obligations in ordinary society, had to be content with offering support to monastic communities in the hope of gaining merit and a more favorable rebirth. This remains the case today. Most Buddhists do not meditate regularly. Instead, they seek to make spiritual progress by supporting Buddhist causes, including monastic orders, and by doing their best to put Buddhist principles into practice in their daily lives. They are inspired by the great achievements of monastics who have developed a remarkable range of meditative techniques, as well as an impressive body of literature on meditation, over the past 2,500 years.

Meditation: *Samatha* and *Vipassana*   From the beginning, Buddhists of many sects have made extensive use of two basic types of meditation: *samatha* (Pali, "calm abiding"); and *vipassana* (Pali, "insight"). These are still widely practiced today and are often employed by the same practitioner.

Samatha cultivates the ability to focus awareness on a single object of concentration. This focal point is often the breath, but any object or sensation is appropriate as it is concentration upon *something* that matters, not the nature of the thing itself. Focused awareness stabilizes the mind, making it less easily disturbed by the disruptive influences of thoughts and feelings.

By comparison, the object of *vipassana* meditation, often called "mindfulness meditation" or "insight meditation," is awareness itself. Typically, the practitioner begins with a focus on the breath, which brings focused concentration and a stable mind. These qualities make it possible to move beyond the thoughts, feelings, daydreams, and other phenomena that normally occupy the attention of the mind and to calmly observe, as if from a distance, the unfolding of all mental and physical phenomena—neither obsessing, reacting, nor judging, but simply allowing them to be. In doing so, the practitioner gains insight into the workings of compulsive and restless thought and the ability to move past the suffering they cause.

Walking Meditation The Buddha taught that meditation should be practiced in four postures: sitting, standing, walking, and lying down. Any activity, he asserted, is an opportunity for meditation. Many Buddhist traditions encourage walking meditation as a means of making the serenity and insight found in the meditation hall possible in the everyday world as well. The foundation of this practice is simply being mindful of and content with what one is doing:

> When walking, just walk.
> When sitting, just sit.
> Above all, don't wobble.
> —*Yunmen (d. 949 C.E.; Tang Dynasty founder of the Yunmen school of Chan Buddhism)*[4]

A large contemporary image of the Walking Buddha in Thailand. Thai images often stylistically craft his right arm to represent the graceful swaying trunk of an elephant.

Some forms of Buddhism, such as Zen, are quite formal in their approach to walking meditation. In most *Zendo*s, or "meditation halls," meditators execute prescribed movements very slowly and deliberately in order to be completely aware of each subtle shift in posture, breathing, and sensation.

Visualization, Deity Yoga, and Inner Mandalas Another important form of meditation entails the practice of visualization. Practices involving the mental contemplation of the body of the Buddha developed early in the history of Buddhism. The visualization of buddhas and bodhisattvas came to occupy a central place in the meditation practices of Mahayana sects as Pure Land Buddhism. But it is in Vajrayana Buddhism that virtuosity in employing visualization techniques developed. By means of a combination of visualization and mantra recitation, "deity yoga" (as it is known in the West) or "actualization" (as it is called in Tibet) creates conditions in which the practitioner's mind comes to embody the deity that is invoked.

Other visualization techniques employ the contemplation of **mandalas**. Mandalas are circular cosmological diagrams that often map out how a Buddhist deity or group of deities manifests both *in* and *as* the universe. As with deities, mandalas are also venerated externally as tapestries, sand paintings, and three-dimensional models, such as the Borobudur Stupa in Java.

Mantra, Liturgical Ritual, and Chanting

Chanting is practiced by almost every Buddhist group. The Three Refuges, in which Buddhists declare their reliance on the Buddha, the Dharma, and the Sangha, are often chanted. Most Buddhist services include liturgical chanting that reflects the philosophical orientation of that particular tradition. The content of the chant and its function can vary greatly. Some forms of chanting consist of entire sutras, whereas others focus on key passages in particular philosophical texts. Still other varieties of chant make use of ritual formulas or simple **mantras** (sacred sounds or syllables).

Conversion and Ordination

As noted earlier, most Buddhists consider a recitation of the Three Refuges to be sufficient in declaring oneself a Buddhist. In most cases, Buddhists seeking to make their conversion public or to be ordained as priests, monks, or nuns participate in formal rites conducted in the presence of the sangha and a revered senior monk, lama, or spiritual teacher.

Typically, there are two different levels of ordination as a monk or nun. The first is that of the novice, which can be conferred on children as young as seven or eight in Theravada. The novice agrees to abide by ten precepts and essentially functions as a student under the direct guidance of a Preceptor. The second, higher ordination of an adult monk requires candidates to be at least twenty years old. In both cases, the recipient of the ordination makes a commitment to embody, maintain, and transmit the Buddhist Dharma.

Women in Buddhism

For much of its history, Buddhism's institutions were formed and controlled primarily by men. In mainstream monasteries, nuns did not have much of a place in the preservation and transmission of the Dharma. But Buddhist women did take on more central roles outside of monasteries, both as lay Buddhists and as wandering ascetics, and their significance is acknowledged in many sources. Powerful political figures such as the Empress Wu Zetian of Tang Dynasty China (late seventh century C.E.) and Camadevi (seventh century C.E.), a legendary queen in northern Thailand, have left an indelible mark in the history of Buddhism as patrons whose support and example helped to spread Buddhist traditions.

But beyond the historical influence of Buddhist women as powerful secular leaders, important female spiritual leaders emerged even at the beginnings of Buddhism. In the early formation of the Pali Canon, one collection called the *Khuddaka Nikaya* canonized a group of early saints in two collections of poems: the *Theragatha* ("Poems of Male Elders") and the *Therigatha* ("Poems of Female Elders"). Thus, even in Buddhism's early years, the tradition acknowledged and preserved the compositions of its women saints. Later, other women saints, particularly in Vajrayana Buddhism, stood out as great virtuosos and innovators of the highest esoteric practices.

In 2003, there were approximately 125,000 Buddhist nuns worldwide. However, centuries ago lineages of Buddhist nuns in many regions either disappeared (such as in the eleventh century in Sri Lanka) or never existed in the first place (as in Thailand). Only in

China, Korea, Taiwan, and Vietnam have nuns traditionally been given full ordination and been regarded with the same respect as their male counterparts. In other countries, only novitiate ordination (that is, a beginning or trial ordination) has been conferred on women. Elsewhere, women have not been eligible for ordination at all. In Tibet, for example, nuns were originally allowed to take only the vows prescribed for laypeople.

Resistance to women taking an active role in Buddhist monastic institutions goes all the way back to the time when Mahaprajapati, the Buddha's stepmother, petitioned for women to be allowed ordination. Though the Buddha eventually relented, he noted that allowing nuns into the order would only hasten the demise of the Buddhist teaching. Even those regions that allowed nuns placed additional constraints on female monastics.

Where there have been some nunneries attached to Theravada monasteries, the nuns have often been relegated to serving the domestic needs of monks, primarily by cooking and cleaning for them. Some women, like the female renunciants of Thailand, have preferred a solitary ascetic life to the limitations of ordination in the male-dominated monastic institutions.

Recently, in most of the Theravada world, full ordination of women has begun to be revived. Women renouncers have been proactive in these regions, adopting ascetic disciplines and formal vows on their own or forming small groups of female practitioners. In addition, there has been an explosion in the number of notable women Buddhist leaders in the West, who have profoundly influenced and empowered Buddhist women around the world. Because of their efforts, new opportunities for women to receive ordination have begun to open up in many countries as women are transforming the Buddhist institutional landscape.

One such example is that of Ayya Khema (1923–1997), who organized the First Council of Buddhist Nuns. Born to a Jewish family in Berlin, Ayya Khema was evacuated from Germany along with hundreds of other children in 1938. Her parents eventually escaped to China, where she was reunited with them in Shanghai. After the war, Ayya Khema studied meditation in the Himalayas. The experiences that grew out of her meditation practice led to her taking ordination as a Buddhist nun in Sri Lanka, where she founded an international training center for Buddhist nuns in 1983. Ayya Khema organized the first international council for nuns in Buddhist history, a conference that led to the founding of a worldwide Buddhist women's organization called Sakyadhita ("Daughters of the Buddha"). In May 1987, Ayya Khema became the first Buddhist nun to ever address the United Nations.

Sacred Places and Objects of Veneration

Like adherents of other religions, Buddhists recognize special places and objects as having a sacred character that makes them worthy of reverence and veneration. The most important of these places are those where important events in the life of the Buddha occurred and that contain the relics of the Buddha.

The principal sacred sites in Buddhism are Lumbini (in modern Nepal), the site of the Buddha's birth; Bodh Gaya, the place where he attained enlightenment; Sarnath, where he preached his first sermon, the "Sermon in the Deer Park"; and Kusinara, the place of the Buddha's death and passing into parinirvana. These sacred places are visited by thousands of pilgrims each year.

The Buddha's followers were said to have collected relics of the Buddha that remained after his cremation. At first, the relics were kept in a single place, but conflict arose when local kings made claims to them. In the end, they were divided into eight portions that were distributed equally among the claimants. According to another account, in the time of Ashoka, the relics were divided again, this time into 84,000 portions that were taken to all parts of the Indian subcontinent. Although we cannot be certain of the accuracy of these stories, there is good evidence that soon after his death the relics of the Buddha were indeed divided and placed in reliquary mounds called **stupas**. In time, the custom arose of placing the relics of Buddhist saints in stupas as well. Today, most stupas are impressive hemispherical structures that resemble the original mounds built on the sites where they stand. The relics they preserve have a powerful and inspiring effect on those who venerate them.

Because the Buddha said that his teaching would serve as his "Dharma-body" after his death, many Buddhists venerate the sacred texts in which the Dharma is preserved. For example, some Mahayana groups place manuscripts of sutras in images of the Buddha or in the structures of shrines, making them a part of ritual worship.

Early Buddhist arts and artifacts tended to represent the Buddha more as an absence than as a presence. For example, the Buddha was often indicated by an empty chair, a pair of footprints, or the bodhi tree he sat under when he obtained enlightenment. In time, though, Buddhists began to make extensive use of images to recall more vividly the physical form of the Buddha and to visualize the appearances of other buddhas and bodhisattvas. Many of these images make use of subtle iconographic cues— such as hand gestures and postures—to symbolize events and functions associated with the Buddha and other enlightened beings.

Buddhists visiting the site of the bodhi tree under which the Buddha is said to have attained enlightenment. This tree is likely a descendant of the original bodhi Tree. Bodh Gaya, India.

From the beginning, Buddhists also venerated images that represent important events in the life of the Buddha and aspects of his teaching. To this day, fig trees continue to be objects of reverence, for it was in the shade of a fig tree that the Buddha attained enlightenment. Another commonly venerated symbol is the wheel. With its eight spokes, the "Dharma Wheel" is an ancient Buddhist symbol that represents the Noble Eightfold Path. The prayer wheel, commonly used in Vajrayana ritual, is a device filled with printed scrolls believed to emit thousands of prayers and mantra recitations when they are rotated.

Holidays and Festivals

The Buddhist year is filled with holidays, festivals, and other special observances. In most countries, their dates are determined by the lunar calendar and therefore fall on different days each year. The most important occasions are commemorations of key events in the life of the Buddha, but there are also celebrations of the birthdays of bodhisattvas, remembrances of historical events, and seasonal observances that have taken on a religious significance.

The Great Stupa of Sanchi, India. Early Andhra Dynasty, first century B.C.E.

Vesak By far, the most important Buddhist celebration is Vesak. Although it originally commemorated the day on which the Buddha was born, Vesak has also become a celebration of the Buddha's death and parinirvana. It occurs on the day of the first full moon in the month of Vesakha, usually in May. On Vesak, Theravada Buddhists decorate local shrines and light lamps to symbolize the Buddha's enlightenment and the spreading of his insight throughout the world. People send out greeting cards that depict key events in the life of the Buddha. Some lay Buddhists observe the same vows as those taken by novice monks. Others stay up all night in meditation as the Buddha had done on the night of his enlightenment.

In Tibet, this festival is called *Saga Dawa*. Tibetan Buddhists light lamps and, like Buddhists in other countries, express their devotion by circumambulating shrines and stupas. They also show reverence and seek to acquire merit through repeated prostrations—lying face down in supplication before a sacred site or object. Many Tibetan Buddhists observe *Saga Dawa* by taking turns bathing an image of the infant Buddha in scented water. In Japan, Vesak is known as Hana Matsuri ("The Flower Festival"). Celebrated on April 8, when it coincides with the blooming of the cherry blossoms, Hana Matsuri also involves the practice of bathing images of the infant Buddha.

Asala In Theravada Buddhism, Asala is a holiday that originally marked the beginning of the three-month rainy season. During this time, monks would cease their wandering and remain in a monastery for an extended period of meditation and introspection. Today, many lay Buddhists in Burma and Thailand take temporary ordinations and live as monks for this three-month period. Asala

Father and child bathe an image of the Buddha as a baby in a Taipei temple during the April 2001 celebration of the Buddha's birth in Taiwan.

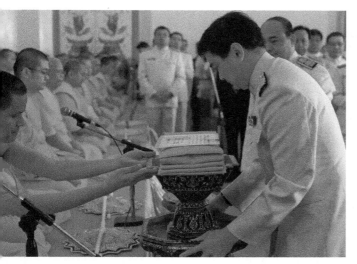

also commemorates the "First Turning of the Wheel of the Dharma," when the Buddha gave his first teaching. Many sermons are given to laypeople at this time.

Other Festivals   The conclusion of the three-month retreat season coincides with other festival observances. During the Kathina ceremony, observed by Theravada Buddhists, the laity offer new robes to monks and make special requests for spiritual guidance and intervention. The Tibetan form of this holiday is called Lhabap and is characterized by feasting and visits to temples.

Prime Minister Abhisit offers Kathina robes to monks at a 2010 Kathina ceremony in Bangkok, Thailand.

There are many important culturally specific festivals that lack corollaries in other regions. To mention just one interesting example, during the "Festival of the Hungry Ghosts" in China and Japan's "Feast of the Dead," the spirits of ancestors are placated with food offerings, and monks are called upon to recite sutras in order to aid the departed in securing a favorable rebirth.

Funerary Rites

When the death of a Buddhist approaches, family and friends will often sit in the dying person's room to offer comfort and assurances that death is a natural part of the life cycle. Monks may be invited to chant sutras. A small statue of the Buddha is often placed near the head of the dying person.

Buddhists practice both cremation and burial. Funeral services may be held either before these events or, in the form of a memorial service, after them. Whatever form a funeral takes, it is always a solemn affair. A photograph or other image of the deceased is usually set upon an altar at the front of the room in which the service is held, as are flowers provided by family and friends. When entering the room, mourners approach the altar, bow with their hands pressed together in a prayerful manner, spend a moment in quiet reflection, and then take their seats. It is customary for monks, family, and friends to speak,

VISUAL GUIDE
Buddhism

The Buddha achieved enlightenment while seated beneath a fig tree that came to be known as the bodhi tree ("Enlightenment Tree"). Here, monks gather at Bodh Gaya in India, the site of the Buddha's enlightenment.

(continued)

129

offering eulogies to honor the deceased. In most cases there is also chanting, led either by monks or family members.

CONCLUSION

We began this chapter with a reflection on the life of the Buddha, which offers his followers an example worthy of emulation. The Buddha's teaching is intended to dislodge the mind from clinging to the illusion of permanence and to empower each individual to find the joy and freedom this realization brings.

For twenty-five centuries, the Buddha's teaching has been elaborated by different schools and sects, each developing its own insights and perspectives on the Dharma. Buddhism has also adapted itself to diverse cultural settings. Its versatility has been fostered in large part by the words of the Buddha himself, who insisted that wherever the Dharma is transplanted, local custom, convention, and religious observance should always be maintained. This has allowed Buddhism to syncretize easily with regional beliefs and customs, as its predisposition has always been to augment rather than to displace. Although we can cite a few notable exceptions, Buddhism has inspired productive and progressive forms of social dissidence and political liberation in the modern era. And, as the world begins to address problems of global significance, Buddhism's central teachings will likely be supportive of efforts to solve them. For example, its doctrine of Interdependent Origination, which describes the fundamental interconnectedness of all things, underscores the responsibility shared by all people for preserving the environmental health of our planet. Indeed, it seems reasonable to hope that the Dharma will combine with the higher teachings of other systems of thought, religious and otherwise, to inspire the changes that will ensure a promising future for ourselves and our world.

Before the Buddha himself was first depicted in works of art, Buddhists venerated his footprints, which symbolized his path into nirvana. The convention of venerating his footprints continues today.

Buddhists of all sects demonstrate their reverence for the Buddha by bowing and prostrating themselves. Some show reverence while walking to a sacred site by bowing or prostrating themselves every step of the way.

As in Hinduism and Jainism, the lotus in Buddhism is a symbol of both purity and enlightenment.

While mandalas are used in Hinduism, where they also function as cosmological diagrams used for meditation, some Buddhists utilize them in other ways. In Vajrayana Buddhism, monks spend weeks constructing sand mandalas such as the Avalokiteshvara Mandala shown here. The sacred image will then be swept toward the center and be destroyed as a reminder that art, like all other things, is impermanent.

What Is Ultimate Reality?

Buddhists often use the Sanskrit word *dharma* in its broader sense (that is, as nature and its laws) to refer to ultimate reality, or reality as it is (rather than as it is usually perceived, or misperceived). According to the doctrine of Interdependent Origination, reality is a web of interrelated and interdependent phenomena in which nothing comes into existence independently of other things. Instead, the origination, or coming-into-existence, of things depends on all other things, as does their continued existence. All things are constituted of elements of other things. Nothing exists in and of itself. Further, according to the Buddha's doctrine of Impermanence, all things are in a constant state of flux and without any underlying or enduring essence or identity.

How Should We Live in this World?

Believing that there is stability and permanence in the world, we seek to possess what we want and to avoid what we do not want. Our inability to do so results in suffering that arises from our ignorance of the true nature of reality. Accordingly, the Buddha's guide to life, the Noble Eightfold Path, begins with the acceptance of a correct view of reality. The importance of striving for goals consistent with this understanding and living according to corresponding ethical principles follows. Finally, the Eightfold Path enjoins Buddhists to cultivate awareness and concentration that lead to enlightenment and an end to suffering.

What Is Our Ultimate Purpose?

For Buddhists, one's ultimate purpose is to break free of samsara and to achieve the end of suffering that is found in nirvana. But Buddhists also recognize that suffering is a condition that afflicts all sentient beings. Moved by compassion for others, they seek to live in a way that allows and encourages them to follow the path that will lead to their own enlightenment and liberation from suffering.

REVIEW QUESTIONS

For Review

1. Describe two ideas of practices that make Vajrayana Buddhism different from Mahayana.
2. Why does the Buddha's doctrine of Interdependent Origination require us to think of ourselves and reality as a whole in a new way?
3. What are the Three Marks of Existence? How do they relate to the doctrine of Interdependent Origination?
4. How does Zen differ from Pure Land Buddhism?

5. What did the Buddha mean by "suffering" (*dukkha*)? How does following the Noble Eightfold Path bring an end to suffering?

For Further Reflection

1. It is sometimes said that Buddhism is a philosophy rather than a religion. Do you agree?
2. What are the most significant ways in which the teachings of the Buddha deviated from those of Hinduism?
3. In what specific ways do the teachings of Mahayana and Vajrayana Buddhism elaborate on those of Theravada?
4. Why is the principle of the Middle Way essential to Buddhism?
5. To what extent are the Buddha's teachings about the nature of reality in agreement with those of modern science?
6. Would you find it difficult to accept the Buddha's doctrine of No-Self? Why or why not?

GLOSSARY

anatman (un-aat-mun) The doctrine that there is no independent, eternal self or soul underlying personal existence. See also No-Self.

arhat (ar'hut) In Theravada Buddhism, one who has attained enlightenment.

bhikku (bi-khu) A Buddhist monk.

bodhichitta (bow-dhi-chit-ta) In Mahayana Buddhism, the wise and compassionate intention to attain Buddhahood for the sake of all other sentient beings.

bodhisattva (bow-dhi-sut-tva) Literally, an "enlightened being." In Mahayana Buddhism, one who has taken a "bodhisattva vow" to remain in samsara in order to work for the enlightenment of all sentient beings. Both Mahayana and Vajrayana Buddhism also venerate a multitude of celestial bodhisattvas.

Buddha (bood-dha) A fully enlightened being.

Chan or Zen (chah-aahn/Zehn) Respectively, the Chinese and Japanese names for the "meditation" school of Buddhism that values meditative experience far and above doctrine.

Dhammapada (dhur-ma pa-da) A collection of sayings of the Buddha found in the Pali Canon.

Dharma (dhur-mah) In the Buddhist context, a term referring both to Buddhist teaching and to Buddhism as a religion.

dukkha (doo-kah) Usually translated as "suffering," a term that can also be understood as anxiety, unease, or dissatisfaction caused by desire.

Four Noble Truths The four truths that form the basis of the Dharma: Suffering is inherent in human life, suffering is caused by desire, there can be an end to desire, and the way to end desire is the Noble Eightfold Path.

Impermanence The Buddha's doctrine that all phenomena are in a constant state of change.

Interdependent Origination The doctrine, also known as Dependent Origination, that reality is a complex of interrelated and interdependent phenomena in which nothing exists independently; instead, the origination of all things depends on other things.

karma (kur-mah) Action; also, the consequences of actions.

lama (laah-mah) In Tibet, a teacher of the Dharma.

Mahayana (muh-haah-yaah-na) Also known as the "Great Vehicle," the form of Buddhism most prominent in China, Japan, Mongolia, Tibet, and Korea.

mandala (muhn-daah-la) Typically, a circular diagram representing the entire universe; often used as an aid in meditation.

mantra (mun-trah) A sacred sound or syllable used as a focus for meditation, as an invocation of a deity, or as a protective spell.

Middle Way The Buddha's principle of the path between extremes of asceticism and self-indulgence that leads to enlightenment.

nirvana (nihr-vaah-nah) The ultimate goal of Buddhist practice: the extinguishing of desire and the suffering it causes.

Noble Eightfold Path The Buddha's prescription for a way of life that leads to enlightenment. Based on the principle of the Middle Way, it is also defined by eight virtues.

No-Self The doctrine that there is no independent, eternal self or soul underlying personal existence. (See also anatman.)

Pali Canon Also known as the *Tripitaka*; the first canon of Buddhist texts consisting of three "baskets" or collections of sutras.

parinirvana (pah-ree nihr-vaah-nah) The full entry into nirvana that occurs at the death of one who has achieved nirvana in his or her lifetime.

samsara (sum-saah-ra) The continuing cycle of birth, death, and rebirth; also, the this-worldly realm in which the cycle recurs.

sangha (suhn-ghaah) The worldwide community of Buddhists; alternatively, the order of Buddhist monks or the membership of a particular Buddhist congregation.

skandhas (skuhn-dhaahs) The five components (body, perceptions, feelings, innate tendencies, and thought) that give rise to a sense of self.

stupa (stooh-puh) A reliquary mound in which the relics of the Buddha or a Buddhist saint are buried and venerated.

sutra (sooh-trah) Discourses or sermons of the Buddha preserved in the Buddhist scriptures..

Theravada (thair-ah-vaah-duh) Theravada, "The Way of the Elders"; the form of Buddhism that is most prominent in Sri Lanka, Cambodia, Laos, and Vietnam.

Three Marks of Existence The Buddha's teachings on impermanence, suffering, and No-Self, the non-existence of an eternal unchanging self or soul.

Tripitaka (See Pali Canon.)

upaya (ooh-paah-ya) The creative application of wisdom in helping others to ease their suffering or cultivate insight.

Vajrayana (vaah-jiraah-yaah-nah) Also known as the "Diamond Vehicle" and "Thunderbolt Vehicle"; the most prominent form of Buddhism in Tibet and Nepal. It incorporates both Mahayana and Tantric ideas and practices.

SUGGESTIONS FOR FURTHER READING

Byrom, Thomas. *The Dhammapada: The Sayings of the Buddha*. New York: Vintage Books, 1976. A very accessible and readable version of a key early Buddhist text.

Lopez, Donald. *Buddhist Scriptures*. London: Penguin Books, 2004. A survey of Buddhist scriptures.

Prebish, Charles, and Damien Keown. *Introducing Buddhism*. 2nd ed. London: Routledge, 2010. An authoritative introduction recommended as the first text to be consulted by those who are new to the study of Buddhism.

Skilton, Andrew. *A Concise History of Buddhism*. Birmingham, UK: Windhorse Publications, 1994. An excellent and accessible history of Buddhism.

Snelling, John. *The Buddhist Handbook: The Complete Guide to Buddhist Schools, Teaching, Practice and History*. Rochester, VT: Inner Traditions, 1998. A guide to Buddhism that includes a detailed directory of contemporary institutions.

Suzuki, Shunryu. *Zen Mind, Beginner's Mind*. New York: Weatherhill, 1997. An excellent introduction to meditation practice.

Williams, Paul. *Mahayana Buddhism: The Doctrinal Foundations*. 2nd ed. New York: Routledge, 2008. A history of Mahayana that places emphasis on the veneration of certain Buddhist texts.

ONLINE RESOURCES

The Wikipedia Buddhism Portal
en.wikipedia.org/wiki/Portal:Buddhism
Collection of articles in the Wikipedia Buddhism series that is generally quite reliable and extensive in scope.

Access to Insight: Readings in Theravada Buddhism
accesstoinsight.org
Readings that include helpful summaries and substantial translated portions of the Pali *Tripitaka*.

The Berzin Archives
berzinarchives.com/web/en/index.html
An excellent collection of translations, teaching, and scholarship on the Vajrayana tradition.

Chinese Religions: Confucianism and Daoism

TODAY IS *QINGMING*, a "pure and bright" day (the literal meaning of this Chinese compound word) that arrives once a year, 105 days after the winter solstice. It is a day for all Chinese families to remember their dead relatives and ancestors by visiting their graves. Spring is definitely in the air. The days have been getting longer and warmer. The rice seedlings, standing in neat rows in ankle-deep water in the paddy fields, wave gracefully in the gentle breeze. Their luxuriant greenness is most pleasing to the eyes of Chen Liang, a peasant from southern China in his early fifties. He and his two sons have been working hard in the past couple of months to plow and flood the paddy fields, seed the nursery plots, and then transplant the young seedlings one at a time into their current location.

But today there will be no work in the fields. *Qingming* marks the renewal of spring. It also celebrates the rekindling of the kitchen fire. Two days earlier the old fire had been put out, so only cold food had been served. Chen Liang and his wife get up today at the crack of dawn to light a new fire in the kitchen. Leftovers from the previous days' cold meals are wrapped in rice pancakes and fried, making "spring rolls" that many Chinese restaurants the world over serve regularly on their appetizer menu. They prepare for an important family gathering at the ancestral graves of the Chen clan. During this annual event, family members gather at and sweep the graves of their relatives and ancestors to renew their kinship ties with both the dead and the living. Plates of fruits,

Woman making offerings in front of her ancestor's tomb.

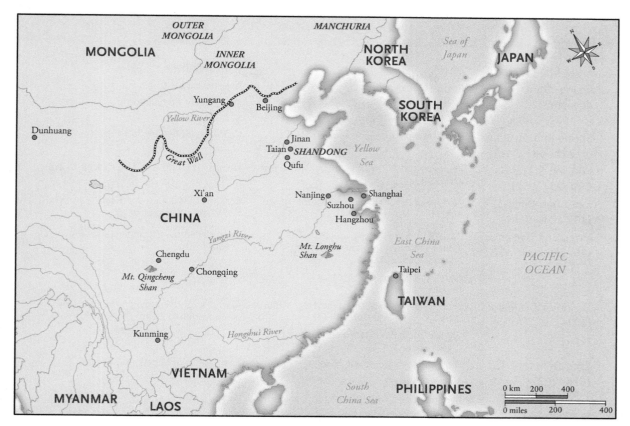

Important Confucian and Daoist sites in China.

freshly steamed chickens, a whole roasted pig, bottles of wine, bundles of incense sticks and bright-red candles, and strings of firecrackers, as well as piles of make-believe paper money and paper clothing for the dead, are all ready to be carried to the lineage burial ground just outside the village.

At the gravesite, where several generations of the Chen clan are buried, Chen Liang meets up with his three brothers, his five cousins, and their families. The children, numbering more than twenty, are all dressed in brightly colored clothing, giggling and playing. They help remove overgrown weeds, clean the tombstones, and arrange food in front of the tombstones. Then, by generation and birth order, all members of the Chen clan bow before their ancestors, address them in silent prayers, offer them wine and food, send them clothing and stacks of underworld money by burning paper imitations of them, and set off firecrackers to scare off wandering ghosts unrelated to the family.

Afterward a picture is taken of the entire gathering in front of the graves. The families divide up the fruits and the meats to be consumed later back at their respective homes. The men linger to talk about the weather and the crops, the women catch up on family news, and the children play. ☀

Era in Chinese History	Daoism	Confucianism
Shang–Zhou dynasties (c. 1600–256 B.C.E.*)	Ancient Chinese religion Shamans	Ancient Chinese religion Beginning of *Ru* tradition
Spring and Autumn (c. 722–481 B.C.E.)	World-escaping recluses and hermits	Confucius (551–479 B.C.E.*)
Warring States (c. 480–221 B.C.E.)	Zhuangzi (365–290 B.C.E.*), *Daodejing* (earliest extant ed. c. 300 B.C.E.)	Mencius (371–289 B.C.E.*), Xunzi (c. 310–238 B.C.E.*)
Early Han Dynasty (206 B.C.E.–9 C.E.)	Worship of Xiwangmu (Queen Mother of the West)	Confucianism declared orthodox (136 C.E.); Five Classics designated
Later Han Dynasty (25–220 C.E.)	Laozi deified as Taishang Laojun. Tianshi [Celestial Master] movement founded by Zhang Daoling (142 C.E.) *Laozi bianhua jing* (Classic of Laozi's Transformations) (170s*)	Confucian classical commentaries and Scholasticism
Period of Disunion (221–589)	Shangqing [Highest Clarity] movement (fourth century) Lingbao [Numinous Treasure] Movement (fourth century)	Confucian texts introduced to Korea and subsequently to Japan
Tang Dynasty (618–907)	First attempt at compiling canon State patronage of Daoism Daoism merged with Chinese folk religion	First stirring of Neo-Confucianism
Song Dynasty (907–1279)	Quanzhen [Complete Perfection] movement founded by Wang Zhe (1113–1170)	Neo-Confucianism: Zhu Xi (1130–1200)
Yuan Dynasty (1279–1368)		Four Books designated as civil service examination curriculum (1313)
Ming Dynasty (1368–1644)	*Daozang* compiled (1445) Daoist sacrificial rituals and notions of health influenced both elites and commoners in Korea, Japan, and Southeast Asia	Wang Yangming (1472–1529), an alternative Neo-Confucian view to Zhu Xi's Confucianism became state orthodoxy in Joseon Dynasty (1392–1897) Korea Confucianism also became state ideology in Tokugawa Japan (1600–1868)
Qing Dynasty (1644–1911)		Civil service examination abolished (1905) Confucianism became dominant ideology in Nguyen Dynasty Vietnam (1802–1945)
Early twentieth century	Chinese intellectuals criticized Daoism as superstition	Chinese intellectuals rejected Confucianism as feudal and reactionary
Communist China (1949–present)	Cultural Revolution (1966–1976) devastated Daoism Daoism gradually recovering since 1980s	Cultural Revolution (1966–1976) devastated Confucianism Confucianism gradually recovering since 1980s

Note: Asterisks indicate contested or approximate dates.

atherings similar to that of the Chen extended family are replicated millions of times throughout China in observance of *qingming*. It is through this activity of remembering the ancestors and reaffirming kinship relations that the Chinese act out one of their most basic religious assumptions. At the core of this ritual is the Confucian notion of filial piety (honoring parents and ancestors) and familial cohesiveness in Confucian teaching. Equally on display is the Daoist (Taoist) attentiveness to changes in season and in nature, as well as the practice of warding off unwelcome ghosts through thunderous explosives. From this single family gathering we see that Confucianism and Daoism can coexist quite harmoniously among the Chinese, with no sense of incompatibility or mutual exclusivity. Indeed, except for extreme partisans in each tradition, most Chinese often embrace both religions with no sense of tension or conflict. How is that possible?

In this chapter you are invited to step into the religious world of the Chinese and to see how these two native Chinese religions both rival and complement each other. (Even though Buddhism is the third main religious tradition in China, we only give passing notice to it in light of its alien origin and its totally different worldviews; see Chapter 5 for a complete treatment of Buddhism.) By focusing on the teachings, history, and practices of Confucianism and Daoism, you can appreciate the true religious nature of the two traditions as well, even though in content and expression they may differ from most other world religions.

THE TEACHINGS OF CONFUCIANISM AND DAOISM

Before Confucianism and Daoism arose, an ancient religion already existed in China. This ancient Chinese religion took shape no later than 1600 B.C.E., fully a thousand years prior to the rise of the two traditions. Both Confucianism and Daoism may be regarded as two divergent outgrowths of this ancient Chinese religion, with Confucianism focusing on interhuman relationship, whereas Daoism emphasizes the relationship between humans and nature. In order to understand Confucianism and Daoism, therefore, this ancient Chinese religion needs to be examined first.

Ancient Chinese Religious Views

The *Book of Changes,* the *Yijing* (*I Ching,* traditionally believed to have been compiled by the end of the second millennium B.C.E.), represents the earliest expression of the Chinese religious mindset. It conveys a worldview that has been described as "organismic," meaning that every single component of the cosmos belongs to an organic whole and that all the component parts interact with one another continuously. Unlike the foundational texts of most religions, the *Book of Changes* does not include a creation myth. This absence of a creation myth may be attributed to the dominance of the spirit of honoring ancestors in China since antiquity. When most of the spirits who populate the supernatural world are former human beings who share the same attributes as the living, the sense of mystery and "otherness" of a creator being may be difficult to envision. Instead, from an original state of "undifferentiated chaos" (*hundun*),[1] two polar yet complementary energies known as **qi** ("breath," "energy," or "force") emerged. One is called **yang** (literally the south-facing, sunny side of a mountain) and the other **yin** (the north-facing, shady side of a mountain). Representing all binary entities and concepts (such as day and night, male and female, hot and cold), yang and yin interact and alternate ceaselessly to form a continuum or spectrum, generating the myriad things in the process.

The yin-yang symbol best represents the Chinese religious mentality. This worldview recognizes differences but also harmony among the differences.

In this kind of a worldview, nothing exists outside the cosmos. This absence of a "wholly other" transcendent creator in the early Chinese cosmological myth has significant implications. That is, the classical Chinese view uses the metaphor of procreation or giving birth, not creation or fashioning something out of nothing, for the beginning of the universe. In this ancient Chinese view, the idea of an almighty god preceding and existing outside of creation is hardly imaginable. Correspondingly, the notion of an active evil dedicated to undermining the plans of a supposedly benevolent creator is also absent. In other words, there is no frighteningly personified devil competing with a benign god to win the hearts and minds of humans. In this world without sin (at least sin as understood by the Abrahamic faiths of Judaism, Christianity, and Islam), humanity is released from an acute sense of guilt. Instead, harmony and balance are good and preferable. Disharmony and imbalance are not.

The cosmic tango of yang and yin, spontaneous and unceasing, is manifested in the ***wuxing*** ("five elements or phases"), the five paradigmatic states of metal, wood, fire, water, and soil. These five states or elements correlate with many categories in nature. In the human body, they correspond to the Five Viscera (heart, liver, spleen, lungs, and kidneys); in the sky, they are the Five Planets (Venus, Jupiter, Mercury, Mars, and Saturn); and in human sensations they are the Five Colors (red, blue, yellow, white, and black) and the Five Flavors (sour, sweet, bitter, spicy, and salty). These five states are at the same time mutually nurturing and mutually destructive. Water sustains wood, wood feeds fire, fire reduces everything back to ashes (soil), soil produces ores (metal), and ores melt into liquid (water). Conversely, water douses fire, fire melts metal, metal chops down wood, wood draws nutrients from soil, and soil blocks water. Ultimately, like the swinging of the pendulum, what drives this dynamic process is the principle of alternation: when one extreme is reached, it reverts to the other. Such is the way the cosmos operates.

Notice in the photo that the two halves of the circle are not perfectly divided right down the middle. Instead, they are interlocked and mutually penetrating. Each half also contains the seed of the other. Thus, the entire cosmos is involved in a ceaseless flow of alternation and change.

Human Body and Soul   As fundamental energies of the cosmos that constantly interact with each other, yin and yang make solid matter when they coalesce and become immaterial when diffused. Their interplay can manifest in concrete and materialistic things, as well as in subtle and spiritual entities. It is in this context that the constitution of human beings can be understood.

All humans have a physical body, the physical manifestation of the interplay between yin and yang. But all humans also have an immaterial aspect, subdivided into *hun* and *po. Hun* reflects the yang component, being light, pure, and upward-rising, whereas *Po* indicates yin, being heavy, turgid, and downward-sinking. *Hun* and *po*, introduced into the physical body when the fetus is gestating, together make up the spiritual aspect of the individual. For lack of a better term, they constitute the soul matter of the individual. As long as they stay with the human body, with only short and temporary absences during the dream state or when in a coma, the individual remains alive. At death, however, *hun* departs from the body permanently, rising skyward, and *po* settles down on earth alongside the interred and decomposing body. Both *hun* and *po* eventually dissipate and become reconfigured in different proportions to form future beings.

The Spiritual World of Gods and Ghosts   After death, as long as the energy remains to keep the current identity of *hun* and *po* intact, the spirit of the deceased lingers. Though only a pale shadow of its former self, the spirit of one who dies at a ripe old age and is properly cared for by the descendants may become **shen**, a benevolent power that protects and brings benefit to the living. In contrast, the spirit of one who dies tragically or prematurely, and one who is not given a suitable burial or sacrifice, will become **gui**, a vengeful and malevolent ghost who visits disasters on people. *Shen* is a generic term for all kindly deities and gods whose power and efficacy are sought to fulfill people's wishes for health, wealth, progeny, and status. Conversely, *gui* refers to all spiteful ghouls, demons, and ogres who wreak havoc in people's lives. Motivated both by longing and fear, the Chinese from ancient times to the present strive to cultivate good relations with both *shen* and *gui*. This, of course, is in addition to their primary obligation to commemorate and honor their ancestors. Thus, the line of demarcation between the spirits and humans cannot be sharply drawn, as there is no separate "sacred" realm in ancient Chinese religious beliefs. Humans can indeed possess or exhibit qualities that in other cultures or beliefs may be considered spiritual, or even divine.

Political Implications of Ancient Chinese Religious Beliefs   During the Shang Dynasty, the earliest verifiable historic period in China to date, whose traditional dates are 1600–1046 B.C.E., the spirits of the ancestors were sometimes asked to carry messages to a higher deity for decision and response. This higher, more authoritative deity was Shangdi, the Lord on High, who was the most powerful god in the Shang spiritual world and who also happened to be the ancient ancestor of the Shang imperial house. This Lord on High was the controlling power in the cosmos. Along with the spirits of the ancestors, Shangdi monitored the behavior of the royal descendants, dispensing rewards and meting out punishments as appropriate. It was precisely for this reason that the Shang rulers needed to maintain close contact and good relationship with Shangdi and the other ancestral spirits, for the spirits were their source of kingly power. This power was termed **de**, commonly translated as "virtue" but more accurately as "potency," which may be more appropriately understood as the charismatic power the king possessed. With *de* the Shang king ruled with authority and legitimacy.

But sometime near the end of the second millennium B.C.E., a former minister of the court staged a rebellion that overthrew the Shang Dynasty and founded the next regime, the Zhou Dynasty (1122–256 B.C.E.). This power shift was rationalized primarily in religious terms. The defeat of the Shang, as the victorious Zhou founders explained it, was in fact sanctioned by Shangdi, who now had a different name and turned out, in fact, to be a different kind of deity. Shangdi was now known as **Tian**, literally, "the sky," but more properly "the force above." (Regrettably, most books and articles written in English on Chinese religion and philosophy translate *Tian* as "Heaven," which is both inaccurate and misleading. In this chapter, we continue to use the term *Tian* rather than any English equivalent in order to avoid any mistaken notion of *Tian* being a paradise-like location.)

Tian was believed to be the source of all things in the universe (not as a creator, but rather as a procreator), the ultimate divine entity that provided order throughout the cosmos. More significantly, *Tian* was also a "will" that would support only the morally deserving as king. This made *Tian* radically different from Shangdi, who was understood to be partial to the Shang kings and amenable to their "bribery" through offerings. *Tian* was not swayed by claimed blood ties or sacrificial presentations; instead, it insisted on moral uprightness as the only condition for its award of political authority and legitimacy, which was labeled **ming**, or **Tianming**. This was the "mandate" or "charge" given by *Tian* to the person and the imperial line that was to rule on *Tian*'s behalf. Moreover, this *ming* could be revoked and withdrawn and could be transferred to another person or family any time its provisional holder was found wanting in moral standing. Known as "*geming*" (the revocation of the "*ming*"), it sanctions and justifies revolution—the withdrawal of the current regime's mandate to rule. Shang's last ruler, who, according to the Zhou founders, was a corrupt and immoral individual, was no longer fit to exercise *Tianming*, hence his removal from power. To this day, this Chinese term means a violent overthrow of the government.

According to the religious mindset of the Zhou, *Tian*'s workings in nature and in the human world are its **dao**, its "way" or "path." It is the dao of *Tian* that provides order and regularity in nature and in human society. By following and obeying this dao, both the natural and the human worlds would reach their optimal potential. This implementation of the dao of *Tian* is the duty and obligation of the human ruler. As the chosen deputy of *Tian* in the human world, the Zhou king (and all subsequent imperial rulers in China) called himself *Tianzi* ("Son of *Tian*"), the person who had been entrusted with the power to rule *Tianxia* ("domain under *Tian*," that is, the entire known world). The king was therefore not just a political leader exercising power over both territory and people; he was also a religious figure who served as intermediary between *Tian* and humanity, as well as the natural world. To fulfill his roles as both king and priest, the Zhou ruler had to observe a set of behavioral practices collectively referred to as **li** ("rituals" or "rites"). It was the correct and sincere performance of *li* that would convince *Tian* of the ruler's moral worth, ensure *Tian*'s continuous favor, and guarantee the ruler's power through his *de*, his "potency." *Li* covered every aspect of kingly behavior—from matters of state to relationships with ancestors to conduct on important familial occasions such as marriage and funerals and even involving military campaigns. It would in time govern all the ritual conduct of the king's ministers as well, as their proper behavior also contributed to the stability and legitimacy of the regime.

Ancient Chinese Texts   Such prescribed rites for the king and his ministers would later be codified into a text known as the *Record of Rites* (*Liji*). However, the beliefs in the source of kingly power and the underlying assumptions of imperial moral obligations are fully addressed in two other texts: the *Book of Odes* (*Shijing*) and the *Book of History* (*Shujing*). The *Book of Odes* is an anthology of poems and ballads expressing the sentiments of both nobles and commoners, whereas the *Book of History* consists primarily of recorded activities and pronouncements of kings and aristocrats. Another work, the previously mentioned *Book of Changes* (*Yijing*), contains early Chinese views of cosmology and the supernatural. Collectively, these texts, which existed in some form after the founding of the Zhou regime, provide most of the information on the ancient Chinese religion from which Confucianism and Daoism would evolve. The Confucians, in particular, would revere these texts as classics and as sacred texts. The four just mentioned, along with the *Spring and Autumn Annals* (*Chunqiu*), purportedly compiled by Confucius himself, would be designated as the Confucian **Five Classics.** The Daoists, while fully aware of the authority of these texts, especially the *Book of Changes*, would create their own corpus of scriptural works focusing more on the constitution of the human body, the basic elements of nature and the cosmos, and the ideal human relationship with the spirits, as you shall see in later sections.

The Teachings of Confucianism

In this chapter, the term Confucianism is used with reluctance. The Chinese refer to this tradition as the "Teachings of the **Ru**" (scholars and ritualists), whose function in the Zhou Dynasty will be discussed later in the History section of this chapter. Even though Confucius has been rightfully credited with giving this tradition prominence and profound religious meaning, he is by no means its founder, nor is he worshiped as a supernatural savior figure like Jesus Christ in Christianity or the Buddha in Mahayana Buddhism. Therefore, "Confucianism" is quite a misleading term. In fact, the name "Confucius" is equally problematic, as it is actually a Latinized way of representing the Chinese reference to "Kong Fu Zi," the honorific way of addressing "Master Kong." Master Kong's full name is Kong Qiu, whose dates are conventionally given as 551–479 B.C.E. You will get a closer look at his life and times later in this chapter; here, we first examine his teachings.

The *Analects* of Confucius Confucius inherited the entire package of ancient Chinese religious views discussed in the preceding pages. This is made clear in the single most important work that contains his main teaching, the *Lunyu*. Literally meaning "comments and sayings" but customarily translated as the *Analects*, this text is believed to have been compiled by Confucius's leading disciples after his death. It serves as a record of statements he had made, exchanges with students he had conducted, and even remarks some of the students had offered. As such, it is an authoritative source for the examination of Confucius's teaching. Despite the possibility of later interpolations and the apparent lack of organization, the extant twenty "Books" of the *Analects*, taken as a whole, reflect a coherent picture of Confucius's major concerns and aspirations. A careful analysis of the content of the *Analects* shows that, while accepting many of the preexisting cosmological notions and religious beliefs of ancient China, Confucius and his immediate followers offered many new insights and creative interpretations regarding them. In the end, these "comments and sayings" contributed to the formation of a distinct tradition with unique views on humanity and its relation to the ultimate reality. The following are some of the most notable topics addressed in the *Analects*.

The Primacy of *Tian*

Confucius lived during the last centuries of the Zhou regime, which was a period of unmistakable dynastic decline. The possible revocation and transfer of *Tianming* was undoubtedly a pressing issue for the elite members of society. What Confucius takes up in the *Analects* is a fresh and innovative understanding of *Tian*, *Tianming*, and their relationship to humans, especially the moral elite.

The *Tian* of early Zhou, as we have seen, was an august and aloof divine power whose interaction with human beings was largely confined to the ruler, who alone could interact with it. By contrast, the *Tian* of Confucius was a far more intimate religious and ethical entity. It had a conscious will that no longer reached out to the Zhou rulers and the various feudal lords (as it had done in the past), but to moral and noble men of diverse backgrounds so that they might revive a moral order that once existed. Confucius saw himself, and encouraged his followers to become, a member of this moral vanguard.

Tian's communication with the moral elite is not verbal or revelatory. Unlike the biblical God or the Qur'anic Allah, *Tian* silently manifests itself in the course of the seasons and in the records of human events to allow perceptive individuals to detect the full content of its command. Once the individual moral person firmly understands that imperative, he becomes the new recipient of the *ming* of *Tian*. He is now an obedient messenger through whom *Tian*'s moral injunctions will be spread, resulting, hopefully, in a general uplifting of society. Various passages in the *Analects* attest to this faith in the primacy of *Tian* in Confucius's life and teachings. The following are particularly illustrative.

A border official from the town of Yi requested an audience with the Master. . . . After emerging from the audience, he remarked [to the Master's disciples], "The world has long been without the ideal Way. *Tian* intends to use your Master like a wooden clapper for a bell [to awaken the world]."

—*Analects 3:24*

When Huan Tui, the Minister of War of the principality of Song, tried to kill Confucius (who was visiting), Confucius exclaimed, "It is *Tian* who has endowed me with virtue. What harm can Huan Tui do to me?"

—*Analects 7:23*

When under siege in the principality of Kuang, the Master declared, "With King Wen (founder of Zhou Dynasty) dead, does not civilization rest now on me? If *Tian* intends to have civilization destroyed, those who come after me will have nothing. But if *Tian* does not intend to have civilization destroyed, then what can the men of Kuang do to me?"

—*Analects 9:5*

The Master lamented, "Alas, there is no one who understands me." Zigong said, "How is it that no one understands you?" The Master continued, "I do not complain against *Tian*, nor do I blame my fellow men. I study what is mundane to reach what is transcendent. If there is anyone who understands me, it is *Tian*!"

—*Analects 14:35*

What these passages show collectively is the centrality of *Tian* in Confucius's thinking. *Tian* is clearly the highest religious authority, as well as ultimate reality, in the *Analects*. The *Analects* suggests a conscious *Tian* who "intends" human beings to have civilization in the form of a perfect order. To that end, it reaches out to a few noble individuals. This is *Tian*'s mandate or imperative (*ming*). For Confucius, *Tianming* is no longer a bestowal of dynastic power to the political rulers but instead a call to moral action to the spiritual elite.

Some scholars of Confucian studies have noted a "prophetic voice" in Confucius and his followers. To be sure, unlike Moses or Muhammad, Confucius did not see himself as the messenger of a personal God. Nevertheless, he criticized the authorities of his time and condemned their departure from the normative ideal by appealing to *Tian*. He invoked his own power as someone who, because of his commission by *Tian*'s command, had that right to do so. In effect, Confucius changed the very nature of *Tianming*. It became the self-ascribed duty of the moral individual to serve as mouthpiece to a *Tian* that did not speak itself, to be inspired and motivated by the sense of mission, indeed of commission, by *Tian*. The men of virtue, the *Analects* insists, must be "strong and resolute, for their burden of responsibility is heavy and the journey is long. Taking upon themselves the burden of humaneness, is that not heavy? Stopping only at death, is that not long?" (*Analects* 8:7). *Tian* in the *Analects* spurned the power holders of a decadent age and instead entrusted the awesome responsibility of protecting the ideals of the human order to a commoner like Confucius.

The Content of *Tian*'s Imperative—the Dao   Just what is this message that *Tian* seeks to convey through the spiritual elite? It is the Dao, the Way. Confucius often complains in the *Analects* that the "Dao is not in practice" (*Analects* 5:7), or the "Dao does not prevail in the world" (*Analects* 16:2). What he means by the Dao is the entire normative social-political-ethical order with the prescriptions for proper ritual behavior publicly, as well as moral rectitude privately. However, when men in power are incapable or unwilling to uphold this order, as was the case during Confucius's time, men of virtue and uprightness must take it upon themselves to protect and preserve this ideal or civilization will be doomed. It is for this reason that Confucius regards the search for and embodiment of the Dao to be the ultimate, paramount task in life. He proclaims: "If I can hear the Dao in the morning, I will die contented that evening!" (*Analects* 4:8).

As Dao represents the entire normative human order, Confucius focuses on certain key aspects for detailed discussion: *ren* and *li*.

Ren   Perhaps the single most important article of faith held by Confucius is **ren** (benevolence, humaneness, virtue)—the kernel of humanity that exists intrinsically in all human beings. It is the germ of moral consciousness that enables human beings to form a perfect human order. Etymologically, it points to the interrelatedness among humans, for in writing it is a combination of the character for person (人) and the character for the number two (二), signaling that it is in a "state of person-to-person" that *ren* (仁) can be enacted. Throughout the *Analects,* the importance of *ren* in Confucius's teaching is evident. Many of his leading disciples ask him about it, and he gives various answers to drive home the idea that *ren* is all-rounded and multifaceted. Indeed, *ren* is so fundamental a concept that Confucius allows the giving up of one's life in order to preserve it (*Analects* 15:9), implying that a life without *ren* is meaningless.

People who can preserve and develop their *ren* can be entrusted to carry out the imperative of *Tian*. "When the root is firmly established, the Dao will grow. Filial piety and brotherly deference, are they not the basis of *ren?*" (*Analects* 1:2). It is the cultivation and nurturing of this root of moral propensity that constitutes the actualization of the Dao. Note that Confucius here is not asserting the perfection of all human beings. Rather, he is advocating their perfectibility through self-effort. This inner moral disposition needs to be expanded and developed before it can sustain the Dao.

How is the Confucian *Tian* different from the Judaic Yahweh, the Christian God, and the Islamic Allah?

What is remarkable about this view is the belief that this moral potentiality is not a monopoly of either the political elite or those of noble birth, but is in fact possessed by all humans. This universal accessibility makes it possible for someone like Confucius to teach others how to achieve *ren* and how to become men of virtue themselves.

Furthermore, this goodness is exemplified by filial piety (**xiao**) and brotherly deference, as well as by a sense of dutifulness (*zhong*) and reciprocity (*shu*). Filial piety stresses one's indebtedness to the family elders and to the parents, and brotherly deference acknowledges the mutual obligations among siblings. Thus, it is within the family that humans first exercise their moral cultivation. Outside the family, one should exert one's utmost effort in interacting with others in society. This effort arises from one's sense of dutifulness and "not doing unto others what one does not want done unto oneself" (*Analects* 15:24), which is the height of reciprocity. *Ren* is thus the entire human moral repertoire, which, when developed and enacted, will produce harmony in the human world and in the relationship that humans maintain with *Tian*.

Li   *Ren* alone, however, is not enough to enable one to preserve the Dao. This inner potentiality for goodness and benevolence has to be manifested by an external performance of prescribed behavior within the family, the community, the entire human society, and the spiritual world beyond. This is referred to as *li* (rites, rituals, normative behavior) in the *Analects*, a word that in ancient China meant only the sacrificial and behavioral rituals of the kings and the nobles. The ideograph for *li* shows a sacred ritual vessel, indicating that the etymological origin of the word has something to do with sacrifice to the gods or the ancestors (禮). In Confucius's understanding of the term, *li* encompasses the entirety of proper human conduct vis-à-vis other human beings, dead ancestors, and the spirits. *Li* cultivates a learned pattern of behavior that, when combined with the moral propensity present in each individual, will produce a magical transformation in interhuman relationships, as well as in relations with the spirits. Once a ritual gesture is initiated in the proper ceremonial context and performed with grace and sincerity, goodwill, trust, and harmony will follow. This is the irresistible and invisible power of ritual itself.

The *Analects* is most optimistic about the efficacy of *li*: In a famous response to his favorite student's question about *ren*, Confucius states: "Restraining oneself and returning to *li*, this is *ren*" (*Analects* 12:1). Only through ritualized interaction with others and with the spirits can one realize one's full potential as a human being. The mastery and performance of *li*, then, is in fact a "process of humanization."[2] *Li* is the external enactment of *ren*. Conversely, *ren* is the inner source of *li*. This is why Confucius asks rhetorically: "A man who is not *ren*, what has he to do with *li*?" (*Analects* 3:3).

Junzi   Confucius uses the term **junzi** (the noble man, the man of virtue, and the superior man) for the noble *ru* on whose shoulders rests the burden of reviving and preserving the Dao. This is Confucius at his most creative and radical in the usage of traditional terminology. Originally used to refer to the scions of feudal rulers, *junzi* in Confucius's refashioning comes to mean men of moral rectitude. From someone highborn, *junzi* becomes someone high-minded. From those of noble birth, *junzi* now means those of noble worth. They are the prophet-like individuals who, though holding no political office or having no privileged positions, nevertheless receive *Tian*'s call. They undertake the most arduous task of implementing *Tian*'s Dao in the human world. The *Analects* puts the issue most plainly: "Without knowing the imperative of *Tian*, one cannot be a *junzi*" (20:3).

The self-cultivation of the *junzi* will earn them a power (*de*) similar to that possessed by the ancient sage rulers. It is a charismatic, noncoercive, potent influence that both inspires and persuades, and coaxes and shames, people into doing what is right. In the *Analects,* Confucius confidently declares: "The *de* of the *junzi* is like wind, while that of the common people is like grass. When the wind blows over the grass, the grass cannot help but bend in the direction of the wind" (*Analects* 12:19). The epitome of the *junzi* is the sage (**shengren** or simply **sheng** 聖), the rarest of human beings who are perfect in their moral standing and kingly in their worldly accomplishments. The traditional Chinese character for sage contains three components: ear, mouth, and ruler (耳, 口, 王). The sage is someone who hears or listens to the Way of *Tian*, conveys it to others through the mouth, and acts in the capacity of the ancient ruler whose job it is to link up the three realms of Heaven, Earth, and Humankind. Thus the sage is decidedly a religious figure, a saintly person who is at once a messenger of *Tian* to the human world and an exemplar of human perfection in the eyes of *Tian*.

The Religious Vision of the *Analects*   Taken as a whole, the vision of the *Analects* offers an amazingly clear picture of Confucius's ultimate concern. The religious aspect of this Confucian vision is unmistakable. It has been justly pointed out that, unlike many other religious figures, Confucius envisaged no escape from the world and human society, nor did he insist on ascetic self-denial as a precondition for spiritual progress. In a similar vein, Confucius did not consider concern with the afterlife or with the spirits to be of primary importance. The following exchange between him and his student Zilu on that subject is famous: "Zilu asked about serving ghosts and spirits. The Master said, 'When we are not yet able to serve fellow humans, why worry about serving the ghosts and spirits?' 'What about death?' [Zilu persisted]. 'When we do not yet know enough about life, why worry about death?' [the Master replied]" (*Analects* 11:12).

In summary, then, you have been shown that Confucius has an abiding faith in the transcendent ultimate *Tian*. He feels an intimate relationship with it. He has a keen awareness of its command (*ming*) given to the moral and spiritual elites (*junzi*) to create the ideal human order (Dao). He firmly believes in the *Tian*-endowed human capacity for perfection and genuine humanity (*ren*) through self-cultivation, and enthusiastically participates in sacrificial rituals and familial and social rites (*li*). These are all components of his religious outlook. To be sure, this religiosity does not express itself in faith in a personal God and the need for salvation through divine grace. Rather, it distinguishes itself as a form of "this-worldly transcendentalism." It treats the "secular as sacred,"[3] and it imparts deeply religious meaning to participation in the mundane. Thus, it expresses a different mode of religiousness. For this reason, it has been paradoxically labeled a "humanistic religion" and a "religious humanism."[4] The distinction between the human and the divine, clearly drawn in the Abrahamic traditions, is not applicable here. For Confucius, the ultimate goal for humans is to heed the instruction of *Tian* by transforming themselves from potential to actual goodness. This process of transformation toward the absolute is the religious nature of the Confucian teaching, and it is right there in the *Analects*.

Admittedly, this religiousness of the Confucian *Analects* has been largely over-shadowed by its familial, social, and political manifestations throughout the course of Chinese imperial history, so much so that Confucianism as a religion is not readily recognized. However, the discussion that follows should further confirm the intrinsic religiosity of the Confucian tradition as it unfolded.

The *Mencius* Mencius (a Latinized rendition of "Master Meng") (371–289 B.C.E.?) was born a full century after Confucius's death. Claiming to be the rightful successor to Confucius, Mencius reaffirmed moral cultivation as a religious calling. He provided the moral elite with a strong sense of mission. Mencius also made one lasting contribution to the Confucian belief system with his insistence on the basic goodness of human beings, thus upholding Confucianism's optimistic view of human perfectibility.

Next to the *Analects*, the *Mencius* (an eponymous work compiled by some of Mencius's leading disciples) is significant as a Confucian scriptural text. Unlike Confucius, who does not regard himself as a sage—a title he reserves only for the few legendary rulers in ancient China—Mencius not only boldly declares his predecessor's sageness but also insists on his own. Indeed, he considers every human being a potential sage, as he believes that each possesses all the innate qualities to become one. It is on the basis of that assumption that he asserts the intrinsic goodness of human nature, which he compares to the natural tendency of water to flow downward (*Mencius* 6A, 2:2). This is Mencius's fundamental article of faith.

Identifying four "sprouts of morality" in all humans—the inborn sentiments of commiseration (inability to bear witness to the suffering of others), shame, deference and yielding, and sense of right and wrong—Mencius proclaims them to be the roots of benevolence (*ren*), righteousness (*yi*), propriety (*li*), and wisdom (*zhi*), respectively. With this belief as his religious premise, he constructs a logical progression from moral cultivation to the ultimate attainment of divine spirituality. He states,

> That which is sought after is called "good." To have it in oneself is
> called "true." To possess it fully is called "beautiful," while making it

shine forth with brilliance is called "great." To be great and be able to transform others is called "sage." To be sage and be beyond understanding by others is called "spiritually divine" (*Mencius* 7B, 25).

Through our moral progress, Mencius suggests, we can become not only good, true, beautiful, and great, but also sagely and ultimately divine. With utter conviction, then, he maintains, "Probing one's heart/mind to the utmost, one will know one's nature. Knowing one's nature, one will know *Tian*. To preserve one's heart/mind and nurture one's nature is to put one in the service of *Tian*" (*Mencius* 7A, 1:1). Once one has embodied the moral imperatives of *Tian*, Mencius reasons, one will find all other concerns secondary. In one of his most celebrated statements, Mencius declares: "I like fish, and I also like bear's paw. If I cannot have both, I will give up fish and keep the bear's paw. Life is what I desire, but so is righteousness. If I cannot have both, I will give up life but cling to righteousness" (*Mencius* 6A, 10:1). With morality as his ultimate concern, Mencius is willing to sacrifice his own life in order to preserve it. This is certainly reminiscent of Confucius's commitment to benevolence (*ren*), for the preservation of which he, too, is willing to suffer death. This is demonstrative of the spirit of the martyr and a deeply held religious sentiment.

The *Great Learning* and the *Doctrine of the Mean*   The remaining two texts of the **Four Books**, completing the Confucian religious corpus designated by the Neo- Confucian scholar Zhu Xi in the twelfth century (see the section on the history of Confucianism later in this chapter), are the *Great Learning* and the *Doctrine of the Mean*, supposedly compiled by two of Confucius's prominent students. Both are chapters from the *Book of Rituals* that have been excerpted as independent texts because of their religious significance. The *Great Learning* refers to learning about what is of primary importance. It prescribes a practical step-by-step roadmap for self-cultivation, starting with individual inquiries and ending with the transformation of humanity as a whole. Listing eight steps in personal cultivation, the *Great Learning* outlines a sequence of individual and social effort made to manifest "illustrious virtue," "love the people," and reach the "ultimate good," which is nothing short of the *Tian*-ordained perfect world order. Thus, learning involves far more than the acquisition of knowledge, but is actually an ethical-religious program of personal and societal perfection.

The *Doctrine of the Mean* begins with a bold declaration: "What *Tian* has ordained is called human nature. Following this nature is called the Dao. Cultivating the Dao is called teaching" (*Doctrine of the Mean* 1:1). These three statements articulate the fundamental Confucian articles of faith, representing what Confucianism regards as self-evidently true. The text asserts that humans are born with a benign nature imparted by *Tian*, the ultimate religious authority. This nature provides them with the inner strength to reach their fullest potential as perfect beings. Furthermore, when extended beyond the individual, this human nature can bring about an ideal social-political-ethical order, the actualization of which is the purpose of education. The text further maintains that the real possibility for achieving perfect goodness exists because of the special relationship between human beings and *Tian*. There is a logical progression from self-generating moral effort to the perfection of the faithful and the world around them: "The *junzi* [noble person] cannot avoid not cultivating his person. Thinking of cultivating his person, he cannot neglect serving his parents. Thinking of serving his parents, he may not avoid knowing other humans. Thinking of knowing other humans, he cannot ignore knowledge of *Tian*" (*Doctrine of the Mean* 20:7). It is clear that to actualize their genuine humanity and divine potential, human beings must fully engage with others.

There are five cardinal human relations for such interaction: three within the family and two outside of the family: that between father and son, husband and wife, elder and younger brothers, ruler and subject, and friends. All these relations obligate individuals to perform their respective roles in society. In other words, the father has to be kind, while the son is respectful; the husband has to be caring, while the wife is submissive; brothers need to be mutually deferential; the ruler needs to have the people's welfare in mind, while the subjects need to be obedient; and friends must maintain fidelity toward one another. It is therefore the entire human community that provides the setting for the Confucian religious quest. The *Doctrine of the Mean* offers a climactic conclusion to the process of self-cultivation:

> Only the most authentic and genuine person can fully develop his nature. Able to fully develop his nature, he can then thoroughly understand the nature of other people. Able to fully understand the nature of other people, he can develop the nature of things. Able to fully develop the nature of things, he can assist in the transforming and nourishing process of *Tian* and *Di* (earth, counterpart to *Tian*). When he assists in the transforming and nourishing process of *Tian* and *Di*, he forms a trinity with them!
>
> —*Doctrine of the Mean* 22:1

This euphoric assurance of the final outcome of human moral cultivation is breathtaking in its grandeur. Not only does the person who realizes his own nature to the full become a paradigm of genuine humanity, but also he actually becomes a "coequal" with *Tian* and *Di* through his participation in their nurture and sustenance of the myriad things. Forming a trinity with the ultimate numinous entity in the cosmos is the highest accomplishment for any religious seeker in the Confucian mode.

In the preceding paragraphs, we have analyzed the content and religiosity of the Four Books. These four texts neatly annotate the later Neo-Confucian goal of **neisheng waiwang**—inner moral cultivation and external skillful management of society and state (see the section on the history of Confucianism later in this chapter).

This is believed to reflect Confucius's original vision, namely, to pursue a personal relationship with the ultimate reality through moral improvement, culminating in an ordering of society and state in accordance with the Way ordained by *Tian*. This religious mission is best expressed by a famous Neo-Confucian scholar by the name of Zhang Zai (1020–1077) who declares that his lifelong goals are:

> To establish the mind of *Tian* and *Di*,
> To inculcate an understanding of [*Tian*'s] command (*ming*) for
> the multitudes,
> To revive and perpetuate the teachings of the sages of the past, [and]
> To provide peace and stability for all future generations.

This is indeed the social-political, as well as religious, aspiration of Confucianism in a nutshell!

Confucianism and Women

The issue of Confucianism and sexism is the elephant in the room that needs to be confronted. Despite its lofty religious teaching, Confucianism has often been criticized for its dismissive and negative attitude toward women. The single most notorious statement made by Confucius regarding women is truly incriminating: "Women and the petty men are alike, in that they are both hard to deal with" (*Analects* 17:23). In addition, one of the most prominent features of Confucianism during the Han Dynasty (206 B.C.E.–220 B.C.E.) and beyond is the oppression of the female by the male. Cleverly manipulating the traditional yin-yang belief into an argument for the priority of yang over yin, hence the male over the female, Han Confucians and their successors in later dynasties insisted that women submit to their fathers when young, their husbands when married, and their sons when old and widowed. This aspect of Confucianism in imperial China became a major cause of criticism of the tradition in the modern period. Since the beginning of the twentieth century, Confucianism has been portrayed as a sexist, patriarchal ideology responsible for the oppression of women in China. The insidious Chinese practices of foot binding (the crushing of the feet of young girls with long binding cloth to make their walking willowy and feminine), concubinage (the keeping of multiple wives by one man), disallowance of women-initiated divorce, prohibition against remarriage, and encouragement of widow suicide have all been blamed on Confucianism.

This view of Confucianism may, however, be too simplistic in characterizing the 2,000 years of Chinese gender history. It makes no distinction between theory and practice, as well as wishful normative values versus actual, living experiences. The oppression of women by Confucian men during China's imperial periods, though real and widespread, should not result in an outright denial of the intellectual and religious dynamism of Confucianism as a teaching of human improvement and self-cultivation with no gender specificity. Some contemporary scholars have taken note of the parallels between Confucian and feminist ethics. Confucianism as a state orthodoxy whose central purpose is social control and political manipulation is indeed incompatible with modern values. However, Confucianism as an ethical and religious teaching, with an emphasis on mutual care, empathy, responsible government, and communal welfare, shares many similarities with feminist care ethics.[5]

The Teachings of Daoism

As asserted earlier, Daoism evolved out of the same ancient Chinese religious mindset as Confucianism did. But instead of regarding *Tian* as the Absolute Ultimate, as the Confucians do, Daoists from the beginning hold Dao to be supreme. It should be recalled that the term Dao is also central to the Confucian tradition. However, the

Laozi riding on the back of a water buffalo as he retires into the realm of the immortals.

Daoists articulate a very different understanding of the Dao. It is this alternative apprehension of the Dao that serves as the point of departure for their entirely different mode of religious experience from that of the Confucians.

Laozi **(Lao-tzu) and** *Zhuangzi* **(Chuang-tzu)**   Traditionally, the best known and earliest identifiable Daoists were Laozi (Master Lao) and Zhuangzi (Master Zhuang). Laozi, more of a composite figure than an actual person, was the reputed author of the **Daodejing** (*Tao-te Ching*; The Scripture of the Way and Its Potent Manifestation), alternatively known as the *Laozi*. Zhuangzi was an obscure individual active in the late fourth century B.C.E. who was credited with authorship of the second most influential Daoist text, the *Zhuangzi*. Both texts are more representative of certain modes of thinking than of individual thinkers, as they are actually anthologies containing different strands of thought rather than coherent and logical teachings of single authors. One point, however, is clear: they are self-consciously non-Confucian in that they express a decidedly alternative understanding of the dao and of ideal human action. In addition, both the *Daodejing* and the *Zhuangzi* also contain descriptions of perfected human beings who possess amazing powers of magic and immortality. Both texts suggest that, through intense inner psychic journeying and mystical conditioning of the human body, individuals can acquire impressive powers of transformation and invulnerability to the decaying agents in nature.

The *Daodejing*   The eighty-one-chapter *Daodejing* is the most translated and most popular Chinese text in the West.

Virtually all the different schools and sectarian lineages within the Daoist movement regard this work as the founding scripture of the tradition.

In contrast to the Confucian Dao, which is the ideal ethical-social-political order ordained by *Tian* for human beings, the Dao of the *Daodejing* antedates *Tian* and acts as the basis of the natural order. Here Dao is the primordial entity that exists in an undifferentiated state prior to the coming into being of myriad things, including *Tian* and *Di*, which now stand for nothing more than nature itself. The lofty primacy of the Confucian *Tian* is supplanted by the nebulous Dao of the *Daodejing*, as indicated by the following celebrated passage:

> There was something undifferentiated and yet complete, which existed before *Tian* and *Di*
> Soundless and formless, it depends on nothing and does not change
> It operates everywhere and does not stop
> It may be regarded as the "Mother of the world"
> I do not know its name; I call it Dao.
>
> —*Daodejing, Chap. 25*

In one broad stroke, the entire Confucian cosmological scheme is turned upside down here. It is Dao, not *Tian*, that gives birth, like a mother, to the myriad things. It is Dao, not *Tian*, that serves as the primal source of the cosmos. Echoing the cosmogonic (concerning the origin of the cosmos) view of the *Book of Changes*, the *Daodejing* gives an even terser summary of the generating process of the cosmos:

> The Dao gives birth to the One [Being, Existence]
> The One brings forth the Two [Yin and Yang]
> The Two give rise to the Three [*Tian, Di,* and Humans]
> The Three engender the Ten Thousand Things [world of multiplicity and diversity]
>
> —*Daodejing, Chap. 42*

Again, the primacy of the Dao as the procreator of the entire universe and everything in it is unequivocally asserted here. As the ground of all beings, this Dao is compared to a "mysterious female," "water," "infant," and "uncarved block," all alluding to the beginning of life and form. However, unlike the Confucian Dao, which requires superior human beings (the *junzi* [men of virtue] and the *shengren* [sages]) to actualize its ideal design, the Dao of the *Daodejing* can only maintain its pristine form when humans leave it alone. Thus, the ideal course of action for insightful and wise human beings is to observe **wuwei** (actions without intention) and **ziran** (natural spontaneity) in their attempt to return to the Dao. These two ideal approaches to life are indicative of the *Daodejing*'s belief in the innate perfection and completeness of the Dao. *Wuwei* calls for a minimalist and noninterventionist attitude in human action, whereas *ziran* rejects any artificiality and contrived undertaking as detrimental to the well-being of humans and nature. Ultimately, the Dao in the *Daodejing* is indescribable, for it defies verbalization and precise definition. "The Dao that can be [verbally] expressed is not the constant Dao," insists the *Daodejing* in its first verse.

Yet the transcendent Dao is, at the same time, manifested in the myriad things through its presence in them as *de*—the very "potent manifestation" of each thing. In contrast to the *de* of the Confucians, which is the charismatic power of the moral elite, the *de* of the *Daodejing* points to the concrete expression of the Dao in all things. *De* is the "thingness" of a thing—that which makes a thing what it is. The combination of Dao and *de*, then, helps to bridge the gap between the transcendent and the immanent for the author(s) of the *Daodejing*. The Dao is the transcendent ground of being; yet through its expression in the *de* of the myriad concrete things, it is also fully immanent.

The *Zhuangzi* The extant version of the *Zhuangzi* consists of thirty-three chapters divided into three sections—"Inner," "Outer," and "Miscellaneous." The first seven Inner chapters are generally believed to be the authentic writings of Zhuang Zhou, the putative author. Yet as in the case of the *Daodejing*, we have only a vague biographical account of the purported author of this text, and little of substance is known about him.

The *Zhuangzi* is overall a different kind of text from the *Daodejing*. Whereas the *Daodejing* is terse and aphoristic in language, the *Zhuangzi* is effusive and vividly narrative. The *Daodejing* idealizes the feminine and regards the Dao as mother, but the *Zhuangzi* does not. The *Daodejing* gives much emphasis to politics and the techniques of rulership; the *Zhuangzi* is deliberately dismissive of politics. The *Zhuangzi* tells stories with a witty, playful, irreverent tone that is totally absent in the *Daodejing*. In terms of basic worldview and cosmological assumptions, however, the *Zhuangzi* shares much in common with the *Daodejing*, hence their grouping together by later historians and bibliographers as representatives of the "School of the Dao."

In the *Zhuangzi*, the Dao is not only the ineffable transcendent entity that gives rise to all things but also the immanent core that exists in all things, from the loftiest perfected beings to the lowliest broken pieces of tile and excrement. It is therefore omnipresent, making all things ultimately equal. As such, the Dao transcends all polarities, dichotomies, and dualities that the human mind is inclined to create. Hence the use of the human cognitive and rational approach to apprehend the Dao is futile and unproductive, as it can only be realized intuitively through the abandonment of the intellect. The mind must be able to be free from all conventional distinctions and established views, hence the advocacy of "carefree wandering" (*xiaoyao yu*) in the *Zhuangzi*. In this connection, the discussion of "fasting the mind/heart" (**xinzhai**) and "sitting and forgetting" (**zuowang**) becomes pertinent, as both practices dispense with rationality and deliberative cognition in order to arrive at the perfect intuitive understanding of the Dao.

Elements of Physical Invulnerability in the *Daodejing* and the *Zhuangzi*
Although both the *Daodejing* and the *Zhuangzi* are best known (in China and in the West) for their sophisticated philosophical discussions of the Dao, much less

known—but no less significant—is their commentary on the physical prowess of the Daoist practitioners. They hint at invulnerability to harm, longevity, and even immortality—the very promises of a Daoist religious movement that began no later than the second century C.E.

We next explore the impact the two have had on the content of Daoism as a religion. The following passages from both texts are highly suggestive:

EXCERPTS FROM THE *DAODEJING*

> He who does not lose his proper place lasts long
> He who dies but does not perish has longevity.
> *—Daodejing, Chap. 33*

> I have heard that people who are good at preserving their lives will not
> encounter wild bulls or tigers when traveling on land, and will not need
> to protect themselves with armor when in the army. Wild bulls will find
> nowhere to thrust their horns, tigers will have no place to sink their
> claws, and weapons will find no point to insert their cutting blades.
> And why is that? Because in them there is no room for death.
> *—Daodejing, Chap. 50*

> He who is richly endowed with *de* is comparable to a newborn baby:
> poisonous insects will not sting him, ferocious beasts will not seize him
> in their claws, and birds of prey will not snatch him with their talons.
> *—Daodejing, Chap. 55*

EXCERPTS FROM THE *ZHUANGZI*

> Far away on Mt. Guye there dwells a divine person whose skin is like
> ice and snow, and who is gentle and shy like a young girl. He does
> not eat the five grains; but [only] inhales the wind and drinks the dew.
> He ascends the clouds, mounts flying dragons, and wanders beyond
> the four seas. His spirit is focused, thus he saves creatures from sick-
> ness and plagues, and guarantees bountiful harvests.
> *—Zhuangzi, Chap. 1*

> The ultimate person is spirit-like. Though the great marshes are
> set ablaze, they will not make him hot. Though the rivers and streams
> freeze up, they cannot chill him. Though violent thunder splits the
> mountains and howling gales churn the ocean, they will not frighten
> him. A man like this rides the clouds and mist, mounts the sun and
> moon, and goes beyond the four seas. Death and life have no effect on
> him, how much less will profit and loss?
> *—Zhuangzi, Chap. 2*

The perfected individuals of old . . . could go up to high places without getting frightened, enter water without getting wet, and go into fire without feeling hot. Only those whose knowledge ascends the height of the Dao can be like this. . . . The perfected breathe with their heels, while the ordinary men breathe with their throat.

—*Zhuangzi, Chap. 6*

Blowing and breathing, exhaling the old and inhaling the new, [imitating the postures of] bear strides and bird stretches—these are all undertaken for the purpose of longevity. They are pursued with fondness by people who practice gymnastic calisthenics and body nourishments in hope of [attaining the longevity] of Patriarch Peng.

—*Zhuangzi, Chap. 15*

A Daoist immortal flying through the clouds, 1750. Portrayed is the sage mother of Dongling, who studied the Way and could cure illnesses. One day, amidst a throng wishing to thank her, she ascended to the clouds.

These passages on Daoist adepts describe their amazing magical power and physical invulnerability.

At the very least, these two texts suggest that the numinous Dao (the holy) is accessible by potent (that is, healthy) individuals and that holiness and robust health are closely related. As described by the *Daodejing* and *Zhuangzi*, the early practitioners of the Dao were people who, through their use of various bodily techniques, acquired powers that enabled them to experience the divine. These techniques and powers would very much become the concern of later Daoists. In short, the *Daodejing* and the *Zhuangzi* can be perceived as "proto-Daoist" texts by virtue of their distinctive view of the Dao and their reference to various practices and powers that anticipate those of the later organized Daoist groups.

Immortality and Alchemy One later Daoist preoccupation is with the notion of *xian* (immortal or transcendent), long a folk religious fascination but articulated most eloquently in the *Baopuzi* (Master Who Embraces Simplicity), a text authored by Ge Hong (283–343 c.e.). Central to the concept of *xian* is the conviction that physical transformation, good health, longevity, and ultimately immortality, can be acquired through proper diet, physical exercise, and drugs. People with the right recipe, formula, or prescription (*fangshi*) would teach these esoteric techniques and provide ready-made elixirs to those who had the financial resources and the necessary devotion to secure their services.

Inherent in the belief in immortality are the ancient Chinese assumptions about the human body and the measures that can be taken to keep it healthy and even immortal. As you may remember from our earlier discussion, the ancient Chinese believed that the human body is the microcosm that reflects the macrocosm of the cosmos. In other words, there is a direct correspondence and parallel between the human body and nature. All the myriad things in the universe are produced by the interaction of the vital energies (qi) of yin and yang. They also manifest the qualities of the five elemental phases (*wuxing*), follow the principle of alternation and constant return, while maintaining balance and harmony with one another. This belief was retained and developed prominently by Daoism and Chinese folk religion. According to this view, there are three central nodal points in the human body called ***dantian*** (locations for the production of pills of immortality)—in the head, the chest, and the abdomen— connected by meridian circuits through which the qi flows. And because the body is the cosmos writ small, just as there are gods and deities inhabiting the physical world outside, there are also numerous spiritual beings residing in various organs of the human body.

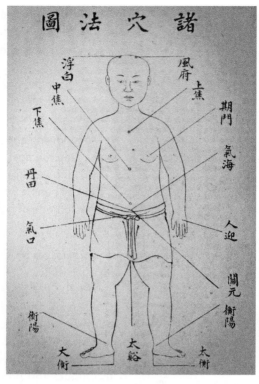

A Daoist view of the major nodal points in the human body through which the qi flows.

Based on this whole series of assumptions, the techniques of ***yangsheng*** (nourishing life) are developed. First mentioned in the *Zhuangzi*, *yangsheng* has the goal of refining the body so that it can overcome its earthly limitations and be in perfect harmony with the Dao, making it last as long as the universe. It involves an entire spectrum of exercises, including deep meditation, controlled breathing, therapeutic gymnastics, dietary regimens, even sexual techniques. All these measures of nourishing life have been practiced by religious Daoists since the second century C.E. and are grouped under the general heading of ***neidan*** (internal alchemy).

While these *yangsheng* techniques aim at the regeneration and reinforcement of the human body by making use of what the body originally possesses, the *fangshi* also focus on the compounding and refining of elixirs with substances (herbal and mineral) from nature. References to "refining gold" and transmuting cinnabar (mercury sulphate) in some Han Dynasty texts indicate a growing practice of alchemy for the purpose of attaining longevity and immortality. This pursuit of alchemical manufacturing of *dan* with minerals and plants would eventually lead to the ***waidan*** (external alchemy) tradition in Daoism.

All the internal and external alchemical techniques discussed here are intended to produce a new body that grows within the old so that, in time, the old self will be replaced by the new in the same way that cicadas and snakes regenerate themselves.

Figurine of Lord Guan as seen in many Chinese restaurants.

Daoist Deities As the Daoist tradition matured, the most exalted god in the Daoist pantheon became the *Yuanshi tianzun* (Celestial Venerable of Primordial Beginning), who is head of a trinity of Three Purities. Below them are innumerable deities of both genders who fill up various ranks in a mind-boggling celestial bureaucracy that loosely corresponds to its human counterpart.

The lowliest among the spiritual bureaucrats is the local earth god, while the head of the celestial government is the Jade Emperor. Many of them have divine origins, of course, but many also are former humans whose merits warrant their promotion to godly status. Some of the deities have national appeal, such as Lord Zhenwu [Perfect Martiality] of Mount Wudang, whereas others are more local in influence, including the Stove god in each household. One ubiquitous Daoist deity, Lord Guan, is honored by business owners as their protector and benefactor. A human turned god, Lord Guan can be seen in the form of a heroic figure with a red face and a cascading black beard, sporting a long robe and holding a long blade. An altar or alcove containing a figurine of him can be found in most Chinese restaurants in North America, where he is worshiped as a patron deity.

Daoist deities not only reside in the heavens, on earth, in the underworld, and in the homes but also inside the human body. They are supposed to protect all the major internal organs from the decaying effect of unwholesome food and old age. The entire pantheon of Daoist deities can be accessed and appealed to through ritual performance for assistance in warding off evil, improving health, guaranteeing harmony in family and community, and attaining immortality.

Daoism and Women

Because of the feminine emphasis of the *Daodejing*, it can be assumed that Daoism's treatment of women is generally better than that of Confucianism. Yet the situation is more complicated than it might first appear. The positions and roles of women in organized Daoism have to be examined in the larger context of Chinese society, which until recent times has indeed been patriarchal and sexist. It is therefore not surprising that women only play limited roles within the Daoist clerical hierarchy.

And yet it is also undeniable that because of women's greater sensitivity to the spirits and their keener communication ability with the divine and invisible world, they do have access to the roles and positions denied to most women in Chinese society at large. Women's special power to intercede with the deities often makes some of them more outstanding and influential practitioners of Daoism than men.

A Daoist movement known as the Celestial Masters (*Tianshi*; see more details in the section on the history of Daoism in this chapter) identified five classes of women suited to be Daoist practitioners: young unmarried women; women unable to marry because of their inauspicious horoscopes; women forced into marriage; rejected (divorced) wives; and widows. All these were vulnerable individuals to whom the Celestial Masters offered an escape and a way to assert their worth. In the Tang Dynasty (618–907 C.E.), women from aristocratic families became Daoist nuns in substantial numbers, either between marriages or as widows. In addition, imperial princesses were ordained as Daoist priestesses.

Equally noteworthy are a number of major Daoist goddesses who play key roles in the religion. Chief among them are Xiwangmu (Queen Mother of the West), best known for granting the power of immortality to the faithful, and Mazu, the virginal protectress of fishermen and merchants who is still very popular in Southeast China and Taiwan today. Some women were actually founders of Daoist sects, most notably Wei Huacun (252–334 C.E.) of the Shangqing [Highest Clarity] tradition and Zu Shu (most active during 889–904 C.E.), who initiated the Qingwei [Pure Subtlety] tradition. Sun Bu'er (1119–1182 C.E.) was a famous female disciple of the founder of the Quanzhen [Complete Perfection] sect who became a senior leader in the movement with the power to teach and ordain other female practitioners. (We examine these other Daoist groups more closely later in this chapter.)

No comparable number of women can be identified as prominent Confucians. It is thus accurate to conclude that women generally fare better in Daoism than in Confucianism.

Xiwangmu (Queen Mother of the West) is one of the most prominent female Daoist deities. She rewards her devout followers with immortality by feasting them with magical peaches.

THE HISTORY OF CONFUCIANISM AND DAOISM

As you may recall, the earliest time in Chinese history for which we have both written records and archaeological evidence is the Shang Dynasty, whose traditional dates are 1600–1046 B.C.E. The head of the Shang spiritual world was Shangdi, the ultimate benefactor of the royal house. Eventually, around the end of the second millennium B.C.E., the Shang Dynasty was toppled by the Zhou. The Zhou founders replaced Shangdi with *Tian* as the overarching spiritual authority. They claimed their victory as a mandate they received from *Tian*, ostensibly because of their moral worthiness. Early Zhou society was idealized as well ordered and harmonious, presided over by men of virtue.

The History of Confucianism

At the time of Confucius's birth, the entire political system and moral framework put in place by the early Zhou kings, as described in the previous section, was in disarray. Powerful feudal lords jockeyed for position to become the next *Tianzi*, the son of

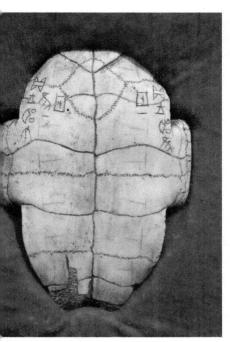

A Chinese oracle bone made of tortoise shell.

Tian, and to replace the current Zhou king. The more capable and ambitious among them actively sought the service of talented men outside the hereditary aristocratic circles, thereby creating upward social mobility for some among the commoners. Conversely, powerful lords could become commoners overnight as a result of their defeat by their rivals, creating a downward social spiral as well.

These critical social developments gave rise to the increasing prominence of a class of experts and specialists known as **shi** (men of service). Drawn from lower aristocratic or commoner backgrounds, they entered the employ of feudal lords and imperial rulers. The *shi* performed two major categories of duties: military and civil. The military men of service, the knights, were referred to as *wushi*, whereas their civilian counterparts, the scholars and ritualists, were known as *rushi*, or simply *ru*. *Ru* were scribes and recordkeepers, masters of religious ceremonies, as well as diviners and spiritual professionals. To perform their duties well, *ru* had to acquire expertise in history, poetry, religious rites, divination, dance, and music.

Confucius, as described in the commonly accepted biography, was just such a *ru* who was born into a family of former aristocrats in the feudal domain of Lu (located in present-day Shandong Province in north China). His father died when he was still an infant, so he had to do menial work as a young man to support himself, his sickly older brother, and his widowed mother. What enabled Confucius to lift himself up from poverty and anonymity was his desire for and success in scholarship. He apparently had an extraordinarily inquisitive mind and a voracious appetite for study, especially of the ancient texts of history, rituals, and poetry. By the age of thirty, he was well known for his expertise as a *ru*. His service in government was limited to a number of minor posts, but his greatest accomplishment was in his vocation as a teacher.

After age fifty, as he realized that the feudal lord of his native Lu did not value his service, Confucius left with a number of trusted disciples in tow and headed for other feudal domains. His hope was that other lords would embrace his ideas and would implement his political blueprint for restoring order to the world. For the next thirteen years he traveled all across northern China, going from one feudal domain to another in search of opportunities to carry out his reform proposals. He met with disappointment everywhere, at times suffering much indignity, deprivation, and even physical danger. In the twilight years of his life, he returned to his home state of Lu with his political ambition unfulfilled. He devoted the remainder of his life to teaching, writing, and editing the ancient texts. Confucius died in his early seventies.

Confucius is believed to have put the major classical works into their final form. He supposedly edited the *Book of Odes* and the *Book of History*, wrote important commentaries on the *Book of Changes*, and contributed to the *Record of Rites,* as well as the no-longer-extant *Book of Music*. He also supposedly authored a book on the history of the late Zhou period from the vantage point of his native state of Lu, which is titled

161

Chunqiu (*Spring and Autumn Annals*). The work covers the years 722–481 B.C.E., a period that has become known as the Spring and Autumn period in Chinese history.

Toward the end of his long life, Confucius gave a telling summary and assessment of his intellectual development as recorded in the *Analects*:

> At fifteen I set my mind on learning
> At thirty I had become established [as a *ru*]
> At forty I was free from doubts
> At fifty I knew the decree of *Tian* (*Tianming*)
> At sixty my ears became attuned [to what I heard from *Tian*]
> At seventy I could follow my heart's desires without transgressing
>   what was right
>
> —Analects 2:4

Statue of Confucius at the entrance to the Confucian Academy in Beijing, China.

This intellectual and spiritual autobiography of Confucius illustrates the pattern of his development from scholar to religious figure. His biography shows that he was a fully human figure with no claim to supernatural origin or power and was the consummate representative of the *ru* tradition and an exemplary teacher. Eventually, however, Confucius would be honored as a sage and the founder of China's most important philosophical and religious tradition.

Later Defenders of the Faith

After Confucius's time, the Chinese world took a turn for the worse. Warfare among the feudal states became more frequent and brutal. The centuries between Confucius's death in 479 and 221 B.C.E. are known as the Warring States period in Chinese history. During this time, Confucius's original vision of moral cultivation and benevolent government seemed impractical and quixotic. Internally, the Confucian tradition was rocked by self-doubt and resignation, as his *ru* followers became mere functionaries for the feudal lords, enjoying little influence or self-esteem. Externally, rival traditions such as Daoism and other more pragmatic schools competed for attention and attacked many of the Confucian ideas.

Into this picture came Mencius (371–289 B.C.E.?), the second most important figure in the Confucian tradition. As the most ardent defender of the faith, he articulated views that would be revered as definitive interpretations of what Confucius had outlined. We have already examined his contribution to the tradition in the section on the teachings of Confucianism in this chapter. His ideas would become orthodox for most future Confucians.

A younger contemporary of Mencius was Xun Qing (310–238 B.C.E.?), or Master Xun (Xunzi), who initially and for a span of several centuries exerted far greater influence on the Confucian movement than Mencius did. Xun Qing's rationalism and pragmatic approach to rituals and learning had given a decisively secular and worldly bent to the Confucian tradition, resulting in a noticeable neglect of its religious nature.

His view of human nature as evil also contradicted the Mencian version. Nevertheless, Xun Qing shared with Mencius an abiding faith in the transformative influence of moral cultivation and the perfectibility of humanity through self-effort. Eventually, however, later Confucians rejected Xun Qing as heterodox, and the text bearing his name was never recognized as a Confucian scripture.

Confucianism as Orthodoxy

When China was unified by the Qin (Ch'in) state in 221 B.C.E., the Confucian tradition was initially a target of state persecution. Its call for benevolent government and individual moral autonomy was rejected by the First Emperor of Qin as impractical and subversive. But the Qin Dynasty soon fell, replaced by the Han (206 B.C.E.–220 C.E.), a much more hospitable regime for Confucian teaching. By the middle of the second century B.C.E., the Confucian tradition finally surpassed all its competitors by becoming the state-designated orthodoxy, in recognition of its usefulness in fostering effective governance and enhancing social cohesiveness. Yet its orthodox status also necessitated fundamental changes in its orientation. From a teaching that called for high-minded personal moral cultivation and benevolent government, Confucianism in the Han Dynasty became a scholastic tradition and a tool for state control and patriarchal authoritarianism. In fulfilling that role, Confucius was showered with grandiose titles by subsequent generations of Chinese rulers who scrambled to outdo one another in their adoration of him, culminating in the breathtakingly exuberant title of "Ultimate

The Apricot Platform (Xingtan) is traditionally identified to be the location where Confucius lectured to his students.

Sage of Greatest Accomplishment, King of Manifest Culture" given to him by an emperor in 1308. "Temples" dedicated to Confucius were built in all the administrative and political centers throughout the empire. Nevertheless, these temples served more as memorials, such as those dedicated to Thomas Jefferson or Abraham Lincoln in the United States, than as places of worship, and Confucius himself remained by and large an exemplary human figure worthy of veneration, rather than a god promising salvation.

The Neo-Confucian Tradition

Although Confucianism served nominally as China's orthodoxy from the second century B.C.E. to the beginning of the twentieth century C.E., a span of over 2,000 years, it coexisted with Daoism and Buddhism during that entire period and at times was even overshadowed by them. Since the twelfth century C.E., however, through a revitalization movement known in the West as Neo-Confucianism, it regained the initiative over its Daoist and Buddhist rivals and became the predominant religious tradition in China until the modern era. Indeed, as advocated by its most eloquent representative, the scholar Zhu Xi (1130–1200), its new scriptural corpus, the Four Books, composed of the *Analects*, the *Mencius*, the *Great Learning*, and the *Doctrine of the Mean*, would constitute the main curriculum upon which the civil service examination of late imperial China would be based. Between 1313 and 1905, all aspiring scholars and government officials in China had to study and were examined on their mastery of

Soon after its elevation to orthodox status in Han Dynasty China (206 B.C.E.–220 C.E.), Confucianism found its way to the Korean Peninsula where, since the beginning of the Joseon Dynasty (1392–1897 C.E.), Confucianism had also become the orthodox ideology of the Korean state, strongly supported by the court and the official-scholar elites. Today, Confucianism's influence in South Korea remains vital. Unlike their fluctuating fate in China, Confucian values have retained their strong presence in South Korean society. Ancestral and familial devotion is an integral part of Korean ethics. As well, educational endeavor, evidenced by the severe competition for entrance into prestigious schools from kindergarten to college, is a national sport unsurpassed in other parts of Asia, including China, Japan, Taiwan, and Singapore. Indeed, one's filial obligation to the family is often a powerful motivating force to strive for academic success.

A national effort has been made in Korea to preserve and promote the filial concept as the foundational principle of the country's morality. Since 1973, May 8 has been designated Parents' Day, when the Ministry of Health and Welfare gives out Filial Piety Awards to exemplary individuals who perform extraordinarily meritorious duties for their parents. In November 2016, the National Assembly also passed a Filial Piety Law to ensure good treatment of ageing parents. Politicians and celebrities tout their filial devotion with no reserve or embarrassment.

Meanwhile, ancestral rites are carried out in the countryside to enhance the bond between the living and the dead. An example can be found in the Son lineage in Yangdong, a UNESCO World Cultural

Ancestral worship at the Naganeupseong Folk Village museum, South Korea.

Heritage site famous for its preservation of Confucian lifestyles and values. At the ancestral house built in 1457 C.E. by the founder of the lineage, Son So (1433–1484 C.E.), a high official in the Joseon court, the current members of the clan gather to commemorate their ancestors of the past six centuries. Dressed in traditional gown and hat, they offer food and wine, read recitations, and prostrate themselves in front of the ancestral tablets. Confucianism is alive and well in South Korea!

this set of canonical works, which provided the basis of their worldview and their outlook on life. To be sure, other voices within the Neo-Confucian movement would challenge Zhu Xi's interpretations, notably that of Wang Yangming (1472–1529). These scholars differed primarily in what they viewed as the best way to attain the same Neo-Confucian goal of "inner sagely moral perfection and outer political ability and administrative skills" (*neisheng waiwang*). Personal moral perfection and universal transformation of the human community formed one continuum in their ultimate religious quest.

Beginning in the fourteenth century, as China entered the late imperial period, the Confucian tradition became fossilized and rigid. The examinations were formulaic wordplays instead of genuine expressions of moral insight or sound administrative proposals. The entire Confucian tradition was turned into a mere tool of state control and social patronage. Political autocracy, patriarchal authoritarianism, and social exploitation were all carried out in its name.

Confucianism as Pan-Asiatic Tradition   Confucian texts had found their way beyond China no later than the turn of the Common Era, along with China's outward expansion both culturally and territorially. But it was in the form of Neo-Confucianism that this religious and philosophical tradition had exerted its most significant impact on China's neighbors such as Korea, Japan, and Vietnam. Thanks to the dynamic influence of Zhu Xi and his intellectual successors, Confucianism became the dominant philosophy and state orthodoxy, beginning with the Joseon Dynasty in Korea (fourteenth century), the Tokugawa Shogunate in Japan (seventeenth century), and the Nguyen Dynasty in Vietnam (nineteenth century). The social organizations, bureaucratic cultures, and religious assumptions of these Asian neighbors of China echoed much of what existed in China during its late imperial period (fourteenth to twentieth centuries).

Confucianism in the Modern World   Confucianism entered a period of sharp decline in the modern age. This process began after the Opium War of 1839–1842, in which China was handily defeated by Great Britain. Other foreign powers quickly followed suit to demand enormous concessions from a weakened and disgraced China. For China's patriotic young generation of intellectual elite, this humiliating development exposed the shortcomings of their Confucian heritage. Confucianism was blamed for China's political, social, and economic backwardness. As a result, the New Culture Movement that began in the second decade of the twentieth century made Confucianism their main target of assault. "Down with Confucius and sons!" was now the popular call for rebellion against the tradition. The logic was that unless the roots of the Confucian tradition were completely eradicated, China would not survive the challenge of modernity. Indeed, the birth of the Chinese Communist movement was in part attributable to this rebellious mode of thinking. From the perspective of the radical revolutionaries, Confucianism was a reactionary ideology of the ruling elite in China's feudal past that should be cast into the dustbin of history.

Confucian influence in East Asia.

But the obituary for Confucianism appears to have been written prematurely. Despite repeated and sometimes violent attempts to rid China of the harmful influence of Confucianism, the "anti-Confucius" campaign of the Cultural Revolution period (1966–1976) on mainland China being the most glaring example, the tradition has survived. As the opening vignette demonstrates, Confucianism as a religious tradition is still very much alive in contemporary China. The central importance of the family, the persistence of ancestral remembrance, and the value placed on education and self-improvement are evidence of the resilience of the Confucian ethos among many Chinese, and even East Asians in general. Some argue that the economic and industrial progress of the "Four Dragons" of Taiwan, South Korea, Hong Kong, and Singapore since the 1980s, and a similar development under way in China as well, might have been brought about by the Confucian heritage in these East Asian countries.

At the same time, an emergent group of "New Confucians," both inside and outside China, has been active as advocates for the revival of the Confucian teaching on philosophical and religious grounds. This group finds a new relevance for the Confucian tradition in the postmodern world on the ground that it expresses values of universal significance. These new defenders of the Confucian faith seek to rearticulate Confucianism for our time in the same way Confucians of the past had rearticulated it for theirs.

Equally notable is the new popularity enjoyed by Confucianism in China within the last decade, in part endorsed by the Chinese government. Academies devoted to the study of the Confucian tradition have been established, instruction on and the memorization of the *Analects* for school-age children are widely promoted, and even TV programs dedicated to the explanation of the relevance of Confucian teaching to contemporary Chinese society are eagerly viewed by a growing audience. The Chinese government also provides partial funding for the establishment of "Confucius Institutes" in European and North American universities to encourage interest in Chinese and Confucian studies.

The History of Daoism

As you have learned in the section on teachings in this chapter, Laozi and Zhuangzi, traditionally recognized as early founders of the Daoist tradition, were shadowy figures whose books bearing their names were actually anthologies containing divergent strands of thought. At best they could be considered proto-Daoists. Laozi was rumored to be a mysterious figure who was already an old man at the time of Confucius's birth (hence his name "Laozi," which literally can mean "old baby"). Late in his life, he reportedly left China beyond its western borders, but not before he dictated to a follower what came to be known as the *Daodejing*. Zhuangzi, whose historicity was more accepted, was believed to have been a fourth-century B.C.E. figure whose wit and irreverence made his comments on the Dao some of the most well-known and celebrated ones. His dreaming of being a butterfly, and upon waking, his questioning of the validity of his human identity was of course the most famous example of his relativistic thinking. In addition, numerous other early commentators of the Dao contributed to the formation of a "Daoist school" or "Daoist tradition" no later than the second century B.C.E.

The Deification of Laozi
A crucial development that led to the rise of Daoism as an organized religion was the divinization of Laozi. Sometime between the second century B.C.E. and the second century C.E., Laozi came to be revered as a human incarnation of the Dao. Remarkably, a belief arose that the Dao could now intervene in human affairs and directly and personally impart teaching to the faithful through its human form. As the Dao incarnate, Laozi was the object of worship, thereby making the Dao, for the first time, a human-like being that demanded and received religious

devotion. In a text entitled *Laozi bianhua jing* (*Scripture of the Transformations of Laozi*), compiled around the middle of the second century C.E., the various incarnations of Laozi over time were recounted. One such incarnation was in the form of a messianic figure dedicated to the salvation of the world; the title Laozi assumed in this case was Taishang Laojun, the Venerable Lord of the Most High.

Even more significantly, Laozi as *Taishang Laojun* could give instructions to selected individuals on the esoteric secrets of the Dao as part of his scheme to save the world. This deified and messianic Laozi thus turned the Daoist teaching into a divine revelation on salvation, which has since become a major tenet of organized Daoism. Once Laozi was venerated as the Dao incarnate, as well as a dispenser of redemptive instructions, Daoism became a salvational faith. A whole pantheon of deities, both in nature and within the human body, came to be worshiped as physical manifestations of the Dao and as agents of deliverance.

Beginning in the middle of the second century C.E., Daoism became an organized and large-scale movement among the common people. In the year 142 C.E., a man by the name of Zhang Ling (or Zhang Daoling) allegedly had a fateful encounter with the deified Laozi, who indicated to him that the world was in great trouble and that he, Zhang Ling, would be taught the right knowledge and proper practice to save it. Zhang Ling was to adopt the title of *Tianshi* (Celestial Master; see the section on the teachings of Daoism in this chapter), and the teaching he was to transmit would be called Orthodox Unity.

Zhang Ling supposedly transferred the *Tianshi* title to his descendants down through the ages until the present day (in Taiwan). The movement would be known variously as "Celestial Master," "Orthodox Unity," or "Five Bushels of Rice," the last derived from the amount of contributions members were expected to make to the organization at their initiation. During the second half of the second century C.E., the movement acted as a theocratic shadow government, providing material aid and physical healing services to its membership, in addition to offering a vague hope of messianic salvation. A contemporary and parallel movement, alternatively known as "Great Peace" (*Taiping*) and "Yellow Turbans" (*Huangjin*), took the messianic message more seriously and rebelled against the Han court in an attempt to usher in a new age. This movement was ruthlessly suppressed, even though the dream of *Taiping* would live on.

Later Daoist Historical Development   The Celestial Masters made an arrangement with the government in 215 C.E. whereby it abandoned its theocratic base in southwestern China and migrated closer to the political center in the north. But soon the Han Dynasty fell, and the subsequent short-lived regimes failed to maintain their power in the face of devastating invasions by nomadic non-Chinese groups such as the Huns, forcing the political and cultural elite to flee south toward the Yangzi River basin. The Celestial Masters followed and became popular there as well, setting up its headquarters on the Dragon and Tiger Mountain in Jiangxi Province in southeast China. During the ensuing Period of Disunion, three centuries when China was politically divided between north and south, Daoism entered a most creative period.

First, the Confucian elites gave new philosophical interpretations to both the *Daodejing* and the *Zhuangzi* that downplayed, if not totally eliminated, the religious elements on meditative transformations and magical physical transmutations in the two texts. Then someone who was much more closely related to the Celestial Masters, a certain Ge Hong (283–343 C.E.), who styled himself the "Master Who Embraces Simplicity" (*Baopuzi;* see his earlier mention in the section on the teachings of Daoism), vigorously asserted the possibility of attaining physical perfection in the form of immortality through various techniques involving alchemy.

But the most significant development in Daoism was in the area of brand-new textual revelations and ritual reforms. Responding both to the competition offered by a rapidly expanding Buddhism and to the need to distinguish itself from the "uncouth" and "coarse" practices of popular religion, Daoist leaders from aristocratic families created new texts and devised new rituals that they claimed were revealed to them through ecstatic encounters with an ever-growing number of Daoist deities.

In the south, the Shangqing (Highest Clarity) and the Lingbao (Numinous Treasure) set of texts and rituals began to emerge almost simultaneously in the fourth century C.E. While the Shangqing emphasized individual experiences of spiritual fulfillment through meditation and mental visualization, the Lingbao focused on ritual precision and use of talismans for the purpose of universal salvation, though the two overlapped considerably as well. In the north, similarly intense and creative activities also took place under the claim of new revelations from Taishang Laojun, the deified Laozi. A Tuoba (a people outside of the Great Wall) ruler, Emperor Taiwu of the Northern Wei Dynasty, was touted as the "Perfect Lord of Great Peace" and declared that the ideal world had arrived.

Common among the various Daoist groups of this period was the belief in and anticipation of an impending cataclysmic disaster that would radically transform the existing world. There was an anxious, yet exciting, expectation of the imminent arrival of a savior-like figure who would protect the devout followers from harm and ensure them a safe journey to the world to come—a perfect world populated by the faithful alone. This eschatological (vision of the end of time) and apocalyptic (revelation of a secret divine design) feature of the Daoist movement resembles many millennial traditions in other cultures.

Because of the proliferation of revelatory texts and the diverse array of rituals, the Period of Disunion also witnessed the first attempts made to classify and standardize them. The Lingbao master Lu Xiujing (406–477 C.E.) was the first to propose the notion of the "three caverns" to categorize the growing corpus of texts. This tripartite principle of organization was a conscious imitation of the *Tripitaka* (Three Baskets), the canonical corpus of Buddhist texts. Subsequent centuries and regimes would see the organization of the texts become more elaborate with the addition of "four supplements." This form of classification would constitute the framework of the entire Daoist canon, known as the ***Daozang***; the most complete and monumental version of this work was printed in 1445 C.E. in 480 sections, 1,120 titles, and over 5,300 volumes.

During China's medieval period, lasting from the seventh to the fourteenth centuries, organized Daoism enjoyed imperial patronage and became very much a part of the cultural life of the elite. Along with a popular Buddhism and the nominal state ideology of Confucianism, it was one of the "three teachings" of the realm. Its emphasis on nature and a free spirit informed much of the art and literature of the time. The breathtaking monochrome landscape paintings and cursive calligraphic art of the elite scholars reflected central Daoist values.

Several new orders also gained prominence during this time, the most influential among them being the Quanzhen sect (Complete Perfection). Founded by a man named Wang Zhe (1113–1170 C.E.), this school of Daoism embraced elements from both Confucianism and Buddhism. From Confucianism it took moral values, and from Buddhism it adopted monasticism and clerical celibacy. In addition to the *Daodejing*, the Confucian *Classic of Filial Piety* and the Buddhist *Heart Sutra* were given the highest prominence by this tradition. The Quanzhen sect was the most popular religious organization in Mongol Yuan China (1279–1368 C.E.), even overshadowing Buddhism. It is one of the only two Daoist groups that still exist today, the other being the Celestial Masters.

During the late imperial period in Chinese history (fourteenth to nineteenth centuries), Daoism was put on the defensive by the triumphant Neo-Confucians. Its clergy was tightly controlled by the state through the highly regulated issuance of ordination certificates. Though individual emperors might have supported Daoism, as evidenced by the printing of the complete *Daozang* in 1445, as a religious tradition it was eclipsed by Confucianism. Although the Confucian elite grudgingly acknowledged the "philosophic" brilliance of the *Daodejing* and the *Zhuangzi*, they regarded organized Daoist groups as nothing more than a corrupted form of pristine, original Daoism. Organized Daoism was marginalized as superstition, unworthy of elite attention. This contempt for Daoism continued beyond the imperial period, was intensified in the early twentieth century, and was adopted as official policy under the Communist regime in 1949.

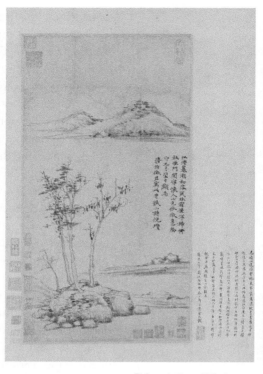

This painting, *Wind among the Trees on the Riverbank* by Ni Zan (1306–1374), is best known for the quietude and balance in nature it expresses. China, Yuan Dynasty (1271–1368), dated 1363.

Daoism as a Pan-Asiatic Tradition Like its Confucian counterpart, Daoism is not confined to the Chinese mainland. The proto-Daoist texts of *Laozi* and *Zhuangzi* had certainly reached Korea no later than the Goryeo Period (918–1392), even though Buddhism was the dominant faith of the time. By the ensuing Joseon Dynasty (1392–1897), when Confucianism was the state orthodoxy, Daoism in the form of shamanism, mountain worship, and immortality practices had become an integral part of Korean folk religion. Even today, the national flag of South Korea contains the Taegeuk symbol of yin-yang complementarity and four of the eight divinatory trigrams. Similarly, in Japan, Daoism was never a dominant, independent tradition when compared with Confucianism and Buddhism. Rather, in its diffused form, it has combined with certain Buddhist groups and indigenous Shinto cults to form specific folk religious traditions since the Tokugawa period (1600–1868). Specifically, the Shūgendō (shamanistic mountain ascetics) and the Kōshin religious practice of controlling the decaying agents of the human body to prevent them from shortening the human lifespan display unmistakable Daoist influences. In Southeast Asia as well, Daoism has found its way into the beliefs of the Xiantian Dao (Way of Prior Heaven) of Malaysia and the Caodai (High Power) tradition in Vietnam. Both are movements promising deliverance from the current age of decadence and corruption.

Daoist influence in East Asia.

Daoism's global reach is evident in two popular practices worldwide: the new age art of building-siting and interior design known by the Chinese name "feng shui," and martial art exercises practiced for their promised benefits in health, mental sharpness, and self-defense. As you may recall, a central concept in Daoist teaching is qi, the vital force and life energy that links all life forms to nature. Feng shui, literally meaning "wind and water," is based on the belief in the efficacy of qi to allow humans to live and thrive in their natural environment. Similarly, Chinese martial art forms such as tai chi, Wudang fists, and qigong (cultivation of qi) call for the harnessing of qi in reducing stress, calming the mind, and protecting oneself from attackers.

By siting a house, a tomb, or a business in an auspicious spot where positive qi is deemed to flow unobstructed, feng shui practitioners believe they will enjoy good fortune and good health. Conversely, they also consider rearranging furniture, mirrors, and doorways in certain directions, or changing the interior partitions of one's dwellings to be effective in warding off evil influences and averting disasters. A whole new industry and an array of merchandise have sprung up to help real estate developers such as Donald Trump to enhance sale of their properties to rich feng shui believers, and Hong Kong Disneyland is known to have moved its main gate by 12 degrees to accommodate the feng shui sensitivities of the local theme park attendants.

The popularity of Chinese martial arts in movies and in exercise gyms, particularly when they feature themes of the soft overcoming the hard, the yielding winning over the aggressive, can be attributed to the global acceptance of the Daoist teachings of the Dao as passive and nonassertive, yet it endures and lasts. The graceful movements of tai chi and the subtle strength of qigong meditational steps have attracted a worldwide following.

A Hong Kong building with a hole to allow the smooth flow of *qi*.

In Paris, France, people gather to practice qi gong and tai chi exercises.

This painting of the poet Li Bo (Li Bai, 701–762) shows him as a Daoist immortal.

Political authorities have embraced both Confucianism and Daoism to legitimize their rule and to impose order on society. How did these religions fare when compared with other major world religions?

Daoism Today Because of elite hostility and government neglect, if not active persecution, Daoism as a religious tradition has generally fared poorly in the modern period. Although the intellectuals still recognized the philosophical ideas in the *Laozi* and the *Zhuangzi* as properly Daoist, they totally ignored the meditative exercises and amazing magical powers of the Daoist seekers of perfection discussed in the two texts, along with the entire corpus of the *Daozang*, the Daoist canon. Daoism was lumped with shamanic popular religion and viewed with disdain. The New Culture Movement of the 1910s and 1920s regarded both Daoism and Confucianism as unwelcome remnants of China's feudal past. The Cultural Revolution (1966–1976) that did so much damage to Confucianism also proved devastating to Daoism. Many historic Daoist shrines and sites were destroyed or sacrilegiously defaced, and all performances of Daoist rituals and liturgies were banned. For all intents and purposes, Daoism as an organized religion ceased to exist in mainland China. Yet the tradition survived amidst China's nebulous folk religion. It also continued to exist, if only barely, outside China among Chinese communities in Taiwan, Hong Kong, and Southeast Asia. Since the late 1970s, however, a Daoist revival of sorts has begun. Daoist ceremonies are once again openly observed in China, and a new generation of Daoist priests has been trained to carry on the tradition and to rebuild the shrines. Academic study of Daoism, primarily by Japanese and French scholars at the beginning, and now joined by Americans and Chinese themselves, has created new understanding of the tradition from the point of view of both doctrines and practices. Some of the scholars have actually become ordained Daoist priests of either the Celestial Master or the Quanzhen tradition to access more accurate and authoritative interpretations of Daoism.

CONFUCIANISM AND DAOISM AS WAYS OF LIFE

The two Chinese religions discussed in this chapter are not just collections of precepts and beliefs, developed over a long history. More importantly, they are lived and practiced traditions. It is in the living and practicing of the two traditions that their true meaning and value can be gauged.

Confucian Rituals

From the very beginning, the Confucian tradition has put great emphasis on ritual as a crucial expression of humanity. As "moral behavior," rituals teach people to conduct themselves with dignity and decorum, making them authentically human. As "holy rites," rituals enable humans to communicate effectively with the spiritual powers and to interact harmoniously with one another. It is in the latter, more overtly religious sense that Confucian ritual is addressed in this section.

In addition to the mundane rituals of familial and social interaction with other human beings in accordance with the prescribed rules outlined in the classic texts, the most important aspect of religious ritual in Confucianism in the premodern period was the sacrificial presentation, or the making of offerings to the spirits, including ancestors, in the form of animals, other food and drink, even jade and silk. These presentation rituals were performed at different levels—the state, the community, and the family. The grandest of the rituals were, of course, conducted at the state level. And chief among the state rituals were those connected with sacrifices to *Tian* and *Di*—and to Confucius once his teaching was exalted to orthodoxy.

The Temple of Tian (*Tiantan*), where the Chinese emperor prayed to *Tian* on behalf of his subjects and in his capacity as "Son of Tian," is now a popular park in Beijing.

The Hall of Praying for an Abundant Harvest (*Qi'nian dian*), Temple of Tian (*Tiantan*), Beijing. The whole complex was built in 1420 under Emperor Yongle and restored in 1530 and 1751. Here the emperor celebrated the sacrifice to *Tian* for a good harvest. The decorated ramp between the two stairways was reserved for the emperor's palanquin.

VOICES: An Interview with Jason Ch'ui-hsiao Tseng

Jason Ch'ui-hsiao Tseng is a Taiwanese man in his fifties with a master's degree from an American university. He engages in educational exchange for Chinese students wishing to study in the United States.

Do you consider yourself a Confucian or a Daoist?

I do not consider myself exclusively one or the other. Both have influenced me deeply, and I regard their teachings as equally valid and complementary.

How is that possible, as their teachings often conflict with each other?

They are not in conflict. They merely represent the polar opposite of the other. They complete each other. For most Chinese, there is no necessity to choose one or the other. We think of them as the two sides of a coin—without both there is no coin. The two together constitute our native Chinese religious outlook. As a matter of fact, we also consider Buddhist teaching a third way of guiding our religious life. These teachings are generally not jealous of one another. They do not demand total exclusive devotion. They provide meaning to different aspects of our lives. There is religious pluralism for most Chinese.

Jason Ch'ui-hsiao
Tseng

How is that so?

We do not believe that one teaching alone corners the market. As a respectful son and an upright citizen, I embrace Confucian values. They teach me to put family and society ahead of myself and to value education as the most important undertaking to improve myself. In my views on how my body works, how my health can be maintained, how different ingredients should be used to achieve balance in my food, and how I can relate to the spirits in the invisible world, I follow the Daoist teaching. And Buddhism gives me hope for a good afterlife. Together they make me a complete person.

Sacrifice to *Tian* and *Di*   *Tian*, you should recall, had been the source of legitimate political power since the Zhou Dynasty. As son of *Tian*, the Chinese ruler carried out *Tian*'s mandate to exercise his imperial prerogatives over the entire realm under *Tian*. The worship of *Tian* thus became the ruler's exclusive privilege and obligation. Later, with Confucianism imbued with yin-yang cosmological ideas in the Han Dynasty, *Tian*, the yang element, was paired up with *Di* (earth), the yin element, and worship of *Di* was added, though with much less pomp and ostentation.

In late imperial China, the worship of *Tian* and *Di* took place annually. On the day of the summer solstice, the emperor made a sacrifice to *Tian* at the Temple of *Tian* (*Tiantan*) located in the southern suburb of Beijing. Correspondingly, on the day of the winter solstice, worship of *Di* was conducted at the Temple of Di (*Ditan*) located at the northern suburb of the capital. The rituals involved nine steps, including purification of the participants, performance of dance and music, reading of prayer documents, and offering of sacrifices.

Sacrifice to Confucius The state cult of Confucius began in the Han Dynasty with the designation of Confucianism as orthodoxy. The descendants of Confucius were first given a hereditary fief, and later the Master himself was given increasingly laudatory titles and ducal honors. Temples commemorating Confucius were ordered to be built in every county and major city throughout the empire. In time, wooden tablets commemorating some of his prominent students, as well

Confucius serves as an object of veneration and commemoration. He is the "Utmost Sage and Late Teacher," as the tablet in front of his statue declares.

as those of successive generations of Confucian worthies such as Mencius and Zhu Xi, were installed in these temples. Although the frequency and elaborateness of the sacrificial rites conducted at these temples varied with time and locale, the traditional birthday of Confucius (the twenty-seventh day of the ninth month) was generally observed. These rites involved dance and music accompanied by drums and bells, proclamations and didactic lectures given by local dignitaries and government officials, and offerings of incense and animals.

The most magnificent Temple of Confucius, as can be expected, is located in his native county of Qufu, not far from Mount Tai in present-day Shandong Province. Built and maintained at state expense, the Qufu Confucian Temple has a main building with a palatial design supported by dragon-decorated pillars, all meant to accord the Master the highest honor comparable to that of a ruler. Stone steles are engraved with the calligraphy or essays of various emperors in Chinese history, all lauding the moral and cultural accomplishments of the sage. This Confucian Temple in Qufu was a pilgrimage site for generations of scholars and aspiring literati and is still popular among tourists today.

Family Rituals The custom of commemorating and honoring ancestors in China goes back to the dawn of recorded Chinese history. But Confucianism, with its discussion of *xiao* (filial piety), lent further theoretical support to the practice. The Confucian teaching maintains that one's filial obligation to parents and ancestors is the core of one's humanity. Thus, while the state monopolized the worship of *Tian/Di* and the educated elites controlled the sacrifice to Confucius, all people could participate in the family ritual of honoring parents and ancestors. Sacrifice to the ancestors is especially important because it gives the descendants a sense of belonging and continuity and thereby a religious appreciation of the chain of life that links them to their forebears.

Confucius's tombstone boldly declares that he is the "Ultimate Sage of Greatest Accomplishment, King of Manifest Culture."

In the *Family Rituals*, compiled by the Neo-Confucian scholar Zhu Xi, detailed step-by-step liturgies are provided for ceremonies associated with ancestor worship. Chapters describe daily "looking in" on the ancestors; more elaborate semimonthly "visits," "reports" on major family events such as births, weddings, and deaths; and formal "offerings" on festival days and seasonal sacrifices. The following is a summarized version of Zhu Xi's instructions for the rites of making seasonal offerings to ancestors.[6]

In the preparatory phase, the date for the sacrifice is selected by divination performed in front of the ancestral shrine in the preceding month. Then, three days before the event, the designated leading man and woman will each lead family members of their respective gender to perform purification rituals in their designated quarters, men in the outer and women in the inner. The men also make the main hall sparkling clean and arrange the place settings for each generation properly. The women will set the incense burner and incense box, as well as prepare wine racks and containers, along with meat plates for the ancestors.

On the day of the event, when the sun is fully up, the wooden tablets containing the names of the different generations of ancestors, separated by gender, are moved to their proper places in the main hall. Then the spirits of the ancestors are greeted, and food is offered to them three times. The ancestors are entreated to eat the food and are given privacy to do so, with everyone from the presiding man on down exiting the main hall, and the door is closed. After a suitable interval, the master of ceremony coughs three times to announce his intention to reenter; then he opens the door, and everyone else comes back in. Tea is offered to the ancestors to supposedly cleanse their mouths. Then the presiding man receives the sacrificed food from the master of ceremony. With reverence, the presiding man bows and prostrates himself to taste the food and drink the wine. Then the entire group takes leave of the ancestral spirits, returns their tablets to their original locations, and clears away the offering tables. The presiding man supervises the division of the sacrificial food to be consumed by all the family members later that day. This brings an end to the ritual of the ancestral sacrifice. The intended effect of this ritual is apparent—to create familial cohesiveness and to recognize the unseverable bond between the living and the deceased family members. You may notice that the scene of *qingming* observance at the beginning of this chapter has similar rituals.

Daoist Practices

Whether it is the amazing feats of the immortals and perfected beings in the *Daodejing* and the *Zhaungzi*, or whether it is the physical-spiritual regimens and alchemical techniques of the later Daoists, it is always understood and expected that the beliefs need to be put into practice to be truly meaningful. Promoting communal harmony, delaying and stopping physical deterioration, and attaining actual immortality involve a whole spectrum of undertakings and practices.

Daoist Communal Festivals and Liturgies

To ordinary believers—those who have no hope of going through the rigor and expenses of pursuing immortality—the Daoist religion as practiced by the Celestial Master sect offers the promise of health, long life, even collective salvation. Membership in these organized movements during the tumultuous centuries after the collapse of the Han Dynasty meant a special sense of belonging to a select group destined to survive those trying times. Noteworthy in their beliefs was the idea of chosenness—that they constituted a special group of people who, because of their embrace of an apocalyptic ideology, were favored by the gods. Referred to as *zhongmin* (seed people), they confirmed their "elect" status through their participation in collective rituals called ***zhai*** (fasts). Lasting several days each, these fasts involved abstinence from food, public performance of penance for past moral transgressions, submission of written memorials to request pardon from the deities, and communal prayers for the salvation of the faithful.

The Fast of Mud and Soot in China's medieval period reflected the general tenor of *zhai* rituals. With hair disheveled and face smeared with soot, believers prostrated themselves like condemned criminals before a raised altar to ask for forgiveness from the gods. Consumed by their agitated emotions, many fell to the ground and rolled about amidst loud wailings. Such public acts of penance were performed to earn pardon and spiritual merit. Another liturgical ritual was the Fast of the Yellow Register, during which the participants performed penitence for their ancestors

VISUAL GUIDE
Daoism and Confucianism

This is an iconic image of Confucius as a learned scholar and an exemplar of human moral accomplishment. Traditionally, the Chinese did not see religion as a separate realm of activity. Hence, the pursuit of scholarship and the enactment of moral behavior within the family and community were very much part of their religious experience.

Though not strictly Confucian, this yin-yang symbol surrounded by the eight trigrams does reflect the Chinese belief in the complementarity of opposites and the harmonious unity of the cosmos. More than any other visual symbol, it represents Chinese religiousness.

Family cohesion and respect for elders are central Confucian values. A daughter and her husband pay a visit to her parents on Chinese New Year's Day to renew her kinship tie with her natal family.

Statue of Laozi carved out of a huge rock in Fujian Province, China. This legendary founder of Daoism symbolizes wisdom and irreverence for conventional thinking. He is understood as the yin to Confucius's yang, and the image of passive acceptance of what nature has ordained to Confucius's active attempt at improving society.

(continued)

Chinese tai chi exercise is perhaps the most representative expression of Daoist beliefs in the human body as a microcosm of the universe. Through harnessing the qi of nature and bringing it into the body for attaining balance and improving health, the tai chi master demonstrates the intimate relationship between humans and the cosmos.

Acupuncture is a good expression of the Daoist belief in the circulation of qi in the human body. By inserting the needles into critical nodal points in the qi circuitry, pain can be diverted and the rejuvenating energy of the body can heal the sick parts.

going back seven or nine generations. The names of deceased ancestors, entered in registers, were read by the officiating priests and were then considered to have gained postmortem immortality. In this way, the filial obligation of the faithful was ritually expressed.

Another communal ceremony, the *jiao* (offering), is popular even in the present day. This public liturgy is usually performed by Daoist priests on behalf of the entire community to petition the gods to bestow good fortune, health, and prosperity on all. Sometimes labeled as a rite of cosmic renewal, the *jiao* brings together the community to participate collectively in a religious ritual that is loud, colorful, and dramatic. Depending on the needs of the community, a *jiao* is conducted at periodic intervals (ranging from once a year for the affluent communities to once every sixty years for the less well-to-do communities) or as special thanks to the deities for having successfully protected the entire community by, for example, warding off an epidemic.

A *jiao* ceremony usually lasts several days. The dates are chosen for their astrological auspiciousness. Daoist priests are contracted to perform the ritual with efficacy and precision. Prior to the official dates of the ceremony, the priests submit "memorials" to the celestial bureaucracy of the gods to give notice of the scheduled *jiao*. Then the location at which the liturgy takes place, usually both the inside and the outside of the largest local temple or shrine, is marked off by hoisted lanterns to signal the enclosure of the sacred space. Afterward, the local deities are invited to take their honored seats within the enclosure; their statues or wooden tablets are carried there by community elders. The procession of the deities through the community is accompanied by lion or dragon dances, made even more boisterous with lots of firecrackers. Then the ritual proper begins in earnest.

Reenacting the beginning of the cosmos in a ritual called *fendeng* (spreading the light), the chief Daoist priest, in full vestment, blows on a buffalo horn and rings his "thunder" bell, to the accompaniment of an entire music ensemble, and repeats the forty-second chapter of the *Daodejing* by announcing that "the Dao gives birth to the One [Being, Existence]; the One brings forth the Two [Yin and Yang]; the Two give rise to the Three [*Tian, Di*, and Humans]; and the Three engender the Ten Thousand Things [world of multiplicity and diversity]." Entering a meditation-induced trance, the priest transforms his body into the body of the Dao. He takes prescribed steps that are dancelike,

A group of Daoist priests perform a ritual service for a member of the community.

spins on himself, and sanctifies the ritual enclosure by requesting the dispatch of heavenly troops to guard the place. At the same time, to placate the wandering ghosts in the neighborhood and to warn them against intrusion into the sacred ground, he provides a feast for them while lecturing them on the reasons for their suffering.

At some point during the ceremony, the names of every member of the community will be posted on a roster and read aloud by the priests to signal their financial and spiritual support of this elaborate and expensive event, as well as to ensure that they will receive their share of the benediction of the gods. There is great interest among the community members in checking the posted name list to make sure that the names are written accurately and that they have not been inadvertently left out.

The climax of the ceremony occurs when the highest of the Daoist deities, the Three Purities and the Jade Emperor, are invited to take part in the ceremony. Piercing prepared talismans with his sword, the chief Daoist priest burns them with great dramatic effect to appeal to the august deities. Once the gods are properly seated, a blanket pardon of every immoral act committed by every member of the community between the last *jiao* and the present one is announced. In grateful response, the community performs a public charitable act of "releasing life"—setting cages of captured birds free and returning to a stream buckets full of live fish. On the last night of the ceremony, a grand feast for all ghosts trapped in hell is hosted by the community. Once again, the Daoist priests exhort the ghosts to behave themselves and to refrain from wreaking havoc in the lives of the living. Balance is restored among the worlds of humans, gods, and ghosts. The rite concludes with sending off the celestial gods and the local deities, distributing food and buns to the spectators, and performing operas for the entertainment of all.[7]

Confucianism and Daoism have together shaped personal conduct and social behavior in China. How do the Chinese allow themselves to be guided by two very distinct religious traditions in their daily lives without much sense of tension and conflict?

CONCLUSION

In this chapter, we have invited you to explore the religious world of the Chinese through a study of their two native religious traditions—Confucianism and Daoism. We have highlighted the religious nature of both traditions. In the case of Confucianism, it is not just a teaching of ethics and good government but is in fact informed by a deep religious faith in a numinous Absolute—*Tian*. Moreover, this faith mandates dedicated human effort to transform the individual and the world. Also documented is the historical unfolding of this tradition over the course of more than 2,000 years. At the same time, the ritual dimensions of this tradition are identified, ranging from the ornate and solemn state observations of the past to the simple familial ceremonies that are still practiced today.

As for Daoism, it is not confined to the metaphysical discussions of the *Daodejing* and the *Zhuangzi*, but rather is richly informed by an elaborate belief in the cosmological importance of the human body, a salvational message of communal redemption, and an abiding yearning for physical transformation and perfection. Moreover, we have examined the historical progression of this tradition as it meandered through the different periods in China. We have also documented the colorful ritual performance of Daoism in the community.

Both Confucianism and Daoism (along with a Chinese version of Buddhism and a syncretized amalgamation of the three teachings in the form of folk religion) have contributed to shaping the Chinese religious mindset. Both have experienced ups and downs in their respective history, at times being the dominant ideology of the realm and at times being eclipsed by other traditions in influence. Nevertheless, both have maintained their central importance to the Chinese people, at no time risking irrelevance or extinction. Despite suffering a brutal critique and rejection in the twentieth century by the modern Chinese intellectual elite in the name of rationalism and egalitarianism, both have remained resilient among the common people. In fact, there are signs of their revival and rejuvenation at the dawn of the twenty-first century. Confucian values continue to inform Chinese familial ethics and social and political behavior, and Daoist concerns for the well-being of the human body and harmonious relationship with the spiritual world shape contemporary Chinese attitudes toward health, medicine, cuisine, and the environment. Indeed, these values and concerns have gone beyond the Chinese world to attain worldwide relevance.

As a final point, we have attempted to justify the inclusion of both Confucianism and Daoism in the study of world religions. Confucianism treats the fulfillment of the human potential as an ultimate concern. The tenacity with which Confucianism exhorts people to strive for human perfection in our mundane lives as a form of divine calling—thereby making the secular sacred—demonstrates an interesting type of religiosity. In addition, its assertion of human coequality with the divine offers an intriguing contrast with other religious traditions. Daoism is similarly a significant world religion. Its perception of the divine Absolute as a life-generating, feminine entity;

its call for a harmonious coexistence between humans and nature; its emphasis on healthy improvement of the human body as a religious mission; and its promotion of communal cohesiveness through ritual participation make it all the more relevant in a postindustrial world. Both traditions fit the definition of religion suggested by Bruce Lincoln and discussed in Chapter 1 of this text. Both possess the four "domains" of discourse, practice, community, and institution.

SEEKING ANSWERS

What Is Ultimate Reality?

Confucianism and Daoism share the same cosmological myth, inherited from ancient China. The natural world is not in a fallen state. There is no almighty creator, nor is there a demonic counterpart. There is no definite beginning of the world, and there is no predicted end. Instead, the world unfolds cyclically and operates like a pendulum, arcing between two extremes and alternating between two polar but complementing opposites. Human beings are not caught in a tug of war between good and evil, and the side they choose does not result in a permanent fate in paradise or hell. Emphasis is placed on balance, coexistence, and harmony. For the Confucians, ultimate reality is *Tian* (Neo-Confucians sometimes use the term *Taiji*, Supreme Ultimate). *Tian* is the procreator of the cosmos and all the myriad things in it. Moreover, *Tian* has a special relationship with humans and communicates with chosen individuals its grand design for humanity. This communication does not occur through dramatic and ecstatic encounters such as that between god and the prophets in Abrahamic traditions. Instead, *Tian*'s message is discerned by perceptive and insightful human representatives through their keen observation of nature and diligent study of human affairs as recorded

in history and enacted in the present. It is in this sense that Confucianism is not a revelatory religion in the conventional sense. In contrast, Daoism, in its organized form, is a revelatory religion. Its ultimate reality is the Dao, the "mother of the universe." Originally formless and undifferentiated, it later takes on human and divine forms, giving instructions and revealing texts to the faithful. Daoism can also be salvational in its message, complete with prescriptions for repentance and thanksgiving.

How Should We Live in This World?

Both Confucianism and Daoism have inherited the ancient Chinese religious view regarding the human condition: human beings, like everything else in the cosmos, are the product of the interaction between yin and yang. They have a corporeal aspect (the body) and an incorporeal aspect (the "soul"), consisting of *hun* and *po*. There is no notion of any alienation from or disobedience of an almighty god; thus, there is an absence of sin. However, this does not mean that human beings are already perfect and need no improvement from their current state. A yawning gap still exists between human beings as they are and human beings as they should or can become. For the Confucians, the right way to live is to live ethically, in accordance with

(continued)

the moral dictates of *Tian*. Humans alone have the responsibility to model and exemplify *Tian*'s moral imperative, thereby making themselves partners in creating harmony and prosperity throughout the cosmos. In concentric circles extending outward from the individual, moral behavior will transform the family, the community, and the world at large. "Do not do unto others what you do not want done to you" is the minimal moral guide for correct living in Confucianism. For the Daoists, the right way to live is to live healthily. To be sure, ethical behavior is part of desirable living, but Daoists also emphasize the human body as a microcosm reflecting perfectly the macrocosm of the cosmos. Thus, taking care of one's body through both internal and external "alchemical" means is a way of living life properly in accord with the Dao. At the same time, focusing on the intimate connection between the individual, the community, and the cosmos, Daoists prescribe diet, exercise, and preservation of health and energy as a way of approaching the holy.

What Is Our Ultimate Purpose?

Confucians and Daoists differ in their answers to this question. For the Confucians, humans are potentially perfect and inclined toward the good. Yet, this potentiality and inclination need to be rigorously nurtured and developed through scholastic learning, moral introspection, and ethical behavior. Learning to be authentically human, to enact the "way" of *Tian*, is the way to improve the human condition and to

perfect it. The highest achievement of human endeavor is to become the coequal of the divine ultimate—*Tian*.

Daoists regard humans on the same level as all the myriad things—they are all concrete expressions of the Dao, the numinous Absolute. Through their ignorance or negligence, however, humans dissipate their primordial endowment of the vital energy, the qi, resulting in their vulnerability to disease and death. Consequently, the Daoist prescription for improving the human condition is to engage in exercises and rituals designed to replenish the body and the spirit, making it once again as immortal as the Dao. Confucians and Daoists also diverge in their beliefs about what happens at the end of life. Confucius himself famously brushed aside a student's inquiry on death. He just did not consider it an issue worthy of exploration. His priority was to pay exclusive attention to life and how to improve it. This "prejudice" has affected all subsequent Confucians, none of whom showed any strong interest in addressing death or its religious meaning. Even the Confucian practice of ancestor worship and respecting the dead can be explained as a way of bypassing the issue, as dead ancestors are treated very much as living members of the lineage and the family. Daoists, in contrast, confront the topic of mortality by emphasizing the possibility and desirability of immortality. Even with the appearance of death as inevitable, Daoists explain it as a stage of transformation to a higher plane of existence, a way of attaining true immortality. Thus, Daoists equally ignore the deeper meaning of death.

REVIEW QUESTIONS

For Review

1. Why should the term Confucianism be used with caution? In what way may it be a misnomer?
2. How do Confucianism and Daoism define such terms as *Tian*, *Dao*, and *de* differently?
3. Why is Daoism more than the teachings of the *Daodejing* and the *Zhuangzi*?
4. Why is Confucianism a religious tradition despite its lack of concern for the afterlife?

For Further Reflection

1. In what ways do Confucianism and Daoism complement each other, and in what ways do they oppose each other?
2. Compare and contrast the Confucian notion of *Tian* with the Christian concept of God.
3. Compare and contrast the Daoist notion of Dao with the Hindu concept of Brahman.
4. Having examined Confucianism and Daoism, have you arrived at any conclusion regarding Chinese religiosity? How does it differ from that of other religious traditions?

GLOSSARY

dantian (dahn'-tee'ən) "Fields for the refinement of the immortal pill"; major nodal points in the human body where the "pill" of immortality can be refined through alchemical means.

dao (dow) A fundamental concept in Chinese religion, literally meaning the "path" or the "way." In Confucianism, it specifically refers to the entire ideal human order ordained by the numinous Absolute, *Tian*. In Daoism, it is the primary source of the cosmos, the very ground of all beings.

Daodejing (dow'-duh-jing) Basic Daoist scripture, lit. "The Scripture of the Way and Its Potent Manifestation"; also known as the Book of *Laozi*, the name of its purported author.

Daozang (dow' zahng) Literally "Treasury of the Dao," this is the Daoist Canon that contains the entire corpus of Daoist texts. The most complete version, still in use today, was first published in 1445.

de (duh) Another fundamental concept in Chinese religions, meaning "virtue" or "potency." In Confucianism, it is the charismatic power of the ruler or the man of virtue, while in Daoism it means the concrete manifestation of the dao.

fangshi (fahng-shər) "Magicians" who allegedly possessed the recipe for immortality.

Five Classics The five canonical works of Confucianism designated in the Han Dynasty. They are the *Book of Odes*, *Book of History*, *Book of Changes*, *Record of Rites*, and *Spring and Autumn Annals*.

Four Books The four texts identified by the Neo-Confucian Zhu Xi as fundamental in understanding the Confucian teaching. Between 1313 and 1905, they made up the curriculum for the civil service examination. They are *Analects*, *Mencius*, *Great Learning*, and *Doctrine of the Mean*.

gui (gwei) Ghosts and demons; malevolent spirits.

jiao (jee'au) Daoist communal sacrificial offerings to signal cosmic renewal and collective cohesion.

junzi (ju'un zee) The personality ideal in Confucianism; the noble person.

li (lee) Etiquette and proper manners; rituals and holy rites.

ming (*see* **Tianming**)

neidan (nay'-dahn) Daoist "internal" alchemy designed to attain immortality through meditation, breath control, gymnastics, diet, and massage.

neisheng waiwang (nay'-sheng' wī'-wahng) Neo-Confucian ideal of "inner sagely moral perfection and outer political skills."

qi (chee) Breath, force, power, material energy.

ren (rən) Human-heartedness, benevolence; the unique moral inclination of humans.

ru (rōō) Scribes and ritual performers of the Zhou period; later used exclusively to refer to Confucians.

Shangdi (shahng'-dee) The August Lord on High of the Shang period.

shen (shən) Gods and deities; benevolent spirits.

shengren (shəng rən) (or **sheng**) The Confucian sage, the epitome of humanity.

shi (shər) Men of service; lower-ranking civil and military officials in the Zhou period.

Tian (tee'ən) The transcendent, numinous entity in ancient Chinese religion; the conscious Will that regulates the cosmos and intervenes in human affairs; conventionally translated as "Heaven."

Tianming The mandate or command of *Tian* that confers political legitimacy to the ruler; also understood by Confucians as the calling to morally improve oneself and to transform the world.

Tianshi (tee'ən shər) "Celestial Master"; reference to a Daoist salvational figure, as well as an organized movement.

waidan (wī dahn) Daoist "external" alchemy involving refining of "pills" with herbs and minerals for ingestion so that immortality can be attained.

wuwei (wōō way) Daoist notion of action without intention; actionless action.

wuxing (wōō shing) The five elemental phases of metal, wood, water, fire, and soil that mutually support and overcome one another.

xian (shee'ən) Daoist immortals and perfected individuals.

xiao (shee'au) Filial piety; respect and care for parents and ancestors.

xinzhai (shin jī) "Fasting of the Mind" in the *Zhuangzi*.

yang (young) Lit. the south-facing side of a mountain, representing the energy that is bright, warm, dry, and masculine.

yangsheng (young shəng) Daoist techniques of nourishing life and attaining immortality.

yin Lit. the north-facing side of a mountain, representing the energy that is dark, cold, wet, and feminine.

zhai (jī) Daoist "fasts" designed to seek redemption of transgressions by the gods.

ziran (zee'-rahn) Daoist notion of natural spontaneity.

zuowang (zoh'-wahng) "Sitting and Forgetting" in the *Zhuangzi*.

SUGGESTIONS FOR FURTHER READING

de Bary, William Theodore. *The Trouble with Confucianism.* Cambridge, MA: Harvard University Press, 1991. A thought-provoking discussion of the "prophetic voice" in Confucianism.

Fingarette, Herbert. *Confucius: The Secular as Sacred.* New York: Harper Torchbooks, 1972. A creative interpretation of the Confucian notion of *li* as holy rites.

Gardner, Daniel K., trans. *The Four Books: The Basic Teachings of the Later Confucian Tradition.* Indianapolis, IN: Hackett Publishing, 2007. A handy translation of important excerpts from the scriptural corpus of Confucianism.

Gardner, Daniel K. *Confucianism: A Very Short Introduction.* New York: Oxford University Press, 2014. A pocket-size introduction to the Confucian tradition for beginners.

Kirkland, Russell. *Taoism: The Enduring Tradition.* London: Routledge, 2004. An impassioned monograph by a specialist to correct many of the misconceptions regarding Daoism and its history.

Kohn, Livia, ed. *Daoism Handbook.* Leiden, The Netherlands: Brill, 2000. A magisterial and encyclopedic collection of essays on various aspects of Daoism, ranging from history to schools to texts.

Schipper, Kristofer. *The Taoist Body.* Berkeley: University of California Press, 1993. An authoritative discourse by an ordained Daoist priest on the rituals and practices of Daoism as they relate to the texts and teachings.

Sun, Anna. *Confucianism as a World Religion*. Princeton, NJ: Princeton University Press, 2013. An authoritative monograph on the issue of Confucianism's religious content and labeling.

Taylor, Rodney L. *The Religious Dimensions of Confucianism*. Albany: State University of New York Press, 1986. A convenient collection of mostly previously published essays by the author to argue for the religiousness of Confucianism.

Yao, Xinzhong. *An Introduction to Confucianism*. Cambridge, UK: Cambridge University Press, 2000. An authoritative basic text on the entire Confucian tradition.

ONLINE RESOURCES

Research Centre for Confucian Studies

cuhk.edu.hk/rih/confucian

This useful website for Confucian studies is maintained by the Research Center for Confucian Studies, Chinese University of Hong Kong. It contains a rich resource guide for Confucian studies.

The Daoist Foundation

daoistfoundation.org

The Daoist Foundation was created by two American academics who, having studied and practiced Daoism for many years, "are committed to fostering the flourishing of authentic and tradition-based Daoist practice, community, and culture with attentiveness to the needs and concerns of Western students."

Center for Daoist Studies

daoistcenter.org

This useful website is the education and research branch of the Daoist Foundation.

187

Judaism

IT IS A SATURDAY morning, and Seth is waiting to read from the Torah—the most ancient of Jewish Scriptures. Seth has spent the past ten months preparing for this moment, and he is about to become a **Bar Mitzvah** (Hebrew, "son of the commandment"). In late antiquity, a young Jewish male became a Bar Mitzvah simply by turning thirteen years old, but by the later Middle Ages a formal rite of passage had developed that signaled a young man's entry into religious manhood. By demonstrating that he can read directly from and comment on the Torah, Seth is proclaiming, before an entire congregation of worshipers, his intention to enter the Jewish community as a literate adult.

Moving a silver pointer shaped like an outstretched hand across the Torah scroll, Seth reads the passage assigned for that particular Sabbath morning. The sacred text before him is especially difficult to decipher because, as in ancient times, it is written in the ancient Hebrew language; however, Seth has reviewed this passage many times and has practically memorized it. After the service, Seth will be joined by friends and family who will celebrate his accomplishments with a party, gifts, and praise. This coming-of-age ritual has been enacted countless times over the centuries in Jewish communities throughout the world, but it is only since the 1920s that the privilege of participating in this ritual has been extended to young women (a **Bat Mitzvah**—a "daughter of the commandment"). Nevertheless, it has become quite common today for

The Bar Mitzvah stands behind a lectern, facing an open Torah scroll, preparing to read his scriptural passage in Hebrew.

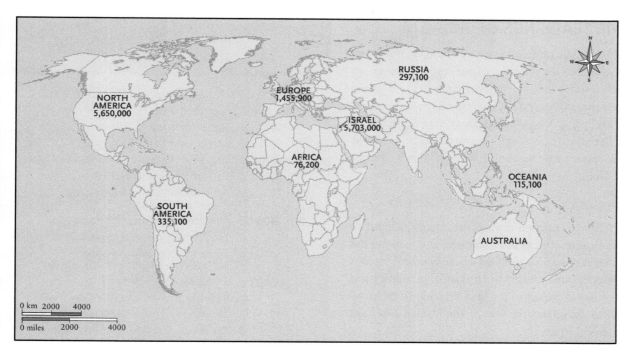

NORTH
AMERICA
5,650,000

EUROPE
1,455,900

RUSSIA
297,100

ISRAEL
5,703,000

AFRICA
76,200

OCEANIA
115,100

SOUTH
AMERICA
335,100

AUSTRALIA

0 km 2000 4000

0 miles 2000 4000

Total number of Jews presently living in the world.

twelve- and thirteen-year-old Jewish girls to perform the same ritual acts that their male counterparts do and to receive the same recognition.

Of all of the life-cycle events in Judaism, the Bar and Bat Mitzvah rite reflects the most fundamental of Jewish beliefs. At the core of the Judaic belief system is the assumption that a very special historical and spiritual relationship—referred to, traditionally, as a covenant—exists between the one God of heaven and earth and the people of Israel. By demonstrating both religious literacy and a willingness to freely embrace a life of sacred duties and obligations, adolescent Jewish boys and girls renew that covenant in a public and deliberate way.

The Bar or Bat Mitzvah ritual is not, however, a prerequisite for membership in the Jewish community. Historically, the only precondition of Jewish identity has been whether or not one has been born to a Jewish mother. Although Judaism has always accepted converts, the majority of the world's Jews have been persons whose ancestors are also Jewish. Nevertheless, this rite of passage has achieved its present popularity because it symbolizes a commitment to a communal religious life and to Judaism as the collective faith experience of the Jewish people. ☀

Judaism is one of the world's oldest extant religions. In addition to examining the teachings and practices of the Jewish religion, we will also survey the historical context out of which they emerged and to which they responded. But first we present an overview of Judaism's teachings.

189

THE TEACHINGS OF JUDAISM

Judaism has undergone many changes in its long history. For the purposes of our study, however, we will start by looking at those concepts and values that the majority of Jews living today would regard as enduring. We will then consider the diversity of belief that increasingly characterizes Judaism in the present age, beginning with Judaism's concept of God.

God

The Jewish religion is most commonly referred to as a type of **ethical monotheism**, as it assumes the existence of a Creator-God whose benevolence and goodness are reflected in His love of humanity and who has imparted to the Jews ethical principles by which they (and the rest of the human race) are expected to live.

As Jewish philosophy developed over the centuries, an understanding of God's nature deepened, and additional qualities—such as **omniscience** and **omnipotence**—were added to the portrait of the deity. Most important for Judaism, however, is the concept of divine "oneness," which can be understood to mean that there is only one divine Being in the universe; this one Being is truly incomparable, and no human being (or anything we can possibly imagine) can be compared to this Being. Judaism's idea of divine **transcendence** presupposes that a fundamental difference in reality exists between God and the world He has brought into existence, and that this difference precludes the possibility of God's embodiment or "incarnation" in a particular human personality.

Yet for all its emphasis on God's "otherness," Judaism is not lacking a sense of God's nearness, or **immanence**. The very fact that Jews pray to God—and do so with the expectation that their prayers will be heard and that those prayers may move the deity to respond—suggests that there are limits to the distance between the divine reality and human consciousness. Moreover, the ancient liturgical tradition

TIMELINE
Judaism

c. 1210 B.C.E.	Pharaoh Merneptah's victory over "Israel."
c. 1000 B.C.E.	King David unites kingdom.
922 B.C.E.	Division of Kingdom of David and Solomon.
722 B.C.E.	Israel conquered by Assyrians.
587 B.C.E.	Destruction of First Temple; Babylonian exile.
539 B.C.E.	Cyrus of Persia conquers Babylon.
333–323 B.C.E.	Alexander the Great conquers Egypt, Palestine, and Persia.
167–140 B.C.E.	Maccabean revolt against Seleucid rule.
140 B.C.E.	Establishment of the Hasmonean Dynasty.
63 B.C.E.	Pompey invades Syria-Palestine; Judea becomes Roman province.
66–70 C.E.	First Jewish War with Rome.
70	Destruction of the Jerusalem Temple.
132–135	Second Jewish War with Rome.
135	The defeat of the would-be Messiah Bar Kochba.
c. 200	Rabbi Judah the Nasi compiles the Mishnah.
c. 500	Completion of the Babylonian Talmud.
882–942	Saadiah ben Joseph serves as Gaon of Sura, Babylonia.
1135–1204	Moses ben Maimon (Maimonides) flees Spain for Egypt.
1492	Jews expelled from Spain.
1570–1572	Rabbi Isaac Luria establishes a community of mystics in Safed, Palestine.
1666	Shabbetai Tzevi declares himself the Messiah.
1700–1760	Israel ben Eliezer establishes the Hasidic movement.
1792	France confers citizenship on the Jews.
1845	Reform Movement of Germany defines the movement's goals and beliefs.
1894–1899	The trial and retrial of Captain Alfred Dreyfus.
1917	The Balfour Declaration.
1939–1945	World War II and Shoah.
1948	State of Israel established.
1951	The Israeli Parliament declares the 27th of Nisan as *Yom HaShoah* (Holocaust Remembrance Day).
1967	Six-Day War between Israel, Egypt, Syria, and Jordan.
1972	Sally Jane Priesand ordained as a rabbi by Hebrew Union College.
1995	The assassination of Yitzhak Rabin

of addressing God through the use of masculine nouns and pronouns (still preserved in many prayer books today) suggests that, at the level of common speech, Jews have long thought of God in human terms. As we shall learn, contemporary feminist critics of traditional Judaism have challenged this practice, arguing that the attribution of gender subverts God's transcendent character. Other critics have also challenged this practice, arguing that any anthropomorphic imaging of the divine is a false representation of an unknowable reality. Such contending views constitute part of an ongoing conversation within modern Judaism over the nature of the one God Jews have long proclaimed.

One of the great constants in Jewish theology, however, has been its assumption that the Creator-God was also the shaping force behind our universe and our human world. Judaism has never conceived of God as a deity who abandoned the universe once it was brought into being. On the contrary, Jews have always assumed that God is determined to see His creative purposes fulfilled in time. Judaism assumes, therefore, that God is moved to respond by every human act of goodness and contrition.

The Problem of Evil How such a God can tolerate the continued existence of evil in a world that He has created is a question that has long troubled Jewish philosophers. The oldest Judaic response to this question—a question that philosophers today often refer to as the "problem of evil"—takes the form of an accusation: the people of Israel have sinned against God by violating His covenant, and therefore God has no alternative but to punish those who have rejected Him and His laws.

However, the Nazi genocide against the Jews during World War II has prompted many Jewish theologians to reexamine this traditionalist argument and to reject this cause-and-effect pattern of thinking. For some, the spectacle of mass murder or, even worse, the possibility of global annihilation makes the biblical idea of a just, compassionate, and omnipotent Creator-God insupportable. Indeed, according to this argument, such a God-concept is no longer acceptable to post-Holocaust Judaism.[1] Still others, unwilling to embrace the agnosticism (or atheism) this argument inevitably leads to, insist on reviving the biblical idea of a divine "eclipse": the belief that God periodically conceals Himself from human understanding, thereby creating a seeming void in which evil, for a time, may prevail.[2]

Nevertheless, according to this counterargument, even during this period of divine "absence," God remains present in many human hearts, and in time God will "return" to our world in the form of humanity's moral striving and severe self-judgment. This alternative view of God's role in the world holds that reconciliation with God, and a renewal of those divine values that reside within all enlightened human cultures, is still possible, and that one should never doubt God's continuing love for, and anguish over, the human race.

Torah

In addition to a commitment to monotheism, Judaism also claims to be a "revealed" religion in that its most basic teachings are believed to be the result of divine revelation.

Most of the twenty-four books that make up the Hebrew Bible advance this claim. Furthermore, when Jews employ the Hebrew word "Torah" (Hebrew, "teaching") in its most inclusive sense, they are referring to the totality of God's revelation to the people of Israel. The very fact that Judaism possesses a sacred scripture presupposes a belief in divine–human communication, as well as a belief in the trustworthiness of those individuals—whether prophets or sages—who served as instruments of divine speech and understanding.

Torah, however, has additional meanings that are crucial to an understanding of Jewish faith. Thus, when reference is made to the scrolls of the Torah (which Seth read from at the beginning of this chapter), what is meant are the parchment copies of the first five books of the Hebrew Bible (known in English as Genesis, Exodus, Leviticus, Numbers, and Deuteronomy). Such scrolls can be found in any synagogue in the world. Jews view this portion of Judaism's ancient scriptures with particular reverence because these scrolls contain virtually all of the sacred legislation contained within the Hebrew Bible. Given the centrality of the idea of sacred law in traditional Judaism, the word "Torah" has often been translated as "the Law."

An even more expansive use of the word "Torah" can be found in the practice of referring to a comprehensive collection of commentaries on biblical law as the "Oral Torah." This multivolume anthology of interpretive and folkloristic writings, more commonly called the **Talmud**, represents the final extension in Jewish history of the idea of revelation. The teachers—known as rabbis—whose comments are preserved in these volumes claimed to be passing on the oral instructions of the biblical Moses, to whom God originally imparted His laws at Mount Sinai. Though not every community of Jews has accepted this claim as historically or theologically valid, the vast majority of the world's Jews have accorded to the Talmud a degree of sanctity and intellectual authority almost equal to that of the biblical Torah, thereby making the Talmud a virtual second scripture in Judaism. Much of the education of rabbis today consists of studying the Talmud, as well as a vast body of interpretive literature (commentaries on a commentary) that has grown up around the Talmud.

Compare the idea of mitzvot in Judaism to the concept of divine commandments in Christianity and Islam.

Mitzvot   At the core of the Torah tradition lies the concept of the **mitzvot** (Hebrew, "commandments"). Judaism can be described as a religion of "divine commandments." By the Rabbinic (or "Formative") Age, the number of such commandments that can be found in the first five books of the Hebrew Bible was fixed at 613, and each of these mitzvot was viewed as an essential link in a chain of religious laws that could not be broken. Today, at least half of these laws are no longer applicable, either to contemporary society or to a Judaism without a temple in Jerusalem, and therefore without a priesthood and a system of animal sacrifice. At the heart of this vast network of sacred laws lie the Ten Commandments, which can be found in two slightly different forms in the books of Exodus and Deuteronomy. For Jews everywhere, these ten pronouncements have served not only as the bedrock of their faith but also as the basis of their social and philosophical ideals.

However, just like the term Torah, the word "mitzvot" (singular, mitzvah) has taken on another, more informal meaning—that of "good deeds." In ordinary conversation, Jews routinely refer to any act of generosity or good will as a mitzvah. A glance at a traditional prayer book will reveal exactly which good deeds the rabbis expected every adult to feel especially bound by in everyday life. The list includes honoring one's parents, visiting the sick, outfitting a bride, and peacefully resolving quarrels between neighbors. But the greatest mitzvah, the rabbis go on to explain, is the study of Torah because it contains all the moral wisdom God has imparted to the Jewish people.

Nevertheless, there are practical limits to how far anyone can go in performing a good deed or fulfilling a divine commandment. Those limits are formally acknowledged in rabbinic law under the principle of "the preservation of life." Thus, the rabbis taught that whenever carrying out a mitzvah entails imminent risk to one's life or health, one is released from that obligation until the threat to life has passed. The only exceptions to this rule—and these exceptions became the basis for the concept of martyrdom in Judaism—are those situations in which a Jew is commanded to worship another god, to commit adultery, or to murder an innocent human being. In all other cases, the traditionalist view is that laws may be bent, but not permanently broken, to accommodate exigent circumstances.

Covenant and Election

Throughout its long history, Judaism has thought of God's relationship with the Jewish people as an intimate contractual relationship (rather like a marriage), freely granted by God and freely entered into by the biblical Israelites and all their remote descendants. In English, this type of relationship is referred to as a **covenant**.

THE TEN COMMANDMENTS

1. I the Lord am your God who brought you out of the land of Egypt.
2. You shall have no other gods besides Me. You shall not make for yourself a sculptured image, or any likeness of what is in the heavens above, or on the earth below.
3. You shall not swear falsely by the name of the Lord your God.
4. Remember the Sabbath day and keep it holy.
5. Honor your father and your mother.
6. You shall not commit murder.
7. You shall not commit adultery.
8. You shall not steal.
9. You shall not bear false witness against your neighbor.
10. You shall not covet anything that is your neighbor's.

In the Hebrew Bible, Israel's covenant with God is often portrayed as a kind of treaty, with reciprocal obligations and expectations. On God's side, an unconditional promise is given to the patriarch Abraham that his descendants would be numerous and that they would inhabit the land God had given Abraham as a legacy. The people of Israel, however, are expected to live up to all of God's demands and to obey His mitzvot. The penalty for disobeying God is a temporary dissolution of the covenant connection, coupled with such punishments as famine, defeat in war, and ultimately exile from the very land first promised to Abraham and his heirs. Clearly, this later understanding of the covenant idea is conditional and even punitive in nature, and for many centuries it provided a theological rationale for the worldwide dispersion of Jews and their subsequent statelessness. Since the establishment of the State of Israel in 1948, contemporary Jewish theology has tended to deemphasize that theme and to stress, instead, the bond of enduring love, trust, and forgiveness that exists between Israel and God.

Much more problematic than the covenant idea, however, is the accompanying belief in Israel's **election**, or, as this idea is more commonly expressed, a belief that the Jewish people have been "chosen" by God to receive His laws and to live in His presence. No concept in Judaism has evoked more hostility and misunderstanding; yet, despite the controversy, it would be difficult to imagine a historically credible form of Judaism that completely lacked this concept. On one level, all that the idea of election in Judaism affirms—and all that the Hebrew Bible attests to—is God's decision to reveal Himself to the people of Israel in a way that is qualitatively different from the way He has related to any other people on earth.

On yet another level of understanding, however, the covenant demands that Israel actively serve God's purposes in history: first, by becoming a "holy nation," completely obedient to His will, and, second, by representing God to the peoples of the world who have no knowledge of His existence. This latter understanding of the doctrine of election is what the biblical prophet Isaiah had in mind when he spoke of Israel becoming a "light to the nations," and after long centuries of living in a stateless Diaspora, Jews have come to see their "chosenness" as an obligation to serve both God and humanity, rather than as an assertion of moral or religious superiority.

Historically, Jews have thought of the covenant in ancestral terms, as most Jews are persons born to Jewish parents. Nevertheless, conversion to Judaism has long been open to any non-Jew who wishes to assume the responsibilities (and the hazards) that are part of membership in the covenant community. Those who enter Judaism by choice are required by tradition to prove their sincerity and to undertake a term of study to prepare for full participation in Jewish religious life. The final stage of conversion customarily entails circumcision for men who are not already circumcised and, for both men and women, immersion in a ritual pool (known as a **mikveh** in Hebrew). From that moment on, the convert is known as a "son" or "daughter" of Abraham, and no Jew by birth is permitted to treat such a convert as anything but a spiritual equal.

Paradoxical as it may sound, therefore, it is possible for anyone to choose to become part of the "chosen people." Nevertheless, because Jewish religious identity is traditionally traced through the mother's line, the conversion of a prospective bride is critical to determining the Jewishness of her offspring. The Reform Movement in the United States, however, has attempted to trace Jewish identity through the male line as well.

Israel

Since 1948, the word "Israel" has been used to identify the Middle Eastern nation-state that bears that name. But for many centuries, beginning with the Hebrew Bible, "Israel" connoted both a political and a spiritual community. In the latter sense, therefore, Israel is that covenant community to whom God imparted Torah and to whom He is bound by promise and affection. Like the idea of election, however, the notion of peoplehood implicit in the concept of Israel can still generate controversy today.

Biblical writers, however, had no difficulty reconciling ethnic identity and religious affiliation: God's covenant, they believed, was established with the "children of Israel" (that is, the lineal descendants of the patriarch Jacob)—and that contractual bond was thought to be unique and without precedent in history. As a consequence, Jews continued to think of themselves over the centuries as members of a single extended family *and* as a faith community held together by a common set of beliefs.

During the modern era, however, Jews found themselves faced with a political dilemma that soon took on religious implications: they could receive citizenship within the now largely secular nation-states of Europe, but only at the expense of their collective historical identity, and by denying all other "political" loyalties. For many Jews, eager to assimilate into modern society and determined to secure civil rights that had been denied them for centuries, the demand that Judaism redefine itself as a religious creed and nothing more seemed a small price to pay for political emancipation.

Orthodox Jews, generally suspicious of secular values and distrustful of the process of acculturation, viewed this new understanding of Jewish identity with alarm. In addition, by the end of the nineteenth century, a very different group of secular dissident Jewish intellectuals—early advocates of Zionism, such as Theodor Herzl—also rebelled, though for completely different reasons, against the notion that Jews had no claim to nationhood and were just another religious denomination among thousands in the world.

Today, many of those who practice Judaism are comfortable with their double identity as members of both a religious and an ethnic community, while at the same time recognizing the inevitable tension between these two perspectives. For those Jews who have chosen to immigrate to Israel and become citizens of a Jewish state, this tension almost disappears, though secular/nationalist and religious values continue to clash with one another in contemporary Israeli society. For those Jews who remain in the Diaspora—a majority of the world's Jewish population—the need to establish a balance between national and religious self-identification remains a challenge.

The Messiah and the Messianic Age

One idea that emerged from ancient Judaism that has had a profound impact on the Western world is the idea of a messiah. From its very beginnings in the Hebrew Bible, however, this concept has meant different things to different audiences. At its root, the term *mashiach* (Hebrew, "anointed one"; translated into English as "messiah") means any person who was ceremonially anointed with oil in preparation for becoming a priest or a king. When most biblical writers used this term literally, that was all they had in mind.

Nevertheless, later prophets such as the Second Isaiah (c. late sixth century B.C.E.) began to use this term metaphorically by applying it to either non-Israelite kings or to an unnamed future "prince" who would redeem his people from subjugation to foreign nations. As the beginning of the Common Era approached, the idea of a messiah continued to evolve. In works that lie outside of the Hebrew Bible, such as the First Book of Enoch and the Fourth Book of Ezra, the term *mashiach* took on explicitly supernatural meanings, signifying a heavenly redeemer figure sent by God to rescue Israel and the world from evil. This more imaginative use of the messiah concept was linked in such books with end-of-the-world visions, complete with predictions of a new world order emerging from a final era of chaos and destruction. Such writers saw the Messiah as an instrument of divine power through whom God would accomplish both the final judgment and the ultimate renewal of life on earth.

When Christianity identified Jesus of Nazareth with this redemptive-supernatural messiah tradition, it prompted the rabbis of the Talmud to reevaluate the very notion of a "messiah." What followed in their writings on this subject was a remarkably diverse collection of views, with some religious authorities identifying the biblical king Hezekiah (late eighth century B.C.E.) as a "messiah," whereas others deferred the appearance of an equally human messiah (albeit one from the line of David) to the indefinite future. Despite this uncertainty over the Messiah's precise identity, a lively debate ensued over which tasks such a messiah might be expected to accomplish and whether his mission would be accomplished within the span of human history or only at the "end" of time. Although centuries of longing for the fulfillment of these messianic visions have produced a succession of "false" messiahs in Judaism, this belief and its advocacy among traditionalist communities has persisted within contemporary Judaism.

The Afterlife

Of all the basic beliefs of Judaism, belief in an afterlife or "world-to-come," along with accompanying beliefs in the resurrection of the dead and the immortality of the soul, are among the most elusive. Historically viewed, these beliefs are not fully articulated until the period of the Talmud. For most biblical writers, the death of the body entailed the passage of the soul into an underworld, where it would remain forever. Still, various biblical texts contain hints of a counter-tradition; for example, the Second Book of Kings depicts the prophet Elijah ascending directly into heaven on a fiery chariot (2 Kings 2:1–12). But such miraculous transitions from life to a mysterious afterlife are exceptional, and it is only in a very late biblical work, the Book of Daniel, that we come upon an explicit reference to the dead rising again to life.

By the rabbinic era, however, mainstream Judaism had already embraced the idea of a postmortem existence in the "world-to-come," though just what this belief entailed remained vague. Thus, questions such as whether the departed enter the world-to-come automatically upon death or only after some ultimate judgment has been passed upon that soul by God, or whether a general resurrection of humankind would precede or follow the Messianic age, were left unanswered.

By the modern era, many reform-minded Jews concluded that any belief in an existence beyond this world was either an archaic folk belief or an insupportable, unscientific hypothesis. Yet despite such opposition, the classic conception of the afterlife, along with references to the resurrection of the dead, persists within most contemporary prayer books. In Orthodox communities, Jews continue to insist that these beliefs are an integral part of the Judaism they uphold.

Jewish Mysticism

The origins of mystical thinking in Judaism can be found in the Hebrew Bible, in which at least one prophet, the sixth-century figure of Ezekiel, recorded visionary trances in which God appeared to him as a figure of infinite mystery, seated upon a throne:

> Above the expanse . . . was the semblance of a throne, in appearance
> like sapphire; and on top, upon this semblance of a throne, there was
> the semblance of a human form. From what appeared as his loins up,
> I saw a gleam as of amber—what looked like fire encased in a frame;
> and from what appeared as his loins down, I saw what looked like fire.
> There was a radiance all about him. Like the appearance of the bow
> which shines in the clouds on a day of rain, such was the appearance
> of the surrounding radiance.
>
> —*Ezekiel 1:26–28*

Visionary passages like these testify to a tradition of ecstatic meditation in biblical Judaism in which a prophetic writer experiences the presence of God in a manner that is at once direct and mysterious. For centuries, Ezekiel's vision of the heavenly throne (which is also a chariot) served as an inspiration to mystics who sought a comparable glimpse of God and of the heavenly beings who, according to biblical tradition, surround His throne.

Another popular biblical text that served as inspiration for Jewish mystics was the opening chapter of the Book of Genesis, in which the creation of the world and of humankind is described. What distinguished the Kabbalistic school of mystical writers from other visionaries was a fascination with the mysterious process of world creation and a deep curiosity about the role of the Creator in this process. This type of mystical inquiry is often accompanied by some form of esoteric biblical interpretation, and it often incorporates some of the boldest kinds of cosmological speculation Jewish writers have ever indulged in.

Key to the writings of the Kabbalah (Hebrew, "received tradition") is one underlying cosmic metaphor, the image of the *Sephirot*. The *Sephirot* are ten in number, and they can be visualized as connected "spheres" of divine power, or as stages in a process of divine self-revelation. As such, they represent at least one of two things: the primary attributes of God and the dynamic emanations of His creative force.

However, the goal of mystical meditation in Kabbalah goes well beyond a desire to describe God or His relation to our world in quasi-mythological terms. The kabbalists were united in their desire to reconnect heaven and earth through a process of contemplative prayer and restorative moral actions. Thus, every blessing that a Jew utters in praise of God, or every mitzvah that is performed in strict accordance with tradition, they taught, can now be invested with an almost magical power to "heal" the world (Hebrew, *tikkun olam*) and is directly related to the soul's longing to reunite with its Creator. The end goal of this longing, kabbalists believe, is *devekut*, or a "clinging" to God that represents the highest state in mystical Judaism of the covenant relationship.

The Lurianic system of Kabbalah, in particular, has had tremendous appeal. In the "beginning" before creation, Rabbi Isaac Luria taught, God (whom kabbalists refer to as the *Ein Sof*, or "Infinite One") withdrew into Himself, thereby creating an empty space within which a material universe could take shape. Having performed this voluntary act of self-contraction (Hebrew, *tzimtzum*), the Creator then allowed rays of light to penetrate the void, resulting in a concentration of this creative force into ten spheres (the *Sephirot*). However, the ten "vessels" God had prepared to hold this *Sephirotic* light mysteriously shattered, leaving the material universe in disarray. According to Luria, this cosmic event was the true origin of evil and disorder in the world, and this partly inexplicable catastrophe resulted in the scattering of divine "sparks" throughout the cosmos and within the human soul. Within each of us, therefore, is an intermingling of good and evil; even the worst human beings, he believed, retain some small portion of divine goodness. With the coming of the Messiah, all of these sparks would be reunited with God. Until that eschatological event transforms the world forever, each person has the potential to liberate that divine "spark" for himself or herself through a process of repentance and return to God (Hebrew, *teshuvah*).

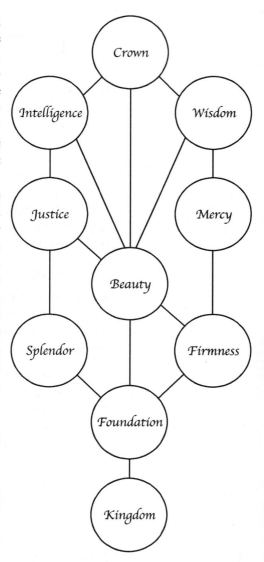

The traditional arrangement of the *Sephirot* is designed to evoke either the tree of life or the human body.

Ideas and images derived from Kabbalah continue to exert some influence on contemporary Jewish thought, and particularly for those associated with the Jewish "Renewal" movement.[3] Admirers of Rabbi Abraham Joshua Heschel (1907–1972) and, more recently, followers of Rabbi Zalman Schachter-Shalomi (1924–2014)— who are determined to bring about a reinvigoration of Jewish spirituality—insist that such concepts as *teshuvah* and *tikkun olam* cannot be confined to the synagogue or to a life of conventional religious observance. For some, *teshuvah* entails a sincere and disciplined internalizing of our longing for God in the form of true piety, affecting every aspect of our behavior. For others, however, *tikkun olam* means, quite literally, actions that benefit humankind and promote peace in the world.

THE HISTORY OF JUDAISM

The earliest reference we have to the Jews—known variously as "Hebrews," "Israelites," and "Judeans" (depending on the era and the context)—dates from the late thirteenth century B.C.E. On a commemorative stone, inscribed at the request of the reigning Egyptian ruler, Pharaoh Merneptah (c. 1210 B.C.E.), the following inscription appears:

Ancient Israel.

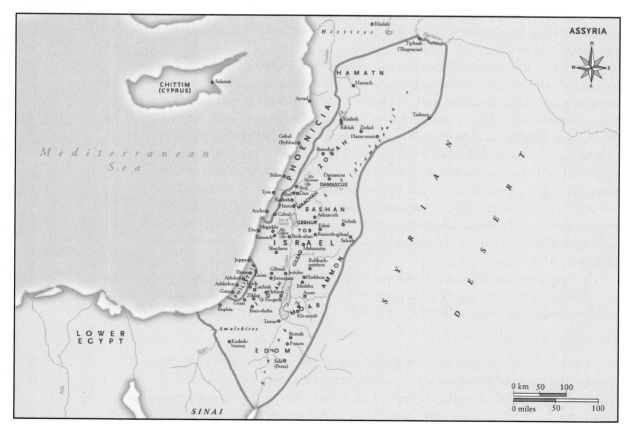

199

"Israel is laid Waste, its seed is no more." No other reference to "Israel" or the "Israelites" appears in Egypt or anywhere else for centuries. Most of what we know about ancient Israel, as well as the beliefs and religious practices of the ancient Israelites, is derived from Jewish Scriptures, referred to in Hebrew as *Tanakh*. In English, we refer to these books as the Hebrew Bible, though Christians commonly refer to these books as the "Old Testament."

Dispersion, Assimilation, and Collective Identity

The composite portrait of ancient Israelite society and its faith that one finds in the books of the Hebrew Bible is one of seemingly endless conflicts and successive divine revelations. For the authors of the Hebrew Bible the central conflict was over one issue: Would Israelites remain loyal to their one God (referred to, in Hebrew, by the consonants **YHWH**), or would they worship the deities of the nations that surrounded them? This was a politically relevant question, as well as a spiritual one, as the people of ancient Israel struggled to maintain their political and cultural independence for several centuries. Eventually, however, the tides of imperial Near Eastern politics swept over them, and after a series of devastating military defeats—first at the hands of the Assyrians in 722 B.C.E. and later at the hands of the Babylonians in 587 B.C.E.—the once-independent Israelite kingdoms of Israel and Judah were destroyed. Thousands of the Israelites were driven into exile or simply absorbed into the Assyrian and Babylonian empires.

Yet, despite this history of conquest and dispersion, the Israelites retained their national identity and their collective memory, and while living in exile they began to assemble a continuous history of their people and of their relationship with their God. Once completed, that history became part of their sacred scriptures. With the earliest copies of these books in hand, exiles from the kingdom of Judah began returning to their homeland after 538 B.C.E., believing that YHWH had at last forgiven them. Over the next few centuries, Jewish communities could be found not only in the historical land of Israel (which Greek and Roman geographers later named "Palestine") but also in Mesopotamia and throughout the Mediterranean. These communities were referred to as the Jewish **Diaspora**, and in the many centuries that followed, the number of Jews living outside of their historic homeland ultimately far exceeded those living within its borders.

For more than two millennia, therefore, dispersion, acculturation, and resistance to total assimilation have formed the larger pattern of Jewish life and must serve as the backdrop to any discussion of Judaism as a historical religion.

The Biblical Period

It has become customary to segment the history of Judaism into several discrete "epochs," each marked by certain key events that help to shape the direction of Jewish religious behavior and thought. The earliest of these epochs is the biblical period, which can be dated (speculatively) from the eighteenth century B.C.E. to the sixth century B.C.E. The key events of this era are the rise of the Patriarchs (Abraham, Isaac, and Jacob); the **Exodus** from Egypt; the formation of the monarchy; and the rise and fall of the two kingdoms—Israel and Judah—that followed. Viewed historically, the Patriarchal period remains shrouded in myth and legend, with the towering figures of Abraham as the principal bearer of the **covenant** that YHWH first establishes with the people of "Israel."

The Exodus from Egypt remains a problematic event for which little credible historical evidence exists today. Nevertheless, in the minds of biblical writers—and in the consciousness of Jews for centuries thereafter—it remained one of the crucial turning points in the history of Judaism. For whether or not it occurred exactly as described in the Hebrew Bible, the escape of Israelite slaves from Egypt marked a significant reversal of fortune for the tribes that called themselves "Israel," and it served as proof of God's power and willingness to intervene in history on their behalf.

More than that, however, the Exodus also marked a decisive moment in Israel's history of divine revelation and lawgiving, for it was on a mountain peak in the Sinai peninsula (variously identified as Mount Horeb or Mount Sinai) that divine instruction was provided to their leader **Moses**, who then imparted these teachings to the assembled Israelite masses. From this era on, "Israel" could no longer regard itself as a simple tribal society, cherishing memories of remote patriarchal leaders. The moment Israel encountered YHWH at Sinai it became a "confessional" community, bound together by a common faith in a Creator-God and committed to His service. As for the land the Israelites were poised to invade, that was understood to be a gift from YHWH, as well as the fulfillment of promises made to their ancestor Abraham. But it was theirs only as long as they remained faithful to the God who had brought them into their "Promised Land" and true to the covenant He had established with them.

Kingdoms of Israel and Judah

As a nation in the making, Israel began to emerge as a distinctive political entity only in the tenth century B.C.E., with the establishment of the dynasty of King David (c. 1000–961 B.C.E.). For a time, David managed to unite a warring tribal society under his leadership, finally passing on the throne to his son Solomon (c. 961–922 B.C.E.), whose even more exalted reign—at least in the eyes of biblical writers—brought a united monarchy to its height of power and fame.

The most important achievement of Solomon's reign, however, was not the extent of his legendary wealth and power, but rather the construction of the First Temple—a permanent sanctuary, designed to replace the portable tent (or "Tabernacle") of Moses's time, wherein prayers and animal sacrifices were offered to YHWH. By building this temple in the capital city of Jerusalem, Solomon ensured not only that the political and religious life of Israel would be geographically concentrated within one "holy" city but also that the Davidic monarchy would forever be associated with the most sacred site in Judaism.

Following Solomon's death, the northern tribes seceded to form a kingdom of their own, subsequently identified as the kingdom of Israel. The southern tribe of Judah remained loyal to the house of David and his descendants, and it bore the name of the kingdom of Judah. Both of these kingdoms, as we have noted, were relatively short-lived, and each in turn was overrun by the armies of more powerful empires. Of the two invasions, it was the second, by the Babylonians (587 B.C.E.), that resonated most powerfully with Jews for centuries thereafter, if only because it was the occasion of the destruction of Solomon's temple. In time, the loss of the First Temple and of the kingdom of Judah became the archetype of all later tragedies of displacement that the Jews were to endure and would be commemorated in both prayer and practice.

The Second Temple Period

The second great epoch in the history of Judaism, known as the Second Temple Period, began with the gradual return of a relatively small band of Judean exiles from Babylonia, following the Persian conquest of the Babylonian Empire in 539 B.C.E. The rebuilding of the First Temple (c. 516 B.C.E.), which the Babylonians had earlier destroyed during their siege of Jerusalem in 587 B.C.E., signaled the renewal of a centralized ritual life for Jews in what was formerly the kingdom of Judah, now merely a province within the Persian Empire. However, the movement of Jews between Babylonia and "Yehud" (as the Persians called Judah) not only provided for the re-population of Jerusalem and its restoration as a center of religious life but also for the passage of ideas and literature from Mesopotamia to the land of Israel.

Even at the beginning of the Second Temple era, a "canon," or collection of sacred Jewish writings, was slowly taking shape. Thus, the formation of Tanakh can be dated most reliably from this period, and the persons most likely responsible for the gathering and editing of these books were scribes and priests. Using the historical and theological perspectives of earlier prophets as their guides, these priestly editors selected works that embodied a recurrent pattern of teachings about divine promise, judgment, and hoped-for restoration, binding together this diverse collection of sacred works with an archetypal vision of Israel's past and anticipated future.

Though politically turbulent, the Second Temple period saw both the growth of the Jewish Diaspora and an increase in the Jewish population of Palestine. In the absence of a Jewish nation-state, religious leadership within the Jewish community fell to the priesthood and to an intellectual class connected to the priesthood. These two groups are said to have formed a leadership "council," known as the "Men of the Great Assembly." Tradition assigns to this body the decision to "close" the canon of divinely revealed (or inspired) scripture. Scholars differ today on the probable period in which religious authorities—whether in Jerusalem or Babylonia—considered the period of prophecy (and therefore the process of revelation) to have ended. However, it is commonly assumed that by the third century B.C.E. the writing and editing of the Torah had already reached a sufficient state of finality to allow Greek-speaking Jews to translate it from Hebrew into Greek. In time, additional portions of Tanakh were translated from available texts; this translation is referred to as the Septuagint, and it played a significant role in introducing Judaism to the larger Greek-speaking world. It was this version of Jewish Scriptures, rather than the Hebrew original, with which most early Christians were familiar.

Division and Revolt One important development within the Second Temple period was the increasing tension within the Jewish community between those who favored social and intellectual assimilation into Greek (and, later, Roman) culture and those who resisted such assimilation in favor of preserving "traditional" values and religious practices. This struggle became openly violent during the Maccabean revolt of 167–164 B.C.E., as the leaders of the revolt found themselves fighting against not only Syrian-Greek armies but also their more assimilated countrymen who sided with the Syrian king, Antiochus IV (c. 215–164 B.C.E.). Although this conflict finally resulted in the reestablishment of an autonomous Jewish state (c. 140–63 B.C.E.), one result of this internal struggle was the gradual appearance of religious "parties" whose influence on Jewish belief and practice grew during the period of Roman domination and occupation of Palestine.

The first-century Jewish historian Josephus (37–c. 100 C.E.) identified the most important of these parties as the Pharisees, who appear to have commanded the attention and loyalty of the Jewish masses. Central to the Pharisees' form of Judaism was their belief in the "Oral Torah"—that is, a body of teachings imparted by God to Moses on Sinai (but never written down) and subsequently transmitted orally to later generations. For the Pharisees, these interpretive readings of scripture were an integral part of "scripture" itself, and therefore just as binding. Thus, the Pharisees taught that Torah—that is, the totality of divine revelation to the Jews—incorporated a belief in both the immortality of the soul and the resurrection of the dead. In the eyes of the common people, the Pharisees' knowledge of the biblical text and their familiarity with biblical law made them more reliable guides than the often corrupt and politically compromised priesthood. It is from the followers of the Pharisees that we derive our sense of what the dominant form of Judaism may have been like by the end of the first century C.E.

A second group that Josephus identified were the Sadducees, whose influence on the Judaism of the time was much weaker. Drawing their constituents largely from priestly families, the Sadducees regarded the written Torah as exclusively sacred and authoritative and therefore rejected the very notion that an "Oral Torah" existed. Unlike the Pharisees, the Sadducees tended toward literalism in their understanding of scripture and therefore could find no warrant for believing in either immortality or resurrection. In politics, they tended to be sympathetic to—or at least accommodating of—Roman authority and therefore less likely than the Pharisees to favor revolutionary leaders.

The third, and most reclusive, community Josephus refers to is that of the Essenes, a general term designating groups of devout Jews who had withdrawn from society in protest against the moral and spiritual corruption of their contemporaries. These traditionalists viewed the temple priesthood with disgust and held the radical view of history that the "End-Time" of divine judgment and global catastrophe was at hand. Such beliefs, which religious scholars refer to as **eschatological**, had become increasingly widespread during the late Second Temple era, particularly when coupled with a belief in a **messiah**. Although such beliefs were

well known throughout the Jewish world, Essenes held to their faith in the imminence of the world's end with particular fervor, and they looked forward to a Messianic Age, when the temple would at last be purified and the Romans defeated by armies of angels.

Masada was the last stronghold the Zealots held before taking their lives rather than yielding to the Roman Army (73 C.E.).

Many historians today associate the Essenes with a community of sectarian Jews who withdrew from Judean society and built a settlement near the northwestern shore of the Dead Sea, at a place called Khirbet Qumran, sometime during the second century B.C.E.[4] The religious literature written and preserved by this group was hidden away in caves near their settlement, and it was not until 1947–1956 that these ancient scrolls were discovered. Collectively, they are referred to as the **Dead Sea Scrolls**, and almost half of them are fragments of books from the Hebrew Bible. These copies of biblical texts are the oldest copies of the Jewish Scriptures known to exist today.

Last, and most transitory in their influence on Judaism, were those revolutionaries Josephus termed the Zealots. Like the Pharisees and the Essenes, the Zealots were eager to see the Romans driven from the land of Israel and looked forward to a restoration of Israel's sovereignty and of its monarchy. However, believing that God would fight on their side, the Zealots sought to expel the Roman army through direct action, and Zealot agitation and rebellion were underlying causes of the First Jewish War against Rome (66–70 C.E.). Even after this war ended in the defeat of Jewish forces and in the destruction of the Second Temple, a group of Zealots continued to hold out against the Romans until 73 C.E., when their mountain fortress of Masada was besieged and overrun by the Roman Army. Rather than surrender, the remnant of the Zealot fighters, along with their women and children, committed suicide (according to Josephus) rather than be taken alive by their enemy.

The Formative Age

The fall of Jerusalem and of Masada, and the destruction of the Second Temple, signaled the end of the Second Temple era and the beginning of the third epoch of Judaism's history, known variously as the Rabbinic Age and the Formative Age (c. late first century C.E.–sixth century C.E.). As long as the temple stood, it served as both a treasured symbol of Israel's biblical past and the operational center of Jewish ritual life throughout the world. Once it lay in ruins, however, the Jewish people needed a new

The Touro Synagogue, built in Newport, Rhode Island, in 1759, is the oldest synagogue in the United States.

institutional center—a replacement sanctuary, until such time as the temple could be rebuilt. The **synagogue**, whose remote origins can be traced back to the beginning of the Babylonian exile, provided just such a substitute, but unlike the temple it was never a place of animal sacrifice, nor was it under the control of a priesthood. In all likelihood, the synagogue began simply as a place of assembly at which Judean exiles could meet and study together. With the temple gone, however, Jews turned increasingly toward the synagogue as the place for religious leadership or for communal prayer.

Unlike the temple, which could stand in only one place (namely, Jerusalem), a synagogue could be built anywhere. Moreover, almost anyone could build a synagogue or serve as a communal leader. Priests had no role to play in the ritual or social life of a synagogue, which made it a more democratic institution from the start.

The Rabbis   In time, the synagogue acquired a clerical leadership all its own, which brings us to the second major historical change that defines the Formative Age: the emergence of a class of religious intellectuals known as rabbis (Hebrew, "my master"). The word was a term of honor conferred on someone whose piety and learning caused him to stand out among his contemporaries and whose teachings (or legal rulings) were sufficiently memorable that subsequent generations viewed him with respect and even reverence.

One such figure, who had come from Babylonia to study in Jerusalem, was Hillel (fl. 30 B.C.E.–4 B.C.E.), whose compassionate nature was as remarkable as his scholarship. According to legend, it was Hillel who, when asked (mockingly) by a pagan to teach him Torah while he stood on one foot, replied: "What is hateful to you, do not do to your neighbor; the rest is commentary"—a version of the so-called Golden Rule. Like Hillel, many of the early rabbis saw themselves as more than just legal scholars whose expertise in biblical law allowed them to advise common folk on matters of correct observance. They also saw themselves as sages or wisdom teachers whose insights into human nature complemented their knowledge of divinely revealed law.

The Compilation of the Talmud   The signature accomplishment of the rabbinic scholar class during the Formative Age was the writing and compilation of the Talmud, a composite work that, in time, was seen as a second Torah, or at the very least, as an indispensable addendum to the Tanakh. On one level, the Talmud is a collection of expansive (and occasionally imaginative) interpretations of biblical law. The format of the Talmud is often dialogical (that is, a series of question-and-answer exchanges). Nearly every page consists of some portion of a rabbinic debate over the alternative ways in which a particular biblical statute can be understood or implemented. The practical objective of all these debates was the creation of an authoritative form of ritual behavior—referred to in Hebrew as **halacha**—that would enable the observant Jew to sanctify daily life and fulfill the commandments imparted to Moses on Sinai. God gave Torah to Israel, the rabbis believed, and now it was their responsibility to clarify its terms and relate them to daily life. In the section of this chapter on sacred practices, we will see how halacha informs the ways many Jews today live their faith.

The Babylonian version of the Talmud, compiled at the beginning of the sixth century C.E., consists of sixty-three separate volumes covering a wide range of legal issues. The historical process by which these volumes came into being, however, can be studied in two stages: the earlier stage, known as the Mishnah (Hebrew, "repetition"), is written in Hebrew and consists of economical formulations of halacha, often accompanied by an attribution to a particular rabbinic scholar; the later stage, referred to as the Gemara (Hebrew, "completion"), is written in Aramaic (a Semitic language, very close to Hebrew), and the rabbinic debates recorded there often take up where the Mishnah leaves off.

This process of recording and summarizing rabbinic debates continued, in both Palestine and Babylonia, during a period of roughly four centuries. As the body of rabbinic commentary evolved toward the next stage of completion—first in Jerusalem in the fifth century C.E. and later in Babylonia at the beginning of the sixth century C.E.—the Mishnah was combined with the far more elaborate text of the Gemara. Together these two scholarly works make up the Talmud. Judaism's greatest challenge during this period, however, was not simply that of preserving the teachings of its religious elite but, more important, it was that of protecting itself from a rival "sister" religion—namely, Christianity—whose political might increased throughout the Roman Empire in the course of the fourth and fifth centuries, at the same time that Judaism's power declined.

The Conflict between Judaism and Christianity

Christianity, as you will learn in Chapter 12, began life as a splinter movement within Judaism, following the death by crucifixion of its central figure, Jesus of Nazareth, in 30 C.E. Over the next two generations the early Christian community gradually pulled away from mainstream Judaism and redefined both the nature and role of Jesus in Christian thought, largely under the influence of an ex-Pharisee known as Paul of Tarsus. Those early followers of Jesus, who may have thought of him as a prophet, or even as a Messiah figure, were soon displaced by those who saw Jesus as the "Son of God," and who eventually came to believe in him as the incarnate human form of YHWH. As the letters of Paul (mostly written between 50 and 64 C.E.) clearly testify, most contemporary Jews viewed these teachings as heresy and quickly banished Jewish followers of Jesus from the synagogue. By the turn of the second century the split between Judaism and Christianity was irreversible, and out of the matrix of Judaism a new (and largely antagonistic) faith had been born.

The philosophical conflict between Judaism and Christianity sprang from a number of incompatible views on the nature of God, the covenant, salvation from sin, and the proper interpretation of biblical texts. For rabbinic Judaism, any material representation of God—either in the form of an image or a living human being—was barely acceptable, and even then only as metaphor. For Christianity, however, the embodiment of the divine in Jesus as the "Christ" soon became a central doctrine of the early Church. As for God's covenant with Israel, Paul argued that the Christian community had—at least at that moment in time—displaced the Jews as true heirs of the biblical promises made to the Patriarchs and the prophets; the Jews, he insisted, had alienated God by their rejection of Jesus and had (if only temporarily) forfeited their intimate relation to the deity. That the Christian and Jewish communities would, before long, rejoin each other in an expanded covenanted relationship with God was Paul's fervent wish and expectation. However, the first four centuries of the Common Era saw only a widening theological and social gap between the two communities.[5]

With the Roman Emperor Constantine's conversion to Christianity early in the fourth century, Judaism found itself facing not only a determined religious antagonist in the Christian Church but also an even more powerful political antagonist, as a succession of Christian emperors sought to stifle Judaism throughout the Roman Empire by imposing punitive legislation on the Jews and by condoning acts of violence against synagogues. In the eyes of the late fourth-century Christian theologian St. John Chrysostom (c. 347–407 C.E.), the Jews were the devil's spawn, their synagogues the dwelling places of all evils, and any civil relations between Christians and Jews, he argued, represented a betrayal of God.[6] Against such a background of institutionalized hatred, the Jews of Christian Europe struggled for the next millennium to maintain not just their faith, but their very lives.

The Age of Philosophy and Mysticism

The fourth great epoch in the history of Judaism, extending from the Early Middle Ages (sixth–seventh centuries C.E.) to the Early Modern period (sixteenth–seventeenth centuries C.E.), can be thought of as the Age of Philosophy and Mysticism. During this period, the Jewish Diaspora stretched from China and India in the East to England in the West. Historians frequently employ the following terms to identify these historical/cultural groupings: Ashkenazim, representing those Jews living in Europe; Sephardim, or Jews living in Spain, Portugal, and parts of North Africa; and Mizrachim, or Jews living in various parts of the Middle East. Each of these communities underwent periods of prosperity and decline, but throughout most of this period some of the most creative developments in Judaism took place: first in Babylonia (present-day Iraq) and later in Spain.

As the Palestinian Jewish community dwindled in numbers and prestige in the course of the sixth and seventh centuries, the center of Jewish intellectual life shifted to Babylonia and to the principal rabbinic academies of Sura and Pumpeditha. And it was Sura, in the early tenth century, that gave rise to one of the major figures in Jewish philosophy: Rabbi Saadiah ben Joseph (882–942). One unavoidable challenge faced Saadiah during his career—one from outside the Jewish community: the advent of an entirely new religion.

The Encounter with Islam   The emergence of Islam in the early seventh century (Chapter 13) posed a significant problem for Jews of Arabia and eventually throughout the Middle East. The founder of Islam, Muhammad (570?–632 C.E.), claimed to have received a new work of scripture—the Qur'an—that was in the form of oral communications from the Angel Gabriel, and that he saw as a more reliable revelation than that given to either the Christians or the Jews. Viewing himself as one in a long line of prophets that included both Moses and Jesus, Muhammad clearly expected the Jews of Arabia to accept his claim to be the last (or "seal") of the prophets and to embrace his revelation as the definitive message of God (or "Allah" as the one Creator-God is referred to in Arabic) to humanity.

When it became apparent that the Jews of Mecca would accept neither him nor his new Torah, Muhammad turned his full attention to his pagan audience, whom he found more receptive to a new monotheistic faith. Muhammad's success in propagating his religious message was matched by his military success in defeating many of his more powerful enemies (which included some of the prominent Jewish tribes of Arabia), and after his death the faith of Islam spread rapidly throughout many of the lands in which Jews had settled centuries before. Although Muhammad's attitude toward the Jews, as expressed in the Qur'an, remained understandably ambivalent, from the eighth century on Jews were accorded a degree of tolerance within Muslim societies that they rarely encountered in Christian lands.

Like many Jewish scholars of his generation, Saadiah had learned a great deal from reading Muslim philosophical literature of the ninth and tenth centuries. Foremost among Saadiah's concerns, therefore, was the need to present Judaism to an educated Jewish audience already familiar with the teachings of both Islam and Greek philosophy, and to do so in a way that did not contradict Jewish Scriptures.

The result of this investigation, which Saadiah published as *The Book of Beliefs and Opinions* (933), is the earliest example of scholasticism in Jewish thought—that is, a systematic attempt to reconcile faith and reason by relating mainstream religious beliefs to contemporary philosophical arguments. Thus, Saadiah sought to prove the unique character of God's revelation to Israel, as well as the rational character of many (though not all) biblical commandments, and thereby strengthen Jewish belief in the uniquely trustworthy nature of Judaism's Scriptures.

Maimonides The tradition of philosophical inquiry produced at least one more intellectual giant during this period: Moses ben Maimon, better known as **Maimonides** (1135–1204). In Maimonides, Judaism found one of its supreme philosophers; much of Orthodox Jewish theology derives directly from his writings. Maimonides, the son of a respected rabbinic scholar, was well prepared for this role by both his background and early education. When his family was forced to flee their native city of Cordoba, Spain, to escape the tyrannical rule of a militant Muslim regime, they found refuge in Egypt under the more tolerant rule of the celebrated Muslim ruler Salah ad-Din (c. 1138–1193). Maimonides was better known to his Muslim hosts as a physician than as a philosopher, though it is the latter role that concerns us here.

Maimonides's passion for logic and intellectual clarity is evident in all of his writings. In his *Mishneh* Torah, for example, he listed every single one of the 613 biblical commandments, revealing (even to the casual reader) that many of these mitzvot could no longer be fulfilled in the absence of the temple in Jerusalem. Similarly, in his *Commentary to the Mishnah*, Maimonides clearly describes what he believed to be the thirteen essential "articles" of Jewish belief, thereby creating a dogmatic framework for any subsequent discussion of Judaism as a faith system.

Though not universally acceptable, even during and after Maimonides's lifetime, this compact statement of belief still serves as a useful reference point in any discussion of what today is called "Torah-true" (or "Orthodox") Judaism.

Ironically, Maimonides's most celebrated work, *The Guide for the Perplexed*, evoked considerable controversy when it finally became public, though Maimonides had not intended it originally for widespread publication. In this philosophical treatise, Maimonides attempted to grapple with some of the more problematic philosophical issues of his day: the existence and attributes of God, the nature of creation and prophecy, the problem of evil, divine providence, and the purpose of human existence. Throughout the *Guide*, Maimonides makes it clear that he distrusts any comparison between humanity and the eternal creator. At best, he argued, we can speak of God mostly in negative terms. For example, instead of saying that God is a being who lives forever, Maimonides advises that it is preferable to say that He has no temporal limits. This particular approach to theology (and, inevitably, to biblical interpretation) emphasizes God's "otherness" and tends to remove God from the material world and beyond the limitations of the human mind.

Like many of his Jewish contemporaries, Maimonides looked forward with some eagerness to the advent of the Messianic Age, though he was shrewd enough not to assign a date to that hoped-for event. Interestingly, however, Maimonides's view of both the Messiah and the era of his arrival is largely naturalistic, and it contrasts sharply with the more supernaturalist traditions that both preceded and followed him:

> The "days of the Messiah" refers to a time in which sovereignty will
> revert to Israel and the Jewish people will revert to the land of Israel.
> Their king will be a very great one, with his royal palace in Zion. . . .

All nations will make peace with him, and all countries will serve him out of respect for his great righteousness and the wonders which will occur through him. . . . However, except for the fact that sovereignty will revert to Israel, nothing will be essentially different from what it is now.

—*Helek Sanhedrin, Ch. 10*

This demythologized version of messianic Judaism was Maimonides's principal legacy to future generations of acculturated Jews. But one important segment of the Jewish community, those drawn to mystical thinking, rejected Maimonidean scholasticism and its celebration of reason and sought to restore to Judaism some of its rich mythological past.

The Kabbalah   Collectively, the many diverse traditions that make up the world of Jewish mysticism are sometimes referred to as **Kabbalah**, but when historians use that term they are thinking primarily of a school of mystics whose beginnings can be traced to twelfth-century France and thirteenth-century Spain. Common to all these writers was an acknowledgment that the hidden "essence" of YHWH—as Maimonides taught—cannot be fully grasped, and certainly never directly perceived or represented.

MAIMONIDES'S THIRTEEN ARTICLES OF JEWISH BELIEF

1. God the Creator exists.
2. God is uniquely "one."
3. God is incorporeal (and therefore all scriptural images of a divine "body" are mere figures of speech).
4. God is eternal.
5. God alone is worthy of worship and obedience.
6. The teachings of the biblical prophets are true.
7. Moses is the chief of all prophets.
8. The Torah comes directly from God (through Moses).
9. Both the Written and the Oral Torah represent the authentic word of God, and nothing can be added or taken away from either.
10. God is omniscient.
11. God rewards the good and punishes the wicked.
12. The Messiah will undoubtedly come (though no exact date can be known for his coming).
13. The resurrection of the dead will occur in the World-to-Come.

In a late thirteenth-century work many regard as the "bible" of Kabbalah—the **Zohar**—this entire structure of divine qualities and emanations is laid out in the form of a biblical midrash, that is, an extended interpretation of select passages from the Book of Genesis. Central to this form of mystical thought is the idea that however imperfect the human race may be, we are still capable of interacting with, understanding, and even influencing God. This theology of immanence—or, more precisely, of divine-human interaction—is quite obviously at odds with Maimonides's view of a profoundly transcendent Creator. Consequently, the kabbalists felt free to evoke the Creator in explicitly anthropomorphic language (i.e., portraying God in very human terms).

By the sixteenth century, the kabbalistic system had matured to the point that a powerful and highly imaginative cosmology emerged, mainly through the teachings of one man: Rabbi **Isaac Luria** (1534–1572). The *Ari* (or "holy lion"), as he was known to his disciples, left no writings at the end of his short life, but his followers disseminated his thought throughout much of the Jewish world, and of all the many variants of Kabbalah, the "Lurianic" system is at once the most influential and the most complex. Luria taught that the individual believer could liberate the divine "spark" within by careful observance of the divine commandments and acts of self-discipline and meditation. In addition, in sharp contrast to mainstream Jewish belief, Luria envisioned each soul undergoing a series of reincarnations, as the soul constantly strives to return to its Source.

The potential danger—as well as the enormous appeal—of Lurianic Kabbalah became quite apparent a century after the Ari's death in the sensationalistic career of a messianic pretender, Shabbetai Tzevi (1626–1676). A Turkish Jew of obviously unstable temperament, Shabbetai became convinced early in life of his extraordinary spiritual powers after studying Lurianic texts. At the encouragement of one of his most fervent disciples (a self-styled prophet named Nathan of Gaza, whom he had met on a visit to Palestine), Shabbetai declared himself the "King Messiah." In 1666, he presented himself before the Sultan of Turkey, asserting his messianic credentials and his "royal" right to the historic land of Israel. The Turkish response to this would-be savior was, first, to imprison Shabbetai for a year and then to offer him a minor position at court following his conversion to Islam. Shabbetai's acceptance of this offer not only exposed him as an apostate, but it also sent shockwaves throughout the Jewish world, particularly among those who had firmly believed that Shabbetai was indeed the messianic deliverer he claimed to be.

The Rise of Hasidism   Shabbetai Tzevi was neither the last nor even the most important religious figure to base his teachings on Lurianic thought. Within two generations of Shabbetai's death, yet another mystical teacher arose, this time in Poland. The **Baal Shem Tov** (c. 1700–1760) also taught the necessity of releasing the sparks of holiness within, thereby hastening the approach of the Messiah. His given name was Israel ben Eliezer, but his disciples commonly referred to him as the "Master of the Good Name" (Hebrew, *Baal Shem Tov*), a title that conveyed to contemporaries the belief that he possessed secret "names" of God that he could use in incantations. Orphaned as an infant, the Baal Shem Tov was given a rudimentary education, and at no time during his career as a spiritual guide was he regarded as a great scholar. Instead, his fame derived from his faith healings and exorcisms. In time, the Baal

Shem Tov gave up the life of an itinerant healer and began to attract a growing number of disciples who were drawn by his reputation for wisdom and spirituality.

At the heart of the Baal Shem Tov's teachings was a profoundly immanental vision of God's omnipresence. For the Baal Shem Tov and his followers—who were soon called **Hasidim** (Hebrew, "pious ones")—God could be found everywhere, and everyone was at least potentially capable of spiritual communion with the Creator. To worship God properly, the Baal Shem Tov taught, one need not be a master scholar; the most ordinary of everyday acts, he insisted, if performed with an awareness of God's nearness and in a spirit of joy and love, become acts of spiritual devotion and serve to make everyday life sacred. No one was too humble or too depraved to turn (or return) to God, who required only a burning desire to perform His will.

At the communal level, the key to success within this system of mystical devotion lay with its leadership, and the Baal Shem Tov urged his disciples to choose a spiritual guide, or *tsaddik* (meaning "righteous one"), to provide a living example for themselves and the rest of the community of what it is like to live a life of intense religious commitment and intimacy with God. After the Baal Shem Tov's death, the Hasidic movement he helped to create spread rapidly throughout Russia and much of eastern Europe. In each major geographical center of Hasidic activity, *tsaddikim* appeared to carry on the teachings of the Baal Shem Tov. Each of these leaders formed a "court," or spiritual circle of followers. In time Hasidic dynasties appeared, as one generation followed another and as the loyalty to the father was transferred to the son. Many of these dynasties, formed in the nineteenth century, still exist today, with the result that virtually all Hasidic communities are centered around the personality and religious leadership of one man—often referred to in Yiddish as the Rebbe—whose authority in all things is largely unchallenged.

Opposition to the Hasidic movement arose soon after the Baal Shem Tov's death, and for the next two generations established rabbinic authorities in Russia and Poland sought to stifle popular interest in Hasidic teachings. Their principal fear was that Hasidism would lead to a revival of a messianic cult like the one that had formed around Shabbetai Tzevi. Yet, despite the determined opposition of the rabbinic establishment, Hasidism flourished, and by the mid-nineteenth century official opposition to Hasidism waned as Europe's rabbinic leadership realized that it faced a far more formidable opponent in the Jewish reform movements that suddenly emerged in response to Enlightenment values during the late eighteenth and early nineteenth centuries.

The Modern Era

The modern era in Judaism can be studied on at least two levels—the political and the philosophical—for until the Jews of western Europe had achieved a certain degree of political emancipation, they were unable to fully acculturate within European society or benefit from the intellectual

Compare the Baal Shem Tov with the Buddha. How are their teachings alike, and how are they different?

A young Israeli Hasid with curled sideburns, commonly worn by men in his community.

revolutions of the seventeenth and eighteenth centuries. For centuries, Jewish life in the West was characterized by both physical and cultural containment, the most visible symbol of which was the Jewish Quarter of many cities (or Ghetto, as it was known after the sixteenth century), where Jews were forced to reside. By law, Jews were also restricted to certain trades and professions, especially money lending, but by the late eighteenth century many of these restrictions began to be removed. As more prosperous and highly educated Jews were permitted to intermingle (and, increasingly, intermarry) with their Christian contemporaries, Judaism itself began to change.

Moses Mendelssohn   No better example of this pivotal transformation in Jewish life can be found than Moses Mendelssohn (1729–1786), the son of a Torah scribe and the principal representative for his time of the Age of Enlightenment (referred to in Hebrew as the *Haskalah*). Because Jews were not yet permitted to attend universities, Mendelssohn was largely self-taught in modern philosophy and several European languages. Before long, his philosophical writings began to attract the attention of non-Jews within his native Germany and beyond. His impact on the Jewish community was just as profound, and through his translation of the Hebrew Bible into modern German and his various other publications, Mendelssohn became one of the most effective advocates for educational reform and the modernization of Jewish intellectual life.

What Mendelssohn is best remembered for today, however, is his eloquent defense of religious freedom, coupled with a defense of the Jewish faith, in a volume entitled *Jerusalem* (1783). In this polemical masterwork, Mendelssohn entered a plea on behalf of religious tolerance and in defense of the integrity of Judaism. He argued that all higher religions share certain common beliefs (such as the existence of a benevolent Creator-God or the immortality of the soul) and that because Judaism also held such beliefs, it was as much an expression of the "common religion of humanity" as Christianity or Islam.

What was distinctive to Judaism, Mendelssohn proposed, was not so much its belief system as its sacred legislation—its Torah, understood here strictly as divinely revealed law—and its emphasis on doing God's will rather than professing correct ideas about God or the afterlife. The essence of Judaism, Mendelssohn insisted, was orthopraxy (correct conduct), and not orthodoxy (correct beliefs). This interpretation of Judaism, it should be noted, was not acceptable to more conservative religious authorities, but it did appeal to more secularized Jewish readers who were prepared, in the next generation to carry the logic of Mendelssohn's argument even further and to attempt to transform the belief structure of Judaism in more radical ways.

Reform Movements in Europe and the United States

The European Enlightenment, and the revolutionary political changes it inspired, affected Judaism in various ways, but its most direct influence can be seen in the early stages of the Reform Movement in the first decades of the nineteenth century. Beginning in Germany, where admirers of Moses Mendelssohn called for the political "emancipation" of European Jews and their gradual assimilation to Western society, the idea of "reforming" Judaism drew support both from lay community leaders and from a younger generation of rabbis who had been permitted to receive a university education. From the outset, the Reform Movement sought to accomplish two goals: first, the modernization of Jewish thought and ritual practice, and second, the acculturation of Jews to the secular culture of nineteenth-century Europe and America. As in any "reformation," however, a split soon developed between those who were determined to achieve these objectives by radical means and those who were not.

At first, reformers seemed content with largely ceremonial innovations, insisting, for example, that rabbinic sermons be delivered in the vernacular language of the nation in which they were living (rather than in Yiddish, the Germanic language of European Jews) or that men and women be permitted to sit together in synagogue during religious services (as opposed to separate seating, which had been the norm for hundreds of years). By the 1840s, however, the demands of the more aggressive reformers became increasingly antitraditionalist and theologically innovative, as reformist rabbis increasingly embraced the idea of Judaism as an evolving religious culture. All of these changes were opposed vigorously by more traditionalist rabbis, who, from this time forward, came to be described as "Orthodox" religious authorities.

Reform Judaism   This more radical type of reformist thinking flourished in the United States after the Civil War. By the late 1880s, Rabbi Kaufmann Kohler (1843–1926) had drafted a set of principles and objectives—known today as "The Pittsburgh Platform of 1885"—that defined the "essence" of Judaism for Kohler and many of his reformist contemporaries. The most important features of this "platform" can be found in its most negative statements, namely, that the Reform Movement rejected the biblical idea of a direct, finite, and exclusive revelation from God—the traditional understanding of the concept of Torah. The reformists opted instead for the concept of an evolving (and therefore universal) revelation, an idea that was easily gleaned from the writings of Moses Mendelssohn. This way, Kohler and his colleagues were able to renounce the dietary code and all other forms of "Mosaic legislation" deemed unacceptable to the Reform rabbinate (such as circumcision and rigorous Sabbath observance) on the grounds that they were "not adapted to the views and habits of modern civilization." And in language designed specifically to suppress any sympathy for Jewish aspirations to return to the historic land of Israel, the Pittsburgh Platform declared boldly that the Jews were no longer a nation and therefore no longer desired to return to, or to restore, a nation-state in Palestine.

Conservative Judaism   However acceptable these innovations may have seemed to those American Jews who identified with the Reform Movement, they were clearly unacceptable to the overwhelming majority of European Jews who began to immigrate to the United States in rapidly increasing numbers during the last two decades of the nineteenth century and the first decade of the twentieth century. As the Jewish population of America increased exponentially, the religious diversity of that community increased as well. By the middle of the twentieth century, the American Jewish community found itself largely divided into three movements: Reform, Orthodox, and Conservative. Of these three, the Conservative Movement had emerged, by the 1950s, as the Reform Movement's principal rival, and its appeal can be explained, historically, as a "counter-reformation" both within and outside of the Reform Movement itself.

Thus, for those Jews who were initially drawn to reformist ideals but who found the more extreme changes advocated by the early Reform Movement distasteful, Conservative Judaism offered a more moderate departure from traditional (or what is now called "Orthodox") beliefs and practices. Like their Reform counterparts, Conservative rabbis acknowledged the evolutionary character of Judaism and embraced the need for substantive change; unlike the leading reformists, however, they were not willing to abandon either principles of faith or religious behaviors that had defined Judaism for many centuries. The result was the formation of a "third way" of responding to the challenges facing Judaism in the modern era, in which a high level of adaptation to secular culture was combined with a selective relaxation of halacha.

In its formative stages, however, the most obvious difference between Conservative Judaism and its Reform and Orthodox counterparts was the public support of both its rabbis and laity for **Zionism**. Throughout its more than 100-year existence, the Conservative Movement has been a fervent advocate for both the formation of a Jewish nation-state in what is now Israel and for the emigration of American Jews to this state.

Reconstructionist Judaism   One of the most important offshoots of Conservative Judaism first emerged in America in the 1930s. Known today as Reconstructionism, this new school of thought centered on the teachings of Rabbi Mordecai Kaplan (1881–1983). By the 1960s, however, the Reconstructionists had formally separated themselves from Conservative Judaism, first by writing their own prayer book and later by establishing their own rabbinical seminary. Though few in number, Reconstructionists have had a far-reaching effect on the thought and religious practices of non-Orthodox Judaism in the United States.

Philosophically, Reconstructionism occupies a position somewhere between Conservatism and Reform. Unlike their Reform counterparts, Reconstructionists held firm to the concept of Jewish nationhood; in fact, for Mordecai Kaplan, the idea that Jews constituted a separate and distinctive *civilization* was central to his belief system. What followed from that assumption was a desire to retain as many traditional "folkways"—which was Kaplan's way of referring to such ritual practices as the dietary code and circumcision—as modern Jews found meaningful. As a consequence, the Reconstructionist Movement tended to place greater emphasis on the historical continuity of religious customs than did Reform Judaism.

At the same time, Reconstructionism developed a much more naturalistic conception of God than either Conservativism or Reform was willing to support. For Kaplan and his followers, God could no longer be thought of as a noun—that is, as a metaphysical "entity," separate from humanity—but rather as the expression of whatever moral and spiritual potential human beings possess in their search for holiness and righteousness. Kaplan's virtual abandonment of the traditional concept of divine transcendence signaled a dramatic break with the Orthodox faith in which he was raised.

For many Jews, Reconstructionist theology seemed to be a contradiction in terms: lacking a true Judaic concept of God, it could be nothing more than a disguised form of secular humanism, and as such, a heretical rejection of Torah. Kaplan's defenders, however, insisted that, as an "evolving religious civilization," Judaism's understanding of God and of the covenant would have to change as well, and in the process absorb contemporary scientific views of the cosmos and of the human mind.

THE VARIETIES OF MODERN JUDAISM

PRACTICE OF HALACHA

ORTHODOXY: Strict observance of halacha, allowing for limited adaptation to changing conditions of life (Sabbath, family purity, and dietary laws)

CONSERVATISM: Serious commitment to observance of halacha, combined with a significant degree of adaptation to changing circumstances of modern life.

REFORM: Liberal view of halacha, generally regarding Sabbath and dietary laws as optional observances.

RECONSTRUCTIONISM: A respectful but liberal view of halacha, coupled with a view of religious practices as "folkways" and facets of Judaism as a civilization.

GENDER SEPARATION

ORTHODOXY: Gender separation and differentiation: separate seating for women in synagogue; opposition to rabbinic ordination of women.

CONSERVATISM: Rejection of gender separation and differentiation; mixed seating in synagogue and ordination of women.

REFORM: Rejection of all forms of gender separation and differentiation; first to ordain women as rabbis and eager adoption of the Bat Mitzvah.

RECONSTRUCTIONISM: Rejection of all gender separation and differentiation: ordains women as rabbis and first movement to support the Bat Mitzvah.

HEBREW LANGUAGE

ORTHODOXY: Retention of Hebrew as language of prayer and strict adherence to traditional prayer routines

CONSERVATISM: Retention of Hebrew as the language of prayer and preservation of most traditional prayer routines coupled with innovative practices (e.g., Bat Mitzvah).

REFORM: Initial opposition to use of Hebrew prayers changes in the course of the twentieth century to greater enthusiasm.

RECONSTRUCTIONISM: Retention of many traditional Hebrew prayers combined with an interest in innovative expressions of faith in English.

(continued)

ZIONISM AND ISRAEL

ORTHODOXY: Some ambivalence toward Israel; fervent opposition toward secular Zionism.
CONSERVATISM: Enthusiastic support of Zionism and Israel.
REFORM: Initially opposed to Zionism, but support increased during the twentieth century.
RECONSTRUCTIONISM: Intense interest in Jewish "peoplehood" and enthusiastic support for cultural and political Zionism.

TORAH

ORTHODOXY: "Torah True": belief in divine revelation at Sinai and in rabbinic interpretation of Torah.
CONSERVATISM: "Positive-Historical" Judaism: belief in divine inspiration of scriptures and acceptance of historical process in the formation of halacha.
REFORM: "Progressive Judaism" committed to an evolutionary view of Jewish belief and religious practice.

RECONSTRUCTIONISM: "Humanistic Judaism" rooted in the belief that Torah is the expression of the religious creativity of the Jewish people.

AFTERLIFE, REDEMPTION, AND THE SOUL

ORTHODOXY: Literal belief in the afterlife, immortality of the soul, resurrection of the dead, messianic redemption of Israel and the world.
CONSERVATISM: Generally, nonliteral belief in the afterlife, immortality of the soul, and resurrection of the dead.
REFORM: Skeptical view of any literal belief in divine revelation, afterlife, resurrection of the dead; figurative view of immortality of the soul and messianic redemption.
RECONSTRUCTIONISM: Generally, agnostic view of any belief in a personal God, combined with a fervent belief in the creative potential of human beings.

The Shoah and the State of Israel

During the twentieth century, two of the most extraordinary events in Jewish history occurred: one traumatic, the other transformative. Both events have had a profound effect on the beliefs and practices of contemporary Judaism. The first event, referred to in Hebrew as the Shoah—or, more commonly, as the **Holocaust**—can be seen as the single greatest tragedy of modern Jewish life: the most successful attempt in history by anti-Semites to rid the world of both the religion Judaism and the Jewish people.

The Shoah   The word "Shoah" itself requires some explanation, if only because it has a different connotation than the more familiar word "Holocaust." In Hebrew the word "shoah" literally means "whirlwind," and as a metaphor it captures—as well as any image can—the insane rage of anti-Semitic hatred that was loosed on Europe's Jews during World War II. Many Jews prefer this term, unfamiliar as it may be to English-speaking audiences, precisely because it avoids the connotation of a divinely commanded sacrifice, which is exactly what the biblical term "holocaust" (or "burnt offering") brings to mind.

For centuries Jews had been the targets of Christian and occasionally Muslim hostility and persecution, but until Adolf Hitler and Nazi Germany embarked on the "Final Solution," no ruler or regime ever entertained the idea of total extermination. In Hitler's autobiography, *Mein Kampf* (1925), he described the Jews as a disease organism within the body of European society that he and his followers proposed to destroy forever. The genocidal policies that his government pursued represented a logical outcome of this essentially racist conception of the Jews

The entrance gate at Auschwitz.

and their faith. To carry out this genocidal campaign, Hitler mobilized not only the resources of Germany but also the support of willing collaborators throughout Europe. There is little doubt that had German armies defeated the United States, Britain, and the Soviet Union during World War II, the annihilation of the world's Jewish population would have been one of Hitler's proudest accomplishments. Even in defeat, however, the Nazis destroyed roughly one-third of the world's Jewish population, and the legacy of torture and mass murder they left behind has deeply scarred the Jewish consciousness.

Contemporary Jewish philosophers have responded to the tragedy of the Shoah in remarkably diverse ways. For one theologian in particular, Ignaz Maybaum (1897–1976), the slaughter of innocents can be seen as a kind of *churban* (Hebrew, "divinely willed sacrifice"), through which the Jews perform an act of vicarious atonement for the sins of the world.[7] For theologian Richard Rubenstein (b. 1924), such logic is morally insane. Rubenstein insists that the random killing of six million Jews (not to mention the untold suffering and murder of many more millions of non-Jews) challenges, at the most fundamental level, Judaism's belief in a just and benevolent Creator who values every single human life. In his book *After Auschwitz*, Rubenstein insisted that Judaism's historic God-concept is "dead" and that no religious philosophy that is still committed to biblical ideas of divine justice and retribution can withstand scrutiny in an age of genocide and mass destruction.[8] For philosopher and rabbi Eliezer Berkovits (1908–1992),[9] however, the mystery of God's presence in history is deepened by the Shoah, not refuted by it, and ours is not the first generation to reflect on God's "hiddenness" or on the terrible consequences of human freedom. For human beings to be capable of choice, he argues, God must "restrain" Himself and allow His human agents to exercise their moral will, even if the consequences of divine restraint are catastrophic.

None of these theologians, however, is willing to see the Shoah as an instance of merited (and therefore inevitable) divine punishment. Their refusal to accept that now-archaic model of God's judgment and response to human sin marks a definitive break with traditional Jewish thought. If much of the world's Jewish population can no longer declare—in the words of the traditional liturgy—"because of our sins were we exiled from the land," then what model of covenant relations can now be invoked to make both human suffering and world redemption meaningful?

For theologian Abraham Joshua Heschel, the only defensible Jewish theology after the Shoah is one that posits God's need for, and yearning after, humankind. The covenant relationship, as Heschel understands it, is a reciprocal one in which human moral intelligence and divine "pathos" join in the act of worship and of love. God's longing for us does not, Heschel insists, annul the reality of evil or the terrible freedom with which human beings have been invested. It does, however, establish what Heschel calls an "analogy of being," that is, a hint of divine likeness in every soul, and thereby the capacity to mend a broken world. If all we knew of God, Heschel argues, was a theory of omnipotence or omniscience, then the Shoah might very well sweep away that merely conceptual reality. But the truth is, he continues, that we know God at a much deeper level of moral consciousness, and that form of the divine presence abides even in the midst of the most appalling evils.[10]

Statehood for Israel   The second pivotal event of modern Jewish history is the establishment of the State of Israel in 1948, what one philosopher has called the "the Jewish return into history."[11] The Zionist philosophy on which the State of Israel rests is really several philosophical/religious arguments in one. In its earliest form, "Zionism" is simply a feeling of attachment to an ancestral homeland in which a vast majority of Jews, past and present, have never lived. Even though a comparatively small population of Jews continued to live in Palestine for centuries after the Exodus, most Jews were content to sing "next year in Jerusalem" at the Passover Seder without ever really contemplating a return to the land of biblical Israel.

A decisive shift in such thinking occurred, however, in the course of the nineteenth century. Two Orthodox rabbis—Yehudah Hai Alkalai (1798–1878) and Zvi Hirsch Kalischer (1795–1874)—argued passionately for a messianic view of Jewish history, urging their contemporaries to emigrate to Palestine in the expectation that the redemption of Israel was about to be accomplished, but only if the Jews took the first practical step of occupying and restoring the land.[12] Their writings were largely ignored within their lifetimes, but the arguments of an assimilated Austrian Jew, writing near the end of the century, attracted much greater attention.

For Theodor Herzl (1860–1904), the rapid growth of anti-Semitism had made the condition of eastern European Jews so precarious that something had to be done—apart from continuing mass emigration to the United States—to deal with the poverty and desperation of the Jewish masses. Herzl's solution was the establishment of an internationally recognized Jewish state, either in Palestine or Argentina. He laid out his ideas in an extended tract entitled "The Jewish State" (1896)[13] and later in a utopian novel, *The Old New Land* (1902).[14] Herzl died in 1904 and never lived to see any of his ideas come to fruition. The Zionist movement he helped to found continued to solicit support for his ideas, and in 1917 British Zionists found a sympathetic advocate in the foreign minister of Great Britain, Lord Arthur Balfour (1848–1930).

Balfour's private letter (now known as the Balfour Declaration) to the most prominent Jew in England, Lord Walter Rothschild (1868–1937), is the earliest sign that any major power was willing, for whatever reason, to validate Zionist claims to a political stakehold in Palestine. In carefully guarded diplomatic language, Balfour declared his government's willingness to establish a "national home for the Jewish people," provided that "nothing shall be done which may prejudice the civil and religious rights of existing non-Jewish communities in Palestine."[15] Within a decade of this proclamation, however, both Great Britain and the rapidly growing Jewish community in Palestine discovered just how intense Palestinian Arab opposition to increased Jewish immigration really was. By the late 1930s, as Great Britain sought to limit sharply the number of Jews who could legally enter Palestine, the stage was set for a succession of wars between Arabs and Jews—wars that have continued to the present day.

This painting of Herzl is one of many that appear on Israeli currency.

As a secular ideology, Zionism (in all its variations) rests on a few basic assumptions. The first assumption holds that anti-Semitism may abate from time to time, but it will never disappear, and as long as Jews are hated anywhere in the world, their lives are in peril. The second assumption is that the only guarantee of physical survival in a hostile world is national sovereignty—because only a nation-state can effectively defend its citizens. Third, the guest-host relationship Jews have lived under, whether in Christian or in Muslim lands, has always been inherently unstable, and on occasion threatening to Jewish survival. If Jews are to have any hope of a secure future, they will have to regain their collective autonomy, which can be accomplished only through political means. And if one adds to all of this the specifically religious belief that the rebirth of the State of Israel represents the beginning stage of messianic redemption of the world, one has a totality of ideas that have been employed to rationalize the transformation of the world Jewish community back into a politico-religious entity. Viewed from this perspective, Jewish history has come full circle in our time, as Jews search for ways to reconnect their religious lives with their enduring sense of peoplehood.

Religious Violence and the Future of Zionism

The assassination of Yitzhak Rabin, Israel's prime minister, on November 4, 1995, laid bare deep ideological differences that had been building in Israel for decades between the generally secular majority of its Jewish population and the more religiously intense segment of Israeli society, often called "Haredi" Jews. The term *haredi* means literally "those who tremble" (before God), and in English they are often designated as "ultra-Orthodox" Jews, whose view of the state of Israel, from 1948 to the present-day, ranges anywhere from violent opposition to its very existence, to an equally fervent and opposite belief in Israel's religious identity, and in its messianic future and goals.

Rabin's assassin, Yigal Amir, belonged to this latter group, and his decision to kill Israel's elected leader sprang from his belief that any peace settlement with the Palestinians—and

Mourners gathered at
Rabin's funeral.

particularly one involving the return of land seized by Israel after the 1967 war, which Rabin had proposed—constituted an act of national betrayal on Rabin's part, and therefore a religious crime deserving of death. In Amir's eyes, Rabin was a *rodef*—a criminal predator, in Talmudic terminology—and one whose very existence threatened the future of the Jewish state. Therefore, for Amir and his supporters, his assassination became a deed sanctioned by political necessity and religious law.

Amir's crime shocked the overwhelming majority of Israelis and was condemned throughout the Jewish Diaspora. At present, he is serving a life sentence in Israeli prisons, but the conflict between theocratic violence and democratic rule which this killing em-bodies remains a troubling shadow hovering over the possibility of political unity in Israel and, more broadly, over the Zionist ideal of collective Jewish renewal.

The Future of Judaism in the Contemporary World

During the last three decades of the twentieth century, and at the dawn of the new millennium, Judaism faced a number of formidable challenges. The sheer loss of human life following the Shoah meant more than just a sharp reduction in the Jewish world population. For some Jews, the possibility of collective annihilation carried with it the secondary possibility of the "end" of Judaism itself, or at the very least the dwindling of what was once a global community. For others, however, the threat of cultural extinction inspired a reexamination of their most basic philosophical assumptions and institutional behaviors. Two of the most far-reaching challenges came from two largely unrelated movements: feminism and radical humanism.

The Challenge of Humanist Judaism   Probably the most far-reaching critique of traditional Jewish concepts and religious practices at the end of the twentieth century came from a very different quarter: the rejection of Judaism's central God concept by secular Jews who found any form of theism philosophically untenable. For some, the renunciation of Judaism's God was a logical response to the insane violence of the Shoah and the absurd wastefulness and cruelty of a world that seemed perpetually at war. No truly just or beneficent God, they argued, could possibly tolerate such slaughter. Therefore, the only reasonable and morally compelling response was to assume that no such deity ever existed—except perhaps in the human imagination.[16]

Of course, anyone who has studied the development of atheism in the modern era has encountered arguments like these. What was new can be found in the insistence of humanist advocates such as the American rabbi Sherwin Wine (1928–2007) that one can remain a Jew, culturally and sociologically, while at the same time rejecting any belief in a supernatural Creator.[17] Taking their cue from Mordecai Kaplan and Reconstructionism, humanistic Jews insist that since Jews are a people first, and only secondarily a religious community, their disbelief in a God should not exclude them from the company of their fellow Jews or prevent them from embracing Jewish ethics and folkways.

At present, the appeal of this approach to Jewish life and values appears to be small. Institutionally, few communities throughout the world have identified themselves with this form of radical humanism or have made the effort to revise their religious calendars and liturgies accordingly. Still, no survey of contemporary Judaism would be complete without some recognition of this radical alternative to mainstream Jewish faith.

Women and Judaism

Traditionally, the status of women in Judaism has been that of respected but subordinate members of the religious community, and for many centuries Jewish women lived in a male-dominant culture. Although two of the books of the Hebrew Bible are named for women (the Book of Ruth and the Book of Esther) and Jewish identity is (traditionally) traced through the mother's line, religious leadership in Judaism has historically been a male preserve. The Orthodox **Siddur** (Hebrew, a single volume that became the primary source of the synagogue liturgy) instructs Jewish males to thank God that they were not born women, and rabbinic tradition released women from all time-bound religious obligations (such as fixed prayer times), based on the assumption that a woman's chief responsibilities were to raise children and maintain the home. The only ritual obligations that women were expected to fulfill were those of baking challah, lighting the Sabbath lights, and attending the mikveh. And although women were never prevented from attending synagogue, their very presence necessitated a physical barrier to separate them from male worshipers, who, it was feared, would otherwise be distracted by their presence. Moreover, the privilege of advanced religious study was reserved exclusively for men, who were thought to be better equipped by nature for the mental rigors of scholarly debate.

The Western feminist movements of the 1970s totally rejected such views on the grounds that they embodied a "patriarchal" view of woman's place in society, and as the influence of feminist thought made its presence felt throughout the Jewish community—particularly in the United States—the exclusion of women from positions of religious authority soon came to an end. The American Reform Movement took the lead by conferring the title of rabbi on Sally Jane Priesand (b. 1946) in 1972, and shortly thereafter both the Conservative and Reconstructionist movements in the United States began to admit women to their rabbinic seminaries. Today, over 300 women occupy pulpits in Reform, Conservative and Reconstructionist synagogues, though as yet very few Orthodox communities have embraced this innovation.

At the same time that women were being admitted to the rabbinate in greater numbers, a new approach to both religious language and the interpretation of biblical literature was beginning to manifest itself within the non-Orthodox spectrum of the Jewish community. Feminist scholars in particular focused on the gendered vocabulary that surrounded the biblical idea of God, as well as echoes of a distinctly masculine image of the Deity in traditional prayers, where God is consistently referred to as "Father," "Lord," and "King." Reform liturgists began to experiment with gender-neutral words such as "Eternal One" and "Source of Life" as alternatives to the obviously patriarchal terminology of the traditional Siddur. In addition, the elimination or revision of prayers that implied the spiritual superiority of the male or that excluded women from the prayer community by omission became part of the same revisionist project. Not all of these innovations have proven universally acceptable, but collectively they represent a serious effort to bring the religious discourse of Judaism into the contemporary world.[18]

GLOBAL SNAPSHOT
Judaism in India

In addition to historically influential communities in Europe, the Middle East, and North America, Jews have also established themselves in places remote from these centers of Jewish life. In India, three culturally distinct groups of Jews have flourished.

The largest of these groups is the Bene Israel (meaning "Sons of Israel"), which claims to be descended from one of the "lost" ten tribes of ancient Israel, and whose ancestors allegedly migrated to India over 2,000 years ago. When travelers from Iraq discovered them in the eighteenth century, the Bene Israel still observed the Sabbath, and continued the practice of circumcision and observance of the dietary code. In the 1830s, Iraqi Jews fleeing Muslim persecution joined the Bene Israel community. Of all of the subgroups of Indian Jews, the Bene Israel appear to have prospered the most under British rule. With Indian independence, however, and the establishment of the State of Israel, the majority of Bene Israel chose to emigrate to Israel, where, at first, their identity as authentic Jews was questioned by rabbinic authorities. By 1964, the Bene Israel were declared historically and ritually Jewish, prompting even further emigration from India.

Two other Jewish communities in India occupy a place in the history of Judeo-Indian culture: the Cochin Jews and the Baghdadi Jews. The Cochin Jews claim to have arrived and settled near the city of Cochin sometime after the division of the two kingdoms (Israel and Judah) following the death of King Solomon. More recent arrivals to this community came from Spain and Portugal after the Jews'

expulsion from both kingdoms in the late fifteenth century, and even later during the seventeenth and eighteenth centuries, when Jewish immigrants from the Middle East found their way to Southern India.

Baghdadi Jews came mostly from Iraq, fleeing Muslim persecution during the nineteenth century. Like their counterparts in the Cochin community, they assimilated to Indian society through marriage. Today, there are very few members of either group still living in India, or retaining Jewish identity. As with the Bene Israel, so with the Cochin and Baghdadi Jews: the attraction of Zionism and of the newly created state of Israel held out the promise for Indian Jews of a more complete and fulfilling Jewish life. It was this promise, rather than any persecution, that prompted them to abandon life in India.

In 2012, New Delhi hosted the first Jewish Indian wedding in fifty years. Here, the bride and groom exchange rings as they are married in the Bene Israel tradition.

Judaism as a Way of Life

As Judaism has historically placed great emphasis on the sanctification of time, any consideration of Judaism as a "way of life" should begin with the ways in which Jews mark the passage of time. Like many ancient peoples, Jews in antiquity employed a modified lunar calendar that allowed them to celebrate each month's appearance of a new moon while at the same time periodically adjusting the lunar year to the solar year. They dated this calendar from what they presumed to be the moment of the world's creation, with the result that the year 2014 in our secular calendar overlaps with the Jewish year 5774. And within this sacred calendar, certain seasons were designated as "Sabbaths," or occasions for religious celebration, during which the Jewish community reaffirms its covenant relationship with God.

The Major Festivals

At the core of this system of seasonal religious observances are five major festivals, all linked to each other and to the cycle of nature—**Rosh Hashanah**, **Yom Kippur**, **Sukkot**, **Pesach**, and **Shavuot**—as well as minor festivals throughout the year. Each major festival is biblical in origin, and on each of these occasions Jews are commanded to cease working and devote themselves to prayer. That said, each major *chag* (Hebrew, "sacred occasion") is as individual as the season it celebrates and the ritual function it performs.

Rosh Hashanah   Commonly referred to as the Jewish New Year, Rosh Hashanah is traditionally celebrated for two days at the beginning of the month of Tishri (September–October), and it is regarded as both a solemn and a joyous occasion. The year begins with a period of self-reflection, signaled by the blowing of a ram's horn (Hebrew, *shofar*) during the synagogue service. The sound of this instrument is designed to awaken the conscience of the worshiper to the need for repentance and reconciliation with God. For that reason Rosh Hashanah is referred to in the liturgy as *Yom Hazikaron*, or the Day of Remembrance. At the same time, the mood created during the two days of Rosh Hashanah is generally hopeful, and it is customary to eat a dish of apples and honey as an expression of hope that the coming year will be one of sweet fruitfulness and fulfillment. On this occasion, it is also customary for Jews to greet each other, at the conclusion of religious services, with the words *l'shanah tovah tikatevu*—"may you be inscribed for a good year." This saying alludes to the ancient belief that, during the ten-day period between Rosh Hashanah and Yom Kippur, God writes the names of those who will live for another year in a "Book of Life."

Covered in a large tallit, this Yemenite Jew blows the shofar on Rosh Hashanah.

The Torah scroll is placed on a table where the reader will use a *Yad* (a pointer) to read each word aloud.

The palm branch, the willow, and the myrtle make up the *lulav*; the citron and the *lulav* are held together during Sukkot prayers.

The Passover plate is prepared for the Seder, with an egg, a shank bone, parsley, chives, and bitter herbs.

The Star of David is a medieval symbol of Jewish identity placed in the center of the flag of Israel.

Yom Kippur Also known as the Day of Atonement, Yom Kippur is the most solemn day in Judaism's sacred calendar and its most important fast day. The purpose of both the dusk-to-dusk fast and the penitential prayers that are recited on Yom Kippur was made clear by the rabbis centuries ago: "For transgressions against God, the Day of Atonement atones; but for transgressions of one human being against another, the Day of Atonement does not atone until they have made peace with one another" (Tractate Yoma 8:9). For repentance (Hebrew, *teshuvah*) to be effective, some restorative action must accompany prayer and self-examination. As a result, the liturgy for Yom Kippur asks forgiveness for all the sins that people are likely to commit against one another, as well as all the acts of defiance that people are likely to display toward God. These confessional prayers, which are recited throughout the day, are collective expressions of guilt and remorse ("Our father, our King, *we* have sinned before You"). But although it is the norm in Judaism to pray as a part of a community, each worshiper is nevertheless expected to internalize the act of repentance and strive for reconciliation with neighbors and with God.

On Yom Kippur a number of restrictions, in addition to fasting, are imposed on observers. Thus, in Orthodox communities, it is customary for married couples to abstain from intimacy, for men to wear white garments (symbolic of purification) to synagogue, and to neither shave nor bathe (as if one were in mourning). In addition, no work of any kind may be performed on Yom Kippur. People who are ill, children under thirteen years of age, and nursing mothers are generally exempt from fasting and other restrictions.

Sukkot Five days after the conclusion of Yom Kippur, Jews undertake a week-long fall harvest celebration known as Sukkot ("booths"). As with any harvest festival,

Sukkot displays symbols of the season, the most important being the palm frond (Hebrew, *lulav*), the citron, and leaves of the willow tree and the myrtle. The sukkah— or temporary hut, from which Sukkot derives its name— is adorned with these plants, and its roof is left partly open to the sky. During the seven days of this holiday Jews are encouraged to eat and sleep in the sukkah, so as to reenact, symbolically, the biblical Exodus. Sukkot thus becomes one of three festivals (the other two being Pesach and Shavuot) that recall the Exodus narrative.

VOICES: An Interview with Rabbi Brad Bloom

Rabbi Bloom, of Temple Beth Yam, Hilton Head, South Carolina, is a graduate of the Hebrew Union College (a Reform Rabbinic seminary). He holds a Master's degree in social work, and for almost thirty years he has served congregations in Illinois and California.

Rabbi Brad Bloom.

How do the High Holy Days evoke feelings of wonder and awe, for you and your congregation?

Rosh Hashanah and Yom Kippur lie at the very core of Jewish religious consciousness. These "Days of Awe," as they are called, challenge us to assess our relationship to God and to each other. We are obliged to ask hard questions and recognize our human frailties, and hopefully discover whatever inner strength we possess to change for the better. The awe and wonder we experience during this period of repentance come from two sources: from our encounters with God and from our communal experience and collective memory, woven together to create a moment of special sanctity.

Of course, our prayers and special rituals are an essential part of that experience. Listening to the *Kol Nidre* chant, for example, we are moved as much by the beauty of the traditional melody as by the thought of unfulfilled vows to God. And similar feelings arise on Rosh Hashanah when the shofar is sounded, echoing throughout the sanctuary. These are all sensory responses, but they evoke powerful emotions and even more powerful moments of introspection.

And how does a sense of God's presence enter into these rituals?

For some, God occupies the center stage in this drama; for others, he is thought of as working behind the scenes, eliciting deep feelings of empathy and belonging through our interaction as a congregation. And for still others, God is not present at all; instead, they experience the assembled presence of *K'lal Yisrael*— the worldwide community of Jews joined in solidarity. Taken together, all of these experiences represent the continuum of awe and wonder that are central to the High Holy Days.

It is traditional religious practice to attend synagogue during the first two days and the last two days of the festival, offering thanksgiving prayers attuned to the fall season. The biblical book of Ecclesiastes is read on the Sabbath of Sukkot, highlighting the festival's themes of the passing of the seasons and the providence of God. At the conclusion of Sukkot, there is an eighth day of prayer and celebration, known as Shemini Atzeret (or "the Eighth Day of Assembly").

Traditionally, Jews living outside Israel divide up Shemini Atzeret into two days, with the second day referred to as Simchat Torah (Hebrew, "Joy of the Torah"); on that day, the annual reading of the first five books of the Hebrew Bible comes to an end, and the cycle of weekly readings begins again. In Israel, and in many Reform congregations, Shemini Atzeret and Simchat Torah are combined into a single day, during which the "gift" of Torah is celebrated.

A decorated sukkah, ready for a midday meal.

Pesach More commonly known as "Passover" in English-speaking countries, Pesach is the second of three pilgrimage festivals, the first being Sukkot and the third being Shavuot. During ancient times, Jews made a pilgrimage to the temple in Jerusalem to offer prayers and animal sacrifices to God. With the Roman destruction of the Second Temple in 70 C.E., the practice of celebrating the Exodus from Egypt then shifted exclusively to the synagogue and to the home. It is in the home that Jews gather on the first two nights of this week-long festival to recount the Exodus story and to partake in a ceremonial meal known as a **Seder**—a practice that may well have begun in biblical times.

Like Sukkot, Pesach is celebrated for either seven or eight days during the month of Nisan (March–April). The first two and the last two days are subject to the same restrictions that govern any *chag*—no work and limited travel. In addition, however, Pesach imposes a dietary requirement: no foods containing yeast may be consumed during this period (reflecting the fact that Jewish slaves, escaping from Egypt, had no time to allow their bread to rise). Most observant Jewish households rid the home of all foods that contain leavening agents and prepare for this occasion by either boiling dishes and silverware or using a separate set of dinnerware reserved for use on Pesach alone. The dietary rules, collectively known as kashrut, are fundamentally important to Jewish practice, as the number of foods sold in supermarkets bearing a "Kosher for Passover" label demonstrates.

Observance of Pesach begins in the evening in the home, where the Seder is celebrated with family and friends, followed the next morning by a festival service in the synagogue. The Seder consists of two rituals in one: a meal, featuring biblical and seasonal foods that reflect the Exodus story, and a liturgy, found in an ancient text called the Haggadah (Hebrew, the "telling"). The Haggadah contains both the story of Israel's escape from Egypt and a collection of hymns and songs and rabbinic commentaries in praise of God, who made that deliverance possible. One of the goals of this ritualized meal is to leave each participant in the Seder with a sense of engagement with the enslaved generation that witnessed not only the liberation from bondage but also the giving of the Torah at Mount Sinai.

Because the Pesach Seder is a family event, children play a prominent role by being given questions to ask, songs to sing, and stories to listen to. During the ceremony that precedes the meal, the prayer leader takes a piece of matzah (a type of unleavened flatbread that, according to biblical writers, the escaping Israelites baked in haste while fleeing Egypt) and breaks it in half, hiding one half of this piece so that children can find it by the end of the meal and exchange it for a gift.

In addition to matzah, other foods displayed or consumed during the Seder meal include bitter herbs (a reminder of the bitterness of slavery); a mixture of wine, chopped nuts, and apples (symbolically representing the mortar used by Israelite slaves to build cities and pyramids); a roasted lamb shank bone (recalling the sacrifice of lambs by the Israelites before their departure from Egypt); and a roasted egg, a green vegetable (usually parsley), and an additional herb or vegetable. These items all reflect the ancient agricultural context of this celebration. Finally, participants consume four small symbolic cups of wine during the Seder meal, each serving as a reminder of the many blessings God bestowed upon ancient Israel and continues to bestow upon the Jewish people. A fifth cup is set aside for the prophet Elijah, whose symbolic presence at the Seder represents the hope that a messiah will someday appear and bring peace and justice into the world.

Shavuot   The last of the three pilgrimage festivals is Shavuot (Hebrew, "weeks"). Between the second day of Passover and the first day of Shavuot, it was the practice in biblical Israel to bring a sheaf of new grain to the temple, and an obvious connection exists between this festival and the later spring harvest. However, during the rabbinic era, Shavuot became associated with the giving of the Torah on Mount Sinai, and from that moment on Shavuot became a part of the ongoing liturgical reenactment of the Exodus that we have traced through Sukkot and Pesach. Given this new historical association, we can understand why the rabbis decided that the high point of the synagogue liturgy for Shavuot would be the public reading of the Ten Commandments.

Traditionally, Shavuot is celebrated for two days (the sixth and seventh of the month of Sivan [May–June]). It is common practice on Shavuot to decorate the synagogue with flowers and to serve meatless meals with honey as a key ingredient—the idea being that the reading of the Torah should be sweet upon the lips. Also common is the public reading of the Book of Ruth, which tells the story of a young Moabite widow who is welcomed into Israelite society and who, centuries later, became the prototype of the ideal convert to Judaism. Finally, there is a custom of staying up the entire first night of the *chag* for the purpose of studying some portion of the Torah.

The Minor Festivals

In contrast to the major festivals, several "minor" festivals serve to fill out the Jewish religious year. Despite their historically subordinate status, they are beloved by the many Jews who observe them. The observance of many of these minor festivals does not entail restrictions on labor, diet, or any other activities. In addition, while the agricultural cycle is clearly embedded within the calendar of major holidays, the minor festivals only indirectly reflect the season in which they appear.

Hanukkah   Of all of Judaism's minor holidays, Hanukkah is probably the best known throughout the Western world. Hanukkah commemorates the Maccabean rebellion that began in 167 B.C.E. against the tyrannical rule of the Syrian monarch, Antiochus IV, who sought to suppress the practice of Judaism within Palestine and who "defiled" the temple in Jerusalem by rededicating it to the Greek gods. For the next two years an armed insurrection, led first by a priest named Mattathias and after his death by his eldest son, Judah the Maccabee, wrested control of the temple from Antiochus's army. Hanukkah celebrates the recovery and cleansing of the Jerusalem Temple and the miracle of the lights that Jewish tradition records. According to this legendary account, once the temple was in Jewish hands it became necessary to rededicate the sanctuary—yet only one flask of the oil necessary to keep lamps lit could be found. Miraculously, however, this one flask continued to burn for eight days, thus attesting to the renewal of God's presence within the temple. In commemoration of that miracle, Jews light a candle each night for eight nights until a ceremonial lamp (known in Hebrew as either a menorah or a *hanukkiah*) is completely lit. This candle-lighting ceremony is accompanied by the chanting of prayers, the singing of songs, and, in more recent times, the giving of gifts. In addition, a traditional game of chance is played with a four-sided top known as a dreidel, on whose sides are inscribed four Hebrew letters, which stand for the words meaning "a great miracle occurred there." In contemporary Israel, however, dreidels bear a slightly altered message: "a great miracle occurred here," referring to the establishment of the Jewish state in 1948.

Purim   Another history-oriented festival is Purim, which occurs on the fourteenth day of the month Adar (February–March). Purim is a carnival-like holiday whose origins can be found within the biblical Book of Esther. Like Hanukkah, Purim celebrates a victory, this time over an antagonist named Haman, who appears in the Book of Esther as a would-be destroyer of the Jewish people. However, unlike Hanukkah, the underlying festival narrative appears to have little or no historical basis. Still, Purim tells an interesting story of adaptation and survival against all odds, and it is a story that has gripped the Jewish imagination for centuries.

For Orthodox Jews, Purim begins with a fast on the thirteenth of the month of Adar. Once the fast is over, the festive aspects of Purim begin. These include a reading of the book of Esther. Congregants interrupt the narration with shouting and foot stamping every time Haman's name is read aloud. In addition, the rabbis, many centuries ago, sanctioned the practice of drinking to excess on Purim, thereby contributing to an atmosphere of barely controlled anarchy, while children are dressed in costumes that suggest the principal characters in the Esther story.

Purim also has its more sedate customs: the sending of gifts to friends, or to the poor, and the eating of triangular-shaped cookies known as hamantaschen, variously thought to represent Haman's ears, or hat, or pockets. Finally, although there is no prohibition against working on Purim, many Orthodox communities will devote the entire fourteenth of Adar to celebrating this festival.

On the final night of Hanukkah, all the candles are lit while children play with the dreidel, a game with toy coins.

Tu B'Shevat   The fifteenth day of the month of Shevat (January–February) is identified in rabbinic literature as the "New Year's Day of Trees." Typically, trees are planted on this day (especially in modern Israel), and monies are set aside for the poor. In some communities Jews hold a special Seder on Tu B'Shevat consisting of recitations from the Bible and the Talmud, combined with the eating of certain fruits and nuts that are native to the land of Israel.

Tisha B'Av   The ninth day of the month of Av (Hebrew, *Tisha B'Av*) is, after Yom Kippur, the most solemn day in the Jewish calendar because it commemorates the destruction of both the First Temple by the Babylonians in 587 B.C.E. and the Second Temple by the Romans in 70 C.E. Each of these events was a tragic turning point in Jewish history, leading to the loss of national sovereignty and the subsequent exile of the Jewish masses from their homeland. On Tisha B'Av (commonly celebrated in July or August), Jews fast from sunset to sunset as they remember not only these tragedies but other terrible losses that they have suffered during their long history. Like Yom Kippur, Tisha B'Av is a day of collective contrition and virtual mourning, as Jews gather in synagogues to read from the Book of Lamentations and sing hymns that reflect on the double loss of Jerusalem and Jewish nationhood.

Yom HaShoah   Holocaust Memorial Day, or *Yom HaShoah* in Hebrew, is the most recent addition to the sacred calendar in Judaism. In 1951, the Israeli Parliament selected this date (the twenty-seventh day of Nisan [March–April]) as a remembrance day for the millions of Jews who were victims of Nazi genocide during World War II. This date was chosen because it coincides with the beginning of the Warsaw Ghetto Uprising of 1943, and Jewish communities throughout the world observe this day of collective mourning and reflection. Yom HaShoah, however, is not a fast day, and

A Jewish mother and daughter light the Sabbath candles.

unlike Tisha B'Av there are no prohibitions on work or other activities. Nevertheless, it has become customary in recent years for Jews to gather on the evening of the twenty-seventh of Nisan and to recite memorial prayers for the roughly one-third of the Jewish world population who lost their lives during the war.

The Sabbath

Although it is neither a major nor a minor festival, the weekly Sabbath (Hebrew, *Shabbat*) forms the core of the sacred calendar in Judaism. Like the major festivals, it is a day of prayer and rest, with its own liturgical tradition and pattern of observance; but, unlike any other sacred occasion in Judaism, its observance is explicitly mandated in the Ten Commandments. The Torah provides two different rationales for Shabbat: in the Book of Exodus (20:8–11), it is identified as the day on which God rested from His creative labors; in the Book of Deuteronomy (5:12–15), however, it is associated with the Exodus from Egypt and liberation from slavery. Each of these explanations provides a distinctive interpretation of the meaning of Shabbat; the first rationale is supernatural, whereas the second, the Exodus, is historical. For both interpretations, however, the commanding lesson of the Sabbath remains the same: God's actions, whether at the beginning of human time or at a turning point in the history of Israel, serve as a model for human behavior. The Creator/Liberator has separated sacred time from ordinary time, and so must we.

Shabbat begins at dusk on Friday and concludes at sundown on Saturday. This 24-hour period is ushered in by the lighting of two candles in the home, reminiscent of the first act of creation. Customarily, it is the woman of the house who lights these candles. Once the Sabbath formally begins, observance shifts to the synagogue, where the *Erev Shabbat* (Sabbath evening) service is conducted. The liturgy for Sabbath evening identifies the Sabbath itself as a "bride," and the feelings aroused by the "joy of the Sabbath" are similar to the emotions evoked by a wedding. With the return of the family from prayer, the Sabbath meal begins with a prayer of sanctification recited over wine and a blessing said over two loaves of bread. Sabbath bread is called challah, and it is usually baked in a shape that suggests a woman's braided hair (yet another allusion to the Sabbath "bride").

Sabbath morning observance shifts to the synagogue, where, in addition to the Shabbat liturgy, a weekly portion of the Torah is read, accompanied by a portion from the prophetic books. That service concluded, the remainder of the day is spent quietly until the evening, when the last two worship services of the day are celebrated, and a separation ceremony, known as Havdalah, is observed with a cup of wine, a braided

231

candle, and a spice box—all reminiscent of the sweetness and calm of the Sabbath. The rabbis of the Talmud once observed that it was not just Israel that had kept the Sabbath but the Sabbath that had kept Israel. As the most direct link to the ancient past, Shabbat serves as one of Judaism's primary symbols of historical and spiritual continuity.

Life-Cycle Events

At each stage in the cycle of living and dying, Judaism offers a distinctive ceremony that marks the passage from birth to death. The ultimate object of these rites of passage is the sanctification of human life and the desire to deepen the covenant relationship between Israel and God.

Birth The ritual process of entering the Jewish community begins, for male babies, on the eighth day of life with the rite of circumcision. Jews are not the only people today who circumcise male infants (nor were they in antiquity), but in Judaism circumcision is much more than a medical procedure. It is a mitzvah, a divine commandment imparted to the biblical patriarch Abraham and incumbent upon all of his male descendants from that time forward.

Historically, circumcision has been one of the distinctive physical marks of Jewish identity. Its importance for Jews can be gauged by the fact that the circumcision ritual takes precedence over the Sabbath or any other holy day in the sacred calendar. The only thing that would delay the performance of this mitzvah would be concern for the health of the child. During this ceremony, after the mohel (a ritual circumciser, who is usually a medically trained professional) has removed a portion of the infant's foreskin, the newborn receives his Hebrew name, which traditionally consists of the child's own name and that of the father (for example, Isaac son of Abraham).

A table set for Shabbat: Challah, candlesticks, and wine.

From this moment on, this is the name by which the child will be known in the Jewish community, particularly on ritual occasions. In many Conservative and Reform communities, it has become the custom to add the mother's name to the father's.

Baby girls enter the Jewish community under slightly different circumstances. There has never been any form of female circumcision in Judaism, nor any fixed naming ritual for the infant female. However, one popular custom today among Jews worldwide is the practice of bringing the newborn to the synagogue on the first (or, in some communities, the fourth) Sabbath after birth. On that occasion, either the child's father or both parents are called up to the Torah and recite the customary blessings. Then the baby girl is given a Hebrew name, and, like her male counterpart's, it is the name that she will use on all ritual occasions for the rest of her life.

Bar/Bat Mitzvah and Confirmation

Compare the Bar or Bat Mitzvah in Judaism with the confirmation ceremony in various forms of Christianity. How are they alike, and how do they differ?

Jewish males traditionally enter the stage of religious maturity at the age of thirteen, whether or not they have engaged in the Bar Mitzvah ceremony. There is no reference to such a ritual in the Hebrew Bible, nor do the rabbis of the Talmud make mention of any specific rite of passage that marks a young man's assumption of responsibilities as an observant Jew. Nevertheless, by the later Middle Ages, something like the Bar Mitzvah ceremony practiced today had already begun to evolve, consisting of some demonstration of Hebrew literacy and an ability to read a weekly portion of the Torah. Of all the commonly practiced rituals of contemporary Judaism, the Bar Mitzvah is the one ritual that is likely to be familiar to non-Jews.

After years of study, the young man who becomes a Bar Mitzvah is taught to see himself as a scholar-in-training whose entry into adult Jewish life is just the beginning of a lifelong program of study. Although the celebration that follows is often joyous, there is a serious underlying purpose: the preparation of a young person to assume what the rabbis have called the "yoke of Torah." Thus, in addition to reading a portion from both the Torah and the prophetic literature, a Bar Mitzvah is expected to deliver a brief scholarly explanation of the portion he has just read, thereby demonstrating a mature comprehension of Jewish Scriptures.

The practice of requiring young women (between the ages of twelve and thirteen) to furnish similar proof of both literacy and religious commitment is of much more recent origin. The first Bat Mitzvah to be performed in the United States was conducted in 1922 for Judith Kaplan, daughter of Rabbi Mordecai Kaplan, the founder of the Reconstructionist Movement. Beginning as a gesture designed to affirm gender equality in modern Judaism, the Bat Mitzvah soon evolved into an alternative form of the Bar Mitzvah ritual, and today the Bat Mitzvah ceremony is as common as the Bar Mitzvah in non-Orthodox communities.

Another innovative practice, known as a Confirmation, is almost as commonplace today in non-Orthodox communities as the Bar and Bat Mitzvah, and it too involves a process of study and ritual performance by both young men and young women. The Confirmation ceremony can be traced back to the early decades of the Reform Movement in nineteenth-century Germany, where some Reform-minded rabbis attempted to find an alternative rite of passage for adolescents rather than the traditional Bar Mitzvah, believing that the latter had become little more than a ceremonial occasion. Their solution was to borrow a practice from the Christian church and to require sixteen-year-old males (and later females) to make a profession of faith during the Shavuot service, thus connecting their religious coming of age with the traditional celebration of the giving of the Torah at Mount Sinai. This practice was integrated into the traditional life cycle after World War II, as many Reform and several Conservative congregations added the Confirmation ceremony to the now-lengthened process of Jewish education. Thus, instead of supplanting the Bar Mitzvah, the Confirmation ceremony simply became a secondary stage of the passage to adulthood.

Marriage and Divorce   In Judaism, marriage is a contractual relationship between a man and a woman, rooted in mutual love and respect, and presumed to be both monogamous and enduring—a relationship on which divine blessings can be invoked. However, like all contracts, the marriage contract can be dissolved.

Over time, Jews have devised formal procedures for regulating and solemnizing the processes of marriage and divorce. Many centuries ago, the marriage ceremony consisted of two separate rites: the betrothal and the actual nuptials. According to this ancient custom, the future bride and groom became engaged to one another through the exchange of a ring. The couple then returned to the homes of their respective parents for a year, after which time the bride and groom gathered, along with their families, under a marriage canopy (known as the chuppah). A rabbi would recite seven blessings, praising God and sanctifying the union, and only at the conclusion of this ceremony would the marriage be consummated. Today, these two ceremonies have been combined and are accompanied by other, largely symbolic rituals: first, having the bride and groom drink from the same wine cup, and second, having the groom present the bride with her marriage contract (Hebrew, *ketuvah*). Finally, at the conclusion of the ceremony, the groom crushes a wine glass with his shoe—traditionally understood to symbolize the destruction of the two temples—whereupon the attending guests shout Mazel Tov (Hebrew, "good luck").

The bride and groom will stand under this chuppah during the wedding ceremony.

From a traditional point of view, the presentation of the *ketuvah* by the groom is the core of the marriage rite in Judaism because it states publicly the groom's intention to provide for his bride's well-being while he lives and her financial security after he dies, or after they divorce. Traditionally, the groom alone vows to set aside monies in escrow as "marriage insurance," but many modern Jewish couples have opted for a very different kind of *ketuvah*, vowing mutual commitment and support, symbolized by an exchange of rings.

Jewish divorce proceedings are no less formal than the marriage ceremony. After marital counseling has been tried and failed, the couple comes before a rabbinic court that hears the case. The divorce document is then drawn up, releasing both parties from any future obligation to one another. At that moment, the husband (or his representative) must hand the divorce document to his soon-to-be ex-wife. He is then declared to be free of their union and eligible to marry again—that very day, if he chooses. The wife, however, must wait three months to marry again, on the presumption that she may be pregnant and therefore carrying the child of her former spouse. Moreover, if her husband refuses to grant her a divorce—or cannot do so because he is missing—traditional Jewish law leaves her few options for dissolving the marriage. She may find herself bound by religious law to a husband who has abandoned her or who may have died without witnesses to his death. Orthodox communities continue to struggle with this legal dilemma today.

Death and Mourning In Judaism the deceased are treated with as much dignity as the living, and the ceremonies associated with the burial of the dead and mourning are invested with sanctity and respect. Whenever possible, a Jewish burial will take place within twenty-four hours of death (unless the Sabbath or a festival intervenes). The body is prepared for burial by being bathed and wrapped in a shroud, then traditionally placed in a simple pine box, thus discouraging ostentation. During the burial service, mourners express their sorrow by a symbolic tearing of their clothes—often wearing a strip of torn black cloth, pinned to a garment—while reciting prayers of praise for God and comfort for the soul of the deceased in the afterlife.

Once burial occurs, those mourners who were closest to the deceased—parents, siblings, children, or spouse—enter into a week-long period of mourning known as shivah (Hebrew, "seven"), interrupted only by the Sabbath. During this period, mourners do not work, remain at home, and receive well-wishers who join with the mourning family in "sitting shivah." Because mourners are not expected, during this week, to attend synagogue, it is customary for friends to join the family in the home to recite morning and evening prayers.

Once shivah is over, however, mourners are expected to return to the world and everyday obligations, with the understanding that for the remainder of that month mourners will abstain from entertainments and remain in a somber state of mind. Once this thirty-day period of diminished mourning is completed, restrictions on the mourner's participation in celebratory events are lifted, though most Orthodox Jews continue a modified mourning protocol until the first anniversary of a parent's death has passed. The erecting of a tombstone does not normally occur until eleven months have passed; thereafter, close relatives are expected to visit the grave at least once a year—usually on the anniversary of the death of that family member—as well as to recite prayers in memory of the dead during memorial services held during all the major festivals. Finally, it is customary to light candles in the home at the time of the yearly anniversary of a loved one's death, and, whenever possible, to place small stones on the gravestone as a sign of one's remembrance of the deceased.

Other Sacred Practices

As a way of life, Judaism seeks to shape every facet of one's behavior: from the food one eats (or doesn't eat) to the way husbands and wives relate to one another. To those living within those traditions, these practices provide a sense of meaning and order, endowing all of life's activities with an aura of holiness.

The Dietary Code   Since antiquity, Jews have observed a restricted diet. Although the details have changed over the centuries, the underlying assumptions behind these practices have not. In the Torah, the people of Israel are told, repeatedly, that God wishes them to be in a state of "holiness," and when that principle is applied to diet, it becomes a discipline of selective food consumption and careful food preparation.

The essentials of the Jewish dietary code are as follows:

1. The only animals that may be eaten are those that have been properly slaughtered; no animal that has been killed by another or that has died a natural death may be consumed.
2. The only quadrupeds that may be eaten are those with split hooves who also chew the cud (like cows or goats), and, once properly slaughtered, their blood must be drained away.
3. No fish may be eaten that does not have both fins and scales.
4. No insects may be consumed at all.
5. No meat dish may be eaten at the same time as a milk dish.

The practical consequences for anyone who observes this diet are obvious: such a person will not dine at a stranger's home without first inquiring whether the food about to be served is really "kosher" (meaning in conformity to rabbinic standards of food selection and preparation) and whether the plates and cooking utensils are also completely free of contamination from forbidden foods. Within all Orthodox and many Conservative Jewish homes, it is customary to find not only kosher foodstuffs on the table but also duplicate sets of ovens, refrigerators, and dinnerware to make it easier to separate meat dishes from milk dishes. Kosher restaurants carry this process one step further by ordering only meat prepared by kosher butchers and by obtaining rabbinical certification that all food preparation procedures have been followed scrupulously. The phrase "kosher-style" food is deceptive: foods and cooking processes are either kosher or non-kosher, but never both. Over the centuries, attempts have been made to rationalize this system of food taboos and culinary practices by suggesting an underlying concern with food safety and dietary well-being. But any benefits derived from not consuming infected meats are peripheral to the primary intent of the dietary code, namely, that of separating the observant Jew from a nonobservant food-consuming culture, thereby making the commonplace act of eating a religiously self-conscious event.

Family Purity   All Orthodox, and some Conservative and Reform, women, in addition to maintaining kosher homes, are also equally attentive to the practice of ritual "purity," and as a consequence attend a mikveh (Hebrew, "pool") at the conclusion of their menstrual periods. In a truly orthodox Jewish home, husband and wife abstain from sexual intimacy not only during the entire period of menstruation but for seven days thereafter, and only then will the wife attend the mikveh. The purpose of this rite of purification, however, is not merely to bathe. Immersion in a mikveh is, rather, a symbolic act of spiritual preparation, and although it is used primarily by women preparing to resume sexual relations with their husbands, it is also used for conversion ceremonies and by orthodox males on the afternoon before Yom Kippur.

The origin of these practices can be found in the Hebrew Bible, where men are warned against having intimate relations with a menstruating woman. Nowhere, however, in either the Hebrew Bible or in rabbinic literature does Judaism suggest that women's bodies are "unclean" in a hygienic sense. As with the dietary code, so with the laws of family purity: the ceremonial discipline of traditional Judaism requires a heightened degree of self-awareness about the routines of everyday life. Among Reform and Reconstructionist Jews, however, such practices are rarely observed, and today rigorous application of the purity laws is only a distinguishing mark of family life within the Orthodox Jewish home.

Prayer

From its earliest beginnings, Judaism developed a distinctive culture of prayer. The Hebrew Bible includes examples of the principal types of prayer that make up the traditional Judaic liturgy: prayers of praise, confession, petition, and thanksgiving. In the Book of Psalms, for example, the legendary King David (to whom much of that book is attributed) petitions God in the following prayer-like poem:

> Hear my cry, O God,
> Heed my prayer.
> From the end of the earth I call to You;
> When my heart is faint,
> You lead me to a rock that is high above me.
> For you have been my refuge,

A tower of strength against the enemy.
O that I might dwell in Your tent forever,
Take refuge under Your protecting wings.
    —*Psalms 61:2–5*

In poems like this, biblical writers addressed God in a language that is at once intimate and awestruck, praising His providential care of those who trust in Him, while requesting His continued protection against evil and misfortune. But no matter what the character of any particular prayer, all prayers in Judaism are addressed directly to God, and all assume His compassion and just concern.

With the destruction of the Second Temple in 70 C.E., the principal site of Jewish prayer shifted to the synagogue, where prayer alone, disconnected from animal sacrifices, became the norm. From that point on, the practice of offering prayer—now no longer primarily the privilege of temple priests—became more democratic. Each community constructed its own house of worship, and before long a recognized liturgy emerged that consisted, in part, of selections from the Hebrew Bible and prayers for various occasions composed by rabbinic authors. By the Middle Ages, these prayers were collected in the Siddur.

The daily routine of prayer appears to have been established during the late biblical period, where we find the exiled Daniel, living in Persia, praying three times a day while turning toward Jerusalem (Daniel 6:11). The architectural arrangement of early synagogues echoed this practice by orienting the entire building in the direction of Jerusalem, though in later centuries Jews were content with placing the Ark—a large, upright cupboard designed to hold several scrolls of the Torah—on the eastern wall. As the rabbinic protocol of prayer developed during the early Middle Ages, the rules governing thrice-daily prayer became increasingly elaborate and formalized, with an additional early afternoon service added on the Sabbath.

Holding a prayer book and wearing a tallit, tefillin, and a kipah, a young man prepares to recite morning prayers.

The most common setting for prayer in Judaism is communal, and although individual prayer is always valid, the full complement of prayers in any prayer service can only be said once a quorum of worshipers has assembled, either in the home or, more commonly, in a synagogue. That quorum is referred to in Hebrew as a minyan, and in Orthodox communities it consists of at least ten males thirteen years of age or older; in Conservative and Reform synagogues, a minyan consists simply of ten adults of either gender.

During the morning service, men traditionally wear a prayer shawl (Hebrew, **tallit**) and phylacteries or prayer-amulets (Hebrew, **tefillin**) throughout, and then remove them at the conclusion of prayers. On the Sabbath it is customary, even in many Reform synagogues, to wear the tallit during prayer services, with tefillin worn only during weekday prayers. In most synagogues today, a head covering (known as a kipah or a yarmulke) is worn during prayer, chiefly by males, and as a sign of respect. Prayer services are conducted in the late afternoon and early evening as well.

One of the most powerful of all the prayers recited during the morning and evening services is the Shema, which consists of biblical verses that first declare the unity of God and then declare Israel's commitment to His service:

> Hear O Israel, the Lord is our God, the Lord is one!
> Blessed is God's glorious kingdom forever and ever!
> And you shall love the Lord, your God with all your heart, with all your soul, and with all your might. Set these words, which I command you this day, upon your heart. Teach them faithfully to your children; speak of them in your home and on the way, when you lie down and when you rise up. Bind them as a sign upon your hand, and let them be symbols before your eyes; inscribe them on the doorposts of your house and upon your gates.
>
> —*Deuteronomy 6:4–9*

This passage is one of the first prayers taught to children and it is, traditionally, the last prayer one utters before death. It is one of several prayers that are recited every day in the week, on major festivals, and on the Sabbath.

In Orthodox and many Conservative congregations, it is customary to read aloud a portion from the Torah every week, on Monday and Thursday mornings, and especially on the Sabbath (morning and late afternoon). In addition, an extra passage from the prophetic books is read on both the Sabbath and the major festivals. On each occasion, the portion selected from the prophetic books either echoes the themes of the Torah portion or reflects the themes of the festival itself. All these readings are normally recited or chanted in Hebrew, with translations in the local language available to the congregation. Today, all Jewish communities employ Hebrew in both the recitation of prayers and in readings from the Torah. Orthodox synagogues conduct services almost entirely in Hebrew, while Conservative, Reform, and Reconstructionist communities use both Hebrew and the congregation's native language.

CONCLUSION

Judaism has not merely survived over a period of three millennia; it has also evolved, responding and adapting to changing circumstances as it developed from a geographically and philosophically circumscribed religious culture into a global faith. As the oldest of the Abrahamic religions, it carries within itself the longest memory of formative events and personalities, and with it an abiding sense of the divine purposefulness of human history. Judaism exists, therefore, at a point of intersection between history and theology, as the life experiences of a people intertwine with their experience of the sacred.

At the summit of Jewish faith lies a singular Creator-God—at once familiar and mysterious, judgmental and forgiving—whose very existence guarantees the order and meaning of the universe; at the heart of Jewish faith lies a covenanted relationship between that God and those who are committed to serving and obeying His will. And even those who doubt the very existence of that God, but who persist in identifying themselves with Jewish history and values, continue to believe in a moral covenant that makes all human communities possible.

SEEKING ANSWERS

What Is Ultimate Reality?

The one God of Jewish faith is understood to be not only the source of all created things but also the highest and most complete form of reality the human mind can imagine. Jewish mystics often refer to this transcendent reality as the *Ein Sof,* or Infinite One. Traditionalists believe that God revealed Himself to the people of Israel at Mount Sinai and that Jewish Scriptures provide a reliable account of that revelation. The biblical view of Creation is, initially, positive: when God views the world He has brought into being He declares it "very good" (Genesis 1:31). However, later mystics, like Rabbi Luria, traced the evil in the world back to a mysterious cosmic error that subverted the design for the created world that God had originally intended. Nevertheless, the presence of divine "sparks" in each of us inspires us to believe that goodness and not evil will prevail.

How Should We Live in This World?

The divine commandments that make up the core of the Torah are designed to enable human beings to achieve true righteousness, that is, to bring the human moral will into conformity with God's will, and thereby ensure that justice and peace will prevail in the world. All ideas of right and wrong—such as the Ten Commandments—must, therefore, be referred back to God's revelation of His will at Sinai and the Torah's laws that govern human conduct. Both biblical writers and their rabbinic commentators believed that human beings are created in the "image of God" and, at the same time, are torn between good and bad impulses. In the mystical tradition, this conflict can be resolved through study, prayer, and meditation, all of which draw us closer to God.

What Is Our Ultimate Purpose?

Judaism has never believed that human beings are hopelessly evil, nor does it support the view that humanity can never make moral progress. The High Holy Days are dedicated to the belief that both individuals and whole societies are capable of changing their behavior and that, through active repentance, they are even capable of drawing closer to each other and to God.

Jews have long believed that the soul is immortal and survives death. The fate of the soul in the "world to come" and God's judgment of that soul remain a subject of speculation and wonder, even today; some, however, regard these beliefs as obsolete and no longer a part of contemporary Jewish faith.

REVIEW QUESTION

For Review

1. What are mitzvot, and where can they be found?
2. What does the word "Torah" literally mean, and how many other meanings can be derived from it?
3. What are Maimonides's thirteen Principles of Faith?
4. Who was Mordecai Kaplan, and to which movement in modern Judaism is he connected?
5. What does the term Shoah mean, and how is it different from the word "Holocaust"?

For Further Reflection

1. What are the implications for Judaism of the concepts of election and covenant? Do Jews see themselves as the only people with whom the Creator-God has communicated? Is it ever possible for a non-Jew to enter into a covenant relationship with Israel's God?
2. How did Judaism recover from the loss of the Jerusalem Temple in 70 C.E.? Why do you think that some Jews living today are hoping to rebuild the temple and resume the practice of animal sacrifice? Why are the majority of the world's Jews content with the synagogue and its prayer routines?
3. How does Maimonides's approach to both God and Torah differ from that of the mystics? Do the kabbalists really believe that it is possible for human beings to seek union with God or to find the presence of God within oneself?
4. Among the varied responses to the Shoah that modern Jewish philosophers have proposed, which response seems the most compelling to you? If you were a Holocaust survivor, what would your view of life and of faith be now? Would you still find it possible to believe in a just and loving God?
5. What does the word "Zionism" refer to, and what role did Theodor Herzl play in promoting Zionist ideas?
6. What are the Ten Commandments, and where can they be found?
7. What is the Talmud, and how many volumes (or tractates) does the Babylonian Talmud contain?

GLOSSARY

Baal Shem Tov (1698–1760) A charismatic faith healer, mystic, and teacher (whose given name was Israel ben Eliezer) who is generally regarded as the founder of the Hasidic movement.

Bar/Bat Mitzvah A rite of passage for adolescents in Judaism, the Bar Mitzvah (for males age thirteen) and the Bat Mitzvah (for females ages twelve to thirteen) signal their coming of age and the beginning of adult religious responsibility.

covenant A biblical concept that describes the relationship between God and the Jews in contractual terms, often thought of as an eternal bond between the Creator and the descendants of the ancient Israelites.

Dead Sea Scrolls Religious literature hidden in caves near the shores of the Dead Sea (c. second–first centuries B.C.E.).

Diaspora A Greek word in origin, it refers to those Jewish communities that live outside of the historical land of Israel.

election The belief that the biblical God "chose" the people of Israel to be His "kingdom of priests" and a "holy nation." This biblical concept is logically connected to the idea of the covenant, and it entails the belief that the Jews' relationship with God obliges them to conform to His laws and fulfill His purposes in the world.

eschatological Any belief in an "End-Time" of divine judgment and world destruction.

ethical monotheism A core concept of Judaism: the belief that the world was created and is governed by only one transcendent Being, whose ethical attributes provide an ideal model for human behavior.

Exodus The escape (or departure) of Israelite slaves from Egypt as described in the Hebrew Bible (c. 1250 B.C.E.).

halacha An authoritative formulation of traditional Jewish law.

Hasidism A popular movement within eighteenth-century eastern European Judaism, Hasidism stressed the need for spiritual restoration and deepened individual piety. In the course of the nineteenth and twentieth centuries, the Hasidic movement spawned a number of distinctive communities that have physically separated themselves from the rest of the Jewish and non-Jewish worlds and who are often recognized by their attire and their devotion to a dynasty of hereditary spiritual leaders.

Holocaust The genocidal destruction of approximately six million European Jews by the government of Nazi Germany during World War II. This mass slaughter is referred to in Hebrew as the Shoah.

immanence The divine attribute of in-dwelling, or God being present to human consciousness.

Kabbalah One of the dominant forms of Jewish mysticism, kabbalistic texts began to appear in Europe during the twelfth and thirteenth centuries. Mystics belonging to this tradition focus on the emanative powers of God—referred to in Hebrew as *Sephirot*—and on their role within the Godhead, as well as within the human personality.

Luria, Isaac A sixteenth-century mystic who settled in Safed (Israel) and gathered around him a community of disciples. Lurianic mysticism seeks to explain the mystery surrounding both the creation of the world and its redemption from sin.

Maimonides A twelfth-century philosopher and rabbinic scholar whose codification of Jewish beliefs and religious practices set the standard for both in subsequent centuries.

Messiah A possibly supernatural figure who will judge and transform the world.

mikveh A ritual bath in which married Jewish women immerse themselves each month, after the end of their menstrual cycle and before resuming sexual relation with their husbands.

mitzvot Literally translated, the Hebrew word *mitzvot* means "commandments," and it refers to the 613 commandments that the biblical God imparted to the Israelites in the Torah (i.e., the first five books of the Hebrew Bible).

Moses The legendary leader and prophet who led the Israelite slaves out of Egypt, Moses serves as a mediator between the people of Israel and God in the Torah and is later viewed as Israel's greatest prophet. It is to Moses that God imparts the Ten Commandments and the teachings that later became the Torah.

omnipotence The divine attribute of total and eternal power.

omniscience The divine attribute of total and eternal knowledge.

Pesach An early spring harvest festival that celebrates the liberation of the Israelites from Egypt, Pesach (better known as "Passover" in English) is celebrated for seven days in Israel and eight days in the Diaspora. The first two nights are celebrated within a family setting.

Rosh Hashanah The Jewish New Year, it is celebrated for two days in the fall (on the first day of the month of Tishrai) and accompanied by the blowing of a ram's horn (a shofar, in Hebrew). It signals the beginning of the "ten days of repentance" that culminate with Yom Kippur.

Seder A ritualized meal, observed on the first two nights of Pesach, that recalls the Exodus from Egypt.

Shavuot A later spring harvest festival that is celebrated for two days and is associated with the giving of the Torah at Mount Sinai. Along with Pesach and Sukkot, it was one of the "pilgrimage" festivals in ancient times.

Siddur The prayer book that is used on weekdays and on the Sabbath.

Sukkot A fall harvest festival that is associated with the huts (in Hebrew, *sukkot*) in which the ancient Israelites sought shelter during the Exodus. It is celebrated for seven days in Israel (eight days in the Diaspora). During that time, Jews take their meals and, if possible, sleep in huts that are partly open to the sky.

synagogue Jewish houses of worship. The focal point of every synagogue is the Ark, a large cabinet where scrolls of the Torah are stored.

tallit A prayer shawl that is worn during morning prayers (traditionally by men). The fringes of this shawl represent, symbolically, the 613 mitzvot found in the Torah.

Talmud A multivolume work of commentary on the laws of the Torah and on the teachings of the entire Hebrew Bible, composed in two stages: the Mishnah (edited in approximately 200 C.E.) and the Gemara (edited, in its Babylonian version, around 500 C.E.). Traditionally, Jews refer to the Talmud as the "Oral Torah" and regard it as an extension of sacred scripture.

Tanakh An acronym standing for the entire Hebrew Bible: **T**orah (the first five books of the Hebrew Bible); **N**eviim (or "Prophets," which includes works of both prophecy and history); and **Kh**etuvim (or "Writings," a miscellaneous gathering of works in poetry and prose). Taken together, the twenty-four books that make up this collection constitute the core "scriptures" of Judaism.

tefillin Taken from the word for "prayer," the term tefillin refers to two small boxes to which leather straps are attached. Traditionally, Jewish males from the age of thirteen wear tefillin during weekday morning prayers. Inside each of these boxes is a miniature parchment containing biblical verses; one box is placed on the forehead and the other is placed on the left arm, signifying that the individual's mind and will are devoted to God.

Torah Literally, the word *torah* means "teaching," and in its most restrictive sense it refers to the first five books of the Hebrew Bible. Less restrictively, it signifies the totality of God's revelations to the Jewish people, which includes not only the remaining books of the Hebrew Bible but also the writings contained in the Talmud.

transcendence The divine attribute of being above and beyond anything human beings can know or imagine.

YHWH These four consonants constitute the most sacred of names associated with the biblical God. The exact pronunciation of this name, according to ancient Jewish tradition, was known only to the High Priest, but after the destruction of the Second Temple the precise vocalization of these letters was lost—only to be recovered in the days of the Messiah.

Yom Kippur Referred to as the "Day of Atonement," it is the most solemn of all of the fast days in the Jewish religious calendar.

Zionism A modern political philosophy that asserts a belief in Jewish national identity and in the necessity of resuming national life within the historic land of Israel.

Zohar A kabbalistic *midrash* based on the biblical Book of Genesis (c. 1280 C.E.).

SUGGESTIONS FOR FURTHER READING

Akenson, Donald Herman. *Surpassing Wonder: The Invention of the Bible and the Talmuds*. Chicago: University of Chicago Press, 2001. An ambitious, and sometimes argumentative, history of the evolution of biblical and rabbinic literature.

Ariel, David. *What Do Jews Believe?* New York: Schocken Books, 1995. An accessible and nuanced account of traditional and nontraditional Jewish beliefs.

Bauer, Yehuda. *A History of the Holocaust*. New York: Franklin Watts, 2001. A well-researched and readable account of the Holocaust, written by the "dean" of contemporary Shoah historians.

Eisenberg, Ronald. *The JPS Guide to Jewish Traditions*. Philadelphia: Jewish Publication Society, 2004. A well-researched and comprehensive guide to traditional and nontraditional Jewish religious practices.

Fredricksen, Paula. *From Jesus to Christ*. New Haven, CT: Yale University Press, 1988. A close scholarly reading of the gospels that traces the separation of emergent Christianity from normative Judaism of the first four centuries.

Neusner, Jacob, and Alan J. Avery-Peck, eds. *The Blackwell Companion to Judaism*. Oxford, UK: Blackwell, 2003. A collection of diverse articles on the history of Judaism, written by some of the leading scholars in Jewish studies.

Plaskow, Judith. *Standing Again at Sinai: Judaism from a Feminist Perspective*. San Francisco: Harper and Row, 1990. A seminal work of feminist reconceptualization of normative Judaism.

Robinson, George. *Essential Judaism: A Complete Guide to the Beliefs, Customs and Rituals*. New York: Pocket Books, 2000. A well-written and comprehensive description of Jewish beliefs and practices.

Sarna, Jonathan D. *American Judaism: A History*. New Haven, CT: Yale University Press, 2004.

The best account to date of the historical development of the Jewish community in the United States.

Strassfeld, Michael. *The Jewish Holidays*. New York: HarperCollins, 1985. A nicely illustrated presentation of major and minor Jewish festivals with detailed accounts of religious observances from around the world.

ONLINE RESOURCES

My Jewish Learning
myjewishlearning.com
A well-researched site for historical subjects and religious practices.

The Jewish Virtual Library
jewishvirtuallibrary.org

A good site for contemporary subjects such as Israel and the Holocaust.

The Jewish Women's Archive
jwa.org
A comprehensive site for research articles on women in Judaism.

12

Christianity

STEVE AND RENEE WALKER have had a lot to look forward to during the past two years. First, there was the long-awaited arrival of little Simone, who brings gladness to her parents and her brother, Brent. Today there will be another exciting event as the Walkers present Simone for **baptism** into a spiritual family that Christians call the Church.

Whereas some Christians prefer to baptize adult believers who understand and accept the essential teachings of Christianity, others such as the Walkers believe that baptism is a special means by which God's love begins to grow even within small children. Wanting Simone to be touched by God in this way, they have arranged for her baptism to take place at St. James's Episcopal Church, where they have found friendship and fellowship with others.

Now the church is filled with worshipers whispering quietly in rows of pews while waiting for the service to begin. When it does, the organist fills the building with resplendent strains of music that seem to shake its foundations, the congregation launches into a favorite hymn, and a procession of clergy makes its way to the front of the church. After welcoming everyone, the priest, Father Robert, pronounces a blessing upon them. Then all eyes turn toward the baptismal font, an elevated basin of water. Steve, Renee, and Brent are waiting there, with Renee holding Simone in her arms.

A priest baptizes a baby girl as her family looks on.

Father Robert now enters into a formal dialogue with Steve and Renee, asking if they will bring up Simone in the Christian faith, if they renounce evil in all its forms, and if they put their trust in the grace and love of Jesus Christ. Answering for themselves and on behalf of Simone, they respond affirmatively. Then, dipping a small silver cup into the water of the baptismal font, Father Robert pours a bit of it three times on Simone's forehead. As he does so, he says, "Simone, I baptize you in the name of the Father, and of the Son, and of the Holy Spirit. Amen." Then, placing his hand on Simone's forehead, he marks the sign of the cross and adds, "Simone, you are sealed by the Holy Spirit in baptism and marked as Christ's own forever. Amen."

Now that the baptismal ritual is complete, Simone's family returns to their seats to await the end of the service. Soon they will be on their way home to join friends and relatives for a festive dinner and celebration of the new life that Simone will live, not just with the Walker family but in communion with more than 2 billion Christians worldwide. ☼

There are three great traditions within Christianity. Historically, the **Roman Catholic Church** has been the dominant **church** in the West. In the East (for the purposes of this chapter, the region extending from the Adriatic to Middle East), most Christians have belonged to the **Orthodox Church** (also known as the Eastern Orthodox Church). **Protestant Christianity**, which consists of thousands of "denominations," grew out of the Roman Catholic tradition in the sixteenth century. Although these churches have been shaped in different ways by complex historical and

World Christian population.

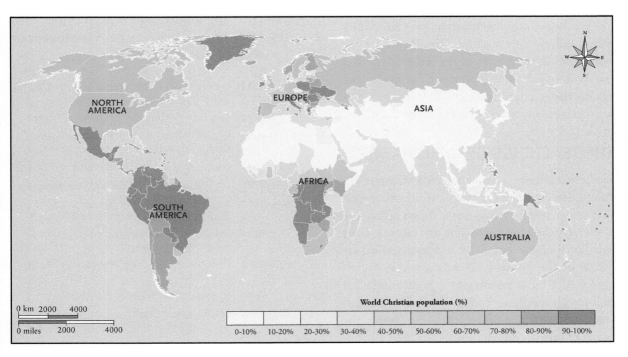

World Christian population (%)

| 0-10% | 10-20% | 20-30% | 30-40% | 40-50% | 50-60% | 60-70% | 70-80% | 80-90% | 90-100% |

cultural forces, they are united by shared beliefs that lie at the heart of Christianity. Christians acknowledge a personal and transcendent God, the creator and sustainer of the universe. The Christian doctrine of the **Trinity** describes God as one in essence but consisting in three "persons": Father, Son, and Holy Spirit. Christians believe that communion with God, in this life and in eternity, is the ultimate purpose of human existence. But there is an obstacle to be overcome: sin. The violation of God's will in thought or action, **sin** is common to all humanity. Worse, sin separates the individual from God. What is needed is the forgiveness that God gives to all who believe that the sacrificial death of Jesus Christ, the Son of God, atoned for all sin. For Christians, the sacrifice of Christ is the supreme expression of divine love. Similarly, they see in his resurrection and ascension into heaven a sign that not even death can separate from God those who respond to God's love. Although they remain imperfect, Christians believe that the destructive power of sin is no longer the primary force in their lives, for they have been baptized into a new "life in Christ."

We begin our investigation of Christianity with a survey of its teachings. We then trace the history of Christianity from the earliest days after the death of Jesus to the present time. Finally, we explore the practices by which Christians give outward expression to their beliefs in their daily lives.

THE TEACHINGS OF CHRISTIANITY

By the first century (as was discussed in Chapter 11), Palestinian Jews had endured centuries of oppression under foreign conquerors, always struggling to preserve their unique religion and culture. Their situation became especially dangerous with the arrival of the Romans (63 B.C.E.), whose brutality fueled a bitter resentment that ultimately led to a Jewish rebellion. Tragically, the revolt ended with the destruction of the Jerusalem Temple, the center of Jewish religious life, in 70 C.E.

TIMELINE
Christianity

c. 30 C.E.	Crucifixion of Jesus.
c. 46–60	Paul's missionary journeys.
70–100	Gospels of Matthew, Mark, Luke, and John written.
313	Constantine decrees religious freedom for Christians.
325	Council of Nicea declares God the Son to be "of the same substance as God the Father."
354–430	Augustine of Hippo, first great theologian of the West and author of the *Confessions* and *City of God*.
367	Contents of New Testament established.
529	Benedict of Nursia writes the *Benedictine Rule*.
949–1022	Simeon the New Theologian and the beginning of Hesychasm.
c. 1000	Conversion of Russia to Orthodox Christianity begins.
1054	The Great Schism divides the churches of East and West.
1095–1272	Western Crusaders repeatedly attempt to free the Holy Land from Muslim rule.
1184	Pope Lucius III inaugurates the Inquisition.
1198–1216	Height of papal power under Innocent III.
1265–1274	Thomas Aquinas writes the *Summa Theologica*.
1453	Constantinople, capital of the Byzantine Empire, falls to the Ottoman Turks.
1517	The Protestant Reformation begins when Martin Luther posts his Ninety-Five Theses.
1534	King Henry VIII establishes Church of England.
1545–1563	Council of Trent, at which the Roman Catholic Church responds to the Protestant movement.
1647	George Fox founds the Society of Friends (Quakers).
1703–1791	John Wesley, founder of the Methodist movement.
1804–1814	Napoleon, Emperor of the French, acts to strip the Roman Catholic Church of its influence.
1834	The Spanish Inquisition, the last stage of the Inquisition, is formally abolished.
1869–1870	First Vatican Council declares doctrine of papal infallibility.
1948	Founding of the World Council of Churches
1962–1965	Second Vatican Council.

Jewish groups responded to these pressures in different ways. Pharisees defended Jewish tradition through strict observance of the Torah. Sadducees cooperated with the Romans in the hope of preserving social stability. Zealots advocated anti-Roman violence. Essenes withdrew to the desert lands outside Jerusalem to wait for divine deliverance.

Believing that God would soon bring an end to unrighteousness, many Jews looked for the coming of a **Messiah** who would inaugurate a new era of justice and peace. Originally, messiah ("anointed one") was a title given to Israel's kings, who were anointed with oil as a sign of God's favor. Later, it came to mean the deliverer God would "anoint" to save the Jewish people from oppression. Some looked for a supernatural Messiah. Others watched for a descendant of David, ancient Israel's greatest king. Most believed the Messiah would rule as king and judge the wicked and the righteous.

The first Christians were Palestinian Jews who believed that Jesus of Nazareth was the Messiah—in Greek, the *Christos*, or "Christ." They proclaimed him as a deliverer not from earthly oppression but from the power of sin. In Jesus, they saw the beginning of a new era of righteousness and peace evident in his teachings, miracles, death, and resurrection.

The Life of Jesus

Our most important sources for the life and teachings of Jesus are the **gospels** of Matthew, Mark, Luke, and John. Written between approximately 70 and 100 C.E., the gospels are early Christian proclamations of the "good news" ("gospel," from Middle English *godspel*, translates the Greek *evangelion*, "good news") about Jesus' teachings, suffering, death, and resurrection. Because their interests are more theological than biographical, the gospels leave much unsaid about the life of Jesus. Still, their essential agreement on many points does allow us to establish the general outlines of his career and teachings.

The gospels report that Jesus was born in the Judean city of Bethlehem. We cannot be certain of the date; Matthew suggests that Jesus' birth occurred before 4 B.C.E., Luke by 1 B.C.E. Jesus spent his youth in the Galilean village of Nazareth. At about the age of thirty, he made his way south to the Judean wilderness, where he was baptized by John the Baptist in the River Jordan. A prophetic figure who warned of God's imminent judgment, John called on sinners to repent and be baptized in water as a sign of spiritual cleansing.

After his baptism, Jesus began a ministry that lasted no more than three years. The gospels say that as he traveled throughout Galilee he performed healings and

Mass baptism of Christians at Yardenit, the site on the Jordan River in northern Israel where Christian tradition says Jesus was baptized by John the Baptist.

miracles that testified to God's presence within him. The gospel accounts also describe Jesus as a charismatic teacher who spoke with authority on the scriptures and urged repentance and baptism in anticipation of the coming **kingdom of God**, a new era of peace and holiness. He was accompanied by an inner group of disciples, sometimes called "the twelve," led by three Galilean fishermen (Peter, James, and John), as well as by people from towns, villages, and the countryside. There were also Galilean women among Jesus' disciples who supported his ministry with their own resources. Indeed, women figure prominently in the gospel accounts of Jesus' ministry. Rejecting the social norms of his time, he befriended women and spoke and ate with them both in public and in private. When even the twelve abandoned Jesus in his final days, it was only the faithful women among his followers who remained with him.

As enthusiasm for his teachings and miracles grew, Jesus' popularity aroused resentment and opposition among members of the religious establishment. Jesus himself appears to have understood that dark days lay ahead. As he prepared to leave Galilee for Jerusalem, he warned his disciples that rejection, suffering, and death awaited him there.

Jesus arrived in the holy city just before Passover in or around 30 C.E. The gospels describe a triumphal entry in which crowds greeted him as the Messiah. Entering the Temple, he caused a great stir by driving out those who did business there, accusing them of making the sacred place a "den of robbers." For several days Jesus taught in the Temple, but then events took an ominous turn. After celebrating a "Last Supper" (perhaps a Passover Seder meal) with his disciples, Jesus was brought before a council of Jewish leaders and then handed over to Pontius Pilate, the Roman governor. Fearing that Jesus was a threat to public order, Pilate ordered his execution. Jesus was crucified less than a week after he had entered Jerusalem.

Palestine during the time of Jesus.

The gospels add theological reflections to this historical outline. Matthew and Luke assert that Jesus' mother, Mary, was a virgin who conceived miraculously in fulfillment of prophecy (Isaiah 7:14). All four of the gospels say that the Spirit of God, or the Holy Spirit, descended upon Jesus at the time of his baptism. According to Matthew, Mark, and Luke, a voice from heaven then declared: "This is my Son, the Beloved, with whom I am well pleased" (Matthew 3:17). In this way, the gospels link Jesus to King David, who is described in Psalms 2:1–7 as God's "anointed" and "son." The gospels also identify Jesus as the "servant" of God who would suffer for the sake of humanity, as foretold by one of Israel's prophets (Isaiah 42:1–4; 53:10–12). Finally, the gospels report that women who had followed Jesus found his tomb empty at dawn on the Sunday following his crucifixion. They and the other disciples were overjoyed when Jesus appeared to them and they remembered what he had once told them: "The Son of Man must undergo great suffering, and be rejected by the elders, chief priests, and scribes, and be killed, and on the third day rise again" (Luke 9:22). Convinced that he was indeed God's Messiah, they began to proclaim the good news that God had acted through Jesus for the salvation of the world.

According to the Acts of the Apostles (found in the Christian scriptures), Jesus remained with his disciples for forty days after his resurrection. Then, having sent them out as **apostles** (Greek *apostolos*, "one who is sent out") to preach to Jews and Gentiles alike, he ascended into heaven. Several days later, as they celebrated the Jewish holiday of **Pentecost**, Jesus' followers were suddenly "filled with the Holy Spirit," the same Spirit of God that had descended upon Jesus at his baptism (Acts 2:2–4). Empowered by the Spirit to carry out the mission Jesus had given them, they found themselves able to speak in languages they had not known before, to prophesy, and to perform miraculous healings. According to Acts, the number of believers grew rapidly, for "many wonders and signs were being done by the apostles" (Acts 2:43). Acts also reports that the first Christians spent "much time together in the temple" (Acts 2:46), reminding us that they were Jews who continued to live and worship as Jews. It did not occur to them that their belief that Jesus was the Messiah had given them a new religious identity outside of Judaism.

The Teachings of Jesus

The gospels describe Jesus as a great teacher who astounded the crowds who gathered to hear him, "for he taught them as one having authority" (Matthew 7:29). Although he engaged in debate with learned Pharisees and Sadducees, Jesus also took great interest in ordinary people. He often taught them in **parables**, stories that employed vivid images from everyday life to illustrate spiritual truths.

The central theme in Jesus' teaching was the kingdom of God (in Matthew, the kingdom of heaven). For Jesus, the kingdom of God was not an ordinary realm but the state of affairs that exists when human beings recognize God's sovereignty over the world and respond in love and obedience to God's will. To put it another way, the kingdom of God means the world as it ought to be, a world in which God's love and righteous rule are fully realized. In the gospels, Jesus sometimes speaks of the kingdom as a future event to be heralded by dramatic signs such as a darkening sun and stars falling from heaven. In the midst of these cataclysmic events, the present age would pass away and the kingdom would be revealed in all its glory. But Jesus also spoke of the kingdom as already present within himself and his followers. Asked when it would come, he replied that it was already present: "The kingdom of God is among you" (Luke 17:21). Though it was still small, Jesus expected the kingdom to grow into something great and wondrous. In one of his parables, he compared it to a tiny mustard seed that "grows up and becomes the greatest of all shrubs, and puts forth large branches, so that the birds of the air can make nests in its shade" (Mark 4:30). Whether speaking of the kingdom of God as present or future, Jesus emphasized its all-surpassing importance. Nothing can compare to the kingdom, he said, and so it is worth any price: "The kingdom of heaven is like treasure hidden in a field, which someone found and hid; then in his joy he goes and sells all that he has and buys that field" (Matthew 13:44).

Jesus taught that the kingdom of God is open to all who repent. By repentance, he meant something more than a mere expression of regret for some wrong one has done. The Greek *metanoia* ("a change of mind") found in the gospels suggests a turning away from anything that might prevent one from doing God's will. Like other Jews, Jesus found God's will expressed in the Torah and its commandments. In his famous Sermon on the Mount (Matthew 5–7), however, he gave the commandments his own interpretation, emphasizing that what God requires is obedience in thought as well as in deed. For Jesus, it was this absolute obedience to the will of God that constituted the true righteousness of the kingdom of God.

Jesus also taught that true obedience to God's commandments was an expression of love. When pressed by a Pharisee to identify the greatest of the commandments, he cited two (Deuteronomy 6:5 and Leviticus 19:18), explaining that they embody the essence of scripture: "'You shall love the Lord your God with all your heart, and with all your soul, and with all your mind.' This is the greatest and first commandment. And a second is like it: 'You shall love your neighbor as yourself.' On these two commandments hang all the law and the prophets" (Matthew 22:37–40).

The nature of love lies at the heart of Jesus' teachings. The gospels use the Greek word *agape*, which denotes the love one has for one's family as well as God's love for humanity. Jesus taught that genuine love knows no limits and is offered freely to everyone: "Love your enemies and pray for those who persecute you, so that you may be children of your Father in heaven (Matthew 5:44–45). Understood in this way, love leaves no room for the condemnation of others: "Do not judge, so that you may not be judged" (Matthew 7:1). Instead, love requires forgiveness: "For if you forgive others their trespasses, your heavenly Father will also forgive you" (Matthew 6:14). These principles are richly illustrated in Jesus' parables. The parable of the Good Samaritan (Luke 10:25–37), for example, demonstrates that even enemies deserve love and compassion. In the parable of the Prodigal Son (Luke 15:11–32), a father greets a dissolute and disrespectful son who has returned home– not with any thought of reproach, but with love and forgiveness gladly given.

The gospels describe Jesus as embodying these principles of repentance, obedience, and love. They also depict Jesus as living in the expectation of his crucifixion. In Mark, he tells his disciples that his death will be "a ransom for many" (Mark 10:45). Jesus spoke of God as Father, sometimes using the Aramaic *abba* ("papa") to suggest a relationship of special intimacy, as well as obedience. He urged his followers to draw close to God as well. They were God's children, he told them. As such, they should approach God in prayer with the words "Our Father" (Matthew 6:9) and with confidence that, like a loving parent, he would provide for their needs (Luke 12:22–31).

As we discuss later in this section, these fundamental teachings of Jesus lie at the heart of what Christians believe about sin, divine love, and salvation. But we first turn our attention to Paul of Tarsus, the first great interpreter of the life and teachings of Jesus, to see how Christian beliefs began to take shape in the years immediately following Jesus' crucifixion.

Paul and the Mission to the Gentiles

The most famous of the Jewish Christians who took the gospel and its teachings to Gentile lands was **Paul of Tarsus**. A Pharisee devoted to Judaism, Paul had been a persecutor of Christians, but after a dramatic experience of the risen Christ (Acts 9:1–19), he dedicated himself to preaching Christianity in Asia Minor (modern Turkey), Greece, and Macedonia. In his letters to young churches in Corinth, Thessalonica, Rome, and other cities, we can see Paul breaking with traditional Jewish thought in emphasizing God's love for Gentiles and disputing the necessity of observing the commandments in the Torah. Because Paul was the first to describe the role of Jesus in the salvation of humanity from sin, some have described him as the second founder—and even the *true* founder—of Christianity. It was due in part to his influence that Christianity was transformed in the middle of the first century from a Jewish sect into a largely Gentile movement.

At the heart of Paul's teaching was his belief that in Jesus Christ God had acted to bring salvation from sin to the world. Paul saw sin as a condition affecting all humanity: "All have sinned and fall short of the glory of God" (Romans 3:23). Controlling human beings and separating them from God, sin corrupts and ultimately destroys human life (Romans 6:23). For Paul, the good news of the gospel was that God's promise of salvation from sin, anticipated in the Jewish Scriptures, had been fulfilled in Jesus' death on the cross. Though sinless and undeserving of death, Jesus had offered himself as a perfect sacrifice in atonement for all sin. Although Paul's language of "sin," "sacrifice," and "atonement" may sound strange today, it is really quite similar to what we might mean when we say we have done some "wrong" to someone and that we must do something to "make up for it." In Paul's time, Jews and Gentiles alike understood that sacrifice was the means of "making up for" an offense against God, or the gods.

Paul was always emphatic in maintaining that salvation cannot be earned by "works," whether human efforts to obey the commandments in the Torah (Galatians 3:10) or good works in general. Instead, he taught that the salvation made possible by Christ's sacrifice is a gift, the ultimate expression of God's love, or **grace**. Salvation is given to those who respond to God's grace in faith, the conviction that God has acted through Jesus Christ to atone for human sin. Although Paul was very clear in teaching that salvation depends on God's grace and the individual's turning to God in faith, he did not dismiss the importance of works. In Romans 2:5–10, for example, he says that people will be held responsible for the good and evil they do. Paul's letters are not always precise about the relationship between faith and works, but they leave no doubt about the priority of faith. In his letter to the Galatians (2:16), Paul wrote that individuals are brought into a right relationship with God "not by works of the law but through faith in Jesus Christ."

For Paul, faith does more than bring salvation; it unites the believer with Christ in a "newness of life" (Romans 6:4) so real that Paul could say, "It is no longer I who live, but it is Christ who lives in me" (Galatians 2:20). Like the apostles who had been filled with the Holy Spirit at Pentecost, Paul believed that the Spirit lives in believers and brings them into union with God. To the Christians at Rome he wrote: "You are in the Spirit, since the Spirit of God dwells in you" (Romans 8:9). As a divine presence within, the Spirit encourages the growth of spiritual virtues, the greatest of which is love (1 Corinthians 12:27–14:1). Paul also believed that the Spirit makes all Christians one in the Church, which he often called the "body of Christ" (1 Corinthians 12:12–27).

Like other early Christians, Paul looked forward to a time when Christ would return in glory to bring an end to evil, sin, and suffering (1 Corinthians 15:20–28). But he also believed that the transformation of the world, signaled by the resurrection of Christ, had already begun. Signs of change were especially evident in the lives of believers, who had been renewed, even re-created, through the action of God's grace: "So if anyone is in Christ, there is a new creation; everything old has passed away; see, everything has become new!" (2 Corinthians 5:17).

God, Creation, and Original Humanity

Christian thought about God, the world, and humanity begins with the first verse in the Bible: "In the beginning God created the heavens and the earth" (Genesis 1:1). Here, and in the story of creation that follows, the Bible makes a clear distinction between created things and their Creator. God is transcendent, existing outside space, time, and the other limiting factors that give the world its order and finitude. And yet God is also immanent, or present in the world, sustaining and caring for all things with a loving benevolence that touches even the least of creatures.

Much as a work of art tells us something about the artist, Christians believe that creation tells us something about God. Paul made this point in his letter to the

Romans: "Ever since the creation of the world his eternal power and divine nature, invisible though they are, have been understood and seen through the things he has made" (Romans 1:20). For Christians, the goodness, beauty, power, and design evident in the world are all expressions of God's nature. But it is God's goodness, and the consequent goodness of the world itself, that are emphasized in the biblical story of the world's beginnings. At the completion of each stage of creation, it says, "God saw that it was good" (Genesis 1:10, 18, 21, 25) and, ultimately, that it was "very good" (Genesis 1:31). Finally, Christianity teaches that the entire order of existing things, and especially human beings, is the deliberate and purposeful expression of a divine love that a grateful creation should return to God in praise. "Let heaven and earth praise him, the seas and everything that moves in them" (Psalms 69:34).

Christians believe that, despite its original perfection, the world as we know it today falls far short of God's intentions, plagued as it is by suffering, injustice, and death. These evils cannot be attributed to God, however, for they are completely opposed to God's perfection. Instead, Christianity points to creation itself—and, more specifically, to humanity.

The story of creation relates that "God created humankind in his image" (Genesis 1:27). For centuries, Christian thinkers have sought to understand all that is entailed by this assertion. Some have found the image of God in the human capacity for rational thought. Others have said it can be seen in the "dominion" God gave to human beings over all the earth (Genesis 1:26), which resembles God's rule over the entire universe. All Christian thought, however, acknowledges that human beings have a unique ability to love God, just as God loves them.

Andrei Rublev's icon of the Holy Trinity (1411) is considered a masterpiece of Orthodox religious art. It depicts (from left to right) God the Father, God the Son, and God the Holy Spirit. On one level, the three figures are the "angels" through whom God appeared to Abraham in the Old Testament. On a higher level, they represent the Trinity in a way that uses color, light, and imagery to give the viewer a glimpse into its unfathomable mystery.

This idea is found in the biblical narrative that describes how God placed Adam and Eve, the first human beings, in a garden-like paradise called Eden. Whether we understand Adam and Eve as literal human beings or as symbols of original humanity—the Hebrew word *adam* means "humankind"—the point of the story remains the same. For as long as human beings related to God in loving obedience, they lived in joyous harmony with their Creator, but their eventual decision to disobey God brought an end to that harmony and, consequently, to the harmony of creation as a whole (Genesis 2:4–3:24). It was through sin that evil in all its forms became a reality in the world. Worst of all, sin separated humanity from God. In the Christian view, the salvation of creation from sin's destructive effects begins with the salvation of human beings. It is only through salvation from sin that they are restored to that original relationship with God in which they find their true place, purpose, and fulfillment. In the words of Augustine, the great fifth-century saint, "You have made us for yourself, and our hearts are rest-less until they find rest in you."[1]

God as Trinity

How do Christian teachings about God compare with those of the related religions of Judaism and Islam and those of Hinduism and Buddhism?

Like Judaism, Christianity is a monotheistic religion. But Christianity differs from its parent religion in defining the one God in terms of three aspects of divinity. For Christians, there is a single divine nature that expresses itself eternally in the "persons" of Father, Son, and Holy Spirit.

The doctrine of the Trinity was not put into precise language until 381 at the Council of Constantinople, one of the meetings at which early Christian leaders as-sembled to establish doctrine. Building on the work of the Council of Nicea (325), the **bishops** at Constantinople produced the **Nicene Creed**, a statement of the doctrine that many Christians continue to recite in public worship:

> We believe in one God, the Father, the Almighty,
> maker of heaven and earth, of all that is seen and unseen.
> We believe in one Lord, Jesus Christ, the only Son of God,
> eternally begotten of the Father,
> God from God, Light from Light, true God from true God,
> begotten, not made, one in Being with the Father.
> Through him all things were made.
> For us and for our salvation he came down from heaven:
> by the power of the Holy Spirit
> he was born of the Virgin Mary, and became man.
> For our sake he was crucified under Pontius Pilate;
> he suffered, died, and was buried.
> On the third day he rose again in fulfillment of the scriptures;
> he ascended into heaven and is seated at the right hand of the Father.
> He will come again in glory to judge the living and the dead,
> and his kingdom will have no end.
> We believe in the Holy Spirit, the Lord, the giver of life,
> who proceeds from the Father [*and from the Son*].
> He has spoken through the prophets.
> We believe in one holy catholic ["universal"] and apostolic Church.
> We acknowledge one baptism for the forgiveness of sins.
> We look for the resurrection of the dead,
> and the life of the world to come. Amen.

As you can see, the Creed is divided into three parts corresponding to the three "per-sons" of the Trinity. It tells us about the relationships among the three persons as well as the functions of each.

Adam and Eve Banished from Paradise. In this fresco, the Renaissance painter Tommaso Masaccio (1401–1428) captured both the shame of Adam and Eve and the fear they felt as they were expelled from the Garden of Eden and separated from God.

The opening statement is about God the Father, the omnipotent ("almighty") Creator of all reality, spiritual as well as material, visible as well as invisible. There is one God, upon whom all things depend for their existence.

The second part of the Creed focuses on God the Son, who is "one in Being with the Father"—that is, of the same divine substance or essence as the Father. For the sake of humanity, the Son became fully human as well as fully divine. As a revelation of divinity on earth, the Son enabled those who recognized him as such to come to a greater understanding of God: "If you know me, you will know my Father also" (John 14:7). Beyond revealing the Father, the Son has three other roles. First, recalling the Gospel of John (1:3), the Creed states that "through him all things were made." Second, the suffering and death of the Son have made salvation possible. Third, the Son, as the risen Christ, will one day return to judge the world.

The final part of the Creed affirms that the Holy Spirit "proceeds" from the Father, implying the Spirit's sameness in substance or essence with the Father. The addition of the Latin *filioque* ("and from the Son") by the Western church, never accepted in the East, underscores the sameness of all three persons of the Trinity. Just as the Father represents God's power in the creation of the world, and just as the Son both reveals the Father and redeems a sinful humanity, the Holy Spirit represents God's continuing presence in the world. Since the beginning, when God breathed the "breath of life" into Adam (Hebrew *ruach* means both "breath" and "spirit"), the Spirit has given life to all of creation. Christians believe that since the descent of the Holy Spirit at Pentecost, it has animated, empowered, and guided the Church. Finally, it is the Spirit within that helps believers as they reach out to God in prayer (Romans 8:26) and that nurtures virtues such as love, patience, kindness, gentleness, and self-control (Galatians 5:22–23).

The Consequences of Sin

Christianity emphasizes the sinfulness of human nature. This may seem a harsh way of thinking about human beings. After all, there are good reasons to believe in their essential *goodness*. Of course, Christians do acknowledge the human capacity to do good things. But they are equally aware of the human capacity for evil and the fact that people are often destructive in their thought and behavior. Christianity teaches that sin is universal; everyone sins. It also insists that the tendency to sin is far more serious than an acquired habit one might overcome through greater self-control or moral effort. The inability of human beings to rise above sin—to be as loving, humble, generous, and righteous as they should be—suggests that something has gone wrong in the perfect world God created and, perhaps, even within human nature. As we will see later in this chapter's section on theology, Roman Catholic and Protestant Christians, on the one hand, and Orthodox Christians, on the other, understand this issue in different ways, though they agree that, because human beings cannot overcome sin on their own, they stand in need of salvation from its power over them—a power that cuts them off from God, the source of all good things.

Grace and Salvation

For Christianity, sin is the fundamental problem of human existence. But it is a problem solved by the good news of God's grace, the love God gives freely to human beings despite their sin. In the Christian view, it is only through reliance on divine grace that salvation from sin becomes possible.

Christianity explains *how* salvation is made possible by using the language of sacrifice, a common Jewish practice in Jesus' time. In the sacrificial ritual, the sins of the people were ritually placed on animals sacrificed as innocent victims for the transgressions of others. For Christians, Jesus' death on the cross was the fulfillment of this sacrificial practice. It is with his crucifixion that the significance of the Christian teaching that Jesus Christ was both human and divine becomes clear. Jesus' divinity allowed him to do for human beings what they could not do for themselves. As the sinless "lamb of God" (John 1:29), he alone could make the perfect atonement for sin that would allow sinners to be restored to their original relationship with God. As a human being, he could suffer the consequences of sin on behalf of humanity. In doing so, Christians say, Jesus fulfilled the words of the Old Testament prophet Isaiah, who spoke of the "suffering servant" of God: "But he was wounded for our transgressions, crushed for our iniquities; upon him was the punishment that made us whole, and by his bruises we are healed" (Isaiah 53:5). Christians see in Christ's suffering for the salvation of humanity the supreme proof of God's grace:

> God is love. God's love was revealed among us in this way: God sent his only Son into the world so that we might live through him. In this is love, not that we loved God but that he loved us and sent his Son to be the atoning sacrifice for our sins.
>
> —*1 John 4:8*

Grace makes salvation possible, but it requires a human response in the form of faith. For Christians, faith is more than intellectual acceptance of the fact that God has made salvation possible through Jesus Christ. Faith in God involves a wholehearted opening of oneself to God so that God's love replaces sinfulness as the prevailing power in one's life.

For Roman Catholic and Orthodox Christians, as well as for some Protestants, good works are an expression of faith, even a part of faith, for a faith that does not involve action is not faith at all. As the New Testament letter of James (2:26) puts it, "For just as the body without the spirit is dead, so faith without works is also dead." Most Protestants, in contrast, make a distinction between faith and good works. Because works, they believe, are not a part of faith, works do not contribute to salvation. In support of this view, Protestants cite New Testament passages such as Paul's letter to the Romans (3:28), "For we hold that a person is justified by faith apart from works." For those who hold this view, good works are something one does *because* one has faith. The differences here are finely nuanced, but they have profound implications that are partly responsible for the separation of the Roman Catholic, Orthodox, and Protestant traditions.

Christians admit that they are no closer to perfection than anyone else, yet they are confident that faith allows them to "walk in a newness of life" (Romans 6:4) on a path that leads toward rather than away from God.

The Church

Christians do not live the Christian life in isolation. Instead, their faith and baptism unite them with all other believers. In its most basic sense, the Church is the sum of all believers, but most Christians believe that the Church is far more than this. Following Paul, they understand the Church to be the "body of Christ," a body whose diverse members are unified by the Holy Spirit: "For just as the body is one and has many members, and all the members of the body, though many, are one body, so it is with Christ. For in the one Spirit we were all baptized into one body—Jews or Greeks, slaves or free—and we were all made to drink of one Spirit" (1 Corinthians 12:13).

VOICES: An Interview with Terrie M. and Father Art

Terrie M. is a member of a Roman Catholic church in Sacramento. Father Art is one of three priests who serve its nearly 3,000 members.

How does the Roman Catholic Church stand in relation to other Christian churches?

Terrie: Some people mistakenly make a distinction between "Catholics" and "Christians," so I want to begin by saying that to be a Catholic is to be a Christian. We share with other Christians our belief in Jesus as Lord. Like other Christians, we believe that salvation comes through faith. We Catholics also believe that God's love and compassion are boundless and given to all, and so we cannot say that the Roman Catholic Church is the only path to salvation.

Father Art: We share with other Christians our reverence for Sacred Scripture, the inspired Word of God, but we have equal reverence for Sacred Tradition, the handing on to each new generation of the wider reality of all that the Church is and believes—that is, its doctrine, life, and worship. The Church's teaching authority [*Magisterium*], guided by the Holy Spirit, is both the servant and the authentic interpreter of the Word of God revealed in Sacred Scripture and Sacred Tradition. This authority, exercised in the name of Jesus Christ, has been entrusted to the bishops in communion with the Bishop of Rome. Catholics grieve that not all Christians share this belief, but I know that all Christian churches recognize some form of tradition and teaching authority, as well as the authority of Sacred Scripture. Our sacred task is to pray and to work for that unity of all Christians desired by Jesus.

What is the great problem of human existence?

Terrie: The great problem we face as human beings is sin, which separates us from God and ultimately results in death. We come into this world, not evil, but certainly with the ability to sin as part of our human condition. Much suffering is caused when we make a choice to live for ourselves. But we are also born with God's grace, an unmerited love that is given freely. Reconciliation is possible for all, and there is nothing that cannot be forgiven. Through the love of God through Christ Jesus, even death has been conquered and the original goodness of humanity is restored.

Father Art: Sin not only separates us from God, it prevents us from being all that God intends us to be. We are justified before God thanks to the gratuitous gift of God's grace in Jesus Christ, crucified and risen, given us by the Holy Spirit at baptism. By the gift of God's grace, we are enabled to live lives of faith expressed in love.

Does being a Roman Catholic give you a heightened awareness or a different way of looking at reality?

Terrie: My reality as a Catholic is grounded in Christ's teaching that we must love and live for each other. We do not go it alone. It is this knowledge and awareness that helps me see that the joys and challenges of life are navigated together. It is perhaps in the celebration of the Eucharist that I am most aware of my union with others, for this ritual is not so much about eating as it is about sharing—our stories, all that we are, and all that we have.

Father Art: Yes, Christ is made manifest to us in the liturgy and the sacraments, and especially in the Eucharist. His presence there heightens our sensitivity to his presence throughout the world, in everyday life, in our work, and in our relationships, so that every moment and every situation becomes an opportunity for praise and worship and for sharing our joy with others.

Father Art and Terrie M.

Scripture

When the first Christians spoke of scripture, they meant the Jewish Scriptures—the Hebrew Bible and its translation into Greek, the Septuagint In Greek, these texts were called *ta biblia*, or "the books"—hence, our English "Bible." It was not long, however, before certain Christian writings assumed an importance equal to that of the Jewish Scriptures. By the end of the fourth century, there was general agreement that twenty-seven of these texts had greater authority than all others. These came to be known collectively as the New Testament. Since then, the Christian Bible has consisted of the Old Testament (the Jewish Scriptures) and the New Testament.

In Christian interpretation, the Old Testament, which tells of God's covenant with the Jewish people, anticipates and is fulfilled by the New Testament, which reveals that the Messiah has come and established a new and universal covenant between God and the Church. Roman Catholic and Orthodox versions of the Bible also include several Deuterocanonical ("secondary canon") texts, which they place in the Old Testament. Protestants call these texts the Apocrypha ("hidden texts") and sometimes place them between the Old and New Testaments in their versions of the Bible.

The first four books in the New Testament are the gospels. Although tradition attributes the gospels to specific individuals, some of them disciples of Jesus, none identifies its author by name. Each gospel portrays Jesus in its own way. In the Gospel of Mark, Jesus is a Messiah who resolutely submits to suffering on behalf of humanity. In the Gospel of Matthew, Jesus is a figure reminiscent of Moses who reveals the true meaning of the Torah. The Gospel of Luke focuses on Jesus' compassion for sinners, women, the poor, and the sick. Finally, the Gospel of John emphasizes the divinity of Jesus. In describing him as God's "Word" (Greek *logos*, "word," but also "divine reason") "made flesh," John presents Jesus as a revelation of God in human form.

The gospels are followed by the Acts of the Apostles, which describe the founding of the Church in Jerusalem and tell the story of Paul's missionary journeys. All but one of the texts that follow Acts are letters, many of them written by Paul. These texts describe the organization of the first Christian churches, tell us about early Christian beliefs and practices, and offer insights into the complex relationship between early Christianity and Judaism. The New Testament concludes with Revelation. Written at the end of the first century, when Christians were beginning to suffer persecution, Revelation is an apocalyptic text that employs vivid imagery in describing the coming of the kingdom of God after a climactic battle between good and evil.

Christians have always seen scripture as the revealed word of God. They turn to the Bible for instruction in doctrine, ethics, and higher truths, confident that this collection of divinely inspired texts has an authority that sets it above all others. But what, exactly, does "divinely inspired" mean? More important, does the Bible make the claim of divine inspiration about itself?

As it turns out, one New Testament text speaks of scripture as "God-breathed" (2 Timothy 3:16), which comes very close to "divinely inspired." Of course, the reference here is only to the Jewish Scriptures, or Old Testament, as the New Testament was not recognized as scripture until long after this text was written. Another New Testament passage describes the prophets of the Old Testament as men who "spoke from God as they were carried along by the Holy Spirit" (2 Peter 1:21). Two Old Testament passages say that God himself wrote the Ten Commandments (Exodus 24:12 and Deuteronomy 5:22). There are also several Old and New Testament texts that describe Old Testament figures as taking dictation from God when writing small portions of scripture (e.g., Ezekiel 11:5, Matthew 22:43). Beyond this, the Bible says little about divine inspiration.

Until the Reformation in the sixteenth century, divine inspiration was not an issue of great importance. The Roman Catholic and Orthodox traditions agreed that the biblical texts were *somehow* inspired by God, who chose their authors and worked *with* and *through* them, and that seems to have been enough. But the Protestant reformers advanced the doctrine that scripture is the only authority on which Christians can completely rely. This meant that that the authority of scripture had to be raised to a level at which it was beyond question. In order to do so, Protestant thinkers formulated a variety of theories to explain just how divine inspiration "works." Some claim that God inspired the biblical writers even to the point of determining every word they chose to use. Others say that God has ensured the truth of the message in the biblical texts but without influencing the means by which the biblical authors chose to communicate it.

Today, there is a broad range of opinion on divine inspiration and the Bible. Some Christians credit the authors of the biblical texts for their spiritual insights and leave little or no room for divine influence. Others downplay the human contribution to scripture, some to the point of attributing every word and idea to God.

The issue of divine inspiration is closely tied to that of biblical accuracy. As you might imagine, the more one emphasizes God's involvement in creating the biblical texts, the more necessary it becomes to insist on their inerrancy. After all, since God cannot lie or contradict himself, a Bible whose ultimate author is God cannot possibly contain even a single error. Of course, there do seem to be errors and contradictions in the Bible. In such cases, Christians who support absolute inerrancy use biblical, historical, and linguistic arguments to show that these are only apparent, not real. Those who endorse a limited inerrancy say that the Bible is inerrant in matters essential to faith and doctrine but may contain insignificant errors relating to geography and history. For the most part, conservative Protestants favor absolute inerrancy. Liberal Protestants, Roman Catholics, and Orthodox Christians tend to support limited inerrancy.

Tradition

Tradition has great authority in the lives of most people. We look to the accumulated wisdom of the past in forms such as laws and constitutions, scientific discoveries, masterpieces of art and literature, and folklore for guidance in organizing society and understanding the world and our place in it. In a similar way, Christians have always looked to their past for guidance in matters of belief and practice. For them, tradition is the "handing on" (Latin *traditio*) and continuing interpretation of the gospel message through the centuries. The idea of tradition is found in the Bible. In one of his letters to the Christians of Corinth, Paul wrote: "I handed on to you as of first importance what I in turn had received" (1 Corinthians 15:3). Although different groups define the content of tradition in different ways, in the broadest sense it includes creeds, forms of worship, doctrines, the decisions of church councils, the works of major theologians, and even the illustration of the gospel in art, music, and literature.

All Christians place great value on tradition. For Roman Catholics and Orthodox Christians, its authority is on the same level as scripture. Some point out that because the earliest Christians were "handing on" the faith even before the first New Testament texts were written, scripture can be seen as a *part* of tradition. Protestants set tradition below scripture but still acknowledge its importance. Most Protestants believe that tradition is helpful in understanding scripture and accept the ancient creeds, basic patterns of worship, and a great many other "traditional" features of belief and practice.

"Last Things"

We have seen that Jesus proclaimed the coming of the kingdom of God—God's loving and righteous rule in the world. Jesus taught that the kingdom was already present in him and in his followers but that its full realization lay in the future. In doing so, he made a distinction between the *now* and the *not yet* that is evident throughout the New Testament.

The Letter to the Hebrews, for example, describes Christians as "those who have once been enlightened, and have tasted the heavenly gift, and have shared in the Holy Spirit, and have tasted the goodness of the word of God and the powers of the age to come" (Hebrews 6:4). Similarly, Paul's letters speak of world-transforming events that had already occurred, such as the resurrection of Christ and the descent of the Holy Spirit upon his followers, but they also look forward to events that would take place at the end of the age. Greek-speaking Christians called these events *ta eschata*, "the last things." They include eschatological events such as the Second Coming of Christ, the resurrection of the dead, the Last Judgment, and the glorious consummation of the kingdom of God.

Most early Christians assumed that the end of their age was not far off. As time passed, however, many came to believe that the consummation of the kingdom would occur within a spiritual context rather than in an earthly kingdom. There is a biblical basis for this view in the Gospel of John, whose "realized eschatology" holds that events such as judgment and resurrection into eternal life have already been realized in the interior lives of believers. Both points of view are still very much alive today, and so it is fair to say that Christians hold a wide range of opinions with respect to the time and nature of the fulfillment of God's purposes in the world.

The Afterlife

Like the adherents of many other religions, Christians believe that human existence extends beyond this life. In the afterlife, the consequences of the choices people make now in relation to God and God's grace will be fully realized. Traditionally, Christians have illustrated these consequences with images of heaven and hell. Some also believe in purgatory, an intermediate state between earthly life and heaven.

Christian beliefs about the afterlife have been influenced by the cultures in which Christianity has developed, as well as by scripture. As a result, they are extremely varied and complex.

Heaven Perhaps it is best to begin with what most Christians believe about heaven. In essence, heaven is perfect and eternal union with God, the fulfillment of the true purpose and deepest desire of human beings. Whether understood as an actual place or a state of being, as physical or spiritual, as earthly or celestial, "heaven" always means the ineffable bliss of everlasting existence in the loving presence of God.

Although the New Testament texts make frequent reference to heaven, they do not describe it in detail. Instead, the New Testament authors provide glimpses of heaven as the city of God, the heavenly Jerusalem, life everlasting, the holy place, and the great reward. In the gospels, Jesus speaks of heaven as "paradise" (Luke 23:43) and as a place he will prepare for his followers (John 14:2–3). Paul's letters describe heaven both as the present dwelling place of God and as the future home of believers. According to Paul, Christians can be certain of heaven because their experience of the Holy Spirit in this life gives them a taste of a future reality in which mortality will be "swallowed up by life" (2 Corinthians 5:4).

For some Christians, heaven is not a place but a spiritual state of being. This view evinces the influence of ancient Greek thought, which held that the true self is an immortal soul that can exist apart from the body and beyond space and time. For other Christians, heaven is the abode of God in the starry firmament above the earth. With roots in both the Old and New Testaments, this conception of heaven as a physical place is associated with the belief that those in heaven will possess physical bodies made perfect and immortal following the resurrection of the dead that will occur when Christ returns to judge the world (1 Corinthians 15; Philippians 3:20). Finally, some Christians understand heaven as an earthly phenomenon. The basis for this view is the vision of "a new heaven and a new earth" in the New Testament book of Revelation (21–22). According to Revelation, the day will come when a "heavenly Jerusalem" will become present on earth. Here, evils such as death and disease will no longer exist, and God himself will live among his people.

Purgatory One of the most striking differences between Christian views of the afterlife concerns **purgatory**. In Roman Catholic thought, purgatory is an intermediate place or state between earthly life and heaven in which the souls of the dead suffer temporal punishment due for sin. Just as a friend might forgive you for some wrong you have done but still expect you to suffer a bit in demonstrating your sorrow, Roman Catholic doctrine holds that sinners must make reparation or satisfaction for sins already forgiven by God. Traditionally imagined as a cleansing fire, purgatory offers the opportunity to complete the work of reparation left undone in earthly life. The scriptural basis for belief in purgatory is found in 2 Maccabees (12:39–45), a deuterocanonical text in which prayer is offered for the dead so that "they might be released from their sin."

Although Orthodox Christianity does not accept the Roman Catholic doctrine of purgatory, most Orthodox Christians believe that after death souls enter a "condition of waiting" in which they can benefit from prayers said on their behalf. Protestant

Christians reject belief in purgatory because they find no basis for it in scripture (most Protestant Bibles do not include 2 Maccabees).

Hell Hell is not so much God's punishment for sin as the self-imposed consequence of rejecting God's grace. Some Christians understand hell as an actual place, others think of it as a state of being, and still others do not believe in hell at all. In describing why hell must exist, one Orthodox writer has said: "God will not force us to love Him, for love is no longer love if it is not free; how then can God reconcile to Himself those who refuse all reconciliation?"[2]

The word translated as "hell" in English versions of the New Testament is Gehenna, the name of a valley bordering Jerusalem where many Jews in the time of Jesus expected that the worst of sinners would one day suffer torment. Thus, Gehenna works well as a way of illustrating the pain of separation from God. Although hell clearly refers to a state of existence, there is little basis in the New Testament for understanding it as an actual place. It was not until the early Middle Ages that hell was transformed in the popular imagination into a subterranean pit of fiery horrors. Although hell has long been understood as a necessary expression of divine justice, many Christian thinkers have found this idea to be inconsistent with God's love. Some have taught that God will ultimately save all people from the consequences of sin.

COMPARISON OF CHRISTIAN TRADITIONS

APOSTOLIC SUCCESSION

ORTHODOX: An important feature of Orthodox belief; ensures continuity with the Church established by Christ through a succession of bishops.

ROMAN CATHOLIC: An important feature of Roman Catholic belief; ensures continuity with the Church established by Christ through a succession of bishops.

PROTESTANT: Rejected by most Protestants.

AUTHORITY OF SCRIPTURE AND TRADITION

ORTHODOX: Tradition is the transmission of divine truth taught by Christ and the apostles. Scripture is just one form of tradition. Others include the liturgy, the Holy Mysteries (i.e., sacraments), doctrines, religious art, and the lives of saints.

ROMAN CATHOLIC: Divine truth taught by Christ and the apostles is transmitted by means of scripture and tradition. Apart from this distinction between scripture and tradition, tradition is understood largely as it is in Orthodox Christianity.

PROTESTANT: Scripture alone is an authoritative source for Christian doctrine.

BIBLE

ORTHODOX: Consists of the Old Testament, New Testament, and Deuterocanonical books.

ROMAN CATHOLIC: Consists of Old Testament, New Testament, and Deuterocanonical books.

PROTESTANT: Consists of Old and New Testaments only.

CHURCH GOVERNMENT

ORTHODOX: Episcopal. Authority is in the hands of bishops (Greek, *episkopoi*), with the Ecumenical Patriarch recognized as the "first among equals."

ROMAN CATHOLIC: Episcopal. Authority is in the hands of bishops. The Bishop of Rome (i.e., the pope) has primacy over all other bishops.

PROTESTANT: Although some Protestants, such as Lutherans and Methodists, recognize the authority of bishops, most reject episcopal government in favor of other forms that place authority in the hands of individual congregations or other independent governing bodies.

CLERGY: GENDER AND CELIBACY

ORTHODOX: All clergy must be male. Priests and deacons may marry but only before ordination. Bishops must be celibate.

ROMAN CATHOLIC: All clergy must be male. Priests and bishops must be celibate, with the exception of priests in the Eastern Rite of the Roman Catholic Church, who may marry.

PROTESTANT: Many churches ordain women. Clergy may marry.

EUCHARIST

ORTHODOX: Christ is truly present in the Eucharist; the bread and wine become the body and blood of Christ by means that are a divine mystery.

ROMAN CATHOLIC: Christ is truly present in the Eucharist; the bread and wine become the body and blood of Christ through "Transubstantiation," the transformation of the inner substance of these elements but not their outward appearance.

PROTESTANT: For most Protestants, the bread and wine are not changed. For some, they are only symbols of the body and blood of Christ. For others, Christ is somehow truly present in the Eucharist.

MARY

ORTHODOX: Venerated as a saint and *Theotokos* (Greek, "Mother of God")

ROMAN CATHOLIC: Venerated as a saint and "Mother of God"

PROTESTANT: Regarded as a woman of great virtue chosen by God to be the mother of Christ. Protestants do not venerate Mary as a saint.

PAPACY

ORTHODOX: The pope is the successor of St. Peter as Bishop of Rome and so enjoys a position of honor among them, but he has no authority over other bishops.

ROMAN CATHOLIC: The pope is the successor of St. Peter as Bishop of Rome and, as the Vicar [i.e., representative] of Christ, has authority over the Church. He is infallible when, through the action of the Holy Spirit, he defines doctrines relating to faith and morals.

PROTESTANT: The pope is the leader of the Roman Catholic Church and has no authority outside the Roman Catholic Church.

SACRAMENTS

ORTHODOX: The sacraments, or "holy mysteries," are ways in which God discloses himself and imparts grace. Although usually said to be seven in number—Baptism, Chrismation, Eucharist, Confession, Holy Unction, Marriage, and Ordination—Orthodoxy regards all that the Church does as sacramental and has never defined the sacraments as seven.

ROMAN CATHOLIC: There are seven sacraments, visible signs and channels of divine grace, which is invisible. The seven are the same as those in Orthodoxy, with some known by different names: Confirmation (Chrismation), Reconciliation (Confession), Anointing of the Sick (Holy Unction), Holy Orders (Ordination).

PROTESTANT: Only two sacraments are generally recognized: Baptism and the Eucharist.

Christianity and Other Religions: Points of Conflict

Existing alongside other religions, Christianity has always sought to define itself in relation to them. This is particularly true of Judaism, within which it originated. The bitterness felt by Jewish Christians after their expulsion from synagogues in the first century can be seen in New Testament passages critical of Jewish piety and religious groups (for example, in Matthew 23 and John 5–8). It must also have influenced the gospel accounts of the crucifixion of Jesus, which place greater blame on Jewish authorities than on the Romans, who actually carried out the execution.

Tragically, the presence of anti-Jewish feeling in scripture continued to influence Christian attitudes toward Jews and Judaism long after the first century. Denounced as Christ-killers and enemies of humanity, seventh-century French and Spanish Jews were subjected to forced baptism. In the late Middle Ages, Jews were expelled from England, Spain, France, and Portugal. Anti-Jewish feeling assumed its most virulent form with the rise of fascism in Germany, Italy, and other parts of Europe in the twentieth century. It was not until after the Holocaust, the genocidal murder of six million Jews carried out by Nazi Germany during World War II, that church leaders began working for an end to hostility toward Jews and Judaism. At its inaugural meeting in 1948, the World Council of Churches declared that anti-Semitism is incompatible with the Christian faith and "a sin against God and man." Today, many Christian groups are engaged in efforts to heal the wounds of the past and to encourage a Jewish-Christian dialogue that will foster mutual appreciation and respect.

As we will see later in this chapter, Christians have found themselves in conflict with adherents of other religions. For example, in the Middle Ages religion contributed to tensions and outright warfare between Christian Europe and the Islamic civilization of the Middle East and North Africa. Later, the expansion of European colonial powers into regions such as Africa and the Americas brought conflict between Christianity and indigenous religions.

Historically, most Christians have believed that there is no salvation outside of the Church, a view based on New Testament passages that speak of Jesus as the only way in which God has been fully revealed to humanity. But the cultural pluralism of today's global society has raised interest in other ways of understanding spiritual realities. In fact, some Christians have found a scriptural basis for the possibility of salvation in other religions. They point to Paul's letter to the Romans, which says that those who follow the dictates of their consciences will be judged as righteous on the last day (Romans 2:14–16). Similarly, the letter of James defines "pure" religion not in specifically Christian terms but as caring for the needy and keeping oneself "unstained by the world" (James 1:27). Biblical passages like these have encouraged many Christians to value the spiritual insights of other religious traditions and to enter into cooperative relationships with them. The spirit of this new attitude, expressed in formal statements by many Christian groups, is represented in the *Declaration on Non-Christian Religions* issued by the Roman Catholic bishops who assembled for the Second Vatican Council (1962–1965):

> Prudently and lovingly, through dialogue and collaboration with the followers of other religions and in witness of the Christian faith and life, we should acknowledge, preserve and promote the spiritual and moral goods found among these men, as well as the values in their society and culture.[3]

Changes in Christian thought remind us that the history of Christianity is a story about the changing ways in which the Church has existed in the world. We turn to that story now in order to discover how the Church of the earliest Christian centuries became the one, or ones, we know today.

THE HISTORY OF CHRISTIANITY

Christianity in the Roman World

Historians agree that Christianity spread steadily throughout the Roman Empire. As it did, Christians met with criticism and persecution that continued until Rome's emperors became Christians themselves. Also, as the Christian movement grew during these early years, it became necessary to define basic doctrines and to adopt a form of church government capable of uniting Christians and promoting uniformity of belief and practice among them.

Conflict with the Roman State The Roman world was often hostile to Christians. Many suspected Christians of disloyalty to Rome because they refused to recognize its gods or participate in public events that involved pagan rituals. Localized persecutions began in the first century and expanded into empire-wide assaults in the third. Despite the terrors of mass arrests and executions, persecution failed to check the growth of Christianity. A dramatic turning point came in 312, when the Emperor Constantine (r. 306–337) defeated a rival after seeing a vision of a cross in the sky. Convinced that the God of the Christians had given him the victory, Constantine decreed religious freedom for Christians and began to promote Christianity by building churches and extending privileges to church leaders.

When Constantine transferred the imperial capital from Rome to Constantinople (modern Istanbul) in 330, he did so in the hope that it would be a truly Christian city free of paganism. Decades later, Theodosius I (r. 379–395) made

The first Christian emperor of Rome, Constantine the Great promoted the spread of Christianity throughout the Roman Empire and founded a new capital at Constantinople (modern Istanbul) in 330. He is represented here with his mother, Helena.

Christianity the official state religion of the Roman Empire and began the suppression of other religions and schools of philosophy.

Diversity in the Early Church

During the first five centuries C.E., Christians formulated many important doctrines, thereby establishing a standard of orthodoxy, or "correct belief." However, some early Christian groups challenged the emerging mainstream Church on issues as basic as the nature of God, the humanity of Christ, salvation, and ecclesiastical (Greek *ekklesia*, "church") authority.

Gnostic Christians produced mysterious gospels and other texts that did not come to light until the late nineteenth century. Many Gnostic Christians believed that Christ's body had been a mere illusion; therefore, he could not have atoned for sin by dying a physical death upon the cross. Salvation came instead from secret knowledge (Greek *gnosis*) that Christ gave only to a select group of *gnostics* ("knowers"), who had passed it down to others. Because Gnostic Christians saw all material reality as evil, they understood salvation as the liberation of souls from human bodies rather than as liberation from sin. Gnostics claimed that the Christianity preached publicly in churches was incomplete, as they alone understood the higher teachings of Christ.

A second group was founded by Marcion (c. 85–160 C.E.), a theologian who had been expelled from the church at Rome for teaching that there are two Gods: the God of the Jewish Scriptures, whom Marcion described as the unjust creator of an evil world, and the supremely good God revealed by Christ. According to Marcion, it was this good God who had sent Christ to rescue human souls. Seeking to cut Christianity off from its Jewish roots, Marcion rejected the Jewish Scriptures and all Christian texts that seemed dependent on them.

A third form of Christianity, known as Montanism, began with Montanus, a charismatic prophet of the late second century who claimed to be the mouthpiece of the Holy Spirit. Montanus prophesied that Christ would soon return to a "new Jerusalem" that was about to appear in southern Asia Minor. The greatest difficulty posed by Montanus was his claim that he preached a *new* prophecy. This raised two critical questions. First, would Christian teaching require ongoing revision in order to accommodate every new group and its revelations? Second, did claims of prophetic inspiration give charismatic figures like Montanus an authority greater than that of church leaders?

Defining Orthodoxy

Resolving questions related to correct belief, scripture, and the authority of the Church was one of the great themes in the early history of the Church. In order to establish its authority and define orthodox belief, the Church created a canon of scripture, formulated creeds, and implemented a system of ecclesiastical government that put authority into the hands of bishops.

We have already seen that a canon of scripture consisting of the Old and New Testaments was in place by the end of the fourth century. Texts widely believed to have been written by the apostles were included, as were writings from the apostolic era that were widely used in public worship. Because the Old and New Testaments were regarded as having a unique authority, they constituted a standard against which the orthodoxy of any new teaching could be judged.

The creeds developed by the early Church were formal and concise statements of essential Christian beliefs. In fact, the word creed itself comes from the Latin *credo*, which means "I believe." Creeds such as the Apostles' Creed and the Nicene Creed served two functions. (1) They proclaimed orthodox doctrine on the incarnation, suffering, and death of Christ, as well as his resurrection and ascension into heaven; and (2) repeated recitation of the creeds by Christians throughout the empire promoted uniformity of belief within the Church.

Finally, the early Church established a form of government that concentrated power in the hands of bishops, who had jurisdiction over large territories called dioceses. According to the doctrine of **apostolic succession**, bishops were the successors of the apostles, who had been commissioned by Christ himself to lead the Church. Claiming to have received both their offices and correct belief through direct lines of transmission, they held an authority that Gnostics, Montanists, and Marcionite Christians found difficult to challenge. Bishops were assisted by priests, who were responsible for individual churches, and every church was served by deacons (Greek *diakonos*, "servant") who assisted priests.

Gradually, the bishops of Rome and Constantinople emerged as the leaders of the churches of the Western and Eastern halves of the empire. Known as "popes" (Latin *papa*, "father"), the bishops of Rome were said to be the successors of the Apostle Peter, the "rock" (Greek *petra*) upon whom Christ had said he would build his Church (Matthew 16:18–19). They claimed the same authority Christ had given to Peter. Other bishops—including the great patriarchs of Constantinople, Alexandria, Antioch, and Jerusalem—acknowledged the bishops of Rome as "first among equals" but without recognizing the right of popes to rule over them.

Early Christian Thought The success of the early Christian movement was due in part to the work of Christian writers who produced carefully reasoned statements of Christian belief. These texts gave Christianity intellectual respectability in a world accustomed to the high standards of Greek philosophy and tended to encourage a search for commonalities linking Christian and pagan culture.

For example, theologians such as Clement of Alexandria (c. 150–215) and Origen (c. 185–254) taught that God had long been at work among the Greeks and Romans, preparing them for the coming of Christ. Just as God had given the Torah to the Jews, said Clement, he had given philosophy to the Greeks as a kind of "schoolmaster" in order to "bring the Greek mind . . . to Christ."[4] Like many thinkers of his time, Clement held that all truth comes from the divine "Word," or **logos**. Thus, truths found in scripture and philosophy were compatible. However, since the logos had become incarnate in Jesus Christ (John 1:18), said Clement, it was only in Christ that seekers of truth would find it fully revealed.

Controversies and Councils   Beginning in the third century, Christian theologians turned their attention to the concept of the Trinity and to the nature of Christ. Discussion of these issues led to ecumenical councils ("worldwide councils") of bishops at which doctrines were defined.

From the beginning, most Christians believed that God the Father, the Creator of the universe, had become present in the world in Jesus Christ, God the Son. They also believed in the Holy Spirit as the continuing expression of God's loving presence and power in the world. But how could the one God also be three? This question was taken up by early theologians such as Tertullian, who gave Latin theology its Trinitarian vocabulary by speaking of God as *tres personae, una substantia* ("three persons, one substance"). Similarly, Greek-speaking theologians described God as a single divine *ousia* ("substance" or "essence") made manifest in three *hypostases* ("subsistences").

This way of thinking about the Trinity sufficed until the early 300s, when Arius, an Egyptian priest from Alexandria, began teaching that God the Son, or logos, was of a different substance than God the Father. Going further, Arius claimed that whereas the Father was eternal, the Son was created in time. Arius's views alarmed other theologians, for they seemed to undermine the unity of the Trinity. If the Father and the Son were so different, they asked, how could God be truly one?

Arius's provocative teachings soon had Alexandria buzzing as people in shops and streets argued theology with an enthusiasm that we today reserve for debates about sports and politics. Fearing that Arianism threatened the unity of the empire, as well as the Church, the Emperor Constantine stepped in and convened an ecumenical council to settle the matter. The Council of Nicea (325) condemned Arius's views, ordered the burning of Arian texts, and formulated a creed affirming that God the Son is *homoousios* ("of the same substance" or "being") with God the Father. An expanded form of this creed, the Nicene Creed (see p. 429), produced by the Council of Constantinople (381), describes God as a Trinity of three distinct yet unified divine "persons."

Even as the Trinitarian controversy was being settled, another debate began over the person of Christ. Christians had long believed that Christ was both human and divine, but they differed in explaining how humanity and divinity coexisted in him. The orthodox position on this issue was determined at yet another ecumenical council at Chalcedon (451): in Christ, two complete and perfect natures, human and divine, were united without separation or fusion in a single person.

Augustine   The drama of the Trinitarian and Christological controversies was played out in the Greek-speaking eastern half of the Roman world and involved many leading theologians. The Latin West produced just one theological giant. This was Augustine (354–430), a North African bishop who laid the intellectual foundations for much of Western Christianity and Western civilization.

Central to Augustine's theology are his views on sin and human nature. Elaborating on the theology of Paul, Augustine argued that sinfulness is a fundamental flaw in human nature that clouds our moral vision and perverts the will by causing us to desire evil rather than good. In the *Confessions*, his spiritual autobiography, he illustrated this point by recalling the pleasure he and some teenage friends once found in stealing and throwing away pears from a neighbor's tree. According to Augustine, the tendency to sin is so deeply ingrained that we are spiritually helpless and therefore completely dependent on God for salvation.

But *how* did human nature become so corrupt? Augustine's answer came in his famous doctrine of **original sin**. All of humanity, it says, participated in the first sin: the sin of Adam and Eve, the first human beings, described in Genesis (3:1–24). At that time, Adam and Eve *were* humanity, with all future generations present in them. Thus, when they made themselves sinners by choosing to disobey God, this original sin transformed human nature in a way that was bound to affect their descendants. Every human being, said Augustine, is born with the "stain" of original sin in the form of a sinful nature. As we will see, although Augustine's teaching on original sin became a foundational feature of Roman Catholic and Protestant Christianity, it was never accepted by the Orthodox tradition.

Augustine's awareness that some people are saved from sin led him to formulate a theory of predestination. Because all human beings are sinful and therefore incapable of responding on their own to God in faith, he reasoned, God must give some people a grace that inspires faith. Divine grace is irresistible, he said, for a love that could be resisted would be incompatible with God's perfection. Thus those whom God touches with his grace are destined to be saved. Augustine conceded that it is impossible to know *why* God extends a saving grace to some people and not to others, but he insisted that God is neither arbitrary nor unjust. Some are allowed a destiny better than they deserve, but no one receives a destiny worse than he deserves.

Augustine was never entirely comfortable with his conclusions about Original Sin and predestination, but his reading of scripture and observation of human behavior made them inescapable. Having seen jealousy in a baby whose brother had taken his place at their mother's breast, he felt he had no choice but to conclude that sin must be something we are born with and not simply a habit everyone happens to pick up. Similarly, though predestination seemed to be the work of an unfair God, Augustine knew that scripture taught that only some would be saved and that God's justice is not always within reach of human understanding.

Augustine's masterpiece was his *City of God*, in which he formulated a Christian philosophy of history. Writing amidst the panic following the sack of Rome by a Germanic tribe in 410, he rejected the pagan claim that Rome's traditional gods allowed the city to fall because they were angry with the Romans for converting to Christianity. Augustine argued that the fall of Rome was part of God's plan for the salvation of the world. God had ordained two "cities": the earthly city, blemished by sin, and the City of God, a spiritual community grounded in love of God. Like all other manifestations of the earthly city, said Augustine, Rome must pass away so that history can move toward the full realization of the City of God on earth. This view of history as progress toward the fulfillment of God's plan for salvation soon became standard in the Christian West.

The Church in the Middle Ages

In the fifth century, Germanic tribes overran the Western half of the Roman Empire. From the resulting chaos, a new medieval civilization emerged that combined Christianity with Roman and Germanic culture. The Eastern half of the Roman Empire survived for another thousand years. Known as the Byzantine Empire, it was Greek in its language and outlook. As the gulf between West and East widened, distinctively Western and Eastern traditions within the catholic ("universal") Church began to take shape.

The Church in the West   The most powerful of the Germanic tribes were the Franks, who controlled most of western Europe by the ninth century. The Franks supported the Roman Church and granted rich lands to bishops and monasteries. In return, the Church sanctioned the rule of the Frankish kings, supplied clergy to serve in their government, and sent missionaries to convert pagan peoples in their kingdom.

The Church's involvement in secular affairs continued after the decline of the Franks and often led to conflict between secular and spiritual rulers, especially the popes. Early medieval popes claimed that their spiritual responsibilities gave them an authority greater than that of secular rulers, but it was not until the eleventh century that the papacy rose to the level they had imagined. The most powerful of popes was Innocent III (r. 1198–1216). Intent on unifying the Christian world under the papal banner, Innocent intervened constantly in secular matters, deposing kings and emperors whenever they displeased him.

An extremely ugly aspect of medieval Christianity in the West was the **Inquisition**, the Church's inquiry into allegations of heresy that began in the twelfth century. Working in partnership with secular rulers, who feared that religious diversity would undermine their authority, the inquisitors sought to eradicate false teachings they believed would endanger the salvation of those who accepted them. The Inquisition also targeted Jews and Muslims. Despite its use of torture and the execution of heretics by burning, the Inquisition could not stamp out heresy. Nevertheless, it persisted in various forms until its final and cruelest phase, the Spanish Inquisition, was abolished in 1834.

The Church in the East   In the East, the patriarchs of Constantinople governed the Church jointly with the Byzantine emperors.

Completed c. 1250, the height and soaring towers of the Gothic cathedral at Chartres in France express the medieval yearning for God. For centuries, pilgrims and secular tourists have come to experience its exquisite, light-filled interior and to see its famous relic, the tunic of the Virgin Mary.

The Byzantine ideal was a *symphonia* ("harmony") of emperor and patriarch based on their shared vision of a holy empire on earth that reflected the glory of the celestial society of heaven. Clashes did occur, but only one threatened the symbiosis of emperor and patriarch. This was the controversy over iconoclasm, or "icon smashing." **Icons**, painted images of Christ and the saints, had long been revered by Byzantine Christians. But some saw this as idolatry. When the Emperor Leo III began removing icons from churches and other public places (726), riots erupted throughout the empire. Leo and his successors responded by deposing uncooperative patriarchs and executing monks, the leading defenders of icons. A formal end to iconoclasm came in 787, when the Second Council of Nicea determined that icons are worthy of veneration but not worship, which must be reserved for God alone.

By the twelfth century, Byzantine missionaries had brought the Slavic peoples of Russia and the Balkans into the Eastern Church. But the position of the Church became increasingly difficult in later years as the Byzantine Empire gradually collapsed under pressure from the expanding Islamic world. The empire fell in 1453 with the capture of Constantinople by the Ottoman Turks. For the next four centuries, most Eastern Christians outside Russia lived in the Ottoman Empire, an Islamic state in which they were tolerated but were denied full religious freedom.

The Great Schism: East and West Divided The Great Schism, the split between Western and Eastern Christianity, came after centuries of gradual separation during which the two traditions developed their distinctive forms. Some of their differences were minor: baptism, for example, was performed by a sprinkling of water in the West but by full immersion in the East, and the West urged priests to be celibate whereas the East preferred them to be married. Far more divisive were the attempts of popes to control Eastern bishops and Byzantine lands. In the end, it was the West's addition of the Latin *filioque* ("and from the Son") to the Nicene Creed that brought a final break. The East rejected this move for theological reasons and because the West had acted without sanction by an ecumenical council. In 1054, angry words over the *filioque* combined with tensions over other issues to force a division of the Church into separate Roman Catholic and Orthodox traditions that remain divided even today.

The Crusades Despite their differences, Eastern and Western Christians did share a common concern over the westward advance of Islamic armies.

The interior of the Cathedral of Hagia Sophia. Dedicated to the "holy wisdom" embodied by Christ, this sixth-century church is the supreme achievement of Byzantine architecture. After the capture of Constantinople by the Turks in 1453, the city was renamed Istanbul and the church first became a mosque, then a museum.

In 1095, Pope Urban II proclaimed a military crusade intended to push the Muslims back and liberate Jerusalem. Crying *"Deus vult!"* ("God wills it!"), armies of knights, peasants, and townspeople set out on the First Crusade. In 1099, they celebrated their capture of Jerusalem with a frenzied slaughter of Muslims and Jews. But the crusaders were unable to defend the lands they had conquered, and subsequent crusades to regain them were often military or moral disasters. Participants in the infamous Fourth Crusade (1204) never made it to the Holy Land, deciding instead to plunder Constantinople. The crusades ended at the close of the thirteenth century, having failed to deliver the Holy Land permanently into Christian hands.

Monasticism and Mysticism One of the most visible features of medieval Christianity was monasticism, a movement that began in the third century when Christians seeking a deeper experience of God withdrew into the deserts of Egypt and Syria. Most early Christian monks and nuns lived solitary lives and practiced a severe asceticism. According to legend, Macarius of Alexandria (d. 395) remained standing for periods as long as forty days, subsisting on a weekly meal of cabbage. The nun Alexandra walled herself up in a tomb for ten years, never seeing another human face.

In the medieval period, monks and nuns were brought together in monasteries governed by "rules" that regularized monastic life and discouraged extreme forms of self-denial. Both the Eastern *Rule* of Basil the Great (330–379) and the Western *Rule* of Benedict of Nursia (480–547) required monks and nuns to take vows of chastity and poverty and to spend their days in communal worship, prayer, and labor. Although the monastic aim of pursuing holiness through the imitation of Christ meant that monks and nuns spent much time in prayer and contemplation, monasteries also served nearby communities, providing them with spiritual guidance, education, shelter for travelers, and care for the poor and sick.

The monastic movement also encouraged mysticism, the direct and intuitive experience of God beyond the limits of mere intellect. Eastern mystics emphasized the absolute "otherness" of God, whom they regarded as so utterly unlike anything else we experience that even concepts as basic as "being" and "nonbeing" are useless in describing divinity. Though remote in his incomprehensibility, they said, God is also near, touching human beings with a love that restores the sinful nature to its original state of perfection in "the image of God" (Genesis 1:26–27). "Love, the divine gift," wrote Maximus the Confessor (c. 580–662), "perfects human nature until it makes it appear in unity and identity with the divine nature."[5] Building on these ideas, Eastern monks such as Simeon the New Theologian

In this fresco by Giovanni Sodoma (1477–1549), Benedictine monks of the Monte Oliveto monastery in Italy eat their meal together—just as they worked and worshiped together in accordance with the Rule of St. Benedict. Note that one of the monks reads to the others from the Bible or some other holy book as they eat.

(949–1022) and Gregory Palamas (c. 1296–1359) practiced Hesychasm, the cultivation of an inner quietude (*hesychia*) that brings an experience of God as divine light.

Western mystics also emphasized the power of divine love. Bernard of Clairvaux (1090–1153) compared Christ to a bridegroom whose love for the soul fills her with a bliss that transcends all earthly feeling. Bonaventure (1217–1274) described how divine love lifts the mind above rational thought, allowing it to unite with God in ecstasy. Many of the great Western mystics were women. Catherine of Siena (1347–1380) described a dialogue between God and a human soul seeking union with the divine in her famous *Dialogue on Divine Providence*. In her *Revelations of Divine Love*, the English recluse Julian of Norwich (1342–1416) spoke of God's love as the only means to abiding joy. "Until I am substantially united to him," she wrote, "I can never have love or rest or true happiness."[6]

On April 29, the feast day of St. Catherine of Siena, four citizens of Siena, Italy, dress in medieval costumes and carry a casket holding the saint's relics in a procession.

Theology   In the West, early medieval theology was centered in monasteries, where learned monks and nuns engaged in debates on issues such as predestination, free will, and the sacraments. In seeking to understand how Christ can be truly present in the Eucharist, for example, medieval theologians formulated a doctrine of **transubstantiation**. According to this doctrine, the bread and wine consecrated by a priest during the Eucharist become the actual body and blood of Christ in substance, though their secondary qualities, such as taste, color, and texture, remain unchanged.

The growth of major universities in the twelfth century created a new setting for theological inquiry. Here, theologians applied the science of logic as developed by Aristotle to grasp the full meaning of truths revealed in the scripture. Known as **scholasticism**, this effort became the chief intellectual enterprise of the West in the Middle Ages. The greatest of the scholastic theologians was Thomas Aquinas (1226–1274), a professor at the University of Paris. In his *Summa Theologica*, Thomas argued that although some truths can be known through reason alone, others can be grasped only through faith. Ultimately, said Thomas, there is a perfect harmony between reason and faith, as both come from God.

The most distinctive feature of Eastern theology was its view that all essential Christian truths had been defined once and for all by seven ecumenical councils that completed their work in the eighth century. After the Second Council of Nicea (787), Orthodox theologians devoted themselves to the analysis and elaboration of the faith as articulated by the seven ecumenical councils.

One of the important ways in which Eastern theology differed from that of the West concerns Augustine's doctrine of original sin. Although both East and West agreed that the original sin of Adam had introduced sin and death into the world, the East did not accept Augustine's view that this involved a corruption of the human nature that everyone assumes at birth. By contrast, the Eastern Church taught that the natural state of human beings is one of spiritual purity. Human beings succumb to the sin and evil of the world in which we live, but this is ultimately due to the choices we make and not to a sinful nature inherited from generations reaching back to Adam that makes it impossible to live as we should. Both East and West agreed that the remedy for sin is baptism, which cleanses the individual from the effects of sin and brings salvation through union with Christ.

The Reformation: Protestant Challenge and Roman Catholic Response

In the sixteenth century, a religious revolution known as the Reformation rocked Western Christianity. The Reformation's first phase is known as the Protestant Reformation because of the protests of reformers against Roman Catholic doctrines and practices. Its second phase was the Catholic Reformation, which included direct responses to Protestantism, as well as reforms undertaken independently of it. Ultimately, the Reformation left Europe religiously divided, destroying forever the ancient and medieval ideal of a united Christendom.

Background to the Reformation Throughout the Middle Ages, the Roman Catholic Church engaged in constant self-examination and reform. Even so, voices calling for change grew louder and more numerous. Some complained of corruption among the clergy. Christians north of the Alps resented taxes imposed by the Church, especially since most revenues were spent in Rome. Many were angered by the luxuries enjoyed by popes. Those who wished to emulate the simple piety of the apostles were discouraged by the example set by church leaders who were more interested in wealth and power than in spirituality. Calls for reform were also encouraged by the revival of humanism—a deep faith in human beings that inspired the Renaissance; this cultural movement was flourishing at the time of the Reformation. Humanists such as Desiderius Erasmus (1466–1536) argued that Christians had no need to rely on the Church. Instead, they were capable of taking charge of their spiritual lives based on their own reading and interpretation of the Bible. By the dawn of the sixteenth century, the desire for religious reform was intense and widespread. The situation was volatile. In 1517, a German monk named **Martin Luther** (1483–1546) provided the spark.

The Protestant Reformation Luther was a member of the Augustinian order but had not found peace in monastic life. Despite his efforts to be an ideal monk, he was plagued by a sense of unworthiness and fear of God's judgment that

Portrait of Martin Luther by Lucas Cranach the Elder (1529). It was Luther who set the Protestant Reformation in motion by posting his Ninety-Five Theses on the door of the All Saints' Church in Wittenberg, Germany.

followed him from his monastery to the University of Wittenberg, where he became a professor of theology. It was in Wittenberg that Luther, reading about "the righteousness of God" in Paul's letter to the Romans (1:17), came to believe that God's righteousness did not consist in his desire to condemn the unrighteous but in his eagerness to forgive them. God does not set before sinners the impossible task of *earning* their salvation, Luther concluded. Instead, he asks only that it be accepted, as an expression of divine grace, by faith. For Luther, it was faith alone, and not good works or sacraments, that "justified" sinners before God.

As Luther considered the implications of "justification by faith," he identified Church practices that he found objectionable. Among them was the distribution of indulgences (certificates of remission of punishment in purgatory). For centuries, popes had claimed the authority to apply the surplus merits of the saints to penitent sinners, thereby releasing them from punishment otherwise due for unconfessed sin in purgatory. By Luther's time, the outright sale of indulgences had become an important means of raising funds to finance the papal office.

In 1517, Luther called for public debate on indulgences and other issues by nailing his Ninety-Five Theses, a statement of his theological positions, to the door of the church in Wittenberg. Supporters quickly rallied behind him. When ecclesiastical and secular leaders ordered Luther to recant his views, he refused, setting the Protestant movement in motion.

Luther now began building a Protestant theology based on three principles. First, salvation is made possible by divine "grace alone." Second, it is "by faith alone" that sinners must respond to grace. Third, "scripture alone," and not papal pronouncements or church councils, is the only authority on which Christians can completely rely. In order to make the scriptures available to the people, Luther translated the Bible into German. Because he found no mandate in the Bible for an ecclesiastical hierarchy, he rejected the authority of bishops and popes, as well as the traditional distinction between clergy and laity. According to Luther's doctrine of the "priesthood of all believers," Christians represented themselves before God and had no need of a special class of priests.

Luther's intention had been to reform the Roman Catholic Church, not to create a new Christian movement, but his teachings cut too close to the heart of Catholicism to make this possible. Moreover, the rulers of many German territories saw in Luther a champion who might end the unwelcome influence of the pope and his ally, the Holy Roman Emperor, in their lands. They therefore encouraged a break with Rome. Fighting between Catholics and Protestants broke out, and by the time it ended in 1555, Lutheranism had triumphed in northern Germany and Scandinavia.

Luther was soon joined by other reformers who expanded the geographical scope of the Reformation. In his *Institutes of the Christian Religion*, **John Calvin** (1509–1564) articulated Protestant doctrines with a power and clarity that put his life in danger in Catholic France. Welcomed by the Swiss city of Geneva, Calvin accepted the essential features of Luther's thought but gave Protestant theology his

The Reformation was brought to England by King Henry VIII, depicted here in a famous portrait by the sixteenth-century painter Hans Holbein the Younger.

own stamp by emphasizing God's sovereignty over the universe and teaching that every honest occupation is a "calling" given by God. Calvinism quickly took root in Switzerland in the Swiss Reformed churches, in the Dutch Netherlands as the Dutch Reformed Church, and in England and Scotland as Presbyterianism.

In Zurich, the Swiss reformer Ulrich Zwingli (1484–1531) denounced all beliefs and practices that were not described in the Bible. Because the Bible makes no mention of images of Christ and the saints, candles, and incense, he removed them from Zurich's churches. A space without symbolic and decorative distractions, he reasoned, would be more likely to bring worshipers into direct communion with God. In teaching that the bread and wine used in the Eucharist were mere symbols, Zwingli went far beyond Luther and Calvin, who joined him in rejecting the doctrine of transubstantiation but retained the belief that Christ is truly in the sacrament.

Alongside the Lutheran, Calvinist, and Zwinglian movements emerged smaller, more radical groups that make up what some scholars call the Radical Reformation. Anabaptists ("*re*baptizers") insisted that Christians baptized as infants must be "born again" and baptized again as mature believers. Refusing to recognize the authority of civil governments and their laws, Anabaptists refused to take oaths and were committed to nonviolence. Other radical groups placed such great importance on the inner presence of the Holy Spirit that they saw little value in the Bible or traditional worship. Still others rejected doctrines as basic as the Trinity and the divinity of Christ.

In England, the Reformation began when the pope refused the request of King Henry VIII (r. 1509–1547) for an annulment of his marriage. Taking matters into his own hands, Henry prevailed upon Parliament to pass an Act of Supremacy (1534) that made the king of England, not the pope, the head of the Church in England. This break marked the beginning of the Church of England and of an Anglican tradition that was later exported to England's colonies. In America, the Anglican Church, as it is sometimes called, came to be known as the Episcopal Church.

Although Henry had wanted to effect only political change, the Church of England soon felt the impact of Protestant thought on the Continent. In the end, a kind of compromise was reached that left the Church of England very "Catholic" in its theology and patterns of worship but clearly influenced by elements of Calvinist and Lutheran theology. Although this arrangement satisfied most Anglicans, there were important groups of dissenters. Calvinist Puritans wanted to "purify" the Church of England of every vestige of Catholicism. Presbyterians, also inspired by Calvinism, wanted to replace the episcopal hierarchy with assemblies of presbyters ("elders"). Quakers rejected all formal worship and all forms of church governance.

The Catholic Reformation   The primary response of the Roman Catholic Church to Protestantism was the Council of Trent (1545–1563), which reaffirmed Catholic teachings but took great care to clarify them. Against Protestant belief in the authority of scripture alone, the council held that tradition is equally authoritative. Against the Protestant reduction of the sacraments to baptism and the Eucharist, it reaffirmed the seven sacraments. In response to the Protestant doctrine of justification by faith, the council insisted that faith must be expressed by good works and cited the New Testament in support of this view (e.g., Romans 2:6; 2 Corinthians 5:10). The council also upheld transubstantiation, confession, priestly celibacy, monasticism, purgatory, and the intercession of saints in heaven on behalf of the living. Although it gave no ground to Protestantism on doctrinal issues, the Council of Trent did take decisive action to end corruption in the Church, to improve the quality of education received by priests, and to ensure that essential doctrines were made clear in the sermons, or homilies, that were a part of the Mass.

Although the Council of Trent left Catholics and Protestants divided, its reforms and clarification of doctrine did reinvigorate the Roman Catholic Church, especially in its efforts to spread the faith. New religious orders such as the Jesuits, founded by Ignatius Loyola (1491–1556), spearheaded the effort to reestablish Catholicism in lands where Protestantism had become popular and to bring Christianity to parts of the world where it had never been known, including China, Japan, India, the Philippines, and Latin America.

How have reformers and reform movements influenced the development of other religions?

Distribution of major branches of Christianity throughout the world.

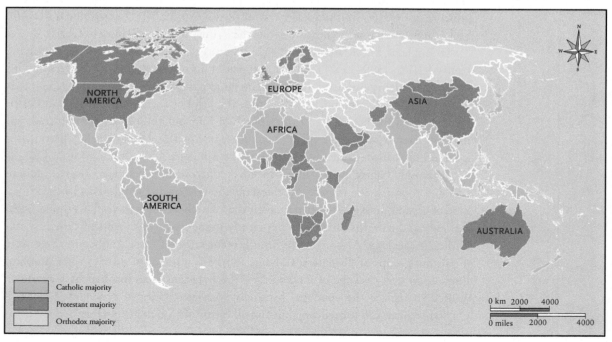

Catholic majority

Protestant majority

Orthodox majority

0 km   2000   4000

0 miles   2000   4000

280

Christianity in the Modern World

The Reformation was only the first challenge faced by Christianity in the modern era. Dramatic scientific, social, political, and intellectual developments also required the Church to respond to a changing world.

As early as the Reformation era, a scientific revolution was beginning to transform the traditional understanding of the universe. For centuries, the Church had endorsed the widespread belief that the universe revolves around the earth—and therefore around humanity, the supreme object of God's love. But this view was abandoned after Nicholas Copernicus (1473–1543) and Galileo Galilei (1564–1642) proved that the earth and other planets revolve around the sun. When Isaac Newton (1642–1727) demonstrated that the universe operates according to laws of nature not found in scripture, science seemed to make the Bible unnecessary to understanding the physical world. The new scientific approach also undermined old ideas about human beings. Charles Darwin's *On the Origin of Species* (1859) challenged the biblical account of the creation of humanity. Later, the work of Sigmund Freud (1856–1939) and the French sociologist Émile Durkheim (1858–1917) suggested that religion did not originate with divine revelation but in the maladjusted psyche or out of a need to create order in society.

The scientific revolution was encouraged by growing confidence in the power of human reason. This was especially evident in the Enlightenment, a philosophical movement of the eighteenth century. Encouraged by Newton's description of nature as entirely rational, Enlightenment thinkers such as Voltaire (1694–1778), Jean-Jacques Rousseau (1712–1778), and Immanuel Kant (1724–1804) believed the way to all truth was through study of the world around us. Unwilling to accept as true any idea that could not stand up under rational scrutiny, they rejected traditional Christianity except for belief in God, whose existence seemed to be implied by the orderliness of nature, and ethical ideals such as honesty and kindness to others.

In the nineteenth century, Christianity felt the effects of liberalism and secularism. Nineteenth-century liberalism held that human beings can create an ideal society if they have the freedom to think and act without interference. For this reason, liberals called for limits on

This mosaic of the Virgin Mary and Christ Child is from the Annunciation Basilica in Nazareth, Israel. It is a wonderful example of the desire of Christians all over the world to understand Jesus in relation to themselves and their own cultures.

In this wood carving from West Africa, an anonymous twentieth-century artist portrays Jesus as African and manages to capture the sorrow and suffering of the savior, who was about to face crucifixion.

the influence of both church and state. Many liberals found it difficult to reconcile Christian beliefs about the sinfulness of human nature and the revelation of truth in scripture with their own views concerning the essential goodness of human beings and the importance of independent thought. Moreover, the progress of democracy across Europe in the nineteenth century brought the implementation of liberal policies that promoted secularism—the belief that religious ideas and institutions should have much less influence in the operation of the state, and especially in public education. The American ideal of the separation of church and state is just one example of this new attitude toward the place of religion in society.

The Missionary Movement   Despite the challenges posed by modern thought and culture, the geographical scope of Christianity grew dramatically in the modern era as European colonial powers expanded their influence into other continents. Most Westerners brought to foreign lands a confidence in the superiority of their own culture and the conviction that they had a moral obligation to share its benefits, including Christianity, with the peoples they found there. As the British poet Rudyard Kipling (1865–1936) put it, "the white man's burden" was to civilize the world's "lesser breeds." Regrettably, the "civilizing" of non-Christians sometimes involved conversions accomplished through intimidation or outright force by colonizers.

Bishops gathered at the Second Vatican Council (1962–1965) in St. Peter's Basilica.

Roman Catholicism in the Modern World   The Roman Catholic Church adapted slowly to the new realities of the modern era. Shaken by the Protestant Reformation and intent on resisting modern influences, it maintained the defensive posture adopted at the Council of Trent until the middle of the twentieth century.

Perhaps the greatest challenge faced by Catholicism was secularization. In France, the Emperor Napoleon (r. 1804–1815) stripped the Church of the authority it had enjoyed for centuries over important aspects of public life. Marriage and divorce became civil procedures, and responsibility for education was assumed by the state, which promoted its own ideals in public schools. In Germany, the state seized vast tracts of land from bishops and monasteries and made priests public employees. Chancellor Otto von Bismarck, outraged by the loyalty of German Catholics to Rome, launched an all-out attack on Catholicism known as the *Kulturkampf* ("struggle for civilization") in the 1870s.

During these difficult years, Catholics turned to Rome for decisive leadership. Intent on providing it, nineteenth-century popes asserted their spiritual authority even as their influence in secular affairs rapidly eroded. This trend culminated under

Pope Francis washed the feet of a dozen inmates, including women and Muslims, at a juvenile detention center in a Holy Thursday ritual during the first year of his papacy. Francis's boldly inclusive gesture just two weeks after his election helped define his papacy.

Pius IX, whose *Syllabus of Errors* (1864) urged Catholics to reject modern evils such as civil marriage, separation of church and state, public education, and Marxism. The climax of Pius IX's reign came with the First Vatican Council (1869–1870), which increased the power of the papacy by proclaiming a doctrine of papal infallibility. According to this doctrine, the pope cannot err when defining doctrines relating to faith and morals.

Later popes upheld Pius IX's conception of papal authority but also attempted to address modernity in constructive ways. Leo XIII (r. 1878–1903), for example, decried the social inequities created by capitalism and industrialization and outlined principles by which justice might be achieved.

A major turning point came when John XXIII convened the Second Vatican Council (1962–1965), which called for recognition of the realities of modern culture. Vatican II urged an openness to dialogue with non-Catholic Christians and described the "high regard" of the Roman Catholic Church for other religions. It also reformed Catholic worship by requiring celebration of the Mass in modern languages instead of Latin and allowing laypeople greater participation in worship. Moving away from the traditional tendency to set the clergy above laypeople, the council emphasized the equality of the faithful. Since Vatican II, the Roman Catholic Church has continued to make its relevance apparent in the modern world while at the same time holding fast to tradition. Thus, Pope John Paul II (r. 1978–2005) was a driving force in bringing about the collapse of communism in eastern Europe at the end of the twentieth century but made no concessions to Catholics who urged a greater role for women in the Church and an end to its stand against birth control.

Pope Francis (r. 2013–) has canonized both John XXIII and John Paul II as saints. A former Archbishop of Buenos Aires, Francis upholds traditional Roman Catholic teachings against abortion, contraception, and gay marriage, but he has also set an extraordinary example in his humility and has called upon all Christians to join him in service to all who are poor and marginalized.

Protestantism in the Modern World   From the beginning, Protestantism encouraged Christians to read and interpret the Bible for themselves. It also resisted the creation of any central authority capable of imposing uniformity of belief and practice. As a result, the number of Protestant denominations grew rapidly. Today, the world's 600 million Protestant Christians belong to thousands of groups. In the United States, the largest Protestant denominations are the Methodist, Lutheran, Presbyterian, Baptist, and Reformed churches.

Despite their many differences, most Protestants share basic doctrines that go back to the Reformation. Following Luther, they believe that salvation from sin is based on faith alone. They regard the Bible as the only authoritative source of revealed truth. Finally, Protestantism allows for diverse forms of church government that give great authority to laypeople and individual congregations.

Since the early 1800s, liberalism and liberal theology have had a significant influence on older and larger Protestant denominations. Interpreting Christianity in the light of modern culture, liberal Protestants have questioned the doctrine of original sin, asked whether a loving God would allow even the worst sinners to suffer in hell, and emphasized the human element in the composition of the scriptures. Embracing the liberal idea that the essential goodness of human beings makes progress toward a better world possible, they have advocated social activism based on the teachings of Jesus as a means of making the kingdom of God a reality. Liberal Protestants have played important roles in the civil rights and antiwar movements and struggled to open the Church to greater participation by women, homosexuals, and other groups.

At the other end of the Protestant spectrum are three important conservative movements: fundamentalism, evangelicalism, and Pentecostalism.

Fundamentalism emerged in the early 1900s as a reaction against liberal theology, the theory of evolution, the academic study of the Bible, and other features of modern culture that conservatives found threatening. The movement takes its name from *The Fundamentals*, a series of booklets that identified five doctrines essential to Christianity: (1) the literal inerrancy of the Bible, (2) the divinity and virgin birth of Christ, (3) Christ's atonement for human sin on the cross, (4) the bodily resurrection of Christ, and (5) the imminent Second Coming of Christ. Seeking to defend these doctrines, leaders such as the television evangelist Jerry Falwell made fundamentalism a powerful force in American culture in the 1970s and 1980s. Fundamentalists also fought to defend what they called "traditional values" against feminism, gay rights, legalized abortion, and the elimination of prayer in public schools.

Pentecostal worship at the Catedral Evangelica de Chile in Santiago, Chile.

Fundamentalism grew out of **evangelicalism**, a much larger movement with roots in the "Great Awakening," a revival of religious fervor that swept through England and North America in the eighteenth century. As its name suggests, evangelicalism encourages the preaching and sharing of the gospel (Greek *evangelion*). It also emphasizes the need for every Christian to have a conversion experience, often described as being "born again" (John 3:3), which leads to a personal relationship with Jesus Christ. Evangelicals regard the Bible as the sole basis of faith, though they do not always insist on its literal interpretation. Like fundamentalists, many evangelicals believe that the end of the age and Second Coming of Christ will occur in the near future. Evangelicalism is a fast-growing worldwide movement that is making its presence felt both in older Protestant denominations and in new movements. It has become a major force in Africa and Asia and is particularly strong in North America. Evangelicals make up as much as one-fourth of the population of the United States,[7] where they have promoted the idea that America is an essentially Christian nation. They have had considerable success in applying their understanding of biblical principles to politics and public policy.

Pentecostalism takes its name from the holy day of Pentecost, which commemorates the descent of the Holy Spirit upon Jesus's followers after his ascension to heaven. According to Acts 1:1–4, these Spirit-filled believers were empowered to "speak in other tongues," to prophesy, and to perform healings in the name of Christ. Since its beginnings in America in the early twentieth century, the Pentecostal movement has sought to reclaim this feature of earliest Christianity. Its most essential belief is that conversion must be followed by a "baptism in the Spirit" made evident by an ability to speak in tongues and at least one of the other "spiritual gifts" described by Paul in 1 Corinthians 12–14. The belief that the ecstatic experience of God belongs at the center of Christian life is unmistakable in Pentecostal churches, where enthusiastic worshipers raise their arms in praise, speak in tongues, and sometimes dance or weep. The phenomenal growth of Pentecostalism during the last century has made it a major force in contemporary Christianity throughout the world. Today, Pentecostalism is the most popular form of Protestantism in Latin America, and it is rapidly gaining converts in Africa and Asia. In America, the most visible Pentecostal denominations include the Assemblies of God, the Church of God, and the Church of the Foursquare Gospel.

Orthodoxy in the Modern World   We saw earlier that the Ottoman Turks completed their conquest of the Byzantine Empire, the home of Orthodox Christianity, with their capture of Constantinople in 1453. The Muslim rulers of the Ottoman state tolerated the Orthodox Church, but they also brought it under government control. When Greeks, Bulgarians, Serbs, and other Orthodox peoples began declaring their independence from the declining Ottoman Empire in the 1800s, they established independent national churches. Today's 225 million Orthodox Christians belong to fifteen autonomous churches, including the Orthodox churches of Greece and Russia and the Orthodox Church in America. The Ecumenical Patriarch of Constantinople retains an honorary primacy among Orthodox bishops but has no real authority over them. Despite this, the Orthodox churches are united by a tradition of shared theology and forms of worship they trace back to the apostles.

Orthodox Christianity resisted the influence of Western rationalism and liberalism in the eighteenth and nineteenth centuries. But Western influence in the form of Marxism had a devastating effect on Orthodoxy after the Bolshevik Revolution in Russia (1917) and the creation of a bloc of communist states in eastern Europe after World War II. Because these states saw all religion as an obstacle to the achievement of their social and political goals, they took drastic measures to strip the Church of its influence. Priests and monks were imprisoned, seminaries were closed, and church property was seized. The collapse of communism in the early 1990s brought a restoration of religious freedom and the revival of Orthodoxy. Since then, a dramatic rise in church attendance has testified to the commitment of millions of Russians, Ukrainians, Georgians, Bulgarians, Romanians, and Serbs to Orthodox Christianity.

Women in Christianity

The historical development of Christianity has occurred largely in patriarchal cultures. Although women have distinguished themselves as mystics, theologians, saints, members of religious orders, and founders of schools, hospitals, and other service organizations, they have generally been excluded from positions of leadership and authority. But women's roles began to change in the nineteenth and twentieth centuries. This is especially true of the Protestant tradition, in which women are now ordained to the clergy and have even founded denominations; good examples are Aimee Semple McPherson and Ellen G. White, founders of the Foursquare Gospel Church and the Seventh-Day Adventist Church (see Chapter 14), respectively. Although the Roman Catholic and Orthodox churches remain opposed to ordaining them to the clergy, women from these traditions have joined Protestants in finding other ways to lead and serve. Perhaps the most notable is their work in the academic world. As scholars specializing in biblical studies, ethics, and theology, women are communicating new ideas and insights that are bringing profound change to Christian thought.

Feminist Theology   Feminist theologians have called for liberation from a Christian worldview based solely on the experience of men. In her *Beyond God the Father* (1973), Mary Daly (1928–2010) argued that the Christian habit of thinking of God as Father allows misogyny to masquerade as a spiritual norm, thereby relegating women to a secondary status in the Church. Rosemary Radford Ruether (b. 1936), another influential feminist theologian, urges a new way of thinking about God as "God/ess" and has suggested the creation of churches open only to women and men committed to the rights and equality of women.

Christianity Today and Tomorrow: Trends and Prospects

We live in a rapidly changing world. What the future holds for Christianity is difficult to predict, though there are signs of the directions it is likely to take. For example, the ordination of women as pastors is becoming increasingly common in Protestant denominations.

Demographic Shifts   Today, approximately half of the world's 2.2 billion Christians are Roman Catholics, 37 percent identify as Protestants, and 12 percent are Orthodox. The remaining 1 percent belong to other Christian groups. Just a century ago, 80 percent of Christians lived in Europe and North America. Today, 60 percent live in Africa,

Branches of Christianity

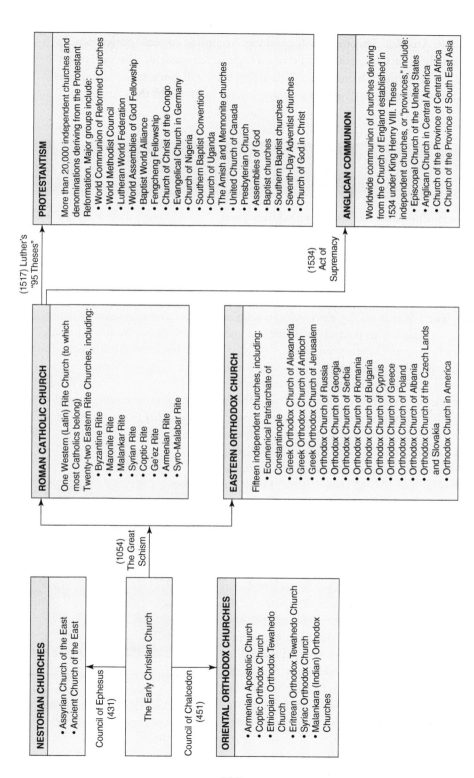

NESTORIAN CHURCHES

• Assyrian Church of the East
• Ancient Church of the East

Council of Ephesus (431)

The Early Christian Church

Council of Chalcedon (451)

ORIENTAL ORTHODOX CHURCHES

• Armenian Apostolic Church
• Coptic Orthodox Church
• Ethiopian Orthodox Tewahedo Church
• Eritrean Orthodox Tewahedo Church
• Syriac Orthodox Church
• Malankara (Indian) Orthodox Churches

ROMAN CATHOLIC CHURCH

One Western (Latin) Rite Church (to which most Catholics belong)
Twenty-two Eastern Rite Churches, including:

• Byzantine Rite
• Maronite Rite
• Malankar Rite
• Syrian Rite
• Coptic Rite
• Ge'ez Rite
• Armenian Rite
• Syro-Malabar Rite

(1054) The Great Schism

EASTERN ORTHODOX CHURCH

Fifteen independent churches, including:

• Ecumenical Patriarchate of Constantinople
• Greek Orthodox Church of Alexandria
• Greek Orthodox Church of Antioch
• Greek Orthodox Church of Jerusalem
• Orthodox Church of Russia
• Orthodox Church of Georgia
• Orthodox Church of Serbia
• Orthodox Church of Romania
• Orthodox Church of Bulgaria
• Orthodox Church of Cyprus
• Orthodox Church of Greece
• Orthodox Church of Poland
• Orthodox Church of Albania
• Orthodox Church of the Czech Lands and Slovakia
• Orthodox Church in America

(1517) Luther's "95 Theses"

PROTESTANTISM

More than 20,000 independent churches and denominations deriving from the Protestant Reformation. Major groups include:

• World Communion of Reformed Churches
• World Methodist Council
• Lutheran World Federation
• World Assemblies of God Fellowship
• Baptist World Alliance
• Fengcheng Fellowship
• Church of Christ of the Congo
• Evangelical Church in Germany
• Church of Nigeria
• Southern Baptist Convention
• Church of Uganda
• The Amish and Mennonite churches
• United Church of Canada
• Presbyterian Church
• Assemblies of God
• Baptist churches
• Southern Baptist churches
• Seventh-Day Adventist churches
• Church of God in Christ

(1534) Act of Supremacy

ANGLICAN COMMUNION

Worldwide communion of churches deriving from the Church of England established in 1534 under King Henry VIII. These independent churches, or "provinces," include:

• Episcopal Church of the United States
• Anglican Church in Central America
• Church of the Province of Central Africa
• Church of the Province of South East Asia

Asia, and Latin America. This trend will continue. According to some projections, by 2050 only one-fifth of Christians will be non-Hispanic Caucasians. The vast majority will live in the southern hemisphere. This global shift will bring major changes as African and South American Christians assume greater influence in the Church.

GLOBAL SNAPSHOT
The Kimbanguist Church in Africa

Although Europeans had traded with Africa since ancient times, it was not until the late 1700s that they began to explore the African continent. By 1900, Europe's colonial powers had brought most of Africa under their control, and missionaries had established European forms of Christianity that flourished until the post–World War II era. By then, African peoples had begun to declare their political independence and to develop their own Christian traditions.

Today, there is an astonishing variety in African Christianity. Ancient churches continue to thrive in Egypt, Ethiopia, and Eritrea, but most of Africa's nearly 12,000 denominations are of recent origin and were founded by Africans. Some of these African Initiated Churches (AICs) blend indigenous religions with Christianity. Some are messianic, emphasizing the Christ-like qualities of their leaders. Many are Pentecostal churches that emphasize the power of prayer and the Holy Spirit, as do Pentecostal churches elsewhere, but have a distinctively African character.

One of the largest AICs is the Church of Jesus Christ on Earth Through His Special Envoy Simon Kimbangu. The Kimbanguist Church was founded in 1921 in what is now the Democratic Republic of the Congo by Simon Kimbangu, a charismatic preacher and healer whose miracles included the revival of a child who had died. Kimbangu was imprisoned for life by the Congo's Belgian rulers who were worried by the thousands who flocked to him for healing, but his movement continued to grow, encouraged by stories of Kimbangu's bodily appearances to followers even while remaining in prison.

Although the Kimbanguist Church embraces features of traditional Christianity, such as the Apostles' Creed and a commitment to providing social and educational services, it radically redefines others. For example, it identifies Simon Kimbangu as the Holy Spirit, his first son as God the Father, and his second son as a reincarnation of Jesus Christ. Like his grandfather, Father Simon Kimbangu Kiangani, the current leader of the Kimbanguist Church is the Holy Spirit in human form.

Like other AICs, the Kimbanguist Church attests both to the enduring appeal of Christianity and its adaptability to the needs and aspirations of particular groups.

Kimbanguists holding bowls of money intended as an offering to Simon Kimbangu Kiangani, the current leader of the Kimbanguist Church, in Nkamba, Democratic Republic of Congo, the birthplace of Simon Kimbangu (May, 2017).

Liberation Theology The beginnings of theological change along these lines became evident in the mid-twentieth century in the form of liberation theology, which grew out of the concern of Latin American priests such as Gustavo Gutiérrez for the plight of the poor. Originating with Gutiérrez's *A Theology of Liberation* (1971), liberation theology calls for radical action to correct the social, political, and economic injustices perpetrated against impoverished Latin Americans by landowners, governments, and the Church itself. It holds that the Church must work to ensure at least the basic necessities of life for all human beings. Moreover, it finds a scriptural basis for its views in the New Testament ideal of the Church as a community of believers committed to caring for each other's material as well as spiritual needs.

The principles of liberation theology have been put to work outside Latin America. In addition to their influence on feminist theology, they are central to black liberation theology, a movement originating in the thought of James Cone (b. 1938). Cone's *Black Theology and Black Power* (1969) and *A Black Theology of Liberation* (1970) offered a scathing criticism of white Christianity and society for their indifference to the problems of race and social injustice. Calling for the application of Christian principles to these problems in *this* world, Cone wrote that "the idea of heaven is irrelevant for Black Theology. The Christian cannot waste time contemplating the next world. . . . Jesus' work is essentially one of liberation."[8]

Ecumenism Another development in contemporary Christianity is ecumenism. Based on the ancient ideal of a single worldwide church, the aim of the ecumenical movement (Greek *oikoumene*, "the inhabited world") is the restoration of Christian unity. It was not until the twentieth century that organizations such as the World Council of Churches began moving deliberately in this direction. In recent decades, most larger churches have declared their interest in ecumenism, and many have established cooperative agreements with each other. There have also been extraordinary ways in which Christians from different traditions have come together in pursuit of unity. A good example is the Taizé Community in France, an ecumenical monastic order of men from both Catholic and Protestant backgrounds. Committed to a shared vision of the essence of the gospel message, the community at Taizé has gained a reputation for holiness that draws thousands of pilgrims every year.

CHRISTIANITY AS A WAY OF LIFE

There is much more to Christianity than the beliefs Christians hold inwardly. Like the followers of other religions, Christians express their beliefs outwardly in a variety of ways. Some are public, such as formal worship in church, participation in rituals, and the observance of holy days. Others are more private and personal, such as prayer and meditation. Together, these practices constitute much of what Christians do in living the Christian life.

Worship

Because the first Christians were Jews, they patterned their worship on the Jewish synagogue service, which consisted of readings from scripture, prayer, and a sermon. To these elements, they added the celebration of the **Eucharist**, a commemoration of the Last Supper Jesus shared with his disciples. The result was a **liturgy** (Greek *leitourgia*, "work of the people") consisting of two parts: the liturgy of the word, including readings from scripture, prayer, and a sermon, and the liturgy of the Eucharist. The Western custom of referring to the liturgy as the "Mass" can be traced back to *missa*, one of the Latin words used to dismiss the congregation: *Ite, missa est* ("Go, the dismissal is made").

Today's Roman Catholic and Orthodox churches are highly liturgical. In worship, members of these traditions are caught up in ritual rhythms of praise and adoration that reach back through more than two millennia. In contrast, most Protestant groups have adopted much simpler forms of worship that emphasize readings from scripture and preaching over ritual.

Christians have always made Sunday, the day of Christ's resurrection, a day set apart for communal worship. Typically, worship in Protestant churches begins with a hymn followed by an invocation or opening prayer. After readings from scripture, congregants might sing another hymn in preparation for the sermon. Informal announcements of interest to the congregation often follow, along with a collection taken up for support of the church and its charitable causes. A recitation of the Lord's Prayer follows the collection. The service concludes with a final prayer and a closing hymn. In Roman Catholic churches, worship begins with a formal procession of the clergy toward the altar (a table used in celebrating the Eucharist) accompanied by the singing of an opening hymn. Next, in a penitential rite,

Early Christians used the "sign of the fish" as a secret symbol to identify themselves during times of persecution. Today, many Christians identify themselves as such by mounting the symbol on their cars. The letters of the Greek word for "fish" (ΙΧΘΥΣ) are the first letters in the words that make up the phrase "Jesus Christ, Son of God, and Savior."

The cross has served as a Christian symbol since ancient times and appears in many forms. With its longer vertical and shorter horizontal arms, the Latin cross is the form favored by the Roman Catholic and Protestant churches. This one stands atop Monte Crocione in northern Italy.

Orthodox Christians use many different forms of the cross. The most common is a simple figure formed by four arms of equal length. This one decorates a small convent on the island of Mykonos, Greece.

The Celtic cross. According to legend, the Celtic cross on the left originated with St. Patrick, who brought Christianity to Ireland. This one serves as a grave marker in a cemetery in Dublin, Ireland.

(continued)

A crucifix is a cross with an image of the crucified Christ. It is used extensively in the Roman Catholic, Orthodox, Anglican, and Lutheran traditions. A vivid reminder of Christ's suffering on behalf of humanity, it is usually displayed prominently in church interiors.

The custom of using alpha and omega, the first and last letters of the Greek alphabet, to symbolize the eternality of God is based on a verse from the book of Revelation in the New Testament (1:8): "I am the Alpha and the Omega," says the Lord God, "who is, and who was, and who is to come, the Almighty."

The Chi-Rho is a symbol of Christ. Its name is based on those of the Greek letters chi and rho, the first two letters in the Greek word Christos, or "Christ." According to legend, the Chi-Rho was revealed in a dream to the Emperor Constantine, who won a military victory after marking it on the shields of his soldiers. Today, the Chi-Rho appears on altars, plaques, vestments, and other items. It is shown here on a Christian stele from Spain, c. 600.

The "sign of the cross" is a ritual hand motion in which the shape of the cross of Christ is traced across the forehead and chest. It is used in both public worship and private prayer. The practice of "signing" oneself as an act of devotion goes back to ancient times. Writing c. 200, the North African theologian Tertullian noted that the Christians of his time "wore out their foreheads" making the sign of the cross.

those present confess their sins and ask God's forgiveness. The liturgy of the word that follows consists primarily of readings from scripture, a short sermon, or homily, and a recitation of the Nicene Creed. At this point, the liturgy of the Eucharist begins with the presentation of bread and wine, which are set on the altar. After the priest blesses these elements, there is a special Eucharistic prayer followed by a singing of the *Sanctus*, a short hymn taken from the Old Testament (Isaiah 6:3). The congregation then recites an affirmation of faith and the Lord's Prayer. In a final preparatory act, members of the congregation wish each other "the peace of the Lord." It is at this point that the bread and wine are consecrated, making Christ present upon the altar. The members of the congregation then share in the rite of communion, in which each person receives a bit of the consecrated elements of bread and wine. Many Roman Catholic Christians say that it is in this solemn moment that they are most acutely aware of God's loving presence. The liturgy concludes with a final prayer, a benediction (blessing), and the formal dismissal of the congregation. The liturgy celebrated in Orthodox churches follows this same pattern, though additional processions, prayers, and blessings make it more elaborate.

Sacraments

Like worship, the special rituals known as **sacraments** are central to Christian life. Understood as visible symbols of God's grace, the sacraments infuse believers with spiritual nourishment and impart a sacred character to transitional moments in their lives. The Greek word for sacrament, *musterion* ("mystery"—the term preferred by Orthodox Christians), helps to explain the significance these rituals have for Christians. Making use of ordinary elements such as bread, wine, water, and oil, they bring the individual into an experience of something extraordinary—the mystery of God's love.

Roman Catholic and Orthodox Christians celebrate seven sacraments. Protestants acknowledge only two: baptism and the Eucharist.

The first sacrament celebrated in the life of a Christian is baptism, a cleansing of sin that marks the beginning of a new spiritual life in which one is united with Christ and sanctified by the Holy Spirit. Baptism can take the form of complete immersion in water or a sprinkling of water on one's head. However it is performed, the priest or minister always follows the instruction of Christ to baptize "in the name of the Father and of the Son and of the Holy Spirit" (Matthew 28:19).

After baptism, a Christian is entitled to participate in the Eucharist, also known as Holy Communion and the Lord's Supper. As we have seen, the Eucharist commemorates Christ's Last Supper with his disciples before his crucifixion. On that occasion, Christ identified the bread and wine they shared with his body and blood:

> While they were eating, he took a loaf of bread, and after blessing it he broke it and gave it to them, and said, "Take; this is my body." Then he took a cup, and after giving thanks he gave it to them, and all of them drank from it. He said to them, "This is my blood of the covenant, which is poured out for many."
>
> —*Mark 14:22–24*

Historically, most Christians have taken these words to mean that Christ is truly present in the Eucharist. Only with the Reformation of the sixteenth century did some Protestant groups adopt the view that the bread and wine are mere symbols of Christ's presence. Although those who believe in the "real presence" have sought to explain

This baptistery basin was built in the sixth century as part of the Basilica of St. Vitalis in what is now Sbeitla, Tunisia. Candidates for baptism were led down the steps and then baptized by full immersion in water.

it in various ways, most acknowledge that it is ultimately a mystery. In a sense, it is similar to the gestures we use to communicate inward feelings in everyday life. For example, most of us believe that the love we feel for someone else can be conveyed by a hug or a kiss, but we would find it difficult to explain in precise terms how our love is present in the gesture. We can understand the Eucharist as a kind of sacred gesture in which God offers grace to human beings. Although Christians have different ways of explaining how this happens, they agree that their participation in the ritual meal of bread and wine brings them into closer union with God and each other.

A third sacrament is confirmation. In the Roman Catholic Church, confirmation is administered to adolescents who have completed formal instruction in the faith. *Because* they understand its teachings, they are recognized as fully responsible members of the Church. In the Orthodox tradition, confirmation usually occurs when an infant is baptized *in order that*, nourished by grace, he or she might grow into a mature understanding of the faith and share in the work of the Church.

The four remaining sacraments are essentially the same in Catholicism and Orthodoxy. Holy matrimony gives a sacred character to marriage. For men who feel called to become priests, the sacrament of holy orders confers a grace that enables them to be effective leaders in the Church. Penance, also known as confession and reconciliation, involves confessing sin to a priest in order to receive his assurances of God's forgiveness and his prescription for the performance of an act of penance or reparation for the sin committed. The final sacrament, anointing of the sick, is meant to strengthen those who are in immediate danger of death.

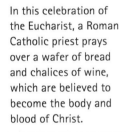

In this celebration of the Eucharist, a Roman Catholic priest prays over a wafer of bread and chalices of wine, which are believed to become the body and blood of Christ.

Church Interiors: Sacred Space

The interior design of a church reflects its theology and liturgical style. Most Protestant churches are quite plain and have rows of seats facing a pulpit in the front as their main features. It is from the pulpit, a raised lectern, that the pastor or minister delivers the weekly sermon. Because Protestants emphasize scripture over sacraments, the pulpit generally has a more prominent position than the altar. Protestant churches make sparing use of decorative effects. There may be candles on the altar and a cross displayed on the wall, but little more. The intention behind this simplicity is to create an environment without distractions in which worshipers can meet God in prayer and in the reading and exposition of scripture.

Roman Catholic churches are more elaborate. Because Catholicism emphasizes the sacraments, and the Eucharist in particular, it is the altar rather than the pulpit that stands out from the worshiper's perspective. Religious paintings and

The design and decor of this small Protestant church are simple. The attention of the congregation is directed toward the pulpit, from which the pastor delivers a sermon based on the scriptures.

statues of saints are commonly found, as are crucifixes, or images of Christ on the cross. To the side of some churches is a stand supporting rows of votive candles set in colored glass. When music is added to these physical features of the church, the senses are filled with sights and sounds meant to lift the mind and heart to God.

This approach to creating a sacred space is even more pronounced in Orthodox churches, whose design and decoration give worshipers a sense of entering into the heavenly presence of God. The main body of the Orthodox church is separated from the sanctuary in the front by a screen, called an iconostasis ("icon stand"), covered with painted images of Christ and the saints. Icons fill the rest of the church as well, reminding worshipers that they belong to a spiritual communion that includes the whole company of heaven. Even the magnificent domes atop Orthodox churches display iconic murals of Christ and the saints. But the main focus of attention is the sanctuary, which can be glimpsed through several doors that provide access to the priest and his assistants. It is in this sacred space that the mystery of the

Like all Roman Catholic churches, this church in St. Maarten in the Netherlands Antilles gives the most prominent place to the altar, where the Eucharist is celebrated. The priest's homily, or sermon, is delivered from a pulpit set to the side. Images of the saints that Catholics venerate can be seen along the walls.

Eucharist is celebrated, with chanting and incense that reveal in the material world the realities of the spiritual realm.

Prayer

For Christians, Jesus provides the ultimate example of the importance of prayer. The gospels describe him as praying frequently, often for hours and with great fervency. On one occasion, he taught his disciples to pray in this way:

> Our Father in heaven,
> hallowed be your name.
> Your kingdom come.
> Your will be done,
> on earth as it is in heaven.
> Give us this day our daily bread.
> And forgive us our debts,
> as we also have forgiven our debtors.
> And do not bring us to the time of trial,
> but deliver us from the evil one.
> —*Matthew 6:9–13*

The interior of an Orthodox church in Odessa, Ukraine. Note the iconostasis, or "icon screen" at the far end of the aisle. In Orthodox churches, the altar is always located behind the iconostasis. Images of Christ and the saints on the interior of the dome remind worshippers of their spiritual communion with heavenly personalities.

This prayer, known as the **Lord's Prayer**, is just one of many forms of prayer in Christianity. In the early Christian centuries, additional prayers were created and formally integrated into the liturgy. Of course, from the beginning, Christians also prayed privately, informally, and silently. Today, it is customary for Christians to offer a prayer of thanksgiving before meals, on rising in the morning, and before going to bed at night. When the troubles and concerns of daily life arise, they ask God for guidance, forgiveness, and peace. In the face of sickness and death, they find in prayer the assurance of God's loving presence.

Most Christian traditions include specialized forms of prayer practiced by those who wish to deepen their spiritual lives. For example, the interior walls of Roman Catholic churches display fourteen images of the passion, or suffering, of Christ during the final hours of his life. During Lent, the period before Easter, Catholics visit these Stations of the Cross in order, reciting prayers and meditating on each incident as a means of coming to a deeper understanding of Christ's suffering. Another form of Catholic devotion is praying the **rosary**. This involves recitation of a series of prayers counted on a string of beads while meditating on important moments in the lives of Jesus and his mother, Mary.

For instruction in prayer, Orthodox Christians turn to the *Philokalia*, a collection of mystical texts written between the fourth and the fifteenth centuries. Containing the words of Orthodoxy's greatest sages, the *Philokalia* is considered a treasury of wisdom concerning the practice of contemplative prayer. Whereas meditation centers on the intellect, contemplative prayer is a "prayer of the heart" in which it is not just the mind but one's whole being that reaches out to God. Its most common form is the Jesus Prayer: "Lord Jesus Christ, Son of God, have mercy on me." Ideally, the Jesus Prayer is recited continually, whether one is driving to work, standing in line, or attending to any other matter. In time, it embeds itself in one's being, and its repetition becomes as natural and effortless as breathing. According to one Orthodox saint, "even when [the practitioner] is immersed in sleep, the perfumes of prayer will breathe in his heart spontaneously."[9] In recent years, the Jesus Prayer and other forms of Orthodox contemplation have become increasingly popular among Catholics and Protestants, who share with Orthodox Christians a yearning for communion with God not only at certain times but throughout the course of each day.

> What similarities do you see between the aims and practices of Christian contemplative prayer and the Hindu recitation of *mantras*?

The Liturgical Year

Just as the life of every Christian is punctuated by the sacraments, each year in the life of the Church is defined by the celebration of holy days and the observance of religious seasons that make up the liturgical year. Built around the two great feasts of **Christmas** and **Easter**, the cycle of the liturgical year draws believers into the experience of Christ, allowing them to relive in a vicarious way the events in his life through which God brought salvation to the world.

> The liturgical year is an annual cycle of holy days and seasons that re-create events and times during the life of Jesus.

The first great season of the liturgical year is Advent, a time of preparation and looking forward to the "coming" (Latin, *adventus*) of God into the world. Advent culminates in Christmas, a celebration of the birth of Christ on December 25, when expectation turns into rejoicing. The Christmas season ends on January 6 with a celebration of **Epiphany** (from the Greek *epiphaneia*, "manifestation"), which recalls the manifestation of Jesus's divinity as an infant (emphasized in the West) and at his baptism (emphasized in the East).

After Epiphany, the liturgical year moves forward to Easter, a springtime celebration of Christ's resurrection. Easter is preceded by the season of Lent, when many Christians practice self-denial as a way of participating vicariously in the suffering of Christ. Awareness of Christ's suffering is heightened during Holy Week, the last week of

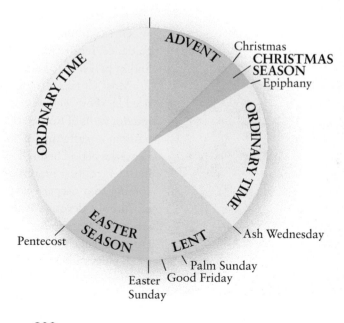

Lent, when most days have special significance. Palm Sunday recalls Christ's triumphal entry into Jerusalem, when enthusiastic crowds placed palm branches on the road before him. Maundy Thursday marks Jesus's institution of the Eucharist at the Last Supper. Good Friday commemorates the crucifixion of Jesus. Holy Week concludes with Easter, the most important Christian holiday because it is in Christ's resurrection that Christians see his triumph over death and the promise of eternal life. Easter is a truly joyous holiday, filled with signs and symbols of new life. In Orthodox countries, Easter mornings resound with the cry, "Christ is risen!" and the response, "He is risen indeed!" Rejoicing continues through the following weeks as Christians celebrate the ascension of Christ into heaven and the coming of the Holy Spirit at Pentecost. After Pentecost, the liturgical year moves into six months of "ordinary time" that ends with Advent, when the annual cycle begins again.

Veneration of Saints

This Greek icon depicts Christ holding the scriptures and raising his right hand in a sign of blessing. The Greek letters outside his halo identify him as Jesus Christ. The letters inside the halo identify him as God.

Like the members of any group, Christians have always had their heroes. Known as **saints** ("holy ones"), they are spiritual role models who have shown how the Christian life should be lived. The greatest of saints is Mary, the virgin mother of Christ, who is considered the foremost example of what God can do in sanctifying a human life. Those who honor Mary point to her virtues of gentleness, humility, and submission to God's will and recall her expression of joy on learning that she had been chosen to bear the Christ: "Surely, from now on all generations will call me blessed" (Luke 1:48). According to Roman Catholic teaching, Mary was unique in being conceived without sin (the doctrine of the Immaculate Conception) and in being taken up bodily into heaven at her death (the doctrine of the Assumption). Orthodox Christians honor Mary with the titles *Theotokos* ("God-bearer") and *Panagia* ("All-holy").

For Protestant Christians, the significance of the saints lies almost exclusively in the inspiring examples they have set for others. In Roman Catholicism and Orthodoxy, the saints have greater significance. These traditions emphasize the eternal participation of the saints in the Church, for though they now exist in heaven, they remain within the mystical communion of believers that is "the body of Christ." Catholic and Orthodox Christians believe that Paul made this point when he wrote that Christians are "citizens with the saints and also members of the household of God" (Ephesians 2:16).

Just as the living pray for the welfare of their fellow Christians, the saints are thought to intercede for them in prayer as well. Belief in the intercession of saints is evident in early Christian literature and in ancient epitaphs found on sarcophagi and grave markers. These implore both saints and departed family members to pray for the living. "Pray for us," says one inscription, "that we may be saved." On the sarcophagus of their little boy, his mother and father wrote: "To our son Philemon, who lived happily for two years with his parents: Pray for us, together with the saints."[10] Belief in the intercession of saints remains an important part of Roman Catholicism and Orthodoxy. Strictly speaking, one does not pray *to* the saints, but *with* them. Saints are not worshiped. Instead, they are venerated with a reverential respect that recognizes their holiness.

The veneration of saints takes a variety of forms. Traditionally, Catholic and Orthodox Christians are given a saint's name at baptism, and their churches are usually named after saints. Many believers honor saints on their feast days. In addition, the physical remains of saints, known as relics, are objects of veneration. Preserved in special containers known as reliquaries, relics are found in many churches, where they bring a sense of the sacred to those who pray in their presence. The relics are often brought out for special observances or processions on the saint's feast day. If this practice seems a bit strange to you, it might be helpful to consider how you might be affected by a more secular "relic." For example, a photograph or keepsake from a loved one you have lost can provide a sense of that person's presence. In some mysterious way, it seems, something of that person's essence remains within the item itself. So it is with the saints, whose holiness is thought to remain in the relics they have left behind.

Images of saints also produce a heightened awareness of holiness. In Roman Catholicism, images take the forms of paintings and statues whose lifelike quality is meant to underscore the experience of earthly existence that the saints share with all other believers. Meditating on a painting or statue, believers are encouraged in the spiritual life by knowing that the saint it represents once experienced the same challenges they experience. The **icons** of the Orthodox, who make no use of statues, are meant to have just the opposite effect. These highly stylized paintings are not intended to be lifelike. Their purpose is to represent not earthly reality but the reality of transfigured and perfected humanity in heaven. Gazing intently at their observers and communicating through symbolic gestures, the saints depicted in icons offer a glimpse of the higher, spiritual realm that is the ultimate goal of every Christian.

Social and Political Activism

Service to others is an important part of Christian practice. According to the New Testament (Acts 4:32–35), the earliest Christians took seriously the command to love one's neighbor as oneself: the wealthy gave all their money to the church, all property was held in common, and no one experienced great need. In the Middle Ages, the churches of the East and West provided important social services by supporting orphans, widows, and the disabled; seeking the release of prisoners of war; and caring for victims of plagues, earthquakes, and other disasters.

This tradition of social service continues today. Most congregations make significant contributions to support the poor, the sick, and the homeless in their communities. On a larger scale, there are hundreds of national and international Christian charities dedicated to fighting social and political injustice, bringing an end to poverty, and providing food, health services, and education to those in need. They include Habitat for Humanity, Bread for the World, International Orthodox Charities, Catholic Relief Services, the Salvation Army, and World Vision.

Christian activism has often brought important social and political change. American abolitionists such as Theodore Weld (1803–1895) and Harriet Beecher Stowe (1811–1896) played leading roles in the American antislavery movement, whose aims were realized in the Emancipation Proclamation of 1863. In the 1960s, it was a black Baptist minister, Dr. Martin Luther King Jr. (1929–1968), who championed the civil rights movement that succeeded in outlawing discrimination against minorities and women in the Civil Rights Act of 1964. Today's Christian activists are involved in causes ranging from placing water for migrants in the deserts of Arizona to protesting nuclear weapons to fighting HIV/AIDS in Africa.

CONCLUSION

With a history reaching back 2,000 years, Christianity has proven to be a durable religion. Like other religions that have met the test of time, much of its vitality lies in the meaning its message has had for countless adherents through the centuries. History, geography, culture, and other forces have produced many forms of Christianity, but they share basic beliefs that go back to Jesus and to the New Testament texts that expound the meaning of his teachings, life, death, and resurrection: there is a single, transcendent, all-powerful, and personal God who created the universe as an expression of divine love and who seeks loving union with humanity.

In addressing the most basic questions arising from human existence, the Christian message has had an incalculable influence on individual lives. But it has also contributed to the formation of entire civilizations, shaping their political and social institutions, informing their cultural values and ideals, and inspiring some of their greatest achievements in art, architecture, and literature.

There are two great issues we must consider, however briefly, in concluding our discussion of Christianity. The first is the role Christianity will play in shaping the world of the future. How will Christians respond to the environmental, social, and political problems our world faces? What actions will they take in promoting justice? How will they apply the gospel message in acknowledging and protecting the rights of women, homosexuals, and the poor—both inside and outside the Church? The second issue is how Christianity will be affected by the rapid change we see all around us. Will its traditional forms and institutions remain solidly entrenched? As the world's Christian population becomes increasingly concentrated in Africa, South America, and Asia, how will the religious and cultural traditions of these regions influence a religion with a history that has been played out largely in Europe and North America? Of course, we cannot be certain of the answers to questions like these. We can be certain only that Christianity, the world's largest religion, will remain a major force in the world in which we live.

SEEKING ANSWERS

What Is Ultimate Reality?

Christianity teaches that there is a single, personal, transcendent, and all-powerful God—a God who is one in essence but threefold in His manifestations as Father, Son, and Holy Spirit. God created a perfect world as an expression of divine love, but it has fallen into imperfection due to human sin. Like Jews and Muslims, Christians believe that God wants to be known in and by Creation, and especially by humanity. For Christians, the supreme revelation of the divine nature is found in Jesus Christ, who was the very incarnation of God. They also believe that God has revealed Himself in other ways, such as through scripture and through the immensity and beauty of the universe.

How Should We Live in This World?

Christians believe that God has reached out in grace (love) to humanity, making atonement for sin through Jesus Christ. For those who respond to God's love in faith, a new kind of life in Christ becomes possible—a life in which the fundamental ethical principle is love. Jesus spoke of love for God and one's neighbor as the essence of scripture and described it in a radical way. Even enemies must be loved and forgiven. This demanding conception of love is one of the essential ideals in Christianity. It is also one that requires great effort. To achieve it, Christians find inspiration in study and reflection on scripture, through prayer, and in fellowship with other Christians who take love seriously. Christians find good examples of love and other virtues in the lives of the saints, whom they seek to emulate. They also believe that the sacraments offer a spiritual nourishment that is helpful in the cultivation of lives they attempt to live in imitation of Christ.

What Is Our Ultimate Purpose?

For Christians, the ultimate goal of human existence is union with God. As Augustine wrote in the fifth century, "You have made us for yourself, O Lord, and our hearts are restless until they find rest in you." The path to reunion with God is through Jesus Christ, whose sacrificial death, an expression of God's love, atoned for all human sin. When human beings respond in faith to God's love, or grace, they are brought into union with the divine. Christians hope to share in the resurrection of Christ, which leads to eternal blessedness in union with God. But there is also the possibility of eternal separation from God. Because the Bible offers few concrete details about these two possibilities, traditionally understood as heaven and hell, they have been interpreted in many different ways.

REVIEW QUESTIONS

For Review

1. What were the means by which the Christian movement defined orthodox belief and established ecclesiastical authority in late antiquity?

2. How did the Roman Catholic, Orthodox, and Protestant traditions within Christianity emerge from the "catholic" or "universal" Christianity of the first millennium? What were the main factors that contributed to the formation of these traditions?

3. What are the seasons and holy days of the liturgical year? What is their significance for Christians? How are they observed?
4. What is the doctrine of the Trinity? Why is this doctrine central to Christianity?
5. What are the major challenges Christianity has encountered in the modern era? How has it responded to them?

For Further Reflection

1. What are some of the more important ways in which basic Christian beliefs are expressed outwardly in worship, the sacraments, prayer, and other devotional practices?
2. If asked by a friend, how would you describe the essence of Christianity? Are there

teachings embraced by all (or, at least, most) forms of Christianity?
3. How do Christian beliefs about God/ultimate reality, human nature, the world, and the ultimate goal or purpose of human existence compare with those of the closely related religions of Judaism and Islam?
4. How do Christian beliefs about these same issues compare with those of religions such as Hinduism, Buddhism, Daoism, Confucianism, Sikhism, and Jainism?
5. Do you think the Christian ecumenical movement has a realistic chance of restoring the original unity of the Christian religion?

GLOSSARY

apostle In the New Testament, Jesus' disciples, sent out to preach and baptize, are called apostles (Greek *apostolos*, "one who is sent out"). Paul of Tarsus and some other early Christian leaders also claimed this title. Because of their close association with Jesus, the apostles were accorded a place of honor in the early Church.

apostolic succession According to this Roman Catholic and Orthodox doctrine, the spiritual authority conferred by Jesus on the apostles has been transmitted through an unbroken line of bishops, who are their successors.

baptism Performed by immersion in water or a sprinkling with water, baptism is a sacrament in which an individual is cleansed of sin and admitted into the Church.

bishop Responsible for supervising other priests and their congregations within specific regions known as dioceses, bishops are regarded by Roman Catholic and Orthodox Christians as successors of the apostles.

Calvin, John (1509–1564) One of the leading figures of the Protestant Reformation, Calvin is notable for his *Institutes of the Christian Religion* and his emphasis on the absolute power of God, the absolute depravity of human nature, and the absolute

dependence of human beings on divine grace for salvation.

Christmas An annual holiday commemorating the birth of Jesus, Christmas is observed by Western Christians on December 25. Although many Orthodox Christians celebrate Christmas on this date, others observe the holiday on January 7.

church In the broadest sense, "church" refers to the universal community of Christians, but the term can also refer to a particular tradition within Christianity (such as the Roman Catholic Church or the Lutheran Church) or to an individual congregation of Christians.

Easter An annual holiday commemorating the resurrection of Christ, Easter is a "movable feast" whose date changes from year to year, though it is always celebrated in spring (as early as March 22 and as late as May 8).

Epiphany An annual holiday commemorating the "manifestation" of the divinity of the infant Jesus, Epiphany is celebrated by most Western Christians on January 6. Most Eastern Christians observe it on January 19.

Eucharist (yoó-ka-rist) Also known as the Lord's Supper and Holy Communion, the Eucharist is a sacrament celebrated with consecrated bread and wine in commemoration of Jesus' Last Supper with his disciples.

evangelicalism This Protestant movement stresses the importance of the conversion experience, the Bible as the only reliable authority in matters of faith, and preaching the gospel. In recent decades, evangelicalism has become a major force in North American Christianity.

fundamentalism Originating in the early 1900s, this movement in American Protestantismis dedicated to defending doctrines it identifies as fundamental to Christianity against perceived threats posed by modern culture.

gospel In its most general sense, "gospel" means the "good news" (from Old English *godspel*, which translates the Greek *evangelion*) about Jesus Christ. The New Testament gospels of Matthew, Mark, Luke, and John are proclamations of the good news concerning the life, teachings, death, and resurrection of Jesus Christ.

grace Derived from the Latin *gratia* (a "gift" or "love"), "grace" refers to God's love for humanity, expressed in Jesus Christ and through the sacraments.

icons Painted images of Christ and the saints, icons are used extensively in the Orthodox Church.

Inquisition The investigation and suppression of heresy by the Roman Catholic Church, the Inquisition began in the twelfth century and was formally concluded in the middle of the nineteenth century.

kingdom of God God's rule or dominion over the universe and human affairs. The kingdom of God is one of the primary themes in the teaching of Jesus.

liturgy The liturgy (from Greek, *leitourgia*, "a work of the people" in honor of God) is basic order of worship in Christian churches. It consists of prescribed prayers, readings, and rituals.

logos In its most basic sense, the Greek *logos* means "word," but it also means "rational principle," "reason," or "divine reason." The Gospel of John uses *logos* in the sense of the "divine reason" through which God created and sustains the universe when it states that "the Word became flesh" in Jesus Christ (John 1:14).

Lord's Prayer A prayer attributed to Jesus, the Lord's Prayer serves as a model of prayer for Christians. Also known as the "Our Father" (since it begins with these words), its most familiar form is found in the Gospel of Matthew (6:9–13).

Luther, Martin (1483–1546) A German monk who criticized Roman Catholic doctrines and practices in his Ninety-Five Theses (1517), Luther was the original leader and one of the seminal thinkers of the Protestant Reformation.

Messiah In the Jewish Scriptures (Old Testament), messiah ("anointed one") refers to kings and priests, who were anointed with consecrated oil. In later Jewish literature, the Messiah is sometimes understood as a figure—in some cases, a supernatural figure—who, having been "anointed" by God, rescues the Jewish people and the world from evil. Christianity understands Jesus of Nazareth as the Messiah.

Nicene Creed A profession of faith formulated by the Councils of Nicea (325) and Constantinople (381), the Nicene Creed articulates the Christian doctrine of the Trinity.

original sin Formulated by St. Augustine in the fourth century, the doctrine of original sin states that the sin of Adam and Eve affected all of humanity, so that all human beings are born with a sinful nature.

Orthodox Church Also known as the Eastern Orthodox Church and the Orthodox Catholic Church, the Orthodox Church is the Eastern branch of Christianity that separated from the Western branch (the Roman Catholic Church) in 1054.

parable According to the gospels of Matthew, Mark, and Luke, Jesus made extensive use of parables—short, fictional stories that use the language and imagery of everyday life to illustrate moral and religious truths.

Paul of Tarsus A first-century apostle who founded churches throughout Asia Minor, Macedonia, and Greece. Paul was also the author of many of the letters, or epistles, found in the New Testament.

Pentecost A holiday celebrated by Christians in commemoration of the outpouring of the Holy Spirit on the disciples of Jesus as described in the second chapter of the New Testament book of Acts.

Pentecostalism A movement that emphasizes the importance of spiritual renewal and the experience of God through baptism in the Holy Spirit, Pentecostalism is a primarily Protestant movement that has become extremely popular in recent decades.

Protestant Christianity One of the three major traditions in Christianity (along with Roman Catholicism and Orthodoxy), Protestantism began in the sixteenth century as a reaction against medieval Roman Catholic doctrines and practices.

purgatory In Roman Catholicism, purgatory is an intermediate state between earthly life and heaven in which the debt for unconfessed sin is expiated.

Roman Catholic Church One of the three major traditions within Christianity (along with Orthodoxy and Protestantism), the Roman Catholic Church, which recognizes the primacy of the Bishop of Rome, or pope, has historically been the dominant church in the West.

rosary Taking its name from the Latin *rosarium* ("garland of roses"), the rosary is a traditional form of Roman Catholic devotion in which practitioners make use of a string of beads in reciting prayers.

sacraments The sacraments are rituals in which material elements such as bread, wine, water, and oil serve as visible symbols of an invisible grace conveyed to recipients.

saint A saint is a "holy person" (Latin *sanctus*). Veneration of the saints and belief in their intercession on behalf of the living are important features of Roman Catholic and Orthodox Christianity.

scholasticism Represented by figures such as Peter Abelard, Thomas Aquinas, and William of Ockham, scholasticism was the medieval effort to reconcile faith and reason using the philosophy of Aristotle.

sin The violation of God's will in thought or action.

transubstantiation According to this Roman Catholic doctrine, the bread and wine consecrated by a priest in the Eucharist become the body and blood of Christ and retain only the appearance, not the substance, of bread and wine.

Trinity According to the Christian doctrine of the Trinity, God is a single divine substance or essence consisting in three "persons."

SUGGESTIONS FOR FURTHER READING

Bowden, John. *Encyclopedia of Christianity*. New York: Oxford University Press, 2005. A one-volume collection of short, scholarly articles on hundreds of topics.

Dowell, Graham. *The Heart Has Seasons: Travelling through the Christian Year*. Worthing, UK: Churchman, 1989. A superb introduction to the significance and celebration of the "seasons" of the liturgical year.

Dowley, Tim, and David Wright. *Introduction to the History of Christianity*. Minneapolis, MN: Fortress Press, 1995. Includes hundreds of photos, maps, charts, and articles on topics of special interest.

Ehrman, Bart. *The New Testament: A Historical Introduction to the Early Christian Writings*. New York: Oxford University Press, 2000. An excellent introduction to the New Testament texts and selected Christian texts from the second century.

Marsden, George. *Understanding Fundamentalism and Evangelicalism*. Grand Rapids, MI: William B. Eerdmans, 1991. Describes the essential features of these two movements and their involvement in politics and science.

McGrath, Alister. *Theology: The Basics*. Malden, MA: Blackwell, 2004. Individual chapters focus on specific issues such as God, Jesus, faith, salvation, and heaven. Emphasizes on Roman Catholic and Protestant thought.

Ware, Timothy (Kallistos). *The Orthodox Church*. New York: Penguin, 1993. A classic presentation of the history, thought, and practices of the Orthodox tradition by one of its greatest spokespersons.

White, James. *Introduction to Christian Worship*. 3rd ed. Nashville, TN: Abingdon Press, 2001. An ideal book for beginners interested in the history and forms of Christian worship.

ONLINE RESOURCES

Virtual Religion Index

virtualreligion.net

An excellent gateway to religion-related sites of all kinds, including collections of texts, religion-specific sites, and academic program sites.

Catholic Online

catholic.org

This online resource provides access to information "on all things Catholic," including saints, holy days, Roman Catholic theology, and announcements from the Vatican.

Orthodox Wiki

orthodoxwiki.org

This online resource includes nearly 4,000 articles on all aspects of Orthodox Christianity. It is a great place to begin an exploration of Orthodoxy.

Theopedia

theopedia.com

An online "encyclopedia of biblical Christianity" with articles on hundreds of topics written from an evangelical Protestant perspective.

Islam

FAINT TRACES OF DAWN light up the tops of tall coconut palms and lush mango trees in a village in Zanzibar, an East African island in the Indian Ocean. Amina, a woman in her early thirties and a devout Muslim, rises from her bed. She was awakened by the sound of the call to prayer from the local mosque. In the open-air courtyard of her house, she begins her morning ablutions to prepare for the first of her daily prayers. She takes cool water from the cistern in the courtyard and carefully washes her face, hands, and feet, and rinses her mouth, nose, and ears. She also wets her head and hair. Before each of the five daily prayers, Amina performs similar ablutions. Although she occasionally wears eye makeup and lipstick, she is careful to avoid nail polish. She explains that all such adornment must be removed to purify herself for each prayer; makeup is easily removed with water, but nail polish is not.

After her ablutions, Amina returns to the house, covers her head and shoulders with a clean cotton wrap, and spreads a colorful woven prayer mat on the floor next to her bed. She removes her sandals, steps onto the mat, and begins the first of the five prescribed daily ritual prayers that are expected of all devout Muslims. The prayers are called *salat* and consist of the recitation of verses from the **Qur'an**, the sacred text of Islam, accompanied by specific bodily movements. Together, the cycles of prayer and movement are called *raka*. Amina has made her daily prayers since she was a young girl. As a child, her mother and elder sisters taught her

Pilgrims circumambulate the Ka'ba in Mecca, Saudi Arabia. The pilgrimage to Mecca, known as the hajj, is a once-in-a-lifetime duty for devout Muslims.

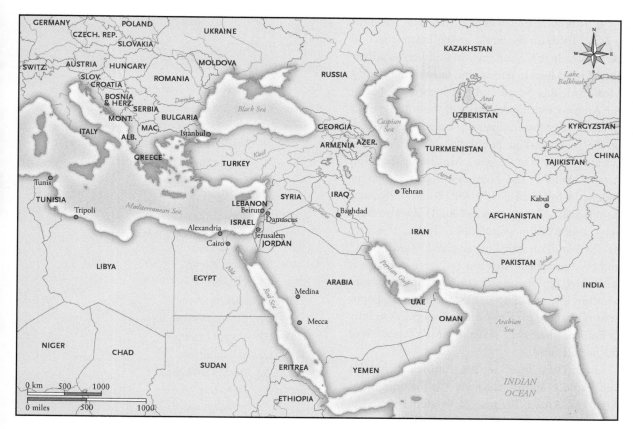

Significant sites in the history of Islam.

how to pray; eventually, she will do the same for her own children. She begins the prayer standing, then kneels, bows her forehead to the ground, and kneels again in accordance with her recitation. Hand movements accompany the bodily postures. Daily prayer is an essential part of Muslim worship. Through prayer, Amina is acknowledging to herself and her community that she is submitting herself to the will of God—an important tenet of the Islamic faith. In fact, the term *Muslim* means "one who submits" in Arabic.

Amina prays alone in her modest home, but men in her community typically gather at the local mosque for each of the daily prayers, which are led by a prayer leader called an **imam**. Like women, most Zanzibari men cover their heads when praying, most often with a brimless, embroidered cap. Although in some parts of the Muslim world women regularly pray in mosques, in Zanzibar, particularly in rural areas, it is uncommon for women to do so. However, women often gather together at mosques for other reasons, such as Qur'an study groups and sessions in religious instruction.

When she completes her prayers, Amina rolls up her prayer mat and sets it aside for later. She reads a few verses from the Qur'an in the early morning light and then begins the first tasks of her day—making tea and sweeping the courtyard. ☀

Amina is one of about 1.6 billion Muslims living in the world today; Islam is second only to Christianity in numbers of adherents. Amina lives in Africa, and most of the world's Muslims live in South and Southeast Asia, not in the Arabic-speaking countries of the Middle East. In fact, Arab Muslims make up less than 20 percent of the total Muslim population worldwide. The country with the largest Muslim population in the world is the Southeast Asian nation of Indonesia, followed closely by Pakistan, India, and Bangladesh. Many countries in Africa also have very large Muslim populations. Today, there are nearly 3 million Muslims in the United States,[1] and the number of Muslims in North America is increasing rapidly, mostly through immigration. Muslims also make up significant minority populations in many parts of western Europe, especially in France, where they make up nearly 9 percent of the population.[2]

Islam developed in the Arabian Peninsula and rapidly spread through the Middle East, Asia, and Africa. Because of its global presence, Islam is practiced, understood, and interpreted in diverse ways in many different countries, cultures, and communities. However, certain beliefs and practices can be considered universal parts of Muslim religious life. First and most important of these is the monotheistic belief in the oneness of **Allah**, which is the Arabic term for God. Second, Muslims recognize **Muhammad**, who received the message of the Qur'an from God, as the final prophet in a long line of prophets sent to humanity by God. The Qur'an is believed to be the word of God and is the holy text of Muslims. In addition, Muslims around the world share the observance of the five pillars of worship practice. The term **Islam** (Arabic, "submission") reflects Muslim belief in the importance of submitting to God's will.

TIMELINE
Islam

570 C.E.	The birth of Muhammad.
610	The first revelations of the Qur'an to Muhammad.
622	The hijra (migration) from Mecca to Medina.
632	The death of Muhammad; issue of succession.
632–661	Period of the Rightly Guided Caliphs.
657	Battle of Siffin.
661	'Ali killed.
661–750	Umayyad period.
680	Battle at Karbala and martyrdom of Husayn.
750–1258	Abbasid period.
1095–1453	Crusades.
1207–1273	Jalalludin Rumi.
1281–1924	Ottoman Empire.
1483–1857	Mughal Empire.
1501–1722	Safavid Empire.
1703–1792	Ibn Abd al-Wahhab.
1849–1905	Muhammad Abduh.
1881–1938	Mustafa Kemal Ataturk.
1923	Huda Sha'rawi unveils at Egyptian train station.
1947	Partition of India and Pakistan.
1979	Iranian Revolution.
2004	France bans wearing of headscarves and other religious identifiers in schools.
2006	Keith Ellison, a Democrat from Minnesota, is first Muslim elected to U.S. Congress.
2009	Green Movement, Iran.
2011	"Arab Spring" pro-democracy movements spread across the Middle East.

THE TEACHINGS OF ISLAM

Islam arose in the Arabian Peninsula in the seventh century, when Muslims believe that a man called Muhammad began receiving communication from God. The primary source of Islamic teachings is the Qur'an, which Muslims believe is the word of God as revealed to Muhammad. According to Muslim belief, Islam was not introduced as a new religion. Rather, the revelations of the Qur'an to Muhammad were a reawakening or reintroduction of the original monotheistic faith of the prophet Abraham, a figure who is also important to Jews (Chapter 11) and Christians (Chapter 12). Islam is considered one of the Abrahamic religions, along with Judaism and Christianity, and the three religions share a great deal. Although many people in pre-Islamic Arabia were polytheists, significant numbers of Jews and Christians also lived in the region. People in Arabia were therefore familiar with biblical stories and characters, and several of these are mentioned in the Qur'an. In the Islamic view, Abraham (or Ibrahim, as Muslims call him) was the original monotheist who received a revelation from God, a revelation that taught him the true religion centering on the oneness of God. Muslims believe that when Muhammad received the revelations of the Qur'an, he was given a reminder for humanity of what God conveyed to Abraham. This section explores what Muslims believe about the revelation of the Qur'an to Muhammad. In a later section, we explore his life, his prophecy, and his leadership roles.

World Muslim population.

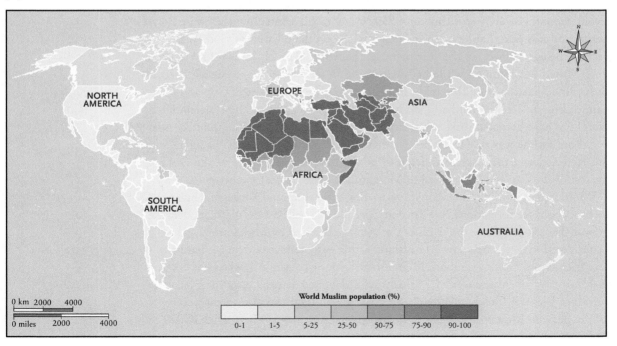

World Muslim population (%)

| 0-1 | 1-5 | 5-25 | 25-50 | 50-75 | 75-90 | 90-100 |

Muhammad and the Revelations

Muslims consider Muhammad (c. 570–632 C.E.) the final messenger in a series of prophets sent by God to humanity. In addition to Abraham, these prophets include many other figures important in the Jewish and Christian traditions, such as Noah, Moses, and Jesus. In Muslim belief, all prophets are solely human—not divine. However, the importance of Muhammad to Muslims should not be underestimated. In addition to receiving the revelation of the Qur'an, Muhammad is considered an extraordinary man in all respects. He was the religious and political leader of the early Muslim community and, even today—fourteen centuries after his death—his life is considered an example for all Muslims to follow.

Some of what we know about Muhammad and his life comes from the Qur'an. We also know something of his life from biographical writings and from what his close friends, associates, and family (who are known together as his *companions*) observed about him and passed on in reports. In addition, there are many stories and legends about the Prophet. Because most of what we know about Muhammad comes from sources that were compiled by Muslims after he became a prophet, we know very little about his early life. Muslims do not believe that Muhammad was divine, but rather consider him to be *al-insan al-kamil*, the ideal human. And although he was a prophet, in many respects he lived the life of a normal man. He had a family, earned a living, and was active in his community.

Most Muslims believe that Muhammad was a spiritual man and a religious seeker even before he began receiving the revelation of the Qur'an. He was considered a devout monotheist even at a time in which many of his contemporaries were polytheists, and it is said that he often meditated alone on the oneness of God. When he reached the age of forty, in the year 610 C.E., the Angel Gabriel (known in Arabic as Jibril) visited Muhammad while he was praying in an isolated cave outside Mecca. Muhammad heard a voice that told him that he was the messenger of God and commanded him to "Recite!" Muhammad is said to have been awed and bewildered. He is thought to have hesitated three times at Jibril's command because as an illiterate man he did not feel he was able to recite. Eventually, he repeated the words the angel told him to recite, and these are considered to be the first revealed verses of the Qur'an. The rest of the Qur'an was revealed to Muhammad over the next twenty-three years.

Muhammad confided in his wife, **Khadija**, a wealthy and successful businesswoman, about the revelations. She listened carefully and believed his message. Because she was the first to believe the truth of the message received by Muhammad, Khadija is considered to be the first convert to Islam. Other early followers were Muhammad's close friends and family members. Muhammad's young cousin 'Ali, who later became his son-in-law when he married Muhammad's daughter Fatima, was the first male convert to Islam. A friend of Muhammad's called Abu Bakr was also an early convert, and he became Muhammad's father-in-law much later in life when, after Khadija's death, Muhammad married Abu Bakr's daughter.

After the first revelations, Muhammad began a life of preaching in Mecca. The verses of the Qur'an that he received during this time emphasized the oneness of God—the central tenet of the Islamic faith. Muhammad preached this idea to the people of Mecca and also taught about morality, social justice for the poor and downtrodden, and the inevitability of the Day of Judgment.

Muhammad was not the only prophet in the Islamic tradition. The Qur'an mentions several prophets by name and refers to the existence of many others. Muhammad, however, is known as the "seal of the prophets," which means that the door of prophecy was closed—or "sealed"—with him because he was the final prophet. Muslims believe that the revelations to Muhammad came at a time when it was necessary to reawaken understanding of God's message to humanity.

The Holy Qur'an

The Qur'an is the sacred text of Islam, and it is considered the literal word of God. The Arabic word *qur'an* means "recitation," and the book is called such because Muhammad received the Qur'an orally and taught it to his followers in the same way. When the Qur'an was eventually written down, the text was corrected by the oral knowledge of those who had committed it to memory. Even today, printed copies of the Qur'an bear the stamp of approval of a person known as *hafidh* or "keeper of the Qur'an." This is a person who knows the entire Qur'an by heart.

The Qur'an was not revealed all at once to Muhammad, but rather gradually over a period of more than twenty years until his death. The language of the Qur'an is classical Arabic, and stylistically it resembles the beauty of the Arabic poetry of the time in which it was revealed. However, it is important to note that Muslims do not regard the Qur'an as poetry. This is because poetry is a human endeavor, and Muslims view the Qur'an as solely the word of God. Reciting, reading, and studying the Qur'an are an important part of daily life for devout Muslims today, in all parts of the world.

This illuminated Qur'an is from the thirteenth century.

The Qur'an is not a narrative text, which means that it does not tell a story from beginning to end (although there are some stories within the text). The Qur'an consists of 114 chapters, each of which is called a **surah**. Each *surah* consists of several verses. The *surahs* are not organized around specific topics or time periods, and they are not arranged in the order of revelation, as one might expect. Rather, they are arranged roughly from the longest to the shortest, with the exception of the opening *surah*, which is quite short. Some *surahs* are only a few verses long, and the longest has almost 300 verses. Each *surah* has a title. The titles were not revealed to Muhammad but were, rather, based on a distinctive element of the *surah*. For example, the third *surah* is called "The Women" because of the many verses within it that reference the status of women.

At the time of Muhammad's death, the revelations of the Qur'an had not been collected into one book. The primary mode of teaching and learning the Qur'an was oral. During the rule of the caliph 'Uthman, however, the revelations were organized into a written text. For centuries, Muslims have considered this text standard. Today, however, some secular scholars think that a number of versions of the Qur'an originally existed and that the written text of the Qur'an emerged gradually in the seventh and eighth centuries.

The most well-known *surah* is the first one, which is called *al-fatihah*, or the "the opening." The *fatihah* is a common prayer used by Muslims in many different contexts. It is the first *surah* that Muslims learn when they begin studying the Qur'an as children or as adults. A devout Muslim will recite the *fatihah* several times during the day's many prayers. The *surah* evokes the oneness of God, the all-powerful nature of God, the Day of Judgment, and God's guidance for a righteous life.

THE OPENING/*AL-FATIHAH*

In the name of Allah, most benevolent, ever-merciful
All praise be to Allah,
Lord of all the worlds,
Most beneficent, ever merciful,
King of the Day of Judgment.
You alone we worship, and to You
alone turn for help.
Guide us (O Lord) to the path that is straight,
The path of those You have blessed,
Not of those who have earned Your anger,
Nor those who have gone astray.[3]

Today, most Muslims consider the Qur'an both inimitable and uncreated. This means that Muslims regard the holy text as unique and eternal. Today and historically, Muslims have believed that the Qur'an's equal cannot be created by human effort, which is considered proof of its divine origins. Most contemporary Muslims also believe that the Qur'an is eternal—that it has always existed. This view has not always dominated, however. The Mutazilites, a rationalist school of Islamic thought that was prominent many centuries ago, argued that the Qur'an was not eternal but was rather created by God. The Mutazilite scholars argued that the idea of an eternal Qur'an compromised the unity of God because God alone was eternal and the creator of all things—including the Qur'an. This view had some support in the tenth century, but eventually the idea of the eternal Qur'an became dominant in the Islamic tradition.[4]

The Teachings of the Qur'an

The major teachings of the Qur'an are found throughout the text. In any number of verses, we can find reference to the nature of God, the reality of the Day of Judgment, and guidelines for moral behavior.

The Oneness of God   Like the other Abrahamic religions, Islam is a monotheistic religion, and the most important principle of Islamic belief is the oneness of God. The Qur'an teaches that God, known in Arabic as "Allah," is eternal, uncreated, all-knowing, and all-powerful, and it is God alone who created the universe and humankind. God is also merciful, just, and good. God is transcendent but also present, or immanent, in the lives of believers. A much-quoted verse of the Qur'an refers to God as closer to humanity "than the jugular vein" (50:16). Muslims believe that it is impossible for God to have a partner, consort, or family because no other being shares God's divinity. Muslims believe that God is the same God of the Jews and Christians. However, to Muslims, the Christian doctrine of the Trinity compromises the unity of God. The Qur'an specifically comments on the impossibility of God begetting a son, as in the following verse:

> He to whom belongs the kingdom of the heavens and the earth: who
> has neither begotten a son, nor has He a partner in kingdom: (who)
> created every thing, and determined its exact measure (25:2).[5]

The Qur'an also teaches that Muslims should strive to acknowledge the oneness of God through acts of devotion. Because the unity of God is the central tenet of Islamic belief, it follows that denying or compromising this oneness is the greatest sin. This sin of associating anything or anyone else with God is called **shirk**. In the Qur'an, *shirk* is noted as the only unforgivable sin in the eyes of Allah. This is because it denies the existence of God and the true nature of God. For the believing Muslim, the worship of God should be given to God alone, and human beings should worship nothing else. Therefore, nature, idols, images, and human beings must not be worshiped.

In Muslim belief, Allah created the universe, the world, and everything in it, including the sun and the moon, the mountains and oceans, and all living things. The natural world is mentioned throughout the Qur'an, and elements of nature are referred to as *ayat*, or signs of God: "We shall show them Our signs in every region of the earth and in themselves, until it becomes clear to them that this is the truth" (41:53). Muslims view the natural world and the entire cosmos as a type of revelation from God. (The Qur'an itself, remember, is another type of revelation.) Therefore, in Muslim belief, the natural world as a whole is evidence of the existence of God, and human beings should be able to realize this simply by observing nature. Even so, human beings cannot truly know the ultimate essence of God, God's ultimate purpose, and ultimate reality. Thus, Muslims may not be able to understand rationally why bad things happen to good people. However, they should have faith in God's purpose, even though they cannot truly know it (2:216).

Prophecy   Prophecy is also an essential component of Islamic belief, and it is mentioned several times in the Qur'an. The belief in prophecy is also important to Judaism and Christianity, and the three Abrahamic faiths share many of the same prophets.

In Islam, it is through the messages revealed to prophets that humanity comes to know the desires of God and the divine laws that govern the universe and creation. The belief in revealed scripture goes hand in hand with the belief in prophecy because Muslims believe that it is through prophets that humanity obtains scripture.

Muslims recognize that there have been many prophets since the beginning of creation. Each prophet received special words from God that were appropriate for humanity at the time in which the particular prophet lived. The prophet Abraham is mentioned several times in the Qur'an. The stories of his life resemble those told by Jews and Christians, and they serve as an important basis for the annual pilgrimage to Mecca (discussed in the next section). The Qur'an also names Jesus as an important prophet (and indeed says that Jesus will return to herald the Day of Judgment), and the Gospels are considered part of God's revelation to humanity. Muslims believe that Jesus was born of the Virgin Mary, who is also mentioned in the Qur'an and is held in very high regard by Muslims. However, Muslims do not believe that Jesus was divine or the son of God. Verse 25:2, which you read earlier, reflects this idea in the passage that God has not "begotten a son."

Muslims believe that all prophets bring communication from God. The Qur'an teaches that prophets fall into different classes based on the nature of that communication. Some are said to bring simply "news" from God. Others, like Muhammad, bring a major message. In addition to Muhammad, prophets such as Moses and Jesus also received major messages. Moses received the Torah as guidance for humankind, and the teachings of Jesus are regarded as a major message from God. Muslims consider all scriptures, including the Torah and the gospels, to be the work of God. Although the Qur'an refers to those peoples to whom scripture was revealed as "Peoples of the Book," the Qur'an also teaches that the earlier messages have been misinterpreted or forgotten by the Christians and the Jews.

According to the Qur'an, Adam and his wife, Hawa (or Eve), were the first two humans. Adam became the first prophet in the Islamic tradition. Adam and Hawa were created separately by God from a single soul (4:1) and were made of dust or clay according to a divine model. Muslims believe that God blew spirit into humanity. Therefore, as in nature, the signs of God are also in humanity. The Qur'an teaches that human beings were created to worship God (51:56) and that the nature of humanity is to obey God and to give thankfulness for God's blessings.

You will recall that the meaning of the term *Muslim* is "one who submits." However, as part of God's creation on earth, Muslims believe that humans should also act as responsible members of society and stewards of the natural world. The Qur'an contains a story that is similar to the one in Genesis, in which the first humans disobeyed God by tasting a forbidden fruit. In the Qur'anic story, Adam and Hawa are both to blame for this disobedience, and they are immediately forgiven for their transgressions by God (71:13–17). Most Muslims believe that, unlike other living creatures, all human beings have free choice and thus must choose to submit to the will of God. Each individual's choices will be evaluated on the Day of Judgment.

The Day of Judgment   The coming of the Day of Judgment and the reality of the afterlife are also central teachings of the Qu'ran. Many of the early *surahs* focus on God's judgment and can be read as warnings to humanity to live a righteous life or suffer the consequences when facing God at the end of days. Despite the dire warning of some of these verses, God's justice is strongly emphasized, and the Qur'an gives details about how to live a righteous life. Greed and hypocrisy are criticized, and kindness and generosity are praised. The Qur'an teaches that all believers, men and women alike, will stand alone in front of Allah and will be judged according to their actions in life. The Qur'an teaches that, after death, a person resides in the grave in a sleeplike state until the end of days, at which time the judgment will take place. The end of days is described in the Qur'an as a time when the world turns upside down in great calamity. *Surah* 99 dramatically describes Judgment Day:

> When the world is shaken up by its cataclysm
> And earth throws out its burdens,
> And man enquires: "What has come over it?"
> That day it will narrate its annals,
> For your Lord will have commanded it.
> That day people will proceed separately to be shown their deeds.
> Whosoever has done even an atom's weight of good will behold it;
> And whosoever has done even an atom's weight of evil will behold that.[6]

On Judgment Day, each person will have a book that details the deeds of his or her life. The book held in the right hand indicates a righteous life, and the book held in the left hand indicates the life of a sinner. The Qur'an teaches that each individual stands alone before God and that no one can intercede on his or her behalf. However, there is some debate about this issue, and some traditions in Islam suggest that Muhammad will be able to intercede on behalf of believers. Some Muslims believe that the Day of Judgment will be ushered in by a person known as the Mahdi, whose just rule will come to the earth at the end of days. The Mahdi is not mentioned in the Qur'an. Rather, the idea developed in Islamic thought in later centuries.

Those who are judged to be righteous will enter paradise. In the Qur'an, paradise is described in much detail as a lush garden with bountiful blessings of food, drink, and beautiful young men and women. Although some take this description to be literal, other Muslims think that it is instead a metaphor for the beauties of paradise. Those who have led sinful lives will be cast into hell, which is often referred to simply as "the fire." Those who are doomed to hell include nonbelievers and Muslims who have rejected their faith by failing to live up to prescribed duties and moral standards. Some Muslims believe that sinners will eventually be forgiven and taken to paradise.

Angels and *Jinn*   The existence of angels is another component of Islamic belief, and angels are mentioned throughout the Qur'an. Angels are part of God's creation, without body or gender. Humans are said to be made of clay and angels from light. Angels serve as important messengers and assistants to God. The most well known of the angels in Islamic tradition is Gabriel, or Jibril. This angel is mentioned several times in the Qur'an and was instrumental in bringing the revelation of the Qur'an to Muhammad from God. Islamic tradition also recognizes supernatural beings called *jinn*, which are said to be created from fire. They are also mentioned in several places in the Qur'an. *Jinn* can take various forms, and, like humans, they can be both good and evil and Muslim or non-Muslim. Much folklore has developed surrounding the *jinn*, and they are represented in tales like *One Thousand and One Nights* as both helping and harming humans. The English term *genie* derives from the Arabic word *jinn*.

Commentary on the Qur'an

The text of the Qur'an is ambiguous in some places and repetitive in others. This has resulted in a long tradition of commentary upon and interpretation of the meaning of the verses. The general Arabic term for commentary on the Qur'an is **tafsir**, which is translated in English as "interpretation." Scholars have been engaging in *tafsir* for centuries, and their commentary takes many forms. In the first few generations following Muhammad's death, scholarly commentary on the Qur'an focused primarily on grammar, language, and explanations of inconsistencies in the text. The goal of this type of *tafsir* was to clarify the meaning of the words of the Qur'an.

Muslims have not always agreed on how the Qur'an should be interpreted and understood. Some scholars have argued that the Qur'an must only be interpreted vis-à-vis itself. In other words, verses of the Qur'an should only be explained by using other passages of the text. Other scholars think that Muslims should use their own reason and rationality as believers to interpret the meaning of the verses. This method of *tafsir* is known as speculative *tafsir*.[7] A famous eleventh-century Persian scholar called Abu Hamid al-Ghazali (1058–1111) wrote that, as rational judgment is a gift from God, people should always use it when considering the meaning of the Qur'an. However, some scholars criticized his approach as preferring human reason over the words of God. Ibn Taymiyya (1263–1328), an Arab scholar, argued that using human reason was not necessary because the entire meaning of the Qur'an could be found within the text. As we discuss later in this chapter, Ibn Taymiyya's approach influenced some Islamic reformist movements in the modern era.

The Sunnah: The Example of the Prophet

After the Qur'an, the second most important source of Islamic teachings is in the **Sunnah**, which refers to the "tradition" or way of life of the Prophet Muhammad. The Sunnah encompasses Muhammad's actions and words. It includes the way he handled disputes in the early community, the way he dealt with his wives, friends, and children, and the way he went about the daily business of life. This extends even to such seemingly mundane matters as how the Prophet cleaned his teeth. To Muslims, Muhammad is considered the ideal human. He is therefore the model of the best way to live. To this day, Muhammad is an inspiration to all Muslims, who strive to follow his example of conduct in their own lives. (Muhammad is discussed in more detail in the section on the history of Islam.)

The Hadith Literature How do Muslims know how Muhammad lived his life, how he treated his family, and how he handled problems facing members of the early Muslim community? Muslims have knowledge of Muhammad's life through a literary tradition known as the **hadith**. Hadith is a form of literature that records in brief reports the details of the life of the Prophet, including his sayings and his deeds. The hadith reports come from the observations of Muhammad's close friends and family, known as his "companions." His companions realized his importance as an example of righteous behavior. They strove to remember his actions and words, and then passed them on through the generations in hadith reports.

A hadith consists of two parts: the *isnad*, or the chain of transmission of the hadith; and the *matn*, the report itself. The *matn* relates Muhammad's words or deeds, and the *isnad* names those people who transmitted the hadith from the time of the Prophet. The *isnad* always originates with one of Muhammad's close companions or a family member. One of Muhammad's later wives, **Aisha,** was one of the most important transmitters of hadith, as she passed on many reports about Muhammad's life. Muslims do not consider all hadith to be equally valid. A complex science of hadith developed in the centuries following the death of the Prophet to evaluate their reliability as true reports of Muhammad's life. Scholars ranked hadith from "solid" to "weak" based on the likelihood of authenticity. The hadith are compiled into collections of several thousand.

Reports known as *hadith qudsi*, or sacred sayings, are also important in the Islamic tradition. Although the name is similar, this is a very different sort of literary tradition from the regular hadith. The hadith *qudsi* are not reports of Muhammad's life but are believed to be words of God. Muhammad is believed to have occasionally transmitted direct words of God that were not intended to be part of the Qur'an. Many of the hadith *qudsi* are succinct and beautiful. They focus on God's love for humanity, God's mercy, and the closeness of God to creation. The following hadith *qudsi* illustrates the quality of God's mercy:

> God says: "If my Servant intends a good deed and does not do it, I write it down for him as a good deed. Then if he does it, I write it down for him as ten good deeds, or up to seven hundred times that. And if my servant intends an evil deed and does not do it, I do not write it down against him. And if he does it, I write it down for him as [only one] evil deed."[8]

Explore the concept of scripture in Judaism, Christianity, and Islam. What important elements do these religions share? How do they differ?

The Five Pillars

The essential teachings of Islam are closely related to Muslim worship practice. The five pillars form the basis of practice. These pillars are

1. *Shahadah:* the declaration of faith
2. *Salat:* the daily prayer
3. **Zakat:** almsgiving
4. *Sawm:* fasting during the month of **Ramadan**
5. **Hajj:** pilgrimage to Mecca

Muslims believe that the foundations for the five pillars were set during the lifetime of Muhammad. The five pillars are carefully articulated in the hadith literature. All of the pillars are equally important. However, they address different elements of religious practice that must be performed at special times. For example, although prayer is a daily requirement, the Ramadan fast happens once per year, and the **hajj** must be performed only once in a lifetime. The pillars are generally required of all adult Muslims. However, individuals are sometimes excused from performing the pillars. For example, someone who is ill, pregnant, or nursing an infant would not be required to fast. Devout Muslims generally aim to observe all of the pillars, but as with every religious tradition, there are variations in levels of observance. Furthermore, there has been some historical variation across communities and cultures in how much emphasis is placed on the pillars. Some Muslim scholars have even debated the relative necessity of observing the pillars, though these scholars have always been in the minority.

The Declaration of Faith   The first pillar is the declaration of faith and is called the *shahadah*. This is the statement of belief: "There is no God but God and Muhammad is the messenger of God." The other four pillars all deal directly with religious practice, but the *shahadah* is different in that it is much more a statement of belief than a ritualized religious practice. To become a Muslim, all one must do is utter the *shahadah* with utmost sincerity in the presence of witnesses. Most new Muslims will first declare the *shahadah*, and then begin a lifetime's journey of learning the Qur'an, the Sunnah, and other aspects of the faith. Many people in North America and elsewhere who have converted to Islam note the simplicity of the faith as something that attracted them to Islam. This simplicity is illustrated by the succinct nature of the *shahadah*.

The Daily Prayer   The *salat*, the mandatory daily prayers, is the second pillar. You encountered the careful preparations for the daily *salat* of Amina at the opening of this chapter. Devout Muslims perform five daily prayers at specific times of the day. Rather than performing all the prayers at once to get them over with for the day, week, or month, Muslims should do them at the required times. The first prayer should be done at dawn every morning. The next prayer is performed at about noon. The remaining prayers are the late afternoon prayer, the sunset prayer, and the final prayer in the evening. Prayer is mentioned in several places in the Qur'an. However, the number of prayers is established not in the Qur'an but rather in the hadith. The hadith literature relates that during a miraculous journey to heaven, known as the **miraj**, Muhammad came into the presence of God. God told Muhammad he should instruct people to make fifty daily prayers. However, when Muhammad told the prophet Moses about the prayers, Moses told him to go back to God to ask for a reduction, as fifty would be too many. Eventually, the number was settled at five, although God said that every prayer would count for ten.

The *salat* are not individualized prayers requesting aid from God or giving thanks, although those personal prayers, called *dua*, are also common among Muslims. Rather, the *salat* prayers are formalized. For each prayer, specific verses of the Qur'an are recited, and special body movements accompany the recitation.

Before beginning the prayers, a Muslim must enter a state of ritual purity. As you learned from Amina at the beginning of this chapter, this purification consists of ablutions, called *wudu'*, which involve cleansing the hands, head, face, and feet. The body should be covered for prayer, and most women and men also cover their heads. The prayer begins with the *takbir*, or the declaration *Allahu Akbar*, which means "God is great." Throughout the prayer, the believer faces the direction of Mecca, where an important structure known as the Ka'ba is located (you will learn more about the Ka'ba later in this section). This means that Muslims in America pray facing the east. In prayer, a Muslim stands, kneels, and bows his head to the floor. These cycles of movements, along with the proper recitation, are called *raka* and vary in number according to the prayer. In some parts of the world, such as regions of Indonesia, the prayer opens with a declaration of intent to indicate that the Muslim is in the right frame of mind for performing the prayer.[9] Not all Muslims declare their intent to pray, but most agree that proper intention is necessary. The intention of the believer is what validates and legitimizes the action of prayer. Many Muslims believe that the intention of the prayer is even more important than the prayer itself. After reciting verses of the Qur'an, the prayer closes with a greeting of peace.

Prayers may be done anywhere—even in a park or airport. However, many Muslims perform prayers at a **mosque** (this English word is taken from the Arabic term *masjid*). A mosque is a place that is designated for prayer. Many people imagine elaborate feats of architectural workmanship when they think of mosques, but a mosque can be as simple as an unadorned room in a commercial building or even a clearing in the woods. Although mosque architecture and decoration vary from the very simple to the very ornate, mosques tend to share some features. All mosques have a prayer space, and most have a fountain

Ablution fountains outside of a mosque.

so that people can perform the required ablutions. The direction of prayer, known as the *qibla*, is marked inside a mosque by a niche called a *mihrab*, which is sometimes beautifully decorated with botanical designs or Qur'anic verses. The floors of a mosque are often completely covered with colorful rugs or woven mats. Because Muslim prayer requires open space for bodily movement, there are usually no seats or pews. Many mosques, particularly those in the Middle East and North Africa, also have a tower called a *minaret*. The minaret is often used to broadcast the calls to prayer.

In much of the world, visitors of all faiths are welcome to enter mosques. Normally, all those entering a mosque will be asked to leave their shoes outside. Sometimes, shoes are placed in a designated cabinet watched by someone who may receive a tip and even clean the shoes. Leaving shoes outside ensures that no outside dirt will enter the mosque to violate the ritual purity of those who have made the proper ablutions for prayer. The prayer space in a mosque is open and peaceful, and people may use the mosque as a place for contemplation and rest throughout the day.

When walking through the hot and dusty streets of busy Cairo, one can see men—and sometimes women—taking a break from the urban noise and bustle by resting in the serene interior of a neighborhood mosque. In many parts of the world, mosques are also used for teaching classes or for other community needs.

Friday is designated as the day for congregational prayer, known as *salat al-jum'ah*. It is incumbent upon Muslim men to attend the midday prayer together, and they may also gather at a mosque for other prayers during the day. In some areas, women also attend the communal prayer, though their attendance is not regarded as mandatory. When Muslims pray in a group in a mosque or elsewhere, it is important that one person act as the imam, or prayer leader. The imam regulates the prayer session and ensures that all believers are praying together. The Friday prayer often features a sermon, which may be delivered by the imam or another preacher. Friday should not be confused with the Christian or Jewish Sabbath. Rather than a day of rest, it is a day for group prayer. In some Muslim countries, Friday is a work day, and businesses are open. In others, businesses are closed.

The five daily prayers are announced in the words of the **adhan**, or the call to prayer. The *adhan* is delivered by a person called a **muezzin**, who calls the faithful to prayer from the door of the mosque or the minaret, sometimes using a loudspeaker. The *adhan* is usually called in a rhythmic, recitational fashion. Hearing the *adhan* several times a day from the wee hours of the morning to evening is very much a part of life in the Muslim world. Many residents and travelers miss it enormously when they move away; non-Muslim travelers often remark that hearing the *adhan* is one of the most memorable experiences of visiting a Muslim country.

The beautiful Shah Mosque, in Isfahan, Iran, was built in the 1600s during the Safavid period.

This small mosque in rural Zanzibar, Tanzania, is built in an architectural style that is similar to houses in the area.

God is most great (repeated four times)
I testify that there is no god but God (repeated twice)
I testify that Muhammad is the messenger of God (repeated twice)
Hurry to prayer (repeated twice)
Hurry to success (repeated twice)
Prayer is better than sleep (repeated twice before the morning prayer)
God is most great (repeated twice)
There is no god but God (once)[10]

Like the other pillars, the *salat* is incumbent upon all Muslims, both male and female. In much of the Muslim world, it is more common for men to pray in mosques than women, although this is not always the case. In such places as urban Egypt and Indonesia, women often pray in mosques. Although females may serve as imam for other women, most Muslims believe that they may not do so for men. When both women and men pray in mosques, usually the genders are separated—either in separate prayer halls or with women praying in rows behind the men. Some Muslims reason that this requirement is due to modesty and concentration. They argue that women and men should not be distracted from their prayers by the presence of the opposite sex. Others argue that men's leadership in prayer is prescribed in the Qur'an. However, some Muslim feminist scholars, such as the American professor Dr. Amina Wadud, are challenging this tradition by arguing that women can lead men in prayer.

The daily prayers are important for Muslims on both an individual and a communal level. Many Muslims feel closest to God during prayer. Although praying five times a day may sound rigorous to non-Muslims, many Muslims welcome the breaks from mundane tasks to focus their attention completely on God. A believer must stop all activity to remember God five times every day. This indicates that submission to God is the most important part of life for a devout Muslim. On another level, praying the same prayers at the same time every day, and often in a group, draws the community of Muslims together in worship of God. Many Muslims report that, in addition to feeling an individual closeness to God during prayer, they also feel at one with the **umma**, the global community of Muslims, in the common purpose of worship.

Muslim men pray together at a mosque in Burma.

Almsgiving The third pillar, zakat, refers to required almsgiving, which is part of a believer's devotion to God and the Muslim community. The rules about zakat are very specific, and the amount of zakat is figured as a percentage (about 2.5 percent) of the value of certain types of property, including cash. Zakat is therefore something like a tax. The wealth on which zakat has been paid is considered to be pure and clean. Therefore, some Muslims describe it as a means of purifying their property. The payment of zakat also expresses a Muslim's commitment to improving his or her community in a real and concrete way. This is because the proceeds from zakat are normally distributed to the poor or are used to maintain public institutions such as mosques and schools. In some countries today, such as Pakistan, the government collects and redistributes zakat funds.[11] Elsewhere, it is up to individuals themselves to make the zakat payments. All adults should pay zakat. However, adults who are mentally ill or unstable are exempt from the requirement.

Fasting during Ramadan The fourth pillar is *sawm*, which is the mandatory fast during the month of Ramadan, the ninth month in the Islamic calendar. Muslims consider Ramadan a sacred month because it was during Ramadan that the Qur'an was first revealed to Muhammad. During Ramadan, all Muslims are required to fast from dawn to sundown. When fasting, Muslims refrain from eating, drinking, and sexual activity. Muslims also strive to avoid arguing and negative thoughts during the hours of the fast.

All adult and adolescent Muslims are generally expected to fast. However, exceptions are made for those who are traveling as well as for women who are pregnant, nursing, or menstruating. In Pakistan, curtained food stalls are set up at train stations during Ramadan. The stalls allow travelers to eat in private, where they are respectfully out of view of those who are fasting and do not wish to be tempted by the sight of someone eating. Individuals who miss fasting days or break the fast are expected to make up the days later. However, children, the sick, the mentally ill, and the very elderly are exempt from fasting entirely. Children are usually encouraged to begin fasting when they show interest, but they are only expected to fast when they are comfortable doing so.

The month of Ramadan is a special time. Although the fast can be challenging, many Muslims find Ramadan to be filled with religious meaning, joy, and sociability. In Muslim countries or communities, the rhythm of daily life changes significantly during Ramadan. Daily activity lessens, and streets are quiet during daylight hours. However, the world awakens at sunset, when the fast ends. Many people share the evening meal with family and friends, and streets are filled late into the evening with well-wishers. Many families eat again around midnight and also before dawn to gain the strength to make it through the day.

Muslims often break the fast with dates before performing the evening prayer. This is because eating dates is Sunnah: Muhammad broke the fast with dates, so many Muslims follow his example. In many cultures, special treats are prepared during Ramadan. Indonesian Muslims look forward to breaking the fast with a

This open-air market in Sumbawa Besar, Indonesia, is very popular during Ramadan, when people buy special delicacies to break the fast.

delectable drink made with coconut milk and tropical fruits. Some Indonesians say that the drink is so sweet because it represents the beauty of a day of focusing solely on God. In Iran and in Persian communities in the United States and Canada, a rice pudding flavored with saffron and rosewater is served during Ramadan.

During Ramadan, Muslims around the world may spend time in the evenings reciting the Qur'an. Many try to achieve the goal of reciting the entire Qur'an during this special month. People may also stay up late into the night visiting friends and enjoying the celebratory and devotional atmosphere of the month. During the last few days of Ramadan, the Night of Power occurs. This is the night when Muslims believe that the Qur'an was originally revealed to Muhammad. Many Muslims believe that a wish may be granted during this special night. The end of Ramadan is marked by an important feast day called *Id al-Fitr*, the feast of fast-breaking, which we discuss later in this chapter.

Like the preceding pillars, *sawm* is important on both personal and community levels. Fasting demonstrates an individual's dependence on God, who provides for humanity. Also, by refraining from food and drink, Muslims become more sympathetic to the plight of the poor and the hungry and learn to appreciate the food they have. Like *salat* and zakat, fasting together also brings a sense of community to Muslims worldwide. A Muslim observing the fast in Los Angeles, for example, will know that his fellow believers thousands of miles away in Malaysia are keeping the fast. In the United States, many mosques and Muslim organizations view Ramadan as a time of outreach to non-Muslim friends and neighbors and as a way of teaching people about Islam. For example, at California State University in Sacramento, the Muslim student organization holds a popular "fast for a day" event every year. Non-Muslims are invited to try fasting for a day and then breaking the fast with a special meal prepared for the entire community. These events often include guest speakers who talk about the meaning of Ramadan and the basics of the Islamic tradition. Guests are also sometimes invited to watch the evening prayer.

Pilgrimage to Mecca The final pillar is called the hajj, which is the holy pilgrimage to Mecca in Saudi Arabia. The Qur'an specifies the pilgrimage as incumbent upon humanity. Every year, millions of Muslims descend upon the city of Mecca in a spectacular display of devotion. The hajj is generally understood to be required of all Muslims who are physically and financially able to make it. A Muslim only needs to perform the hajj once in his or her lifetime, but many Muslims who are able to do so repeat it. Pilgrims describe the event as one of unparalleled spiritual significance, and they experience intense feelings of connection to God and humanity during the hajj. Muslims who return from the hajj often use the title hajj (for men) or hajja (for women) before their name to indicate that they have made the journey.

The hajj must be undertaken at a particular time of year, namely, during the second week of the month *Dhu al-Hajj*, which is the final month in the Islamic calendar. A person must be physically and financially able to make the trip, or else it is not valid. One may not borrow money to make the pilgrimage, but it is appropriate to accept financing for the trip as a gift. In addition, the money set aside for the hajj must be purified by paying zakat on it. As a means of organizing the millions of travelers who come for hajj, the government of Saudi Arabia today requires pilgrims to join a travel group to make the hajj. Planned excursions depart from every corner of the world, and tour companies arrange everything from air travel to bus transfers to accommodations. In Saudi Arabia, a great deal of planning is involved because of the sheer numbers of Muslims who arrive in Mecca and its environs during the week of hajj. Only Muslims may make the journey; curious tourists are not allowed to partake in the experience.

When making the hajj, pilgrims must leave behind indicators of their social and economic status to properly enter a state of ritual purity. This state is called *ihram*. All men must wear special clothing, also called *ihram*. This consists of two very simple pieces of white cloth—one is worn above the waist and one is worn below. Women may wear what they choose, and most dress in simple clothing and avoid makeup, jewelry, and perfume. Pilgrims should also refrain from sexual activity, arguing, and frivolous conversation while in a state of *ihram*. Ideally, these restrictions are meant to ensure that the pilgrim's mind is solely on God and the hajj. The state of *ihram* also

Muslim pilgrims prepare for prayer at the Haram mosque in Mecca.

emphasizes the equality of all Muslims before God because all status markers, such as expensive jewelry, are removed.

The pilgrimage involves a number of highly specific, ritualized acts. Muhammad determined the sequence of the events of the hajj before his death, and some events reenact moments from his life. Many of the rituals also recall the actions of Abraham and his family. In this way, the rituals connect the believer to the distant past and the origins of monotheism with Abraham.

Perhaps the most important focus of the hajj is the structure known as the Ka'ba, which was a focus of pilgrimage in Arabia even before the time of Muhammad. It is a cubical building about thirty feet by thirty feet, and Muslims believe it was originally built and dedicated to Allah by Abraham and his son Ishmael. Today, the Ka'ba is covered by a cloth embroidered with gold thread that is replaced every year by the Saudi government. When a pilgrim first arrives in Mecca, he enters the Great Mosque that encircles the Ka'ba while reciting verses of the Qur'an. The pilgrim then circumambulates the Ka'ba seven times in a counterclockwise direction. This is known as

the *tawaf*. This ritual is an act of devotion that is believed to be in imitation of the angels circling God's throne. The *tawaf* is performed three times during the course of the pilgrimage.

Another important rite of the hajj is called the *sa'y*. This rite commemorates the story of Hagar, mother of Ishmael, who frantically searched for water in the desert by rushing seven times between two hills. During Hagar's search, God made a spring appear, and Hagar and Ishmael were able to quench their thirst. Pilgrims visit this spring to this day, many taking the special waters home as a symbol of Mecca. Today, the route between the two hills is enclosed as part of the Great Mosque.

Another part of the hajj involves a journey to the plain of Arafat, where a tent city is established every year to house millions of pilgrims from around the world. It is here that Muslims recollect a story about Abraham that is also prominent in Jewish and Christian traditions. In all three traditions, Abraham is believed to have been commanded by God to sacrifice his son. (Most Muslims believe he intended to sacrifice Ishmael, but Jews and Christians usually regard Isaac as the object of sacrifice; the Qur'an does not mention which son was the intended sacrifice.) As Abraham prepared to make the sacrifice, the Angel Gabriel (Jibril) appeared at the last minute, and a ram was substituted for the son. Abraham's willingness to sacrifice his beloved son is regarded as a model of faith in Islam, and this is a solemn, reflective time of the hajj. The pilgrims perform the "standing ceremony," in which they remain standing from noon until sundown in praise of Allah. The hajj ends with the most important holiday of the year, the Feast of Sacrifice, which we discuss later in the chapter.

Now that we have covered the major teachings of Islam, let us turn to the history of the religious tradition, beginning with the birth of Muhammad.

THE HISTORY OF ISLAM

Muhammad ibn Abd Allah was born around the year 570 C.E. in the town of **Mecca**, a city in the southern Arabian Peninsula. At the time of his birth, the peninsula was not politically united, and much of the population was made up of nomadic herders, known as Bedouins, who lived in remote desert areas. Despite this lack of political centralization, the region was by no means isolated. The peninsula was situated between the Byzantine Empire to the northwest, the Persian Sassanian Empire to the northeast, and the Christian Abyssinian kingdom across the Red Sea in Ethiopia. In addition, the city of Mecca was a significant trading center and place of religious pilgrimage. Although there were Christians and Jews in Arabia at the time, the majority of the people living in Arabia were polytheists who worshiped several deities. Trade fairs regularly took place in Mecca, and people passing through often left representations of deities at the temple called the Ka'ba, which, as noted earlier, was a large cube-shaped building in the center of town; today, this is the site to which all Muslims turn as they pray, and toward which they make a hajj at least once in their lives, as you learned in the preceding section. Tradition holds that at the time of Muhammad, more than 300 deities and spirits were represented by idols in the Ka'ba. Muslims call this period before the revelation of the Qur'an the **jahiliyya**, or the "age of ignorance."

Muhammad was born into a tribe called Quraysh, a powerful extended family that was very influential in Mecca. His father died before he was born, and his mother died when he was a young child. After her death, Muhammad went to live with his grandfather, who was his appointed guardian. When his grandfather died, Muhammad was raised by his uncle, a man named Abu Talib. Although he spent most of his early life in the city of Mecca, as a young boy Muhammad was sent out to the desert to live with the Bedouin, who many considered to live the ideal Arab lifestyle. At the time, sending children to the Bedouin was considered an important way to impart Arab values and culture to young city dwellers.

Muhammad is known to have been a hard worker, and he was active in business and trade. Indeed, he met his first wife, Khadija, while he was working for her in a trading caravan. Khadija was a widow about fifteen years older than Muhammad, and she was so taken with the integrity and dignity of the young man that she proposed to him. They married when he was about twenty-five years old and she forty. Their marriage was thought to be one of close companionship and deep love, and they had several children together.

As was discussed earlier, Muhammad began preaching in Mecca after receiving the first revelations. His preaching was not welcomed, however, and was even controversial in some quarters of Mecca. The reason was that he criticized both the polytheistic beliefs held by many Meccans and the disregard that wealthy Meccans showed toward the poor. The controversy led to persecution of the small but growing community of Muslims. Because they held much power in Mecca, Muhammad's own clan, the Quraysh, stood to lose the most with the social change that Muhammad's teachings advocated. The Quraysh were thus particularly active in ridiculing and persecuting Muhammad's followers.

This persecution inspired some Muslims to flee to Abyssinia (Ethiopia), where they were granted refuge by the Christian king. Others tried to resist. One well-known Muslim who resisted persecution was Bilal, an Abyssinian slave who had converted to Islam. The man who owned Bilal forced him to lie in the hot sun with a stone on his chest and told him to renounce his Muslim beliefs by denying the oneness of God. Bilal refused, crying out "One! One!" until he was rescued by Abu Bakr, who purchased him from his tormentor and then freed him from slavery. Bilal is remembered by Muslims to this day for his devotion and is also known as the first muezzin—the person who calls the faithful to prayer.

The Hijra and the Growth of the Muslim Community

Because of the troubles in Mecca, Muhammad eventually encouraged his followers to leave and make a new home elsewhere. The people of a little settlement north of Mecca with a small Jewish population welcomed him, and he encouraged his followers to go there. This town became known as **Medina** (from the term *medinat al-nabi*,

What is the role of prophecy in Islam, Christianity, and Judaism? Consider the figures Abraham, Moses, Jesus, and Muhammad. How are they understood in each tradition?

which means "the city of the Prophet"). The Muslims moved from Mecca to Medina in the year 622 C.E., and this migration is called the hijra. The hijra is a very important event in Islamic history; as you have learned, the Islamic lunar calendar begins not with Muhammad's birth but with the hijra. The reason is that the hijra marked the beginning of a distinct Muslim community, or *umma*, with Muhammad as its leader.

Muhammad did not travel with the first group that went to Medina; he and some of his companions waited for a few weeks to make the trip. When they finally left for Medina, angry Meccans from the Quraysh tribe pursued them. A popular story recounts that during Muhammad's journey to Medina he hid from the Quraysh in a cave for three days. When his pursuers reached the cave, they did not look inside because a kindly spider had spun a web to hide the entrance, thus saving Muhammad. Even today, some Muslims will not kill spiders because of their appreciation for the spider's important role in protecting the Prophet from the Meccans. Stories about the hijra and the foundational period of Islam are well known and inform the way many Muslims live their lives. Today, Muslims around the world recall the hijra as a difficult but very important time.

What happened to the Muslim community with the move to Medina? With the move, the growing Muslim community took on a new political and social form. Additionally, Muhammad's role expanded over the years as he became the leader of the new community. In Mecca, Muhammad had primarily preached and taught the revelations to his followers. In Medina, however, he took on a wide variety of new roles and oversaw political, social, and religious matters. In addition to his role as prophet of God and religious leader, Muhammad became the political head of the community. He continued to receive revelations from God for twenty more years. Reflecting these changes, the verses of the Qur'an that Muslims believe were revealed to Muhammad in Medina concern the regulation of community life.

The migration to Medina did not end the Muslim community's problems with Mecca. Muhammad and the Muslims lived a perilous existence for several years as they suffered economic hardships in Medina and threats from Mecca. With the aim of providing economically for the community, the Muslims had begun to raid trade caravans bound for Mecca, though with limited success. Although it may sound surprising to the modern reader, raiding was a common and even acceptable economic practice in Arabia at that time, especially in times of hardship. Most often, however, raids did not involve bloodshed.

Conflicts with the Meccans continued, primarily with the Quraysh tribe, who still viewed the Muslims as a threat. Furthermore, the raids caused many economic problems for the Meccans and increased the tension between the two cities. The result was one of the most famous clashes in early Muslim history, the Battle of Badr in the year 624 C.E. The Muslims had planned a raid on a Meccan caravan at a place called Badr. The Meccans, learning of the plan, sent a force of more than 900 men to protect the caravan. The Muslims, though badly outnumbered at only 300 strong, soundly defeated the Meccan forces. The battle is mentioned in the Qur'an, which reports that angels helped the outnumbered Muslims win the battle (8:9). The Qur'an also notes this as a critical moment in the development of the spirit and destiny of the Muslims. After this dramatic battle, Muhammad's reputation as a great leader grew.

A few years later, in 628 C.E., Muhammad attempted to lead the Muslims back to Mecca for a pilgrimage. The people of Arabia had been making pilgrimages to the Ka'ba for centuries. The Meccans, expecting an attack, proposed a negotiation with the now more powerful Muslims. Muhammad agreed, and the pilgrimage was postponed through the signing of a treaty between the Meccans and the Muslims. Two years later, in 630 C.E., the Muslims returned, and the Meccans surrendered when they saw Muhammad's even greater political and military strength. Muhammad accepted the surrender and allowed the Meccan people to go free if they would convert to Islam. Upon entering Mecca, Muhammad and the Muslims destroyed the polytheistic idols housed at the Ka'ba and rededicated the building to the one and only God and the religion of Abraham.

Muhammad lived for only two more years after his victorious return to Mecca. At the time of his death, he had a large family. Khadija had died several years earlier, and after her death Muhammad married several more wives. Some of his marriages were contracted for political alliances, and others to care for widowed and divorced women who had no one else. The best known of his later wives was a woman called Aisha, who was the daughter of Abu Bakr. She was much younger than Muhammad, which was not unusual in marriages at the time. Aisha was a very important early figure in Islamic history and is thought to be one of Muhammad's most beloved wives. As mentioned earlier, she was the source of much information about Muhammad's life and was often consulted by other Muslims because of her vast knowledge of religious matters. In 632 C.E., Muhammad is believed to have died peacefully in Aisha's arms after returning from a final journey to Mecca. He was buried under her home in Medina, and to this day, some Muslims visit this site as a place of pilgrimage.

By the time of his death, Muhammad was the political and religious leader of much of Arabia. After the move to Medina, Muslim rule had spread rapidly across the Arabian Peninsula through both nonviolent political alliances and military conquests. Many people of Arabia had converted to Islam. Some did so because they believed in the truth of Muhammad's message, and others converted for political reasons, namely, to form alliances with Muhammad and the powerful Muslim community.

Not all people living under Muslim rule converted to Islam, however. Significant Christian, Jewish, and other religious minority populations remained. From this early period, Muslims have considered Christians and Jews to be People of the Book, a designation that means that they are a people who have received scripture from God and are thus close to the Muslim community. Later, Hindus and Buddhists were also considered People of the Book, as Muslim rule spread into South Asia. Under Muslim rule, these minority communities were governed by what are termed *dhimmi* laws; the term *dhimmi* refers to their status as protected peoples. These laws allowed non-Muslims in Muslim territories to worship how they chose, provided they paid taxes and submitted to Muslim authority. The *dhimmis* did not enjoy all the privileges of Muslims—they were not allowed to bear arms, for example—but they were entitled to the protection of the Islamic state.

The Crisis of Succession and the Rightly Guided Caliphs

At the time of Muhammad's death, communities throughout Arabia were united under Islam, but it was unclear to Muhammad's followers who should succeed him to lead the Muslims. When he died, most Muslims thought that Muhammad had not designated a successor. The companions of the Prophet thus chose the highly respected Abu Bakr to lead the Muslim community. Recall that Abu Bakr was one of the first converts to Islam and was Muhammad's father-in-law. A minority of Muslims, however, believed that Muhammad had designated his cousin 'Ali to succeed him. 'Ali was also Muhammad's son-in-law because he had married Fatima, Muhammad's daughter by Khadija. Although 'Ali was highly regarded even by those who did not think Muhammad had designated him to be his successor, he was much younger than Abu Bakr. Therefore, many considered him too young to lead the community.

This controversy over leadership of the Muslim community is often known as the crisis of succession, and it led to the development of the two major branches of Islam: the **Sunni** and the **Shi'a**. The majority group became known as the Sunni, which remains the larger of the two major branches. The minority group became known as the Shi'a, a name that comes from the term *Shiat 'Ali*, which means the "party of 'Ali." The Shi'a is the smaller of the two major branches of Islam. Later in the chapter, we discuss how this dispute over succession led to other differences between the Sunni and the Shi'a.

The leaders who came after Muhammad were not viewed as prophets. They were known rather as **caliphs**, who ruled as the representatives of God and the Prophet and had both religious and political authority. This was a new form of government called a caliphate, and it remained the model for Islamic society for several hundred years. The designation of Abu Bakr as caliph started a historical period that came to be known as the time of the Rightly Guided Caliphs, who were Abu Bakr and his successors: 'Umar, 'Uthman, and finally 'Ali.

As caliph, Abu Bakr sought to strengthen relationships with the communities and tribes of Arabia who had formed alliances with Muhammad. Abu Bakr faced the potential breakdown of Muslim unity because some of these tribes, particularly those in parts of Arabia far from Medina and Mecca, wanted to break their ties to the Muslim community when Muhammad died. After the death of Abu Bakr, which was only two years after he had been appointed caliph, the Muslims chose a man called 'Umar to lead. Like Abu Bakr, 'Umar had been close to Muhammad. Also like Abu Bakr, he was confronted with the problem of some communities wanting to break away from Islamic rule. However, he managed to preserve unity and expand Muslim rule, conquering the lands of Egypt, Syria, and Iraq. When 'Umar died in 644 C.E., another of the Prophet's companions, a man called 'Uthman, was selected as the new caliph.

'Uthman led the Muslims for twelve years, from 644 to 656 C.E. He continued the rapid political expansion that 'Umar had begun, but he also faced many problems. Muslim rule now extended from the Mediterranean and North Africa into Central Asia. Because the *umma* now reached beyond Arabic-speaking lands, there was a great deal of cultural and linguistic diversity among the Muslims. This situation made leadership a far more complex undertaking than it had been in the time of Muhammad and Abu Bakr, when nearly all Muslims were Arabs. This eventually led to charges that the caliphs discriminated against non-Arab Muslims. Furthermore, many accused 'Uthman of nepotism when he appointed his nephew Mu'awiya as governor of Syria. 'Uthman also placed other relatives in key posts, many of whom grew rich as a result. A few years into his rule, 'Uthman faced a number of rebellions in outer provinces of the empire, and in 656 C.E. he was killed by insurgents who had marched on Medina.

After 'Uthman's death, 'Ali was named caliph. During the time of the first three caliphs, 'Ali's supporters grew in numbers. Despite this growing support, 'Ali's time as caliph saw many fractures in the Muslim community. Supporters of 'Uthman were upset that 'Ali had never punished his murderers. This controversy resulted in the Battle of the Camel. This traumatic moment in Islamic history was the first to pit Muslims against Muslims. In the battle, 'Ali defeated an army led by Aisha and other prominent Meccans. Aisha directed the battle from her mount on a camel, from which the battle took its name. 'Ali's forces attacked and brought down her camel in order to hinder her leadership, and his forces were victorious. Mu'awiya, 'Uthman's nephew, also challenged 'Ali's authority. This conflict reached a peak in the Battle of Siffin in 657 C.E. When they met on the battlefield in Syria, Mu'awiya asked 'Ali for an arbitration of their dispute, and he accepted. However, some of 'Ali's followers disapproved of the arbitration, which they viewed as a surrender to Mu'awiya. This group formed a splinter group known as the Kharijites, which means "those who seceded." In 661 C.E., 'Ali was murdered by a Kharijite.

The Umayyads and the Abbasids

After 'Ali was killed, Mu'awiya claimed the caliphate. His leadership gave birth to what is known as the **Umayyad** Dynasty. This marked the end of the period of the Rightly Guided Caliphs. The institution of the caliphate survived, but the divisions in the community of believers that had worsened under 'Ali remained.

The Umayyad period lasted over a century, from 661 until 750 C.E. Umayyad leaders ruled from the city of Damascus in Syria. Although they were considered fairly effective leaders who expanded the Muslim Empire farther east to India and farther west to Spain, the reign of the Umayyads was controversial. For example, many Muslims thought that the Umayyads did not truly represent the diversity of the Muslim people, favoring Arab Muslims over non-Arab Muslims. Such criticism arose in part because Mu'awiya had designated his son Yazid as his successor instead of letting the community select a leader. This turned the caliphate into a dynasty.

Many Muslims who were opposed to the Umayyad Dynasty felt that the leadership of the *umma* should come from the line of Muhammad through Fatima and 'Ali. They argued that, therefore, their sons, Hasan and Husayn, should lead the *umma*. With the support of the Shi'a, **Husayn** eventually challenged the Umayyads for authority. However, he was slain in 680 C.E. when Yazid's armies ambushed him on the plains of Karbala in what is now Iraq. This tragic event is referred to as the "martyrdom of Husayn." This is a moment in Shi'a history that is solemnly commemorated to the present day as Husayn's sacrifice for the Muslim people. With the death of Husayn, the number of Muslims who believed the leader of the *umma* should be from the family of the Prophet grew. It was at this point that the Shi'a formally broke away from the Sunnis and established a line of successors to the Prophet that remained within Muhammad's family.

In the late seventh and early eighth centuries C.E., many more Muslims began to criticize the Umayyad Dynasty. This group included those who were critical of the Umayyads for their perceived discrimination against non-Arabs and also those who supported the family of 'Ali as rightful leaders of the *umma*. Muslims opposed to the Umayyads became known as the **Abbasids**, taking the name of one of Muhammad's uncles, al-Abbas ibn Abd al-Muttalib. In 750 C.E., the Abbasid Revolution succeeded in removing the Umayyads from power.

The first caliph of the Abbasids was a man named Abu al-Abbas, and during his rule the Abbasids moved their capital from Damascus to Baghdad. Baghdad became a cultural capital of the world. Islamic arts and sciences flowered in this time, which became known as the classical period of Islamic civilization. One of the most well-known pieces of literature from this period is the *One Thousand and One Nights*. These colorful tales celebrate the reign of the most famous Abbasid caliph, Harun al-Rashid, who ruled for twenty-five years in the late eighth century.

Many of these intellectual and artistic developments had an enormous impact on world history and the cultures of Europe and Asia. Islamic scholarship in science, philosophy, and medicine built on earlier knowledge from Greek and Persian sources and was very influential in European schools and universities for many centuries. The time of the Abbasids was also the period during which many Islamic religious doctrines were developed into forms that are still accepted today. For example, it was in this period that the Islamic legal schools of thought, which we discuss later in this chapter, were formalized.

Abbasid rule continued for several centuries, but not all Muslims were united under the Abbasid Caliphate. In 950 C.E., for example, rulers in Cairo and Spain also claimed the title of caliph. Furthermore, the Abbasid period saw the influence of the Crusades in Syria and Palestine, when European Christians sought to win control of the Holy Land. Christian forces captured Jerusalem from Islamic control in 1099. The holy city was later recaptured by Salah ad-Din (also known as Saladin), a famed Muslim military leader, in 1187. The rule of the Abbasids ended in 1258 C.E. when Baghdad was sacked by a Mongol army from the east led by the grandson of Genghis Khan.

By the end of the Abbasid Caliphate and the beginning of the fourteenth century, Islam was the majority religion in a vast region stretching from Spain and the western edge of North Africa all the way to Iran in Central Asia. The religion was also gaining converts in sub-Saharan Africa and South and Southeast Asia. Although military conquest expanded Muslim rule in some areas, it is incorrect to think that the historical spread of Islam around the globe was solely by the sword. In the earliest years of the *umma*, many tribes in Arabia joined the Muslims through political alliance. The growth of Islam throughout much of Asia and sub-Saharan Africa was gradual and peaceful. Often, Islam was introduced largely through traveling preachers, teachers, and traders.

Later Islamic Empires: The Ottomans, the Mughals, and the Safavids

After the fall of the Abbasids, several powerful Islamic empires arose in the next few centuries. These were the Ottoman Empire in the Mediterranean region, the Safavids in Iran, and the Mughal Dynasty in India.

The Ottoman Empire spanned over 600 years, from the fourteenth to the twentieth centuries. The early empire was marked by rapid expansion, and at the height of its power, the Ottomans controlled much of the Middle East and Mediterranean, reaching into southeastern Europe and Africa. The empire reached its height during the fifteenth and sixteenth centuries, and in 1453 the Turks took the city of Constantinople, the former capital of the Byzantine Empire. The city, now called Istanbul, became the Ottoman capital and an important seat of Islamic learning and Islamic power. The Ottoman Empire did not come to an end until after World War I.

At the same time that the Ottoman Empire reached its height, another Muslim empire arose thousands of miles away in South Asia. This dynasty, known as the Mughals, ruled much of India from the early sixteenth to the eighteenth centuries, even though the Muslim population was in the minority. The Mughal Dynasty, though not as long-lived as the Ottomans, saw a growth of literary and artistic development in South Asia. Mughal architecture is considered to have created some of the world's most impressive buildings such as the Taj Mahal in Agra, India. The stunningly beautiful Taj Mahal

The Sultan Ahmed Mosque in Istanbul, Turkey, was built in the 1600s and is a fine example of Ottoman architecture. It is also known as the Blue Mosque because of the blue tiling inside.

was built in the 1600s by the Mughal emperor Shah Jahan as a memorial and mausoleum for his beloved wife, Mumtaz Mahal. The Mughal Empire reached its peak in the eighteenth century, and although there was a Mughal ruler until 1857 in India, Mughal power and territory saw a decline with the advent of British occupation of South Asia.

To the west of the Mughals during the same period, the Safavid Empire flourished in Iran. Perhaps the most notable aspect of the Safavid rule was the establishment of Shi'a Islam as the religion of Iran; to the present day, the vast majority of Iran's Muslims are Shi'a. The Safavid period saw significant developments in Shi'a religious and philosophical thought. As with the Mughals, the period saw the development of great works of art and architecture.

Islam and Nationalism

In the twentieth century, the nation-state came to dominate the political organization of the world. Muslim leaders took different positions on the ideal relationship between religion and the nation-state. In many places, religion has served as a means to unify people across ethnic, class, and social boundaries. Some Muslim nationalists and political leaders envisioned a close link between their ideals of new states and Islam. Their vision involved a state government based on the principles of Islam and Islamic law as the basis for the legal system. Other leaders sought to distance nationalist policy from Islam and favored European secular states as political models.

The Taj Mahal, a mausoleum in Agra, India, was built in the 1600s by the Mughal emperor Shah Jahan as a memorial and mausoleum for his beloved wife, Mumtaz Mahal.

When the Ottoman Empire collapsed at the end of World War I, Turkey moved toward embracing European ideals of secular nationalism. A man called Mustafa Kemal, better known as Ataturk, the founder of modern Turkey, embraced this ideal. He argued that Turkey should follow the path of the western European nations and separate religion from politics. Ataturk disbanded the powerful religious brotherhoods, which had been very important in Turkey, and embraced a secular legal system that did not incorporate Islamic law at any level. He also required Turkish people to dress in a European style, which meant that women had to abandon headscarves and men had to stop wearing the traditional hat called a fez.

Although these policies were far reaching, they did not eradicate Islam from public life in Turkey. For example, although **Sufi** religious brotherhoods had been made illegal, many Turkish people still followed the mystical path known as Sufism, which we discuss later in this chapter. Although Islamic courts were no longer a part of the official legal system, Muslims still took disputes to Islamic legal authorities, particularly in rural areas. During the late twentieth and early twenty-first centuries, many Turks reembraced their Islamic heritage. The Justice and Development Party, which has been supportive of reintroducing Islam into public life, has been the majority party in the governing coalition since the early 2000s.

Other Muslim countries followed a very different path than Turkey. For example, in the Indian subcontinent, which was colonized by Great Britain, discussions of independence and nationalism early in the twentieth century focused a great deal on religious divisions in the region. With India's independence from Great Britain in 1947, two countries were formed: India and Pakistan. Pakistan was created as a Muslim homeland for the millions of Muslims who lived in South Asia. An important thinker behind the creation of Pakistan, Muhammad Iqbal, argued that Muslims needed a separate country to protect them from the majority Hindus in India. An organization called the Muslim League was instrumental in the early twentieth century in launching the idea of a separate state for the Muslim people of India. That ideal became a reality with independence. At first, Pakistan was divided into East and West Pakistan. In the 1970s, East Pakistan became the country that is now known as Bangladesh. Today, Pakistan and Bangladesh are among the largest Muslim-majority countries in the world, and India still has a significant Muslim minority.

Iran is an important case study of Islam and nationalism in the twentieth century. Throughout much of the century, the *shah* (or king) of Iran was Reza Pahlavi. The *shah* embraced the ideals of the Western world and looked to Europe and the United States as models for development. However, Iran's Shi'a religious scholars were critical of the monarchy for marginalizing religious learning and religious authority in Iran. Iranian liberals and Marxists also criticized the *shah* as a corrupt leader who was entranced with the Western world and closely tied to Western governments, particularly the United States. In 1978, a coalition of clerics, intellectuals, and women's groups formed with the goal of removing the *shah* and his family from power. The revolution they staged in 1979 deposed the *shah* and ushered in the leadership of Islamic clerics. Not surprisingly, after the revolution, many of those people who had supported the overthrow of the *shah* felt neglected when the religious clerics took charge and formed an Islamic Republic.

A religious scholar known as Ayatollah Khomeini (1902–1989) headed the new government. The term *ayatollah*, which literally means "sign of God," refers to Shi'a religious scholars who have achieved a very high level of religious learning and scholarship. Khomeini had been one of the most outspoken critics of the *shah* among the religious scholars, and he argued that it was the duty of the religious scholars to build an Islamic state in Iran. This is precisely what happened in the aftermath of the revolution. The new government instituted strict reforms, which they argued reflected Islamic rules of behavior. Women were required to dress in a full-length black garment known as the *chador*. Many Iranians, among them intellectuals and professionals, left the country and made their homes abroad in places such as the United States and Canada.

Today, people in Iran are divided as to how much authority religious scholars should have in the government. The supreme leader of Iran remains an ayatollah; the current supreme leader, Ayatollah Ali Khamenei, succeeded Khomeini in 1989. Iran also has a president. In 2009, huge numbers of Iranians took to the streets to protest the disputed reelection of President Mahmoud Ahmedinejad, and many have interpreted the protests as criticism of the Islamic Republic. The protest has been called the Green Movement, or Green Revolution, after the color adopted by the opposition presidential candidate, Mir-Hossein Mousavi. In 2011, Mousavi openly supported the pro-democracy Arab Spring movements in other Middle Eastern countries and called for more protests. He was then placed under house arrest for the next several years, and he remains detained at the time of writing. The current president of Iran is the moderate Hassan Rouhani, who was reelected in 2017.

Islamic Reform Movements

In the last two centuries, many movements have aimed to reform local Muslim communities and the worldwide *umma*. As we discussed earlier in this chapter, in their early history, the Muslims rapidly grew into an important world power. Various Muslim empires remained powerful for many centuries, through the Abbasid period and into the later Ottoman, Mughal, and Safavid sultanates. European powers were generally eclipsed by the Islamic world during this time. However, in the eighteenth century, European empires began to gain prominence as economic and political world powers. European power continued to grow with the advent of industrialization. Eventually, the British, French, and Dutch empires colonized much of the Muslim world. The British and French colonized much of Muslim Africa and the Middle East; the British and the Dutch controlled Muslim lands in South and Southeast Asia.

Wahhabism   During the eighteenth century, several Muslim reform movements developed. These movements were spearheaded by factions concerned about what they viewed as a decline in Muslim communities and in Muslim power worldwide. One of the most well-known reforms was the Wahhabi movement. It was originated by a scholar named Muhammad Ibn Abd al-Wahhab (d. 1792), and it is still influential today. Ibn Abd al-Wahhab disapproved of Muslim practices that he perceived as falling outside of the Qur'an and Sunnah and that had developed after the time of Muhammad. The Wahhabi movement was especially critical of venerating saints and visiting tombs. Al-Wahhab argued that these practices and others were considered innovations and had contributed to the decline of Islam and the Muslim world. As a result, al-Wahhab's followers razed many saints' tombs and shrines, including those of Muhammad, his companions, and Husayn.

In the late eighteenth century, followers of al-Wahhab formed significant ties with the ruling family of Arabia. To this day, the movement remains influential in Saudi Arabia and in other parts of the Muslim world, where it has sent teachers and established schools. Followers of the movement call themselves Muwahiddun, though they are commonly called Wahhabis in the news media. Sometimes, movements like the Wahhabis that advocate living according to models from the past are known as **salafi** or **salafist,** from the Arabic term *salaf al-salih*, which means "righteous ancestors."

The Wahhabi movement is often characterized as very conservative and "fundamentalist." However, we must be careful in using the term *fundamentalist* when discussing any religious movement. This is because not all movements called fundamentalist are the same. The Wahhabi movement is often termed "fundamentalist" because of its emphasis on the primacy of the Qur'an and the Sunnah and its criticism of later developments in Muslim thought and practice. The movement thus emphasizes the "fundamentals" of Islam—the Qur'an and the model of the Prophet. Today, the Wahhabi movement is often portrayed very negatively in the Western media, owing to its influence on notorious extremists such as Osama bin Laden and the emphasis some Wahhabis place on bringing their version of Islam to other parts of the Muslim world. Although followers of Wahhabi Islam are generally more conservative than other Muslims, not all embrace a political version of Islam.

Resisting Colonialism and Westernization   During the nineteenth century, European powers increasingly dominated Muslim lands. Many Muslim thinkers lamented the loss of a cohesive and powerful *umma* and regretted the decline of several important Muslim empires. The Mughals had dominated much of South Asia for several generations, but the introduction of British rule in the nineteenth century saw the end of the Mughals. The Ottoman Empire, too, had thrived in the eastern Mediterranean and North Africa, but by the early nineteenth century it was threatened by increasing European power.

As a result, reformist movements developed that prioritized revitalizing the *umma*. Some focused on trying to revive the lost glory and power of the *umma*. Other movements directly resisted European imperialism and, later, American expansion and influence. And some reformers tried to deflect the criticism of the Islamic world that was coming from powerful Western governments. European leaders and scholars were often quick to criticize Islam and Muslim cultures as being "backward," and some Muslim reformers made concerted efforts to combat these developing stereotypes.

These movements took several forms. One reformer was Muhammad Ahmed ibn Abdallah (1844–1885), more commonly known as the Sudanese Mahdi. The Sudanese Mahdi organized a powerful military uprising against the Egyptian and British forces that occupied the Sudan in the nineteenth century. Many people have claimed the title of Mahdi over the years, and Abdallah convinced people that he was indeed the Mahdi heralding the end of days. In this way, he was able to recruit a large number of followers. His movement emphasized social equality, and he entirely revamped the five pillars. For example, he incorporated a declaration of himself as Mahdi in the *shahadah*, and he dropped the hajj as a requirement. His revamping of the pillars was highly controversial, and many Sudanese Muslims did not support his efforts. However, his aims were more political than religious, and he successfully took the city of Khartoum in 1885 from the British and Egyptian armies.

Jamal al-din al-Afghani (1838–1897) was a reformer who sought to inspire Muslims by convincing them that the roots of revitalization were within their own faith and their own history. Born in Iran, al-Afghani traveled extensively in the Middle East and Central Asia and advocated the idea that all Muslims worldwide should join together with the goal of revitalizing the *umma* and defeating Western imperialism. He called upon his fellow Muslims to unify against Western influence. Al-Afghani is often considered the originator of the anti-imperialist sentiment among many Muslim thinkers of the time. In addition, he argued that Islam was the religion most amenable to scientific knowledge. Al-Afghani was also well known as an activist for the poor and downtrodden, and he called for social reform in Muslim countries to alleviate their plight.

Through calling for unification of the *umma*, al-Afghani is often considered the father of pan-Islamism, and he was a great inspiration to other reformers. Perhaps the best known of his followers is Muhammad Abduh (1849–1905), who was born in Egypt and achieved great renown as an advocate of Egyptian nationalism. Like al-Afghani, Abduh saw no conflict between religion and science, and he asserted that Islam had always embraced scientific methodologies. And like many reformers of his time, Abduh thought that the Qur'an should be interpreted in light of social changes. Abduh argued that although certain Islamic doctrines were absolute and unchangeable, some teachings should change with the times. For example, he is well known for his criticisms of polygamy, discussed in more detail later in this chapter.

A third reformer of the same period was the modernist thinker Sayyid Ahmed Khan (1817–1898). Khan is best known for his educational reforms in South Asia and his support of the British. Unlike reformers such as al-Afghani, Khan admired the West, particularly the British, and attempted to bring Western ways of thought and education to his native India. Although he did not advocate imperial rule, he believed that the Muslims of South Asia could only move forward through embracing certain Western ways. In light of these views, it is not surprising that he was criticized by other reformers of his time as being too sympathetic with the British. He is also known for advocating interpretation of the Qur'an in a rational way in light of social changes. Like Abduh and Afghani, he embraced developments in science and argued that there was no conflict between Islam and science.

The Muslim Brotherhood

The reformist spirit of the nineteenth century carried over into the twentieth. Several important and wide-reaching twentieth-century movements responded to and built on the developments of the nineteenth century. A key goal for many twentieth-century reformers involved finding a path to economic development for Muslim countries that did not follow Western models. More specifically, many thinkers have sought a path that allows Muslim countries and cultures to maintain their Muslim identities and still embrace certain ideas and technologies that originated in the West. Even in the postcolonial world, Europe and the United States are criticized for cultural imperialism because Western cultural models and products are spread throughout the world, particularly through business and media.

One of the most influential contemporary movements has been the Muslim Brotherhood. The Brotherhood has been in existence for several decades. It is based in Egypt, though it has been influential all over the globe. The founder was Hassan al-Banna, who organized the movement in 1928 to revitalize Islam from within by focusing on a return to the Qur'an and the Sunnah. Like other reformers of his time, al-Banna was opposed to Western imperialism. He argued that encroaching Western values were contributing to the decline of Islamic societies.

Sayyid Qutb, one of the more influential members of the Brotherhood and an outspoken critic of Western influence, aimed to revitalize the Islamic world solely through Islamic principles. Qutb was executed in 1966 by the Egyptian government after being repeatedly accused of treason, terrorism, and a plot to kill President Gamal Abdel Nasser. Qutb's writings have continued to influence certain Islamic activists and some extremists, including those highly critical of Western influence on the Muslim world, such as Osama bin Laden and members of al-Qaeda. However, it is important to note that many members of the Muslim Brotherhood have been very critical of Sayyid Qutb's radical views.

Throughout its existence, the Brotherhood has had a fractured relationship with the Egyptian government. It was banned in the 1950s, after members of the Brotherhood attempted to assassinate Egyptian President Nasser. Despite this ban, the Brotherhood remained active, and in later years it attempted to reconcile with the government of President Hosni Mubarak, who was deposed in 2011. In 2012, Muhammad Morsi was the first member of the Brotherhood to be elected president in Egypt. He was ousted in 2013, however, and the Brotherhood was again banned by the new government.

Varieties of Islam: Sunni and Shi'a

Most of what we discuss in this chapter is applicable to both major branches of Islam, the Sunni and the Shi'a. Although the essential beliefs of the two branches are the same—notably, the oneness of God, the Qur'an as the word of God, and Muhammad as the messenger of God—there are some important differences between them.

Who Are the Sunni?   Sunnis make up the majority of Muslims worldwide, about 80 percent, and the Shi'a about 20 percent. As you learned earlier, the Sunni and Shi'a split began over the leadership of the Muslim community after the death of the Prophet Muhammad. The majority of Muhammad's companions thought that he had not chosen a successor, and so they supported Abu Bakr as the next leader. However, Sunnism did not develop into a distinct branch of Islam until about 300 years later. At that point, certain scholars emphasized that Muslims should primarily follow the example of the Prophet Muhammad, the Qur'an, and the opinions of earlier scholars with regard to engaging in rationalist thought like that of the Mutazilites. The word "sunni" comes from this emphasis on the Sunnah of the Prophet.

One of the differences between Sunni and Shi'a Islam concerns the sources of Islamic law, which we discuss in more detail in a later section. In short, although both branches agree on the importance of the Qur'an and the Sunnah, in Sunni Islam an additional source is the consensus of the community. This became a source of law because of a hadith that reported the Prophet saying, "My community will never agree upon an error." Of course, it is impossible to solicit the opinion of every Muslim on a particular legal question, so Sunnis have generally agreed that the community in question consists of the *ulama*, or legal scholars.

Who Are the Shiʻa? Shiʻa Muslims are in the majority in Iran and Iraq, and they form significant minorities in other countries, including Pakistan and India. In addition to believing that Muhammad designated ʻAli to be his successor, the Shiʻa believe that Muhammad passed on special religious knowledge to his relatives through ʻAli. Therefore, to the Shiʻa, only Muhammad's family and their descendants should lead the Muslim community. This belief in a continuing spiritual leadership of the Muslim community through the line of successors is the most significant contrast between Sunni and Shiʻa Islam. For the Shiʻa, the rightful leaders of the Muslim community are known as imams, the same term used for someone who leads prayer. In Shiʻa Islam, the imam is both the political and the religious leader of the community, and he possesses the special religious knowledge that Muhammad passed on to the members of his family. ʻAli is regarded as the first imam. It is important to note that, although the imam has a very prominent role in Shiʻa Islam, he is not a prophet.

The authority of the Shiʻa imams has a special role in Shiʻa law that we do not see in Sunni approaches to Islamic law. The Shiʻa schools do not recognize consensus as a source of law but instead focus on the infallibility of the imam. Islamic scholarship is highly important in the Shiʻa tradition. Also, although scholarship and learning are valued among Sunni Muslims, there is a more formal religious authority structure in Shiʻism that we do not find in Sunni Islam.

The Shiʻa community itself has several branches, which differ in how they trace the line of imams in descent from ʻAli. The largest branch is known as the Twelvers, who

World Sunni and Shiʻa distribution.

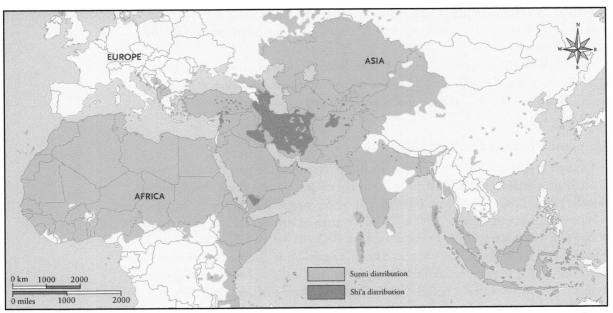

Sunni distribution

Shiʻa distribution

make up the majority of Muslims in Iran and Iraq. The Twelvers believe that the line of imams went through several generations until the twelfth imam disappeared in the ninth century. This twelfth imam is considered to be in "occultation," or hiding. Twelvers believe that he will eventually return. In the meantime, the Islamic scholars are considered responsible for the leadership of the Muslim community. This idea was important in the new government set up in Iran after the 1979 revolution.

Another branch of Shi'ism, known as the *Ismailis*, believes that there has

An Iraqi soldier stands guard as Shi'a pilgrims approach the holy city of Karbala.

been an unbroken line of imams from 'Ali until the present day. They take their name from the seventh imam, a man named Ismail, whom the Twelvers do not recognize as an imam.

The month of the Islamic calendar known as Muharram is especially significant to Shi'a Muslims. This is because the martyrdom of Muhammad's grandson Husayn, discussed earlier in this chapter, is recalled on the tenth of the month. This date is called **Ashura**, and the entire month of Muharram is recognized as an important and somber time. At this time of year, the death of Husayn is commemorated in many ways by Shi'a Muslims in places such as Iran and Iraq. Husayn's story is retold through passion plays and street processions, called Ta'ziya, in which Muslims reenact the events of Husayn's death.

For Shi'a Muslims, the tombs of the Prophet's family are popular sites for pilgrimages. Through these pilgrimages, Muslims commemorate and honor the Prophet's family. Karbala, where Husayn was martyred and is said to be buried, is an important pilgrimage site in Iraq.

Islam and Political Conflict Today

In Chapter 1, we considered Bruce Lincoln's theory regarding the potential of religion to facilitate violent conflict. And as nearly every chapter in this book shows, individuals, groups, and nations have invoked religion to engage in or to justify warfare, colonization, and other forms of violence. At the time of writing, ISIS (Islamic State in Iraq and Syria) is frequently in the news. Like al-Qaeda before it, ISIS has claimed responsibility for many terrorist attacks around the world, including suicide bombings. Political scientists define terrorism as a premediated act of violence, often against civilians, that has a specific political goal. Perpetrators may believe that there is a religious basis or reward for their violent actions, or they may attempt to justify the violence with religious ideologies. In the 9/11 attacks on the United States, Osama bin Laden and al-Qaeda used religion to explain their actions, and bin Laden claimed to be influenced by the writings of Sayyid Qutb.

In the early 2000s, ISIS was established as an umbrella movement for al-Qaeda in Iraq and other Sunni insurgent groups. In 2014, ISIS leaders claimed to have established a "caliphate" in northern Iraq and to be applying Islamic law. However, ISIS has taken an extremely violent approach to dealing with adversaries (both Muslim and non-Muslim) and even journalists. Muslims worldwide have denounced ISIS, just as they did with al-Qaeda. And although al-Qaeda and ISIS claim to be founded on Islamic principles, it is important to understand the rise of such groups in their historical and political context. Many political scientists think that the war in Iraq, launched in 2003, further destabilized an already precarious state, exacerbated Sunni and Shi'a tensions, and contributed to the devastating conditions under which ISIS arose and gained support.

Muslims around the world have expressed dismay and frustration at the use of Islam to facilitate or justify violence, contending that terrorist attacks are antithetical to the teachings of Islam, which prohibit the killing of innocents. Muslims cite scriptural evidence for this stance in a Qur'anic verse (5:32) that equates the killing of one innocent person to the killing of all of humanity. Empirical evidence also exists showing that contemporary Muslims condemn violence committed in the name of Islam. For example, in 2014, Heraa Hashmi, a student at the University of Colorado, began compiling a spreadsheet of Muslim activists, leaders, and thinkers worldwide who have condemned such violence. As of November 2016, she had recorded nearly 6,000 public statements of condemnation by Muslim political leaders, religious leaders, thinkers, and activists. Others joined her effort, and the list is now maintained as a website, MuslimsCondemn.com.

Muslims in North America

Today, about 2.6 million Muslims live in the United States, and close to 1 million live in Canada. Both populations are growing rapidly, primarily through immigration. American Muslims are making social contributions in both their home communities and regional and national politics. Many Muslims live in large urban areas, but significant populations also live in smaller towns and more rural areas. The Muslim population in the United States is not limited to one particular city or even one particular region. Muslims live everywhere, from Los Angeles to Salt Lake City to Dearborn, Michigan, the city that has the largest Muslim population in the United States.

The African American Muslim population grew significantly in the twentieth century. Scholars estimate that from 10 to 30 percent of the Africans who were enslaved and brought to the United States from the seventeenth to the nineteenth centuries were Muslims. Once in the United States, however, many slaves were not permitted to freely practice their religion, although some were literate in Arabic and tried to maintain their religious practice. Many slaves were also forced to convert to Christianity or converted by choice.

In the twentieth century, African Americans were attracted to Islam and converted for a variety of reasons. For example, many people regarded Islam as the likely religion of their African ancestors. Thus, Muslim religious leaders often stressed these ties to Africa; some claimed that Islam was a more "authentic" religion for African Americans, for Islam was not the religion of the European American slave owners. Today, about half of the Muslims in the United States are African Americans.[12] The Nation of Islam has played an important role in the U.S. Muslim community. However, the majority of African American Muslims are not members of the organization. The Nation was founded by a man who was known by several different names, among them Wallace Ford and Wali D. Fard. In the 1930s, Fard established the Temple of Islam in Detroit, Michigan, and he preached that all black people were originally Muslims. Eventually, a student of his named Elijah Muhammad succeeded him as the leader of the Nation of Islam. The Nation differs significantly from mainstream Islam on several key teachings. Most significantly, followers regard Fard as God incarnate, and Elijah is considered his prophet. The Nation of Islam has been controversial in the United States because of teachings that suggest the natural supremacy of black people and encourage the rejection of white society. Despite its controversial nature, the Nation has been active in improving the lives of African Americans.

When Elijah Muhammad died in 1975, the Nation of Islam split. One group, led by his son Warith Deen Muhammad, moved away from the teachings of the Nation toward mainstream Sunni Islam and became known as the American Muslim Mission. This is the largest organized group of African American Muslims today. Louis Farrakhan, a radical preacher who is very controversial for his espousal of black supremacist ideas and politics, has led the other group, which retained the name Nation of Islam, for many years.

An American Muslim soldier praying.

Malcolm X, a leader in the black power movement of the 1960s, was perhaps the most famous American Muslim and the most famous member of the Nation of Islam. He was raised a Christian with the name Malcolm Little and converted to Islam while serving a prison sentence. He took the name X as a statement decrying his "slave name" of Little, in reference to the historical practice of slaves being given the surnames of their masters. He eventually took the name Malik al-Shabazz. Malcolm X was affiliated with the Nation of Islam for several years and became an influential public figure. However, after he made the hajj to Mecca in the 1960s, he moved toward mainstream Islam and eventually separated himself from the Nation. In his autobiography, he movingly describes the sense of harmony and unity he felt while on hajj with Muslims of all colors, ethnicities, and cultural backgrounds.[13]

Islam is truly a global religion. Through population growth, Muslims are becoming a significant religious minority in the United States, Canada, and Europe, and are playing an increasingly important public role. In 2006, the United States saw the election of the first Muslim member of Congress, Representative Keith Ellison of Minnesota. In 2015, eleven Muslims were elected to the Canadian Parliament—the highest number ever. And in 2017, the mayors of both London and the large Dutch city of Rotterdam are Muslim. However, as with many immigrant groups before them, immigrants from the Muslim world face challenges in Europe and North America.

In the United States, Muslims are not only a religious minority, but also must contend with the added difficulty of an American population that does not know much about Islam except for unflattering stereotypes. In the aftermath of 9/11, North American Muslims faced suspicion and hostility from their non-Muslim neighbors. Some non-Muslim Americans mistakenly viewed the terrorist attacks as representative of Islam and Muslims, and in turn targeted Muslim communities, breaking windows in mosques and threatening teachers at Islamic elementary schools. In 2010, a controversy about the building of an Islamic center in lower Manhattan turned especially heated. Many non-Muslim Americans were vehemently opposed to the center because it was a few blocks away from the site of the September 11 attacks on New York.

Despite these difficulties, many Americans have expressed increased interest in understanding other faiths and cultures—particularly Islam. Also, many American Muslim individuals and communities have made concerted efforts to educate other Americans about their faith, beliefs, and religious practices and to explain that the vast majority of the world's Muslims regard terrorist acts as distinctly un-Islamic with no basis in the faith. Through these outreach efforts and the efforts of non-Muslim Americans to understand Islam and Muslim peoples and cultures, meaningful religious diversity in the United States may become possible.

In 2015, several hundred members of the Muslim community of Hamtramck, Michigan, rallied at City Hall to condemn terrorism and ISIS.

As noted earlier, most African American Muslims are not members of the Nation but are rather Sunni Muslims whose beliefs and practices are like those of other Sunni Muslims around the world. Many American Muslims today are either immigrants or the descendants of immigrants. Like all immigrants to the United States, Muslims have come in waves from many parts of the world; most are from the Middle East,

South Asia, Southeast Asia, and Iran, though others came from eastern Europe, Africa, and elsewhere. In the late nineteenth century, people migrated from the Middle East, namely, Syria, Jordan, and Lebanon, to the Americas for economic reasons. Most of them were uneducated, and most were single men. This resulted in much intermarriage between these Muslim newcomers and people of varied cultural and religious backgrounds.

In the middle of the twentieth century, Muslim immigrants began to come from other areas of the Middle East, the Soviet Union, and eastern Europe. Many in this wave of immigrants were educated and from wealthy families, and many had a great interest in assimilating to the wider American population. In later years, Muslim peoples came to the United States from South Asia, Iran, and other parts of the world. Many in this most recent wave have had less interest in assimilating to mainstream American culture, instead hoping to preserve their cultural and religious heritage.

ISLAM AS A WAY OF LIFE

What does it mean to be a practicing Muslim? What does one do on a daily basis? In this section, we discuss worship practice, the Islamic year and important holidays, and Islamic law. We also explore gender roles and family life and the complex concept of jihad.

VOICES: An Interview with Dola K. and Taslima S.

Dola was born in Bangladesh and has lived in the United States since she was two years old. She is now twenty-four and holds a BA in Anthropology and eventually hopes to complete a PhD in that field. Taslima is twenty-two and is studying for a BA in international business. She moved to the United States from Bangladesh when she was sixteen years old and hopes to become an investment banker.

Taslima S. (left) and Dola K.

In your view, what is the essence of Islam? What should students understand about Islam?

Dola: For me, the first thing is the belief in a supreme being that is all powerful, all-knowing, and has a hand in what happens in the universe. Islam is also about how you live your daily life according to guidelines and principles. To me, the essence of Islam is being a loving and kind person, and seeing the good in everything and everyone. Living your life with love is how I understand Islam. Islam is not homogeneous —it contains many beliefs, and many interpretations can be derived from those beliefs; how you practice it is personal, and I don't believe it's necessary for everyone to follow Islam in the same manner.

Taslima: To me, Islam is a set of guidelines that helps you achieve your daily goals. Islam is kind of a reality check for me: I think that God will not give you what you do not work for. You have to work for your goals, and you earn your own dimes. God never oppresses—rather, you oppress yourself if you do not take initiative. God told me I can be a businesswoman someday. Muhammad's first wife was a businesswoman! She went to war, she was a merchant, she had her own values and her opinions. God did not oppress her, so who are we to oppress ourselves?

What is humanity's place in the world? How does being a Muslim shape your worldview?

Dola: Humanity's place in the world is to help each other. Even though we live in this big wide world of billions of people, we should be one community. We should treat each other kindly and lovingly, and I think that is what Islam teaches.

Taslima: Islam stresses equality for all. To me, the main purpose of being a Muslim is that I have the opportunity to share with others. If I am eating one day and I see my neighbors are not eating, then I will be there for them. Islam has taught me regardless of what other people's point of view is, to be respectful and to harm no one because of their views. I have learned to see the best in people.

From your perspective, what is it like to be a Muslim in North America today?

Dola: In the current political atmosphere, I find that I am cautious of how I approach people. I have no problem admitting that I am Muslim, but it has made me more cautious about how I talk about culture, politics, and society. I haven't experienced any discrimination, but members of my family have. But I also find that I am more accepting of others. Being Muslim in the US has helped me become more accepting of people who are different in other ways.

Taslima: I agree with you. You can't always practice your religion by the book. A French imam recently argued that we need to reevaluate our religion in terms of Western culture. The adaptability is something I like about Islam.

When I started high school in the US in 2011, people would ask me if my father was Osama bin Laden. I would respond by joking about it. When I used to work at a fast food restaurant, someone once chanted "terrorist" at me in the drive-through. I wear hijab in everyday life, but since I work at a very conservative place, I have chosen to not wear it at work. My family is not religious, but when I was a child I had a religious friend, and once I started learning more about Islam I decided to try wearing hijab. My parents were so upset!

Dola: Oh, my parents would be so happy if I did! I don't wear hijab, and nobody in my family wears hijab. I do speak Bengali out in public with my family, but I don't have an accent; I have perfect American English. People don't tell me to "Go back to where you came from!" But people have told my mom that because she has an accent.

What opportunities and challenges do you face as a young Muslim woman in the United States?

Dola: I struggle with guilt on this subject. In Bengali culture, Islam is not very restrictive, but there are still values that clash. I date, but culturally it is not appropriate, and dating is still taboo in my family. However, I am letting my parents arrange my marriage. As Westernized as I am, I would like to marry a Muslim Bengali man. My parents never pressured me, but they were so happy when I asked them to arrange the marriage. And it made my heart so happy!

Taslima: My family is more liberal, and are okay with us dating. They don't think dating is bad, but they are focused on the future, and they want dating to lead to a long-lasting marriage. But they want me to finish my education first. My parents don't want me to have to rely on a man.

Dola: My family holds Islam above our Bengali culture. But I think they are so intertwined that you can't really tell the difference. I think religion should adapt to culture, not the other way around.

Taslima: As American Muslims, we can adapt our religion. As an American woman, I have freedom to do what I want. Yes, I have my own religious and cultural views, but I am also an American. I want other Muslims to know that it is okay to be a Muslim and an American—it is never a bad thing to be an American. It is never a bad thing to be a woman of color, or a Muslim woman who is dating someone different. Your sexual orientation is not a bad thing. If you are a Muslim, you pray and you believe in the five pillars, and that's it. I came to America to be an American, and I'm going to be the best possible American.

Dola: That's how I feel. I can be Bengali, I can be Muslim, and I can be American. I try to be an example for the younger girls in my community, and I tell them they can be themselves and stand up for themselves.

The Qur'an in Daily Life

The Qur'an is an important part of the daily life of all Muslims, and the text itself is treated with great reverence and respect. To Muslims, the Qur'an is authentic only in the original Arabic. This means that a translation, such as an English version of the Qur'an, is not the holy book itself but merely an interpretation of the meaning. In many Muslim countries, children are encouraged to attend Qur'an schools, where they are often introduced to religious study through learning to memorize and recite sections of the Qur'an. In most communities, both boys and girls study the Qur'an, and people will often continue to study the Qur'an throughout adulthood. Indeed, Muhammad encouraged all Muslims to pursue a life of learning.

To Muslims, the true meaning of the Qur'an can only be understood in the original Arabic. The beauty of the language is said to lend itself to the spiritual nature of the words of God. Thus, Muslims around the world learn to recite the Qur'an in Arabic—even if they do not speak or understand the language. (Often, a teacher will explain the meaning of the text in the local language.) Verses of the Qur'an are recited during the daily prayers, and the Qur'an is also recited at numerous other occasions, including weddings, funerals, birth celebrations, holidays, and political events.

Hearing the Qur'an recited by a talented person can be a moving experience for people of all faiths, even if they do not understand the words. Although people can achieve great fame for their ability to recite beautifully, Muslims do not normally regard recitation as entertainment or singing. In many places, children and adults recite the Qur'an in highly organized competitions that can resemble an American spelling bee. Amina, the woman introduced at the beginning of the chapter, has studied the Qur'an for years and has great skill in recitation. As a teenager, she once won a sewing machine in a recitation contest.

What Is Jihad?

The term **jihad** comes from an Arabic verb meaning to "struggle" or "strive" and has historically had complex meanings. The concept of jihad is often distorted in contemporary Western media. In general, the term jihad means exerting oneself in the name of God. Jihad can refer to several types of struggle on both personal and social levels. The term is used only rarely in the Qur'an, and nowhere is it explicitly linked to armed struggle. Rather, it was early in Islamic history that the term became associated with defensive military endeavors against the enemies of the growing Muslim community. Some Muslim groups both today and throughout history have called for a military jihad against nonbelievers, even out of the context of defense of the Muslim community. You can see how the term is used in different verses of the Qur'an:

This building in Zanzibar, Tanzania, houses both Islamic and secular primary courts, as well as government offices.

> O Believers, go out in the cause of God, (whether) light or heavy, and strive (jihad) in the service of God, wealth and soul. This is better for you if you understand.
>
> —9:41

> And strive (jihad) in the way of God with a service worthy of Him. He has chosen you and laid no hardship on you in the way of faith, the faith of your forebear Abraham. He named you Muslim earlier, and in this (Qur'an) in order that the Prophet be witness over you, and you be witness over mankind. So be firm in devotion, pay the zakat, and hold on firmly to God. He is your friend: How excellent a friend is He, how excellent a helper!
>
> —22:78

So do not listen to unbelievers and strive (jihad) against them with greater effort.

—25:52

Muslims often refer to the *greater* jihad as one's struggle to become a better person by striving against one's own sinful tendencies and to live in accordance with the will of God. Although we often see the term jihad translated into English as "holy war," Muslims regard the military connotations of the term as the *lesser* jihad. The idea of "greater and lesser" jihad comes from the hadith literature. Muhammad is reported to have said, upon returning home from a battle, "We return from the little jihad to the greater jihad."

The Islamic Year and Holidays

The Islamic calendar begins with the hijra, that is, the migration of Muhammad and the early Muslim community from Mecca to Medina in 622 C.E. The Islamic calendar is lunar because the Qur'an stipulates that the moon should be the measure of time. In most of the Muslim world, however, people use both the lunar and solar calendars. The Qur'an also designates the names of the twelve months of the year.

Several important celebrations and feast days occur throughout the Islamic year, and Muslims around the world celebrate these days in a variety of ways. The Feast of Sacrifice, or *Id al-Adha*, is the primary holiday of the Muslim year. The feast takes place at the end of the hajj season, and it is celebrated by all Muslims—not just those who made the pilgrimage that year. The feast commemorates Abraham's willingness to sacrifice his son at God's command. In many countries, offices and shops close for two days, and people spend time with their families and friends. In commemoration of the ram that was sacrificed instead of Ishmael, Muslims are expected to slaughter an animal to mark the holiday. However, because this is not always possible, Muslims may make charitable donations as a substitute.

The second most significant holiday in the Muslim calendar is *Id al-Fitr*, the Feast of Fast-Breaking. This holiday marks the end of the month of Ramadan. This feast is a time of joy and forgiveness and is celebrated in many different ways around the world. Muslims mark the day by attending congregational prayers, visiting friends and family, or celebrating in public festivals and carnivals. Often, Muslims will wear elegant clothing for the holiday, and children are dressed in their finest new clothes. In some places, children are also given special treats, money, or gifts.

The Prophet's birth is also an occasion for celebration in many parts of the Muslim world, such as North Africa, East Africa, and South Asia. This celebration is known as *Mawlid al-Nabi* and takes place around the twelfth day of the third month of the Islamic calendar. The birth of the Prophet may be marked by state-sponsored ceremonies. Elsewhere, the birthday is marked by all-night recitation sessions, at which participants recite the Qur'an and devotional poetry. Some Muslims criticize the celebration of the Prophet's birth. They argue that such celebration of Muhammad risks elevating the Prophet to the status of God. Muslims in Saudi Arabia, for example, do not generally celebrate *Mawlid al-Nabi*. As you learned earlier in this chapter, the month of Muharram is particularly important for Shi'a Muslims as a time to commemorate the martyrdom of the Prophet's grandson Husayn.

The Shari'a: Islamic Law

Muslims believe that God, as the creator of the universe and humanity, established a wide-ranging set of guidelines for human beings to follow. These guidelines are known as the shari'a. The literal translation of the Arabic term *shari'a* is the "road" or "way." In English, it is most often translated as "law." However, the shari'a encompasses a much broader range of law and legal activity than what is normally associated with law in the Western world. The shari'a regulates almost every aspect of daily life for believers. Proper religious practice is included in the shari'a, and so are areas of law that North Americans find more familiar, such as marriage and divorce, inheritance, commerce, and crime. However, few countries actually apply Islamic law in full, either today or in the past.

In Islamic belief, God is the sole legislator. In theory, this means that while humanity can interpret law, humans cannot legislate or make new laws. The shari'a is drawn from several sources. The Qur'an is the primary legal source. In the early Meccan *surahs*, general legal principles are introduced. These include the importance of generosity, of obeying God's command, and of performing prayer and religious duties with sincerity. In the later Medinan *surahs*, many technical legal matters are presented in great detail. Some of these *surahs* contain specific laws governing community relations, marriage and family, and inheritance and commerce.

Although the Qur'an is the primary source of law, Islamic scholars throughout history have recognized that it does not address every legal situation. As a result, there are also other sources of Islamic law. Different branches of Islam, such as the Sunni and Shi'a traditions, and different schools of thought within them have recognized different sources as more or less important. For example, in Sunni Islam, many scholars have referenced the Sunnah as a very important additional legal source, which is second only to the Qur'an in importance. For centuries and up to the present day, Islamic jurists have consulted the Sunnah for answers to legal questions that are not explicitly addressed by the Qur'an. The Sunnah is important because Muhammad is considered the ideal human, the person closest to God, and the recipient of the revelation of the Qur'an. For that reason, his words and actions became an important legal source as a model for human behavior. Furthermore, Muhammad acted as a judge and a mediator of disputes in Medina, and the way he resolved legal conflicts is recorded in the hadith.

There are also other sources of Islamic law. In the sections on Sunni and Shi'a Islam, we discussed sources of law that are distinct to each. For example, many Sunni scholars agree that if a legal matter is not addressed by the Qur'an or the Sunnah, then it is appropriate to use human reason to find an analogous situation; this reasoning by analogy is known as *qiyas*. In addition, Sunni Muslims recognize the consensus of the Muslim community as a source of law; this is known as *ijma* and is recognized as a source of law because a hadith reports that Muhammad said, "my community will never agree upon an error." Law for Shi'a Muslims is somewhat different. For example, Shi'a legal traditions do not recognize consensus as a source of law but do recognize the imams as an important source of law, as they are considered infallible.

Because Islamic legal scholars have not always agreed on the merit of sources of law such as reasoning by analogy and consensus, several schools of Islamic law developed in the centuries following the death of Muhammad. Among the Sunni, there are four schools, each named after the legal scholar who founded it. The schools were formalized by the tenth century, and all the schools recognize the validity of the others.

Both historically and today, studying shari'a is an important part of Islamic education. Those who gain expertise in the law may have a special status in the community. The term *ulama* refers to Islamic legal scholars. Among these scholars are legal practitioners known as *qadis*, court judges who issue rulings on various matters. A *mufti* is an expert in Islamic law who is qualified to give nonbinding legal opinions, known as *fatwas*.

Today, many Muslim-majority states include Islamic law and courts in the state legal systems. However, in most countries in which Islamic law is applied, Islamic courts handle only matters of family law and only for Muslims. Family law includes issues such as marriage, divorce, child custody, and inheritance. Only in a very few countries, such as Iran and Saudi Arabia, is Islamic criminal and commercial law recognized in the state legal system. One reason is that many countries that were colonized by European powers adopted European legal codes for criminal matters. Also, some countries have determined that centuries-old laws are not appropriate for modern contexts.

Many Muslims live in accordance with Islamic law in their personal lives, even if they do not live in a country with Islamic courts. As noted earlier, Islamic law informs the daily life of the believer and regulates how a Muslim worships God. In addition, much like Jewish law, Islamic law regulates what a believer should eat and drink. For example, Muslims are prohibited from consuming pork and alcohol. Much of the legal basis for the prohibition on pork comes from the Qur'an. The prohibition on alcohol, though mentioned in the Qur'an, is more thoroughly developed in the hadith literature.

Case files from an Islamic court in East Africa.

Sufism

Muslims have sometimes described the shari'a, or Islamic law, as the "outer" way to God because it regulates a person's "outer" existence: how he or she should handle relationships with other people, how he or she should live in a community, and how he or she should worship. For many Muslims, however, there is also an "inner" way to God. This is the mystical tradition of Islam, which is known as Sufism. Like traditions of mysticism in other religions, the goal of a follower of Sufism, a **Sufi,** is to draw close to and personally experience God. However, unlike mystics of other religions, Sufis base this spiritual quest on the sources of Islam, namely, the Qur'an and the example of Muhammad.

It is likely that Sufism arose in the years after the death of Muhammad as a response to the worldly excesses and materialism of the Umayyad Dynasty. Many early Sufis were ascetics who taught that a simple way of life was in keeping with the way Muhammad lived. One famous eighth-century Sufi was Hasan of Basra. (Basra is a city in Iraq.) He was known for preaching asceticism and for his constant weeping out of fear of God. A renowned early female Sufi was Rabia al-Adawiyya, also of Basra. Rabia was known for her almost giddy happiness in the love of God. There are many wonderful stories about Rabia. In one, she criticized Hasan of Basra by telling him that his constant weeping and fear of God drew the focus to himself rather than to God. This theme is echoed in another story, in which she walks through the streets of Basra carrying a pitcher of water and a flaming torch. When asked why she was doing this, she explained that she wanted to set paradise ablaze and put out the fires of hell so people would love God solely for the sake of God—not out of hope of paradise or fear of hell.

After Rabia's time, this ideal of intense love for God became a primary focus for Sufis. Love is often expressed in Sufi poetry, which is one of the premier art forms in Islamic history. The following poem, by the great thirteenth-century Sufi poet Jalalludin Rumi, describes the beauty of submitting to God. Those who love and submit to God are compared to a moth who is drawn to a candle's flame.

> Love whispers in my ear,
> "Better to be a prey than a hunter,
> Make yourself My fool.
> Stop trying to be the sun and become a speck!
> Dwell at My door and be homeless.
> Don't pretend to be a candle, be a moth,
> so you may taste the savor of Life
> and know the power hidden in serving."[14]

Sufis ground their belief and worship practice in the teachings of the Qur'an. Sufi readings of the Qur'an have often searched for the inner, or hidden, meaning. This approach to interpreting the Qur'an often focuses on God's love for creation and God's closeness to humanity. Sufis often emphasize the teachings of the hadith *qudsi*, which focus on these themes.

Like all Muslims, Sufis consider Muhammad the ideal human, and they strive to emulate the way he lived his life. Sufis emphasize the story of the miraculous night when Muhammad journeyed from Mecca to Jerusalem and from there ascended to heaven to meet God. The ascension to heaven is known as the *miraj*. Muslims believe that the Angel Gabriel came to Muhammad one night while he was sleeping and took him to Jerusalem. From there, Muhammad ascended upward through the many levels of heaven. He met earlier prophets like Jesus and Moses. Eventually, Muhammad came into the presence of God. God gave him significant blessings and special spiritual knowledge that he later passed on to his companions, particularly 'Ali. Because Muhammad is believed to have personally experienced the presence of God, Sufis consider him to be the first Sufi and the source of the special spiritual knowledge they seek. In East Africa and the Middle East, Muslims learn of the *miraj* through epic poems, which are recited on special occasions like *Mawlid al-Nabi*. Because Muhammad ascended to heaven from Jerusalem, it is recognized as a holy city for Muslims, along with Mecca and Medina.

The Dome of the Rock in Jerusalem.

The night journey is mentioned in the Qur'an (17:1) and the hadith literature and is considered by many Muslims to be the greatest of all Muhammad's spiritual experiences. Because Muhammad ascended to heaven from Jerusalem, the city holds a special place in Islam, and it is one of the three Muslim holy cities, along with Mecca and Medina. In the year 691 C.E., the beautiful shrine known as the Dome of the Rock was built over the spot from which Muhammad ascended to heaven. The Dome of the Rock is located on the place known as the Temple Mount, where the ancient Jewish temples were located. It is therefore easy to understand why this place in the center of Jerusalem is special to both Muslims and Jews. This is one of the primary reasons that the status of Jerusalem is so central to the Arab-Israeli conflict today: practitioners of both faiths (as well as Christians) consider the city to be holy and long to have unfettered access to it.

Most Sufis agree that an individual needs guidance along the spiritual path to God. As a result, a master–disciple relationship is very important in Sufism. The *shaykh*, or master, directs the spiritual training of the novices. In the early centuries of Islam, respected *shaykhs* would guide several pupils, and as a result a number of Sufi orders, *tariqas*, developed around particular Sufi masters. Each order traces a spiritual lineage of learned leaders back to Muhammad and from Muhammad to God. Muhammad is believed to have passed on his special religious knowledge to his companions, who then passed it down through the generations from master to disciple.

Although members of all the orders have the same goal—personally experiencing God—they emphasize different meditation techniques and spiritual practices. Some orders are widespread and have members all over the world. Others are limited to a particular region. The most well-known order in the Western world is perhaps the Mevlevi order, which is based on the teachings of Jalalludin Rumi.

Sufi orders emphasize the necessity of some type of *dhikr*. The term means "recollection" and refers to Sufi meditation in which the believer strives to "recollect" God

Mevlevi dhikr; Mevlevis are sometimes known as Whirling Dervishes.

Pilgrims at the shrine of Hazrat Mu'in ud-Din Chishti in Ajmer (Rajasthan), India.

so completely that he forgets himself. *Dhikr* can take many forms and varies from order to order. Sometimes *dhikr* is as simple as the recitation of the *shahadah*, and sometimes it is much more elaborate. The Mevlevis have an elaborate *dhikr*. In the West, they are often called the "Whirling Dervishes" because their *dhikr* involves controlled whirling. For all Sufis, the goal of *dhikr* is to lose the sense of self entirely in complete remembrance of God.

Not all Sufi practice takes place in the formal context of the orders. In many parts of the world, Muslims may participate in Sufi practice without affiliation to an order. A good example is the practice of saint veneration. Many Sufis venerate *shaykhs*, or saints, who were well known and respected for their religious learning and spirituality. In some areas, such as Pakistan and northern India, the tombs of deceased *shaykhs* have become places of pilgrimage. At the tombs, people seek blessings from the saints. Tomb visitation is very common in South Asia, when the celebration of the saints' death date can draw thousands of pilgrims. Many pilgrims are not affiliated with a Sufi order, and some are not even Muslim; people of all faiths may recognize the power of a saint.

Throughout Islamic history, occasional tension has arisen between Sufis and other Muslims. For example, the practice of saint veneration has drawn criticism from some, who argue that the celebration of saints compromises the oneness of God by raising mere mortals to the level of the divine (recall al-Wahhab's criticism of saint veneration). Of course, those involved in saint veneration do not regard saints as divine. Rather, they view saints more as close friends of God, who are filled with blessings that can be transferred to others. Historically, Sufis have sometimes been criticized by other Muslims for neglecting the five pillars in favor of more esoteric religious knowledge and practice. Some early Sufis rejected adherence to the shari'a on the grounds that the technical laws merely served to veil God from the believer, not draw him or her closer. However, this was not a majority opinion among Sufism. Indeed, some Sufis, especially the eleventh-century scholar al-Ghazali, have made a specific effort to reconcile the shari'a and Sufism. In his writings, al-Ghazali established Sufism as a branch of formal learning in the Islamic sciences.

Marriage and Family

Marriage and family life are the cornerstones of Muslim communities. Devout Muslims, who strive to follow the example of the Prophet in their daily lives, consider Muhammad to have set the example of marriage and to have been the ideal husband and father. As a result, marriage is generally regarded as incumbent upon all Muslim men and women when they reach adulthood. Celibacy is not normally encouraged, and sexual pleasure is considered a gift from God to be enjoyed within a marriage.

Much variation exists throughout the Muslim world concerning marriage arrangements, weddings, and the organization of the family life. In some areas, marriages for young people are arranged by their parents, whereas in others, women and men select their own marriage partners. However, in most Muslim communities, dating is not an acceptable practice—even among Muslims living in North America. Furthermore, adult children in many Muslim families live with their parents until they marry, even if they are financially able to live on their own. Regardless of the method of arranging marriages, according to the shari'a, young men and women may reject a marriage partner they deem unsuitable; the consent of both the bride and the groom is necessary for the marriage to take place. However, this legal right does not always coincide with community or cultural norms. In some cultures, a bride's silence about her parents' choice of a marriage partner is considered to indicate acceptance of the proposal.

In Islam, a marriage is considered a contractual relationship. For the marriage to be valid, the bride, the groom, and witnesses must sign a marriage contract. The contract designates the *mahr*, which is the gift a bride will receive from the groom and his family. The gift may be cash or other property. The marriage contract may be considered invalid without the *mahr*, though the amount may vary greatly from family to family and culture to culture. The amount depends not only on the family's wealth but also on community norms. For example, urban Muslims in the Middle East might give a *mahr* of thousands of dollars, whereas the normal amount in a small African village might be only fifty dollars. According to shari'a, the *mahr* is solely the property of the bride. However, in many cultures, a bride's parents may take some of the *mahr* due

A Muslim bride signs her marriage contract.

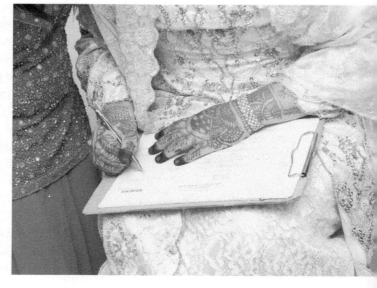

to customary practices and local expectations the wedding day, the bride and groom may be separated for most of the festivities. The groom usually signs the marriage contract in a mosque in the company of his male friends and relatives. The marriage official, often an imam, then takes the contract to the bride in her family's home, where she is accompanied by her female relatives and friends. Wedding celebrations are often large affairs, and feasting, Qur'an recitation, and sometimes music and dancing may accompany the signing of the contract. In many communities, men and women celebrate entirely separately. This is because some Muslims do not consider it acceptable for men and women to socialize together. In some cultures, the bride is taken to the groom's home in a big procession at the end of the day. There, the new couple shares a special meal and begins their life together.

According to most interpretations of Islamic law, Muslim men are allowed to marry up to four wives. However, this is only under certain conditions, and only if the man can support all his wives and treat them equally. For example, the verses in the Qur'an concerning polygamy suggest that the practice is appropriate in times of warfare when there may be many unmarried women. Furthermore, the Qur'an states, "Marry such women as seem good to you, two, three, four; but if you fear you will not be equitable, then marry only one" (4:3). A later verse says that "You will not be equitable between your wives, even if you try" (4:129). Some thinkers, such as the Egyptian reformer Muhammad Abduh (about whom you read earlier in this chapter), argued that these two verses actually prohibited polygamy because the later verse stated that no man could possibly treat multiple wives equitably, which is a necessary condition of polygamy. Abduh also contended that although polygamy may have been necessary in the time of the Prophet to protect women who had no one to care for them, it was destructive in the modern context. However, most Muslims have considered polygamy legal, though the occurrence of the practice varies tremendously around the world, and some countries, like Tunisia, have banned it entirely.

Several types of divorce are permitted in Islam. Guidelines for divorce come from both the Qur'an and hadith literature. One type is divorce by male unilateral repudiation. In this type of divorce, a man writes or pronounces the formula "I, (the man's name), divorce you, (the wife's name)." In classical Islamic law, this type of divorce does not need the approval of the wife or a legal authority. However, in many countries today, unilateral divorce is no longer permissible, and men and women must both file for divorce in court. According to shari'a, women may seek divorce from Islamic judges on a variety of grounds. Stipulations for divorce are occasionally written into the marriage contract. For example, a woman may specify that she can divorce her husband if he marries another wife. Divorce is common in some Muslim countries and uncommon in others. In some places, a divorced man or woman is dishonored and finds it difficult to remarry, whereas in others there is little or no stigma attached to a divorced man or woman.

Women and Islam

There is much variation in how gender roles are perceived and interpreted throughout Muslim cultures. As in other religious traditions, such as Judaism, Christianity, and Hinduism, patriarchal cultural norms are sometimes justified in terms of religion. When we consider the historical context in which it was revealed, the Qur'an introduced many legal rights and privileges to women that they had not previously enjoyed. For example, women were given the right to divorce their husbands on a variety of grounds; they were allowed to inherit and hold property that remained theirs even in marriage (women in England did not gain this right until the late nineteenth century); and they were given the right to refuse arranged marriages. The Qur'an also prohibited female infanticide.

According to Islamic belief, women and men are viewed as equals in the eyes of God and will be judged on their own accord. In the Qur'an, verse 35 of *surah* 33 addresses this issue:

> Verily for all men and women who have come to submission,
> Men and women who are believers,
> Men and women who are devout,
> Truthful men and truthful women.
> Men and women with endurance,
> Men and women who are modest,
> Men and women who give alms,
> Men and women who observe fasting,
> Men and women who guard their private parts,
> And those men and women who remember God a great deal,
> For them God has forgiveness and a great reward.[15]

The Qur'an requires all Muslims, women and men, to live a righteous life and to seek education. Women may work outside the home, though this is still uncommon in some areas. According to religious law, all of a woman's earnings remain her property. Thus, women are not required to use their earnings to support the family and maintain the home; it is a man's legal duty to provide for his family, even if his wife is wealthier than he. Of course, in practice, many women contribute their earnings to the household.

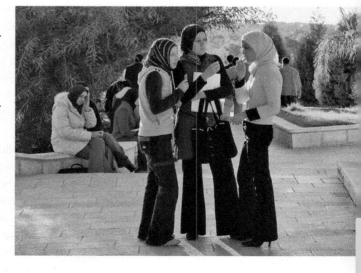

Three young Palestinian students in modest dress.

Despite all these rights, the place of women in Islam has sometimes been interpreted in very strict fashion. The most blatant case is that of the Taliban in Afghanistan, who deny women the right to work outside the home, the right to be educated, and even the right to walk freely in the street. However, this strict interpretation of religious texts and traditions is far from mainstream. Most Muslims view the Taliban's orders as radical and even religiously unlawful.

Along these same lines, much cultural variation exists in the practices regarding interaction between Muslim men and women. In some parts of the world, Muslim men and women live very separate lives. The seclusion of women is called *purdah* in South Asia and is practiced by some Hindus and Sikhs, as well as some Muslims. Elsewhere, as in many parts of Southeast Asia and Africa, Muslim men and women intermingle freely.

The Qur'an encourages both men and women to dress and behave modestly. The verses concerning dress—particularly that of women—are interpreted in many ways. Modest women's dress takes many different cultural forms. In some cultures, modest dress is interpreted as long pants and a modest top. In other contexts, Muslim women wear a type of cloak over their clothing when they leave the home. And some Muslim women choose to cover their heads and hair with a scarf. But this is not solely a Muslim practice: in the Middle East and Mediterranean, women covered their heads long before the time of Muhammad.[16] Covering the head has also been common practice among many Christian, Jewish, Hindu, and Sikh women. The terms used for elements of modest clothing vary from culture to culture, but several terms derived from Arabic are in common usage around the world. For example, the Arabic term *hijab* may refer simply to modest dress or more specifically to a scarf that covers the hair. The term *niqab*, also from Arabic, normally refers to a covering of the nose and mouth. The term *burqa*, also from Arabic, usually refers to a full-length garment that covers the head, body, and most of the face.

Many Muslim women dress modestly strictly out of religious commitment. For others, wearing modest dress is an important move toward gender equality in the workplace and the public sphere. Such women believe that when they are dressed modestly, they are valued by others on their merit alone, not on their appearance. To others, maintaining modest dress makes a statement of resistance to Western scholars and activists by demonstrating that feminism can be defined in myriad ways in different cultural and religious contexts. Some Muslim women say they pity Western women, who they believe must dress in a way that serves men's pleasure in viewing the female form.

We should not consider the status of women in any religious tradition without also considering historical change; this is particularly true of Islam because of the many negative stereotypes Muslim women have faced in recent years.

Reform and Women's Status   Several important reformers in the nineteenth and twentieth centuries sought to improve women's status in Muslim countries and cultures. Many of these reformers have focused on proper understanding of religious sources and Islamic law concerning women.

In much of the twentieth century, particularly in the first half, Muslim feminists were upper-class women who had the time and leisure to deliberate these issues, not working-class women whose labor was necessary to support their families. One of the most famous of these early Muslim feminists was Huda Shaarawi (1879–1947), an educated upper-class Egyptian woman who symbolically removed her face veil in an Alexandria train station in 1923. Shaarawi was president and founder of the Egyptian Feminist Union and did not believe that veiling was an Islamic requirement. When she removed her veil, she had just returned from a women's conference in Rome. She encouraged women

Compare the role of women in the Islamic tradition with that of women in other religions. How are the roles of women similar or different?

to cast off their headscarves in a quest for liberation. Many Egyptian women, particularly educated and elite women, were inspired by her example and ceased wearing face veils and headscarves. Shaarawi remained an activist and feminist leader throughout her life. She founded schools and medical facilities in Egypt and also advocated for women's rights throughout the Arab world.

Beginning in the later years of the twentieth century, many Muslim feminists have sought paths to equality that diverge from Western models. In their view, Islam itself provides the necessary means for women to achieve their rights. Many argue that the Qur'an must be reinterpreted in an attempt to eradicate cultural practices that are detrimental to women but have been justified as appropriate Islamic practice. Some have argued that women's status would be much improved only if Islamic laws were properly followed. As discussed earlier, many women in recent decades have, in a sense, reembraced modest dress as a feminist statement. In Egypt, this idea became prominent in the 1980s, and many mothers and grandmothers who had consciously decided against wearing veils or headscarves were dismayed that their daughters were wearing them, ironically with the same rationale their grandmothers used to discard it.

Muslim feminists differ in their approaches to Islam. Zaynab al-Ghazali (1917–2005) was an Egyptian feminist who advocated increasing women's rights and improving women's status through Islam. Nawal al-Saadawi (b. 1931), also Egyptian, is a woman who maintains that women can achieve equality only by rejecting what she views as the patriarchal tendencies of religion. Al-Saadawi is both a medical doctor and a writer, and her novels and stories have been both influential and controversial in the Arab world because of her focus on feminist issues and problems facing Arab women. Recently, al-Saadawi was active in the 2011 Egyptian revolution that overthrew the thirty-year presidency of Hosni Mubarak.

Calligraphy developed as an important art form in Islam because of a widespread understanding that imagery is prohibited by the sacred sources of Islam. This example is the word "Allah." Beautiful calligraphy decorates pages of the Qur'an, mosques, and other items.

Throughout the daily prayer, the believer faces the Ka'ba in Mecca and stands, kneels, and bows his head to the floor. These cycles of movements, along with the proper recitation, are called raka and vary in number according to the prayer.

The direction of prayer, known as the *qibla*, is marked in a mosque by a niche called a *mihrab*, which is sometimes highly decorated with designs or Qur'anic verses, like this *mihrab* at a mosque in Cairo, Egypt.

The Ka'ba, a cubical building in Mecca that measures about thirty feet by thirty feet. Many Muslims believe it was built and dedicated to the one God by Abraham and Ishmael.

CONCLUSION

In this chapter, you have learned about the historical development, beliefs, and practices of Islam and Muslims. Islam is truly a global religion and is among the fastest growing religions in the world. Many Muslim-majority countries are experiencing rapid population growth, but numbers are also increasing because of conversions. One of the most marked characteristics of the Muslim world today—its diversity—is unlikely to change. In fact, the ethnic diversity of the Muslim world is likely to increase. Muslims live in nearly every country in the world and on every inhabited continent.

Muslims everywhere, however, are responding to a rapidly changing world and increased globalization. Today, Muslims are facing questions about the role of religion in private and public life, relationships with other religious communities in plural environments, and what it means to be a person of faith in the modern world. Some of these issues are common to many religions. Others, such as the role of Islamic law in modern governments, are specific to Muslims. How will Muslims address these issues in years to come? One matter that has received much attention in the press lately is that of Islamic dress in western Europe. In France in 2004, schoolgirls were prohibited from wearing headscarves because officials argued it violated France's commitment to secularism. (Other religious symbols, like the yarmulke worn by Jewish boys, were also banned.) Many Muslims, however, thought this was a violation of their freedom to practice religion. The headscarf question has also been debated in other European countries. In 2015, Germany's highest court reversed its 2003 ban on female teachers wearing headscarves. Today, German teachers can wear headscarves as long as they are not disruptive. A related challenge Muslims face is the negative perceptions some Westerners hold about Islam and Muslim life. How will Muslims living in religiously plural societies grapple with this sort of challenge? In the United States, some Muslim Americans who have been invited or have volunteered visit churches, synagogues, schools, and community centers with the aim of teaching people about Islam and increasing their familiarity with Muslim ways of life. Muslim communities around the world struggle with competing interpretations of Islam's teachings. Sometimes young Muslims who go abroad to study in places such as Saudi Arabia, Indonesia, or Egypt come back to their home communities with different ideas about the way in which Islam should be practiced and taught. In many countries, as exemplified by some participants in the "Arab Spring" demonstrations of early 2011, Muslims are considering the relationship between Islam and democracy. Although some argue that Islam is inherently compatible with democracy because of examples such as the historical emphasis on consensus, others argue that democracy is a Western concept that is not compatible with an Islamic system of government.

As you have learned, Islam is a unique religious tradition, but it also shares a great deal with Christianity and Judaism. Will these similarities lead to greater communication and cooperation between Muslim and other religious communities? Although it is difficult to predict what the future will bring, it is clear that Islam will remain a dynamic and diverse religious tradition. Throughout history, Muslim thinkers, artists, and practitioners have contributed greatly to global human culture, and they will continue to do so in the future.

SEEKING ANSWERS

What Is Ultimate Reality?

Muslims believe that God is the creator and sustainer of the universe, the world, and all that is in it. Muslims believe that elements of the beautiful natural world are signs of God. Humans can learn something about ultimate reality through God's revelations, which are communicated to humanity through prophets. The Qur'an is the source of God's teachings about the nature of ultimate reality and the nature of the world.

How Should We Live in This World?

Muslims believe that human beings are part of God's creation. The Islamic tradition offers many guidelines concerning the right way for human beings to live. People should worship God, be generous to the needy, and live righteously. The life of the Prophet Muhammad, especially as related in the Sunnah, serves as an example for Muslims of how to live. The five pillars of Muslim worship practice are the foundation for how Muslims live their faith.

What Is Our Ultimate Purpose?

Muslims believe in an afterlife and a Day of Judgment, when all humans will be judged on their actions and deeds in this life. Those who have lived righteously will enter paradise, and those who have led sinful lives will be cast into the fire. Some Muslims think that human beings have free choice and must choose to submit to the will of God. The choices that individuals make will be evaluated on the Day of Judgment, when God will judge each person independently. Other Muslims do not adhere to an idea of free will. Devout Muslims aim to live righteous lives by submitting to the will of God, adhering to the five pillars and following the example of the Prophet Muhammad.

REVIEW QUESTIONS

For Review

1. What are the essential principles of belief in the Islamic religion?
2. What are the key religious practices in Islam? How do beliefs relate to religious practice and expression?
3. What are the most important sources of spirituality for Muslims?
4. What is a prophet in the Islamic tradition? What role does Muhammad play in Islam and in the life of Muslims today? How do Muslims know about the life of Muhammad, and how does he differ from other prophets?
5. What is Sufism, and how is it rooted in the Islamic tradition?

For Further Reflection

1. How do the teachings of Islam inform religious practice? How might the daily life of Muslims reflect their commitment to Islamic ideals? How do Islamic teachings about God compare with those of other monotheistic traditions?

2. What important challenges do Muslims face in the modern world? Why do you think Islam has been so stereotyped in North America and the West?

GLOSSARY

Abbasids An important Muslim empire that ruled from 750 to 1258 C.E.

adhan (a-than; Arabic) The call to prayer.

Aisha A beloved wife of Muhammad who is known for transmitting many hadith.

Allah (a-lah; Arabic) The Arabic term for God.

Ashura The tenth day of the month of Muharram, recognized by Shi'a Muslims as the anniversary of the martyrdom of Husayn.

caliph (ka-lif; Arabic) Leader of the Muslim community after the death of Muhammad.

hadith (ha-deeth; Arabic) Literary tradition recording the sayings and deeds of the Prophet Muhammad.

hajj (hahj; Arabic) The annual pilgrimage to Mecca, one of the five pillars of Islam.

hijra (hij-rah; Arabic) Sometimes spelled hegira. The migration of the early Muslim community from Mecca to Medina in 622 C.E.; the Islamic calendar dates from this year.

Husayn Grandson of Muhammad who was killed while challenging the Umayyads.

imam (ee-mam; Arabic) Prayer leader; in the Shi'a tradition, one of the leaders of the Muslim community following the death of the Prophet Muhammad.

Islam (is-lahm; Arabic) Lit. "submission"; specifically, the religious tradition based on the revealed Qur'an as Word of God.

jahiliyya (ja-hil-ee-ah; Arabic) The "age of ignorance," which refers to the time before the revelation of the Qur'an.

jihad (jee-had; Arabic) Lit. "striving"; sometimes the greater jihad is the struggle with one's self to become a better person; the lesser jihad is associated with military conflict in defense of the faith.

Khadija Muhammad's beloved first wife.

Mecca The city in which Muhammad was born; place of pilgrimage for Muslims.

Medina The city to which Muhammad and his early followers migrated to escape persecution in Mecca.

miraj (mir-aj; Arabic) Muhammad's Night Journey from Mecca to Jerusalem and from there to heaven, where he met with God.

mosque (mosk; from the Arabic term *masjid*) Place of prayer.

muezzin (mu-ez-in; Arabic) The person who calls the adhan.

Muhammad The prophet who received the revelation of the Qur'an from God; the final prophet in a long line of prophets sent by God to humanity.

Qur'an (kur-an; Arabic) The holy text of Muslims; the Word of God as revealed to Muhammad.

Ramadan (rah-mah-dan; Arabic) The month in which Muslims must fast daily from dawn until dusk; the fast is one of the five pillars of Islam, the month in which the Qur'an is believed to have been revealed to Muhammad.

salat (sa-laht; Arabic) The daily prayers, which are one of the five pillars of Islam.

sawm (som; Arabic) The mandatory fast during the month of Ramadan; one of the five pillars of Islam.

shahadah (sha-ha-dah; Arabic) The declaration of faith: "There is no God but God and Muhammad is the Messenger of God"; the first of the five pillars.

shari'a (sha-ree-ah; Arabic) Lit. "the way to the water hole"; specifically, Islamic law.

Shi'a (shee-ah; Arabic) One of the two major branches of Islam. The Shi'a believed that 'Ali should have succeeded as leader of the Muslim community after the death of Muhammad. That is, only the family and descendants of the Prophet Muhammad should lead the Muslim community.

shirk (sherk; Arabic) The sin of idolatry, of worshiping anything other than God, the one unforgivable sin in Islam.

Sufi (soof-i) A follower of the mystical tradition of Islam, Sufism, which focuses on the believer's personal experience of God and goal of union with God.

Sunnah (sun-na; Arabic) Lit. "way of life" or "custom"; specifically refers to the example of the life of the Prophet Muhammad; important religious source for Muslims.

Sunni (soon-e; Arabic) One of the two main branches of Islam. The Sunnis believed that the Muslim community should decide on a successor to lead after the death of Muhammad.

surah (soor-ah; Arabic) Chapter of the Qur'an; there are 114 *surahs* in the Qur'an.

tafsir (taf-seer; Arabic) Interpretation of or commentary on the Qur'an. There are several types of *tafsir*, which aim to explain the meaning of the Qur'an.

Umayyad Dynasty Controversial Muslim dynasty that ruled from 661 to 750 C.E.

umma (um-mah; Arabic) The worldwide Muslim community.

zakat (za-kaht; Arabic) Regulated almsgiving; one of the five pillars of Islam.

SUGGESTIONS FOR FURTHER READING

Armstrong, Karen. *Muhammad: A Biography of the Prophet*. San Francisco: Harper San Francisco, 1993. A detailed and readable account of Muhammad's life.

Denny, Frederick M. *An Introduction to Islam*. Englewood Cliffs, NJ: Prentice Hall, 2010. A thorough introduction to Islam aimed at college students.

Ernst, Carl W. *Following Muhammad: Rethinking Islam in the Contemporary World*. Chapel Hill: University of North Carolina Press, 2003. A readable introduction to Islam for the general public, focusing on Islam in the modern world.

Netton, Ian Richard. *A Popular Dictionary of Islam*. Chicago: NTC Publishing Group, 1997. A useful dictionary of key terms, people, and places in the Islamic tradition.

Renard, John, ed. *Windows on the House of Islam*. Berkeley: University of California Press, 1998. A collection of primary source materials from early Islamic history until the present; includes poetry, essays, philosophical writings, and more.

Schimmel, Annemarie. *Mystical Dimension of Islam*. Chapel Hill: University of North Carolina Press, 1975. A classic and comprehensive overview of Sufism.

Sells, Michael. *Approaching the Qur'an: The Early Revelations*. Ashland, OR: White Cloud Press, 2002. Translation and explanation of the earliest *surahs* of the Qur'an.

ONLINE RESOURCES

Oxford Islamic Studies Online
www.oxfordislamicstudies.com
A comprehensive source with contributions from top scholars on all topics related to Islam.

Center for Muslim-Jewish Engagement
http://cmje.usc.edu/
Useful site from the University of Southern California with databases for searching English translations of the Qur'an and hadith collections.

Index

6

613 biblical commandments, 209

A

Abbasids, 330-332
Abduh, Muhammad, 308
Ablution fountains, 319
Abraham, 163, 194, 255, 309-310
Abu al-Abbas, 331
Abu Bakr, 326
Abu Talib, 326
Act of Supremacy, 279
Acts of the Apostles, 251
Acupuncture, 179
Adam and Eve, 255
Adhan, 320-321
Advaita Vedanta, 46
Advent, 17, 208-209, 296-297, 333
African American Muslims, 342-343
African religions
    as a way of life, 72, 289, 344
    diversity of, 19, 82, 190, 359
    history of, 11, 35, 99, 268-269, 307
    myths of, 27
    teachings of, 18, 36, 95, 139, 190, 269, 309
    women and, 26, 283, 354-356
Afterlife
    in Confucianism, 174
    in Islam, 314
    in Judaism, 196-197
Age of Philosophy and Mysticism, 207
Agni, 52
Aisha, 317
Akbar, 319
Alchemy, 157-158
Alexander the Great, 36, 190
Al-fatihah, 312
Al-Ghazali, Zaynab, 358
'Ali, 308
Allahu Akbar, 319
Alpha and omega, 291
Altan Khan, 117
Altars, 62-63, 111, 291
Alternative Christianities
    The Family, 137
American Muslim Mission, 342
Amir, Yigal, 220
Amitabha Buddha, 107-108
Amito, 108
Ammachi, 79
Anabaptists, 279
Analects
    religious vision of, 148
angels, 15, 204, 315-316
Angkor Wat temple, 113
Anglican Church, 279
Antiochus IV, 203
anti-Semitism, 219-220
Anwar, 113
Apocrypha, 261
Apostles, 254
Apostolic succession, 265
Apricot Platform, 163
Aquinas, Thomas, 248

Arafat, 325
Aramaic, 206, 253
Aranyakas, 52-53
Arati, 54
Arhats, 102
Arianism, 271
Arjuna, 41
Artha, 50
Arya Samaj, 35
Asala, 128
Ascension, 248, 351
Ashkenazim, 207
Ashoka, 90
Ashrama, 76
Ashura, 340
Assumption, 8, 149, 189, 297
Assyrians, 190
Atharva Veda, 52-53
Atheism
    New, 32, 221-222
Atisa, 117
Atman
    as Brahman, 47
Atomism, 18
attachment, 42-46, 92, 219
Augustine, 248
Avalokiteshvara, 104-106
Avalokiteshvara Mandala, 130
Avatars, 40
aversion, 94
Ayat, 313

B

Baal Shem Tov, 211-212
Babri Masjid, 35
Babylonian Talmud, 190
Baghdad, 307
Balfour, Arthur, 219
Balfour Declaration, 190
Baptistery basin, 292
Bar Mitzvah, 188
Basil the Great, 275
Bat Mitzvah, 189
Battle of Badr, 327
Battle of Siffin, 308
Battle of the Camel, 330
beats, 118
Bedouins, 325
Benedict of Nursia, 248
Berger, Peter, 13
Berkovits, Eliezer, 218
Bernard of Clairvaux, 276
Bhagavan, 37
Bhagavata Purana, 53
Bhajan, 34
Bhakti, 35, 112
Bhakti marga, 43-45
Bharata, 54
Bharatiya Jana Sangh, 69-70
Bharatiya Janata Party (BJP), 70
Bible
    Hebrew, 17, 192, 255
Biblical period, 200
Bilal, 326
Bindi, 72

Bishops, 256
Bloom, Brad, 226
Blue Mosque, 332
Bön religion, 116
Bodh Gaya, 17, 89
Bodhi tree, 113
Bodhichitta, 107
Bodhidharma, 90
Bodhisattvas, 98
Bolshevik Revolution, 285
Bonaventure, 276
Bongeunsa Temple, 25
Book of Changes, 139
Book of History, 143
Book of Music, 161
Book of Odes, 143
Book of Rituals, 150
Borobudur Temple, 115
Brahma, 38
Brahmanas, 52-53
Brahmins
    bhakti and, 63
Brahmo Samaj, 35
Bread for the World, 299
British East India Company, 65-66
Buddha-Nature, 110
Buddhas/The Buddha
    enlightenment of, 132
    life of, 17, 45, 90-91, 169, 189, 249,
        310-311
    statues of, 23, 114-115, 294
Buddhism, 7, 41, 88-90, 139, 256
Buddhist Councils, 100
Buddhist Councils, period of the
    Chan, 90
    Confucianism and, 139
    Daoism and, 138
    Gelugpa, 114
    gods in, 74
    Hinduism and, 63
    in East Asia, 103
    in India, 39, 90, 223, 332-334
    in the world today, 119, 308
    Islam and, 208, 329
    Jodo, 107
    Kadampa, 114
    meditation in, 126, 197
    Nichiren, 90
    ordination in, 126
    Pure Land, 90
    rebirth in, 42, 107-108
    Seon, 115-116
    significant sites of early, 89
    the Four Noble Truths, 93
    the Noble Eightfold Path, 93
    the Northern transmission, 114
    the Southern transmission, 113
    the Western transmission, 117
    Three Marks of Existence, 131
    Three Refuges, 111
    Tibetan, 99-100
    Zen, 19, 90
Buddhist Power Force, 119
Burial, 77, 137, 235
burqa, 357
Byzantine Empire, 248, 325

C

Calendars
    of Hinduism, 78
    of Judaism, 223
Calligraphy, 108, 176, 358
Calvin, John, 278
Calvinism, 279
Camadevi, 125
Caodai, 171
Catholic Reformation, 277
Catholic Relief Services, 299
Celestial buddhas, 98
Celtic cross, 290
chador, 334
Chag, 224
Challah, 222
Chan Buddhism, 124
Chanting, 75, 111, 229, 295
Chen Liang, 136-137
Cherry blossoms, 128
Chiang Mai, 88-89
Chinese religions
    ghosts in, 180
    texts of, 139
    the divine in, 39
Chi-Rho, 291
Chit, 38, 132
Chodron, Pema, 122
Christianity
    God in, 141, 197, 246
    grace in, 254
    in Africa, 285-286, 308
    in the East, 207, 247
    in the Middle Ages, 267
    in the modern world, 24, 281-283, 359
    in the West, 247
    Judaism and, 206-207, 256, 309
    other religions and, 268-269
    prayer in, 284, 318
    saints in, 280
    the church in, 261
    theology of, 271
    tradition in, 139, 247
    worship in, 289-290
Christmas, 296
chuppah, 234
Churban, 218
Church interiors, 291
Circumcision
    female, 232
Civil disobedience, 68
Civil Rights Act of 1964, 299
Civil Rights movement, 299
Classic of Filial Piety, 170
Clement of Alexandria, 270
Comic books, 82, 119
Confucian Academy, 162
Confucianism
    as a religion, 149
    as orthodoxy, 163
    as pan-Asiatic tradition, 165
    Doctrine of the Mean, 150
    Five Classics, 138
    Four Books, 138
    Great Learning, 150
    later defenders of the faith, 162
    Mencius, 138
    neo-, 150

    rituals of, 174
Confucius
    sacrifice to, 174
Conscience, 19, 224
Conservative Judaism, 214-215
Constantine, 248
Constantinople, 248, 332
Copernicus, Nicholas, 281
Council of Constantinople, 256
Council of Trent, 248
Creeds, 262-263
Cremation
    in Buddhism, 92
Crucifixion of Jesus, 248
Crusades, 274-275, 308
Cuba, 9
Cultural anthropology, 29
Cultural revolution, 138

D

dé, 284
Dalit, 84
Daly, Mary, 286
Dantian, 158
Dao
    of Tian, 146
Daozang, 138
Darshan, 72-74
Dasharatha, 54
Dates, 80, 90-91, 138, 322
David, 68, 190, 249
Deacons, 266
Dead Sea Scrolls, 204
Declaration on Non-Christian Religions, 267
Demons, 15, 55, 98, 141
Des Moines Balagokulam, 71
Devanampiyatissa, 113
Devekut, 198
Devi, 51
Devi Mahatmya, 56
Dhammapada, 103
Dharamsala, 100
Dharma Shastras, 53
Dharmakaya, 104-105
Dharmakirti, 114
Dharmasvamin, 113
Dhikr, 352-353
Dhimmi laws, 328
Dhritarashtra, 55
Dhu al-Hajj, 324
Di, 176
Diamond Sutra, 107-108
Diaspora
    Hindu, 69-70
    Indian, 69-70
    Jewish, 193
Din-I-Ilahi, 65
Dioceses, 270
Divination, 161
Divine inspiration, 217, 261-262
Divorce document, 235
Doctrines, 14, 36, 103, 173, 262, 331
Doi Suthep Mountain, 89
Dome of the Rock, 352
Dongling, 157
Dragon and Tiger Mountain, 168
Dreidel, 230
Dua, 318
Durga, 51

Durga Puja, 62
Dussehra, 80-81
Dvaita Vedanta, 46

E

Ear piercing, 76
Easter, 295
Eck, Diana, 72
Ecumenical councils, 271
Ecumenical Patriarch of Constantinople, 285
Ecumenism, 289
Eden, 19, 255
Egyptian Feminist Union, 357
Ein Sof, 198
Election, 70, 193-195, 283, 343
Eliade, Mircea, 17
Ellison, Keith, 308
Emancipation Proclamation, 299
empathy, 28, 153, 226
Endogamy, 48
Enlightenment (experience)
    of the Buddha, 88-89
environmentalism, 18
Epicureans, 16
Epicurus, 18
Epiphany, 296
Episcopal church, 246
Erev Shabbat, 231
Essenes, 203-204, 249
Ethical monotheism, 190
Eucharist, 260
evangelicalism, 284-285
Exodus, 16, 192, 261
Ezekiel, 261

F

Faith
    reason and, 210, 276, 316
Falwell, Jerry, 284
Family Rituals, 176-177
Fangshi, 157-158
Farrakhan, Louis, 342
Fascinans, 20
Fast of Mud and Soot, 178
Fast of the Yellow Register, 178
Fatima, 310
Fatwas, 350
Feast of Fast-Breaking, 323
Female infanticide, 356
Feminist theology, 286
Fendeng, 179
Festivals and holidays
    of Daoism, 138
Fez, 333
Fire sacrifice, 62
First Buddhist Council, 90
First Crusade, 275
First Jewish War, 190
First Vatican Council, 248
Five Activities of Shiva, 73
Foot binding, 152
Ford, Wallace, 342
Forehead markings, 72
Formative Age, 204-205
"Four Dragons", 167
Foursquare Gospel Church, 286
Fourth Crusade, 275
Francis, Pope, 283

Franks, 273
Freud, Sigmund, 14, 281

G

Galilei, Galileo, 281
Ganesh Chaturthi, 34-35
Ganesha, 16, 34-35
Ganges River, 57
Ge Hong, 157
Gemara, 206
Genesis, 17, 192, 254-255, 314
Genghis Khan, 117, 331
Ghee, 74-75
Ginsberg, Allen, 108
Global snapshot
    Confucianism in Korea, 164
    Daoism in feng shui and martial arts, 172
    emergence of Western Buddhism, 121
    Judaism in India, 223
    Kimbanguist Church in Africa, 288
    Muslims in the West, 343
globalization, 25-26, 82, 359
Gnosis, 269
God
    fear of, 277, 351
Godse, Nathuram, 69
Good Friday, 296-297
Goryeo Period, 170
Gospels, 243, 248-253, 314
grace, 108, 147, 247
Great Mosque, 324-325
Greater jihad, 348
Guan, Lord, 159
Guanyin, 106
Gui, 141
Gupta Empire, 62, 112
Gyatso, Tenzin, 118

H

Habitat for Humanity, 299
hadith, 317-318
Hadith qudsi, 317
Hagar, 325
Haggadah, 228
Hajj, 306
Halacha, 206
Hall of Praying for an Abundant Harvest, 174
Haman, 229
Hamantaschen, 230
Hampi Bazaar, 48
Han dynasty, 114-115, 138
Hana Matsuri, 128
Hanukkah, 229-230
Hanuman, 54-55
Haredi, 220
Harijans, 48
HarperCollins Dictionary of Religion, 12
Harun al-Rashid, 331
Harvest Festival, 39, 225
Hasan of Basra, 351
Hashmi, Heraa, 341
Hasidism, 211-212
Haskalah, 213
Hatha yoga, 47
Havdalah, 231
Hawa, 314
Headscarf, 359
Heart Sutra, 107, 170

Hebrew language, 188
Heian period, 116
Helena, 268
Henotheism, 15
heresy, 206, 273
Herzl, Theodor, 219
Hesychasm, 248
Hezekiah, 196
"Hidden texts"
    of Christianity, 66, 268-269
Hierophany, 17
Hijra, 308
Hillel, 205
Himalayas, 39, 117
Hindi, 64-65
Hinduism
    future of, 71
    Hindutva and, 69
    icons of, 80
    in the United States, 16, 71
    nationalism and, 70
    pilgrimage in, 77
    sects of, 56, 115
    significant sites in, 60
    Vedic period, 62
Hindutva, 69-71
Hippies, 118
Hitler, Adolf, 218
Holi, 81
Holocaust Memorial Day, 230
Holy orders, 266
Holy Week, 296-297
Horeb, Mount, 201
Huangjin, 168
Humanism, 149, 216
Humanist Judaism, 221
Hun, 10, 141
Hundun, 140
Huns, 168
Husayn, 308

I

Ibn Taymiyya, 316
Iconoclasm, 274
Iconostasis, 294-295
Icons
    Christian, 8, 275
Id al-Fitr, 323
ignorance, 41, 94, 183, 326
Ihram, 324
Ijma, 350
Imams, 339-340
Immaculate Conception, 297
imperialism, 336-338
Impermanence, 94
India
    Buddhism in, 90
    Golden Age of, 63, 115
    Hinduism in, 67
    Jainism in, 65
Indian National Congress, 70
Indian Uprising, 66
Indra, 52
indulgences, 278
Indus River, 36
Indus Valley civilization, 35
Inquisition, 248
Interdependent Origination, 93
International Orthodox Charities, 299

Iqbal, Muhammad, 334
Isaac, 190, 281, 325
Isaiah, 194, 250-251
Ishmael, 324-325
Islam
    and political conflict, 340
    Christianity and, 19, 192
    in North America, 318
    Nation of, 342
    reform movements in, 213
    varieties of, 338
    Wahhabi, 335-336
Ismail, 340
Ismailis, 340
Isnad, 317
Israel
    concept of, 190

J

Jacob, 195
Jade Emperor, 159
Jahan, Shah, 333
Jahiliyya, 326
James, William, 8
Japan
    Confucianism in, 163-165
    Daoism in, 170
Jatis, 48
Java, 90, 166
Jesus Christ
    as the messiah, 250
    icon of, 255
    mosaic of, 281
Jesus Prayer, 296
Jewish Quarter, 213
Jiao, 179-180
Jinn, 315-316
Jnana, 43
Jnana marga, 43
Jodo Shinshu, 121
John the Baptist, 249
Jones, William, 35
Jordan River, 249
Joseon Dynasty, 164
Josephus, 203-204
Judah the Maccabee, 229
Judaism
    Conservative, 213-215, 262
    in the modern era, 215, 301, 316
    Orthodox, 8-9, 195, 255
    Reconstructionist, 215-216
    Reform, 190
Julian of Norwich, 276
Junzi, 147-148

K

Ka'ba, 306
Kabbalah, 198-199
Kabir, 35
Kailasha, Mount, 57
Kali, 58-59
Kalki, 40
Kama, 50
Kanishka I, 114
Kannada, 64
Kaplan, Judith, 233
Kaplan, Mordecai, 215
Karbala, 308

Karma marga, 43-45
Kartikeya, 16
Kashrut, 227
Kathina, 129
Kauravas, 55
Ketuvah, 234-235
Khadija, 326
Kharijites, 330
Khema, Ayya, 126
Khotan, 100
Khuddaka Nikaya, 125
Kimbanguist Church, 288
Kingdom of God, 250-252
Kipah, 238-239
Kirtan, 34
koans, 108
Kohler, Kaufmann, 214
Kolam, 48
Krishna
    in the Mahabharata, 57
Kshatriyas, 48
Kōshin, 170
Kulturkampf, 282
Kumbha Mela festival, 77
Kumbhakarna, 55
Kusinara, 127
Kustana, 114

L
Lakshmana, 54-55
Lakshmi, 51
Lakshmi Puja, 80
Lalita Sahasranama, 51
Lamas, 99
Lang Darma, 117
Lankavatara Sutra, 107
Laos, 10, 60, 89, 137
Laozi bianhua jing, 138
Laozi (Daoist master)
    image of, 114, 178
    statue of, 162
Last Supper, 290
Laws of Manu, 42
Lent, 176, 295-297
Lesser jihad, 348
Lhabap, 129
Li, 147
Li Bo, 173
liberalism, 281
liberation theology, 289
Lincoln, Bruce, 13
Linga, 57
Logos, 261
Lord's Prayer, 290-291
Lotus, 45, 89-90
Lotus position, 45
Lotus Sutra, 90
Loyola, Ignatius, 280
Lu, 161
Lu Xiujing, 169
Lulav, 225-226
Lumbini, 89
Luria, Isaac, 190
Luther, Martin, 118, 277
Lutheranism, 278

M
Macarius of Alexandria, 275

Maccabean revolt, 190
Madhva, 46
Mahadevi, 37
Mahaprajapati, 126
Maharishi Foundation, 71
Maharishi Mahesh Yogi, 71
Mahasabha, 69-70
Mahayana Trikaya, 105
Mahinda, 113
Mahisha, 80
Mahishasura, 58
Mahmud of Ghazni, 64
Mahr, 354
Maimonides, 190
Maitreya, 105-107
Malcolm X, 342
mandalas, 109
Manjushri, 111
Mantras
    Buddhist, 65, 108-110
Mara, 92
Marathi, 64
Margas, 43-44
Markandeya Purana, 53
Marriage contract, 234, 354-355
Marx, Karl, 14
Marxism, 283
Masada, 204
Mashiach, 196
Masjid, 35, 319
mass, 191, 249
Mataji, 37
Material dimension of religion, 23
Matn, 317
Matsuri, 128
Mattathias, 229
Matzah, 228
Maundy Thursday, 297
Mawlid al-Nabi, 348-349
Maximus the Confessor, 275
Maya, 42
Maybaum, Ignaz, 218
Mazel Tov, 234
Mazu, 160
Medina, 307-308
mediums, 108
Meera, 79
Mendelssohn, Moses, 213-214
Menorah, 229
Merneptah, Pharaoh, 199
Messiah
    Jesus as, 206-207, 250-251
Messianic Age, 196-197
Mevlevi order, 352
Middle Way, 92
Midrash, 210
Mihrab, 319
Mikveh, 194
Ming, of Tian, 144
Ministry of Health and Welfare, 164
Minyan, 238
Miraj, 318
Mishnah, 190
Mitzvot, 192
modernization, 25-27, 82, 213-214
Modi, Narendra, 70
Mohel, 232
monism, 16, 36-38
Monotheism

ethical, 190
Montanism, 269
Montanus, 269
Morsi, Muhammad, 338
Moses, 21, 145, 190, 261, 310
Mosques, 70, 307
Mousavi, Mir-Hossein, 335
Mu'awiya, 330
Mubarak, Hosni, 338
Muezzin, 320
Mufti, 350
Mughal Empire, 308
Muhammad, Elijah, 342
Muhammad ibn Abd Allah
    revelations of, 308-309
    successors to, 331
Mumbai , 34
Mumtaz Mahal, 333
Mutazilites, 312
Muwahiddun, 335
Mysterium tremendum, 20

N
Namaste, 72
Nara period, 116
Nataraja, 39
Nathan of Gaza, 211
Nation of Islam, 342
National League for Democracy, 119
Nationalism
    Islamic, 68, 332-338
Native American religions
    balance in, 175
    myths in, 82
Navaratri, 51
Nazi Germany, 218, 267
Nehru, Jawaharlal, 69-70
Neidan, 158
Neisheng waiwang, 165
neo-Confucianism, 138
Nestorian churches, 287
Neti, 38
New Age, 168
New Culture Movement, 173
New Religious Movements
    atheism in, 221
    in Japan, 108, 165
    modernization and, 25, 82
    number of, 18, 46, 119, 160-161, 189, 251,
        308
New Testament, 18, 248
Newton, Isaac, 281
Nguyên dynasty, 138
Ni Zan, 170
Nicene Creed, 23, 256
ninety-five theses, 248
niqab, 357
Nirmanakaya, 103-105
Noah, 310
Nontheistic belief systems, 16
Northern Wei Dynasty, 169
Numinous experience, 20
Nuns
    Daoist, 114, 159-160

O
Omnipotence, 219
Omniscience, 57, 190

One Thousand and One Nights, 316
Opium War, 165
Oral Torah, 210
Oriental Orthodox churches, 287
Origen, 270
original sin, 272
Orthodox Church
    churches of, 248
    saints of, 85
Orthodox Judaism, 215
Orthodoxy
    Confucianism as, 152-153
orthopraxy, 213
Oshita, Bob, 121
Osho Rajneesh Movement, 59
Otto, Rudolf, 24
Ottoman Empire, 274, 308

P

Pahlavi, Reza, 334
Palamas, Gregory, 276
Palestine, 190, 250, 331
Pali, 90
Palm Sunday, 296-297
Panagia, 297
Pandavas, 55
Pandu, 55
Pan-Islamism, 337
pantheism, 15
Parables, 251-252
Paradise, 108, 142, 255, 315
Parents' Day, 164
Parinirvana, 93
Parker, Trey, 119
Parvati, 35
Passover plate, 225
Patanjali, 47
Paul of Tarsus, 253
Pentecost, 251
Pentecostalism, 284-285
Perfection of Wisdom Sutra, 106-107
Period of Disunion, 138
Persian Empire, 202
Pesach, 224
Pharisees, 203-204, 249
Philokalia, 295-296
Po, 182
polygamy, 67, 337
Pontius Pilate, 250
popes, 270
Prajna, 97
Prajnaparamita Sutra, 106
Prayag, 77-78
Predestination, 272
Prophecy, in Islam, 326
Protestant Reformation, 248
Puja, 34
Pulpit, 293-294
Pumpeditha, 208
Puranas, 35
Purdah, 357
Pure Land Buddhism, 104
Pure Land Sutras, 107
Purgatory, 19, 263-265
Purim, 229-230
Purusha, 48
Purusha Sukta, 48

Q

Qadis, 350
Qi, 140
Qibla, 319
Qin Dynasty, 163
Qingming, 136
Qiyas, 349
Quraysh tribe, 327
Qutb, Sayyid, 341

R

Rabbis, 192-193
Radical, 55, 148, 204, 279, 338
Radical Reformation, 279
Rahula, 93
Raja Yoga, 47
Raka, 306
Ram Lila, 81
Ramadan, 6, 317-318
Ramakrishna, 35
Ramakrishna Math, 68
Ramanuja, 59
Rangoli, 48
Ravana, 54-55
Reconstructionist Judaism, 215
Record of Rites, 143
Reform Judaism, 214-215
Reformation
    Catholic, 247-248
    Protestant, 247-248
Relics, 89, 276
Religion
    dimensions of, 22, 181
    historical development of, 286
    individual nature of, 12
Religious violence, 220
Reliquaries, 298
Renaissance, 257
Resurrection
    of Jesus Christ, 247
Revealed ethics, 18-19
Rig Veda, 35
Rightly Guided Caliphs, 308
Rinpoche, Mingyur, 99
Rishis, 42
rén, 147-149
Roman Catholic Church/Catholicism
    Eastern Rite, 266
Roman Empire
    Christianity in, 268, 308
    Judaism in, 190
Rosary, 295
Rosh Hashanah, 224
Rothschild, Walter, 220
RSS (Rashtriya Swayamsevak Sangh), 35
Ru, 138
Rubenstein, Richard, 218
Rumi, Jalalludin, 308

S

Sacred time, 231
Sacrifice
    fire, 62
    to Tian and Di, 175
Sadducees, 203, 249
Safavid Empire, 308
Saga Dawa, 128

Sages, 36, 91, 152, 205, 295
Sailendra Dynasty, 114
Sakyadhita, 126
Salat, 306
Salat al-jum'ah, 320
Salvation Army, 299
Sama Veda, 52-53
Samadhi, 47
Samboghakaya, 104-105
Samhitas, 52-53
Sanctus, 291
sand paintings, 124
Sangh Parivar, 70
Sangha
    beginnings of, 92
    in Theravada Buddhism, 132
Sanghamitta, 113
Sannyasis, 50
Sanskrit, 35, 90
Sarasvati, 77
Saraswati, 35
Saraswati, Dayananda, 35
Sarnath, 89
Sat, 38, 92
Sati, 67
satori, 108
Satyagraha, 68
Sawm, 317
Sa'y, 325
Schachter-Shalomi, Zalman, 199
Scholasticism, 138, 208, 276
science, 25, 99, 276, 317
Second Buddhist Council, 90
Second Coming of Christ, 263
Second Council of Nicea, 274
Second Temple period, 202
Second Vatican Council, 248
Sect, 82, 90, 170, 253
secularization, 26, 282
Seder, 219, 250
Seekers, 114, 173, 270
Sei, Katherine, 98-99
Separation of church and state, 282
Sephirot, 198
September 11 attacks, 343
Septuagint, 203, 260
"Sermon in the Deer Park", 127
Sermon on the Mount, 252
Shah Mosque, 320
Shahadah, 317-318
Shakti Peethas, 77
Shaktism, 56-58
Shamanism, 109, 170
Shang dynasty, 142
Shangdi, 141-142
Shankara, 46
Sharada, 51
Sha'rawi, Huda, 308
Shari'a, 349-350
Shatrughna, 54
Shavuot, 226-228
Shema, 239
Shemini Atzeret, 227
Shen, 141
Shūgendō, 170
Shinto
    medieval, 169
    State, 115-116, 169-170
Shirk, 51, 313

Shiva
  Five Activities of, 73
  Shaivism, 56-58
Shivah, 235
Shofar, 224
Shruti, 52
Shu, 147
Shudras, 48
Siddur, 222-223
Sign of the cross, 247
Sikhism
  scriptures of, 18
Silk road, 100
Simeon the New Theologian, 248
Sinai, Mount, 192
Sita, 54-55
Skanda, 57
Skandhas, 95
slavery, 228, 326
Smriti, 52-53
Snyder, Gary, 108
Social aspects of religion, 14
Sociological study of religion, 12
Sodoma, Giovanni, 275
Solomon, 190
Son So, 164
Sonam Gyatsho, 117
South Korea, 25, 110, 164
Spain
  Jews in, 224
Spanish Inquisition, 248
Speculative tafsir, 316
Spring and Autumn Annals, 143
Star of David, 225
Stations of the Cross, 295
Stoicism, 15
Stone, Matt, 119
Stupas, 115
Sudanese Mahdi, 336
Sufism, 350
Sukkah, 226-227
Sukkot, 224-228
Sumatra, 113-114, 166
Summer solstice, 175
Sun Bu'er, 160
Sun god, 40
Sura, 190
Surahs, 311
Sutra Pitaka, 102-103
Sutras, 47, 102-103
Svami, 38
Svetaketu, 41
Synagogues, 207, 267, 359

T
Tafsir, 316
Tai chi, 172
Tai, Mount, 176
Taiji, 182
Taiping, 168
Taishang Laojun, 138
Taj Mahal, 332-333
Takbir, 319
Tallit, 224
Talmud, 190
Tamil, 39
Tang dynasty, 124-125, 138
Tariqas, 352
Tawaf, 325

Tefillin, 238
Temple Mount, 352
Temple of Di, 175
Temple of Jerusalem
  First, 35, 90, 190, 248, 308
  Second, 39, 90-91, 190, 248, 308
Temple of Tian, 174-175
Temples
  Confucian, 116, 162
Ten Commandments, 16, 192-193, 261
Tertullian, 271
Teshuvah, 198-199
Thangkas, 121
The Great Schism, 248
Theodosius I, 268
Theophany, 17
Theotokos, 266
Theragatha, 125
Therigatha, 125
Third Buddhist Council, 90
"Third eye", 72
Thirteen articles of Jewish belief, 210
Tian
  Dao of, 154
  in the Analects, 146-147
  primacy of, 154
Tianming, 142
Tianxia, 142
Tianzi, 142
Tikkun olam, 198-199
Tillich, Paul, 12
Tisha B'Av, 230-231
Tokugawa shogunate, 165
Tomb visitation, 353
Torah
  Oral, 192
  written, 204, 248-249
Touro Synagogue, 205
transcendence, 20-21, 39, 190
Transcendental Meditation (TM), 71
transcendentalism, 149
Transubstantiation, 276
Trikaya, 103-105
Tripundra, 72
Trisong Detsen, 116
Trump, Donald, 172
Tsaddikim, 212
Tu B'Shevat, 230
Tulsidas, 65
Twelvers, 339-340
Tzevi, Shabbetai, 190
Tzimtzum, 198

U
Ulama, 338
Umayyad dynasty, 330-331
Umma, 321
United States
  Protestantism in, 283
Untouchables, 69
Upanayana, 76
Upanishads
  spread of, 63
Upaya, 123
Urban II, Pope, 275
urbanization, 25

V

Vaishyas, 48
Vajrayana Buddhism
  Kadampa sect of, 114
  Mahayana and, 111-112
Valmiki, 54
Varanasi, 60, 92
Varnashrama dharma, 47-49
Varuna, 52
Vedanta Society, 68
Vedanta Society of New York, 68
Venkatesan, Jayashree, 51
Vernal equinox, 80
Vesak, 88-89
VHP (Vishwa Hindu Parishad), 35
Vietnam War, 118
Vijayadashami, 80
Vinaya Pitaka, 102
Violence
  Hindu nationalism and, 70
  religion and, 21, 248
Vipassana meditation, 123
Visakha Bucha Day, 88
Vishishta-Advaita, 46
Vishnu
  Vaishnavism, 46
Visualization, 109, 169
Vivekananda, Swami, 35
Voltaire, 281
Vrindavan, 78

W
Wahhabism, 335
Waidan, 158
Walking meditation, 124
Wang Yangming, 138
Wang Zhe, 138
Warring States Period, 162
Wat Phrathart Doi Suthep, 89
Watts, Alan, 119
Wei Huacun, 160
Weld, Theodore, 299
Western Buddhism, 121
Wine, Sherwin, 221
Winter solstice, 175
World Council of Churches, 248
"World religions discourse", 29
World Vision, 299
World War I, 332-333
World War II, 190-191, 267
Wudu', 319
Wushi, 161
Wuxing, 140
wúwéi, 154

X
Xian, 157
Xiantian Dao, 171
Xiao, 147
Xiaoyao, 155
Xinzhai, 155
Xiwangmu, 138
Xun Qing, 163

Y
Yad, 225
Yajur Veda, 52-53
Yama, 58
Yangsheng, 158

Yangzi River, 168
Yardenit, 249
Yarmulke, 239, 359
Yasodhara, 91
Yazid, 330
YHWH, 200-201
Yi, 145
Yiddish, 212
Yoga
    death, 36, 108-109
    deity, 35, 109
    guru, 58-59, 109
    Raja, 47
Yoga Sutras, 47
Yom HaShoah, 190
Yom Kippur, 224-226
Yuan dynasty, 138
Yuanshi tianzun, 159

Z
Zakat, 317
Zealots, 204, 249
Zen Buddhism, 19, 108
Zendos, 124
Zhai, 178
Zhang Ling, 168
Zhang Zai, 152
Zhenwu, Lord, 159
Zhi, 149
Zhong, 147
Zhongmin, 178
Zhou dynasty, 142-143
Zhu Xi, 138
Zilu, 148
Zionism, 195
Ziran, 154
Zohar, 243
Zoroastrianism
    community of, 66
    rituals in, 64
Zu Shu, 160
Zuowang, 155
Zwingli, Ulrich, 279